New Hollywood violence

Published in our
centenary year
~ **2004** ~
MANCHESTER
UNIVERSITY
PRESS

Inside Popular Film

General editors Mark Jancovich and Eric Schaefer

Inside Popular Film is a forum for writers who are working to develop new ways of analysing popular film. Each book offers a critical introduction to existing debates while also exploring new approaches. In general, the books give historically informed accounts of popular film, which present this area as altogether more complex than is commonly suggested by established film theories.

Developments over the past decade have led to a broader understanding of film, which moves beyond the traditional oppositions between high and low culture, popular and avant-garde. The analysis of film has also moved beyond a concentration on the textual forms of films, to include an analysis of both the social situations within which films are consumed by audiences, and the relationship between film and other popular forms. The series therefore addresses issues such as the complex intertextual systems that link film, literature, art and music, as well as the production and consumption of film through a variety of hybrid media, including video, cable and satellite.

The authors take interdisciplinary approaches, which bring together a variety of theoretical and critical debates that have developed in film, media and cultural studies. They neither embrace nor condemn popular film, but explore specific forms and genres within the contexts of their production and consumption.

Already published:

Thomas Austin *Hollywood, hype and audiences*
Harry M. Benshoff *Monsters in the closet: homosexuality and the horror film*
Paul Grainge (ed.) *Memory and popular film*
Julia Hallam and Margaret Marshment *Realism and popular cinema*
Joanne Hollows and Mark Jancovich (eds) *Approaches to popular film*
Mark Jancovich, Antonio Lázario-Reboll, Julian Stringer and Andy Willis (eds)
    Defining cult movies: the cultural politics of oppositional taste
Antonio Lázaro-Reboll and Andy Willis *Spanish popular cinema*
Nicole Matthews *Gender in Hollywood: comedy after the new right*
Rachel Moseley *Growing up with Audrey Hepburn*
Jacinda Read *The new avengers: feminism, femininity and the rape-revenge cycle*
Andy Willis (ed.) *Film stars: Hollywood and beyond*
Aylish Wood *Technoscience in contemporary film: beyond science fiction*

6129276

New Hollywood violence

Edited by
Steven Jay Schneider

Manchester University Press
Manchester and New York
distributed exclusively in the USA by Palgrave

Published by Manchester University Press
Oxford Road, Manchester M13 9NR, UK
and Room 400, 175 Fifth Avenue, New York, NY 10010, USA
www.manchesteruniversitypress.co.uk

Distributed exclusively in the USA by
Palgrave, 175 Fifth Avenue, New York,
NY 10010, USA

Distributed exclusively in Canada by
UBC Press, University of British Columbia, 2029 West Mall,
Vancouver, BC, Canada V6T 1Z2

British Library Cataloguing-in-Publication Data
A catalogue record for this book is available from the British Library

Library of Congress Cataloging-in-Publication Data applied for

ISBN 0 7190 6722 7 *hardback*
     0 7190 6723 5 *paperback*

First published 2004

13 12 11 10 09 08 07 06 05 04   10 9 8 7 6 5 4 3 2 1

Typeset in Sabon with Frutiger
by Northern Phototypesetting Co. Ltd, Bolton

Printed in Great Britain
by Bell & Bain Ltd, Glasgow

For Elyse & Stuart, with love

Contents

Illustrations

Notes on contributors

Martin Barker is Professor of Film and Television Studies at the University of Wales, Aberystwyth. He is the author of many articles and books on controversial media and their audiences, most recently *Knowing Audiences: "Judge Dredd," its Friends, Fans and Foes* (with Kate Brooks, University of Luton Press), *Ill Effects: the Media Violence Debate* (with Julian Petley, edited and contributed, Routledge), and *The Crash Controversy: Censorship Campaigns and Film Audiences* (with Jane Arthurs and Ramaswami Harindranath, Wallflower Press).

Nick Browne is Professor of Film and Television at the University of California, Los Angeles. His diverse list of publications includes *Refiguring American Film Genres* (University of California Press), *New Chinese Cinemas: Forms, Identities, Politics* (Cambridge University Press), *Cahiers Du Cinema, 1969–1972: The Politics of Representation* (Harvard University Press), and *The Rhetoric of Filmic Narration* (UMI Research Press). He is also directing a comprehensive study of violence in contemporary film.

Sylvia Chong is an Assistant Professor in American Studies and English at the University of Virginia. Her book project, tentatively entitled *The Oriental Obscene: Violence and the Asian Male Body in American Popular Culture During the Vietnam Era*, focuses on the circulation of violence in Vietnam War news coverage and the martial arts film.

Susan Felleman is Assistant Professor in the Department of Cinema and Photography at Southern Illinois University-Carbondale. She is the author of *Botticelli in Hollywood: The Films of Albert Lewin* (Twayne).

Geoff King is Course Director, Film & TV Studies, Brunel University. His publications include *New Hollywood Cinema: An Introduction* (I. B. Tauris), *Film Comedy* (Wallflower Press), *Spectacular Narratives: Hollywood in the Age of the Blockbuster* (I. B. Tauris), and, as co-editor, *ScreenPlay: Cinema/Videogames/Interfaces* (Wallflower Press).

Thomas Leitch teaches English and directs the Film Studies program at the University of Delaware. His most recent books are *The Alfred Hitchcock Encyclopedia* (Facts on File) and *Crime Films* (Cambridge University Press).

Paula J. Massood is Associate Professor of Film Studies in the Film Department of Brooklyn College, City University of New York. Her articles on African American film have appeared in *Cinema Journal, African American Review*, and *Cineaste*. She is the author of *Cities in Black: Visualizing African American Urban Experiences in Film* (Temple University Press).

Todd Onderdonk is currently writing his dissertation at the University of Texas at Austin on modernist masculinities in the works of Hemingway and Fitzgerald.

Fred Pfeil is Professor of English at Trinity College. He has written extensively on popular culture and is the author of *White Guys: Studies in Postmodern Domination and Difference* (WW Norton) and *Another Tale to Tell: Politics and Narrative in Postmodern Culture* (Verso).

Murray Pomerance is Chair and Professor in the Department of Sociology at Ryerson University. He is author, editor, or co-editor of numerous volumes including *Enfant Terrible! Jerry Lewis in American Film* (New York University Press); *Sugar, Spice, and Everything Nice: Cinemas of Girlhood* (Wayne State University Press); *Ladies and Gentlemen, Boys and Girls: Gender in Film at the End of the Twentieth Century* (SUNY Press), *Closely Watched Brains* (Pearson), *Bang Bang, Shoot Shoot! Essays on Guns and Popular Culture* (Pearson), and *BAD: Infamy, Darkness, Evil, and Slime Onscreen* (SUNY Press). He is editor of the Horizons of Cinema series at SUNY Press and, with Lester D. Friedman, co-editor of the Screen Decades series at Rutgers University Press.

Stephen Prince is Professor of Communication Studies at Virginia Tech. He is the author and editor of numerous books of film history and criticism, including *Screening Violence* (Rutgers University Press) and *Movies and Meaning: An Introduction to Film*, 2nd edn (Allyn & Bacon).

Jacinda Read is Lecturer in the Department of Cinema Studies at Nottingham Trent University. Her book *The New Avengers: Feminism, Femininity and the Rape-Revenge Cycle* was published by Manchester University Press.

Thomas Shatz is Professor of Communication and Chair of the Radio-Television-Film Department at the University of Texas, Austin. His books on Hollywood films and filmmaking include *The Genius of the System*

(Pantheon), *Hollywood Genres* (McGraw-Hill), and *Boom and Bust: The American Cinema in the 1940s* (Scribner). He also holds regular seminars in the US and abroad on the American film and television industries, and has done extensive work on various media-related PBS documentary programs and series.

Steven Jay Schneider is a PhD candidate in Philosophy at Harvard University and in Cinema Studies at New York University's Tisch School of the Arts. He is the editor of *The Horror Film and Psychoanalysis: Freud's Worst Nightmares* (Cambridge University Press) and *Fear Without Frontiers: Horror Cinema Across the Globe* (FAB Press); co-editor of *Underground U.S.A.: Filmmaking Beyond the Hollywood Canon* (Wallflower Press), *Horror International* (Wayne State University Press), and *Understanding Film Genres* (McGraw-Hill); and author of *Designing Fear: An Aesthetics of Cinematic Horror* (Routledge).

J. David Slocum is Assistant Dean in the Graduate School of Arts and Science at New York University, where he teaches cinema studies and humanities. His writings on violence, film, and culture have appeared in *American Quarterly*, *Cineaste*, *Social Research*, and *The Times Literary Supplement*. He is editor of the AFI Film Reader *Violence in American Cinema* (Routledge) and is currently completing *Community and Carnage: A Cultural History of Violence in American Movies, 1896–1950*.

David Tetzlaff is Assistant Professor of Film Studies in the Theater Department of Connecticut College. He is a former co-editor of *The Journal of Communication Inquiry* and has contributed to such volumes as *The World Wide Web and Contemporary Cultural Theory* (Routledge) and *The Madonna Connection* (Westview Press).

Theresa Webb is a postdoctoral researcher at the Southern California Injury Prevention Research Center at the University of California, Los Angeles. Her current work is focused on the effectiveness of the Motion Picture Association of America's voluntary rating system.

Ken Windrum is a PhD candidate at the University of California, Los Angeles, currently writing his dissertation on American Cinema of the late 1960s and early 1970s.

Preface

Steven Jay Schneider

As the second Persian Gulf War rages in Iraq and on television sets around the world, the present volume seems ever more timely, ever more relevant. For surely, what we are watching (to say "witnessing" would be naïve) on the small screen will be coming soon to a theater near you, though rarely in a literal or even instantly recognizable form.

The essays collected herein are devoted to an interrogation of various issues, questions, and concerns – historical, empirical, conceptual, aesthetic, cultural, ideological – relating to the depiction of violence in what has come to be known as New Hollywood cinema. The somewhat restricted notion of "New Hollywood" employed in the title has been articulated most concisely by Murray Smith (following Thomas Schatz) in terms of a return to genre filmmaking following America's flirtation with European art cinema in the late 1960s and early 1970s, albeit a return "now marked by greater self-consciousness, as well as supercharged by new special effects, saturation booking, engorged production budgets and, occasionally, even larger advertising budgets."[1] Thus the focus is on violence – its motivations, formal and stylistic attributes, cultural politics, appeal and effects on viewers, etc. – primarily as it appears in studio-produced genre films released from around 1969 (the year of Sam Peckinpah's groundbreaking Western, *The Wild Bunch*) to the present.

But rather than seeking to impose or even settle on an all-encompassing characterization of film violence, much less on violence generally, the individual contributors to this volume respect the term's often intimidating complexity, shedding new and much-needed light in the course of performing close readings of particular films (Onderdonk, Read, Schneider, Tetzlaff, Windrum), auteur analyses (Chong, Massood, Pfeil), genre and cycle studies (Browne and Webb, Felleman, King, Leitch), and historical-theoretical investigations (Barker, Pomerance, Schatz, Slocum). Although the conclusions arrived at are of necessity always partial and frequently open to discussion and debate, the sum total suggests a more complete and more nuanced portrait of violence in New Hollywood filmmaking than has previously been available.

1 *Natural Born Killers* (1994): a simultaneously self-conscious and excessive display of violence in recent Hollywood cinema

The four sections of this book – "Surveys and schemas," "Spectacle and style," "Race and gender," and "Politics and ideology" – represent just one possible way (though I think the most intuitive one) of dividing up the fifteen chapters. These sections are bracketed by an Introduction by Thomas Schatz that historically situates the discussions to follow, and an Afterword by Stephen Prince that looks back at these discussions and points the way towards areas of future inquiry.

This collection was first conceived in discussions with Frank Grady and Paul Roth, organizers of the University of Missouri-St. Louis "Violence, Cinema, and American Culture" conference, held on April 6–7, 2001. I am deeply indebted to them both. I also wish to express my sincere thanks to the following people: Mark Jancovich, for encouraging me to submit the proposal to Manchester University Press's "Inside Popular Film" series; Matthew Frost, Fiona Morrice, and Kate Fox at the Press, for all their help along the way; Kristi Long at Palgrave/St. Martin's, for her prompt and positive feedback; Thomas Schatz and Stephen Prince, for kindly agreeing to the Introduction and Afterword, respectively; everyone who submitted drafts during the planning stages (an embarrassment of riches, truly); and in particular, to all the contributors, whose hard work and patience made this project a pleasure the whole way through. Finally, I would like to thank my family and friends, especially (and as always) Katheryn, Elyse, Pam, and Stuart, for their unconditional support and love.

Notes

1 Murray Smith, "Theses on the Philosophy of Hollywood History,"
   Contemporary Hollywood Cinema, ed. Steve Neale and Murray Smith
   (New York: Routledge, 1998), 11.

Introduction

Thomas Schatz

From *The Great Train Robbery* (1903) a century ago to the current spate of summer blockbusters, Hollywood movies have been fundamentally "about" violence. In fact, violence has been a defining characteristic and signal feature of Hollywood cinema since the silent era. And in a medium so utterly geared to narrative conflict and melodramatic excess, in a nation whose history and foundation myths are so rife with savagery and bloodshed, how could it be otherwise? Endlessly reworked in a vast repertoire of popular genres and narrative formulae, violence itself has become a venerable social problem that defies resolution, a tangle of binary oppositions and cultural contradictions that crucially informs our national character and our shared vision of an "imagined community."

Movie violence in America has involved, since its inception, something of a holy trinity of necessary participants: a culture industry determined to depict and exploit it, moviegoers equally determined to experience it and social watchdogs determined to regulate it. Indeed, Hollywood's twin taboos of sex and violence have evolved in an intense symbiosis with film censorship, and various flashpoints have marked watershed moments or key transitions in American film history. The title of this collection, *New Hollywood Violence*, speaks directly (albeit implicitly) to this point, suggesting that the treatment of violence in American film has changed in significant ways with the emergence of the so-called "New Hollywood" some three decades ago. Not coincidentally, several essays in this volume directly relate the emergence of the New Hollywood with "ultraviolent" releases like *Bonnie and Clyde* (1967), *Night of the Living Dead* (1968), and *The Wild Bunch* (1969), films that ignited firestorms of controversy and were harbingers – along with *The Graduate* (1967), *2001* (1968), *Midnight Cowboy* (1969), *Easy Rider* (1969), and *M*A*S*H*

(1970) – of a full-blown cinematic revolution.[1] These films scarcely emerged *sui generis*, of course, and we can only gauge their impact and importance when we understand the conditions and context – what might be termed the "generative mechanisms" – that facilitated and shaped their creation.[2]

From a critical political economy perspective, the regulation of movie content, and particularly film violence, has been a crucial factor throughout the history of the American film industry. In fact Hollywood's classical era was bracketed by a number of key regulatory decisions that marked both its emergence and its eventual collapse. Crucial formative events included the Supreme Court's *Mutual* decision of 1915, which denied movies protection under the First Amendment, identifying them instead as "a business pure and simple, originated and conducted for profit," as well as the creation in 1922 of the MPPDA (Motion Picture Producers and Distributors of America), a "trade organization" created to stem the public outcry over salacious movie content. These developments served not only to facilitate the self-regulation of movie content, but also the integration of the studio system and the assertion of studio control over the entire US movie marketplace. Decades later, the studio system would be dis-integrated by the Supreme Court's 1948 *Paramount* decision, which forced the studios to sell their theater chains and prohibited trade practices so essential to their hegemony and market control. And the Court's 1952 *Miracle* decision effectively reversed its 1915 ruling, granting movies the same First Amendment protections granted the press and the other arts. These rulings loosened the studios' collective (and codified) control over production and thus the constraints over cinematic expression that had prevailed for decades.[3]

Those constraints were a function of the MPPDA's infamous Production Code, which was written in 1930 but not effectively enforced until 1934 with the formation of the Production Code Administration. The PCA was created in response to threats of external censorship by the local and federal government, and also by the Catholic Legion of Decency, created in 1933 in direct response to Hollywood's increasingly direct treatment of violence and sex in a wide range of films, from gangster sagas to women's pictures. The Code modified both the narrative logic and the moral calculus of Hollywood movies, although the PCA was equally significant as a public relations ploy that served to ensure industry self-regulation. Not surprisingly, perhaps, the PCA granted filmmakers far more license in their depiction of violence than sex – a fact borne out by the remarkable numbers of crime films, war films, and Westerns that the studios cranked out. In fact the Western, a genre fundamentally attuned to violent confrontation, accounted for roughly one-quarter of all films produced in Hollywood from the early 1930s to the mid-1950s.[4] Another indication was the wartime relaxation of constraints put on "war films" – initially newsreels and documentaries (at the direct behest of FDR), and eventually in dramatic features as well. This in turn affected other genres and trends, most notably in what was then called the "red meat" cycle of urban crime thrillers – films like *Double Indemnity* (1944) and *Mildred Pierce* (1945) – which would later be termed *film noir*.

Throughout the classical era, Hollywood's portrayal of violence was heavily genre-coded, as was its depiction of sexual courtship and coupling. The studio system was geared to mass consumption for a generalized "mass audience" that consumed films at the phenomenal rate of 80 to 100 million moviegoers per week (when the total US population was about 125 million) – some eight to ten times the current rate of consumption. Thus the workings of the Production Code and the studio production mode were geared to children and adults alike, and strategies of genre-coding served both to convey and contain (if not conceal) acts of violent brutality and sexual intimacy.

The postwar era brought massive changes to the American culture industries, and the impact on movie violence was particularly acute. The Supreme Court's 1948 dis-integration of the studio system coincided with the emergence of commercial television, which in the span of a decade completed dislodged "the movies" as America's preferred form of habituated narrative entertainment. TV's growth was fueled by suburban migration and a housing-family baby boom, along with a booming economy and surging consumer culture. Meanwhile, Hollywood dramatically reduced production operations, relying on fewer, "bigger" pictures – widescreen Technicolor spectacles, precursors to today's blockbusters – as well as smaller-scale independent production (most of them financed and distributed by the studios) geared to increasingly specialized audiences. The big-budget spectacles relied on established genres and tended simply to ratchet up familiar genre-coded violence and sexual content, but the low-budget independent realm – 1950s exploitation films and teenpics, art films and imports – aggressively challenged a wide range of Code-related taboos.

The marked influx of foreign films in the 1950s and 1960s, and the cross-fertilization between Hollywood genres and those of other national cinemas, had a particularly pronounced effect. While the impact on sexual content gained the most notoriety, foreign films and filmmakers were radically redefining the parameters of movie violence. Consider the generic interplay of Hollywood Westerns and Japanese samurai films in the 1950s, for instance, and their curious offshoot in the form of the "Spaghetti Western" in the 1960s – a hyper-violent, hyper-masculine genre variation that took the US by storm in late 1967 and early 1968 with the release in quick succession of Sergio Leone's *A Fistful of Dollars* (1964), followed by his *For a Few Dollars More* (1965) and *The Good, the Bad, and the Ugly* (1966). Or consider the concurrent development of the horror genre, from the recombinant sci-fi/horror films of the early 1950s (e.g., *The Thing from Another World* [1951], *Them!* [1954]) to the subsequent emergence of AIP's horror teenpics (*I Was A Teenage Werewolf* [1957], etc.) and the late 1950s influx of Hammer Studios' horror films from England (beginning with *The Curse of Frankenstein* in 1957), the latter with their savvy, stylized blend of sex and gore for the burgeoning teen and drive-in crowds. AIP responded with Roger Corman's "Edgar Allen Poe cycle," bringing a Grand Guignol dimension and witty irony to American horror cinema.

The American horror film that defined the moment and truly reinvented the genre, of course, was *Psycho* (1960), Alfred Hitchcock's experiment in terror whose success and impact surprised even him. (It was Hitchcock's most successful film, second only to *Spartacus* at the box office in 1960.) The influence of *Psycho* was immediately evident, not only in the predictable run of low-grade facsimiles but also in a range of innovative psycho-sexual thrillers, from Robert Aldrich's neo-gothics (*Whatever Happened to Baby Jane?* [1962]; *Hush . . . Hush, Sweet Charlotte* [1964]) to such European art-cinema variations as Roman Polanski's *Repulsion* (1965) and Michelangelo Antonioni's *Blow-Up* (1966). Polanski eventually migrated to Hollywood, where he enjoyed immediate success with *Rosemary's Baby* (1968), a film which, along with *Psycho*, recast American horror in a distinctly modern idiom – and a domesticated

2 Cannibalism and zombies in one of 1968's most violent and disturbing American features: George Romero's *Night of the Living Dead*

one at that, where the prospect of violence (mental as well as physical) was far more immediate and frightening than in traditional horror. *Rosemary's Baby* actually surpassed *Psycho* in its canny blending of genre motifs and narrative conventions, its effective blending of melodrama and comedy, and its obliteration of any clear distinctions between art cinema and exploitation.

Rosemary's Baby was one of many mainstream 1968 releases, including *Bullitt*, *In Cold Blood*, *If*, *Point Blank*, *Night of the Living Dead*, *Hang 'Em High*, and *The Good, The Bad, and the Ugly*, that signaled the movies' more aggressive and graphic depiction of violence. *Variety*'s page-one banner headline in its inaugural 1968 issue referred to 1967 as a "Year of Violence," and that trend quite obviously intensified over the ensuing year.[5] This surge in movie violence was one clear indication that Hollywood was entering a period of unprecedented innovation, experimentation, and accomplishment – a period that has been variously described as the American New Wave, the Hollywood Renaissance, the New American Cinema and, inevitably, the New Hollywood.[6] More so, perhaps, than at any time in its history, Hollywood was attuned to the larger social and cultural climate, as well as to the changing values and sensibilities of its core audience, as the "youth culture" shifted from a subculture to a genuine counterculture. Movies were distinctly in sync with the violence and turmoil of the era, and in fact Hollywood in the late 1960s was exceptionally attuned to the larger cultural climate. Americans in their teens and twenties during this period were at the forefront of a range of social movements – civil rights, antiwar, feminist, environmentalist, *etc.* – that ushered in a period of massive cultural transformation; nowhere on the US cultural landscape was that transformation more evident than on movie screens. Among the more insightful (if sensationalistic) appraisals of the era is Peter Biskind's *Easy Riders, Raging Bulls: How the Sex-Drugs-and Rock 'n' Roll Generation Saved Hollywood.* The subtitle is both playfully ironic and altogether serious, suggesting that a new generation of filmmakers and moviegoers, caught up in a widespread change in the cultural zeitgeist, redirected and energized a moribund film industry.

A wide range of social and industrial factors contributed to Hollywood's sea change in the late 1960s. Chief among these was the radical revision of the Production Code in 1965 and the subsequent dismantling of the PCA (along with the Catholic Legion of Decency), which left Hollywood without a self-censorship mechanism until the installation of the MPAA ratings system in 1968. By then the proverbial horse was out of the barn, and the MPAA's newly installed ratings system – then limited to G (General), M (Mature), R (Restricted), and X (no admission to anyone under sixteen) – foundered woefully in its efforts to regulate the newly liberated industry, as indicated by the "X" ratings assigned to films like *If* and *Midnight Cowboy.*[7] Other factors included a new "generation" of filmmakers and moviegoers, as Hollywood's old guard faded and the industry entered an "auteurist" phase that was vociferously supported by the hip, young, cine-literate audience. Remarkably enough, given the strictures of the classical studio system and the current television industry, the American cinema became a "director's medium" to an unprecedented degree, as filmmakers like Penn, Peckinpah, Robert Altman, Bob Rafelson, Mike Nichols, Paul Mazursky, Hal Ashby, Francis Ford Coppola, William Friedkin, Martin Scorsese, and others wielded more influence and creative control than at any time before or since.

The youth market was a key factor as well, not only because younger moviegoers were more receptive to innovative and occasionally subversive films, but also because they were so utterly out of sync with mainstream America (in this era of the "generation gap" and Nixon's "silent majority"). Moreover, various "niche markets" developed within the general youth market, often geared to blatant excess in terms of sex and violence – from the low-budget horror teenpics like *Night of the Living Dead* and *The Texas Chainsaw Massacre* (1973), to blaxploitation films like *Shaft* (1971) and *Superfly* (1972), to sexploitation films like *Deep Throat* (1972) and *The Devil in Miss Jones* (1973).[8]

The final and perhaps most important factor in Hollywood's late 1960s transformation was the literal and figurative "bottom line." Simply stated, the late 1960s and early 1970s marked a period of severe economic distress for the American movie industry, due mainly to the crippling failure of big-budget blockbusters and the surging youth market. As Hollywood lost touch with the mainstream and catered to more dependable but increasingly rebellious younger moviegoers, revenues dwindled and the box-office charts were dominated by an eclectic mix of modestly performing films. The top twenty box-office films of 1973, for example, included a few solid hits like *The Exorcist* and *The Sting*, but also films like *Magnum Force* (the sequel to *Dirty Harry* [1971]), the X-rated *Last Tango in Paris*, and the triple-X *The Devil in Miss Jones*, Bruce Lee's breakthrough kung fu film *Enter the Dragon*, and a hyper-violent right-wing vigilante fantasy, *Walking Tall*.

The Exorcist is important here because, as both a solid commercial hit and a hyper-violent horror film, it signaled the imminent recovery of the industry and the re-codification of movie violence. It was, in other words, a film that both mainstream adult America and the MPAA ratings board could handle, a film that reveled in but finally contained and denied its own violent impulses. While a few major films of the era such as *Taxi Driver* (1976), *Apocalypse Now* (1979), and *Raging Bull* (1980) pushed the logic of genre-coded violence beyond the manageable limits of taste and cinematic license – and thus under-performed commercially – many others, including *The Godfather* (1972), *Jaws* (1975), *Rocky* (1976), *Halloween* (1978), and *Alien* (1979), found ways to package ultraviolence in the familiar conventions of genre (and the increasingly ubiquitous "R" rating), rendering it suitable for general consumption. These were the hits that spawned the "new" New Hollywood, with its commercially savvy producer-auteurs like Lucas and Spielberg, its obsession with big-budget blockbusters and multi-media franchises, its multiplexes and younger-skewed youth market, its increasingly stabilized ratings system, its ever-growing ancillary markets and a resurgent "studio system" geared to an era of global media consumption. As Biskind and others note, the American New Wave had ebbed by the late 1970s, and in fact Scorsese's searing study in violence, *Raging Bull*, was released within days of the disastrous premiere – and consequent non-release – of Michael Cimino's *Heaven's Gate*, the film that bankrupted United Artists and marked the definitive end of Hollywood's auteurist phase. *Raging Bull* itself was a critical and commercial disappointment, and along with a few other gems in 1979–80 such as *All That Jazz*, *Apocalypse Now*, *Manhattan*, and *The Shining*, it marked the last gasp of the New American Cinema.

Violence continues to fuel Hollywood movies, of course, from mainstream male action-adventure blockbusters to high-gore, niche-market fare. A governing paradox of the New Hollywood has been the consolidation of power by a cartel of global media conglomerates geared to franchise-scale blockbusters on the one hand, and the steadily increasing diversification, fragmentation and localization of both media products and media audiences on the other; and the essays in this volume well indicate that violence permeates all sectors of the industry. While radical, innovative and offbeat films no longer dominate as they did in the 1970s, they are alive and well on the margins of the New Hollywood in commercially viable "specialized" markets, ranging from Hong Kong action films and art-cinema imports to slasher teenpics and hip-hop gangsta films. And the farther reaches of ultra-low-budget and straight-to-video fare have given exploitation filmmakers more license than ever before.

Many of those on the margins display much the same modernist impulse as the New American cineastes of the 1970s in their penchant, as director George Romero once put it, for "taking the old genres, the old horses, and baring all the nerves."[9] But the far more pervasive manifestation of movie violence is found in mainstream films, from high-end horror to action-adventure spectacles. It is altogether remarkable, in fact, how ubiquitous violence has become in American cinema, to a point where the term "action" is basically a euphemism for violence. And while the turmoil and social upheaval of the 1960s are long gone, multiplex screens across America suggest that we are still obsessed with violence – more so, perhaps, than at any time in our nation's history. As Richard Slotkin aptly notes in *Gunfighter Nation*, his epic study of America's long-standing culture of violence, the Western may no longer pervade the cinema, but "the underlying mythic structures it expressed remain more or less intact. Action in the imagined world of myth-symbolic play still takes the form of captivities and rescues, still evokes the three-part opposition in which the American hero stands between extremes of bureaucratic order and savage license."[10]

Notes

1 See Stephen Prince, "Graphic Violence in the Cinema: Origins, Aesthetic Disigns, and Social Effects," *Screening Violence*, ed. Stephen Prince (New Brunswick: Rutgers University Press, 2000), 6–19.

2 See Robert C. Allen and Douglas Gomery, *Film History: Theory and Practice* (New York: Knopf, 1985).

3 Garth Jowett, *Film: The Democratic Art* (Boston: Little, Brown, 1976). On the *Mutual* decision, see 119–20; on the formation of the MPPDA, 166–7; on the *Paramount* decision, 277–8 and 345–6; on the *Miracle* decision, 406–7.

4 For data on Hollywood's production of Westerns, see *The BFI Companion to the Western*, ed. Edward Buscombe (London: BFI, 1988), 426–7.

5 Abel Greene, "Year of Violence & Mergers," *Variety* (Jan. 8, 1968): 1.

6 David A. Cook in *A History of Narrative Film* (New York: Norton, 1981) directly relates the emergence of the "New American Cinema" to the release of *Bonnie and Clyde*, 877–9. James Monaco in *American Film Now* (New York: New American Library, 1979) associates the "American New Wave" with the emergence of the group of "whiz kids" directors (Bob Rafelson, Dennis Hopper, *et al*.) in 1968–69. Peter Biskind, in *Easy Riders, Raging Bulls: How the Sex-Drugs-and Rock 'n' Roll Generation Saved Hollywood* (New York: Simon & Schuster, 1998), alternately opts for New American Cinema as well as New Hollywood. See also my essay, "The New Hollywood," in *Film Theory Goes to the Movies*, ed. Jim Collins, *et al.* (New York: Routledge, 1993), 8–36.

7 On the 1965 revision of the Production Code, the 1966 installation of Jack Valenti as President of the MPAA, etc., see Jowett, *Film*, 413–20. The newly created National Catholic Office of Motion Pictures officially supported the MPAA ratings system when it was installed in 1968, but withdrew its support in 1971, publicly criticizing the new system as ineffective.

8   According to *Variety*'s regular listings of all-time "film rental champs,"
    both *Deep Throat* and *The Devil in Miss Jones* were among the top-ten
    box office films of their respective release years.
9   Quoted. in Steve Fore, CinemaTexas Program Notes for *Ulzana's Raid*,
    19.2 (Oct. 21, 1980), 76.
10 Richard Slotkin, *Gunfighter Nation: The Myth of the Frontier in 20th-
    Century America* (New York: HarperCollins, 1992), 642.

I

Surveys and schemas

1

The "film violence" trope: New Hollywood, "the Sixties," and the politics of history

J. David Slocum

This essay reconsiders the cinema of bloodletting, bodily pain and invasiveness, and death, which emerged in the 1960s and 1970s, and arguably replaced an earlier suggestiveness with what some have seen as more direct, viscerally engaging and confrontational images of violence. Writing in 1967, Pauline Kael memorably called this a shift toward a cinema of "blood and holes"; more recently, scholars like Paul Monaco and Stephen Prince have approached the changes by highlighting the development of, respectively, the "cinema of sensation" and "ultraviolence."[1] For these observers and others, the arguably new aesthetics and politics of imaging violence constituted a signal break in film history that consigns other and especially earlier representations of brutality, violent action, and death to the realm of the tame, quaint or inchoate. In the process, and notwithstanding the varied approaches and terms employed to describe the changes, broader public and scholarly understandings of "film violence" at the time and subsequently have been recast and circumscribed according to what happened during the period starting with *Psycho* (1960), continuing through *Bonnie and Clyde* (1967) and *The Wild Bunch* (1969), and ending with *Taxi Driver* (1975) or even *Halloween* (1978).[2] Without minimizing the achievement or originality of these productions, the aim here is to elucidate the historical grounding of both individual films and the multiple contexts – institutional, intellectual, discursive – from which they emerged and in which they circulated.

Beyond asking why these changes appeared on screen when they did, in other words, the call here is to probe why and how they have captured critical and popular attention as *the* predominant aesthetic and representational forms for conveying "film violence." These forms, first privileged in the 1960s, have provided a crucial legacy to the public, to scholars, and to policymakers, so it is fair to ask how they have persisted in framing critical and popular understanding. While attending to the evolution of film techniques, industrial concerns, cultural referents, and visual and representational issues, such questions must also address the weight of critical and public-policymaking approaches to film violence that grew to prominence after World War II. The result will be an interrogation of some familiar histories of "film violence" and, particularly, the question of behavioral effects on which they are grounded. Reflections will follow on whether the continuing predominance of those histories is partly a result of scholarly and policymaking neglect of the power relations structuring media and society.

My remarks are framed by what Eleanor Townsley has called "'the Sixties' trope" operative in both historiography of the last half-century and the analysis of contemporary social and political narratives.[3] Building on the writings of intellectual historian Hayden White, Townsley uses "trope" to refer to "a figurative use" of words or images that move meanings away from the literal or immediate. The trope's "function is to compress and inscribe historically developed critical understandings in a very short space," Townsley writes. "It reduces complexity and represses contentious detail in favor of what everyone knows."[4] Tropes are importantly to be distinguished from narratives. While narratives serve a similar organizational function by giving coherence and meaning to events and to history, their production, especially in political (or cinematic) realms is overt and self-conscious. In contrast, Townsley argues, "tropes produce the historical effect by hiding the moment of their own construction and the processes of their institutionalization and reproduction."[5] It is perhaps similarly worth differentiating "tropes" from "discourses": whereas tropes are specific figures or expressions, discourses are the constellations of elements (including tropes) that generate, circulate, and bind meanings of an object or event in a given historical moment and culture. In other words, tropes move and reconfigure discourses, often by mobilizing specific moral tensions. Central to my argument is the process by which the "film violence" trope ascendant in the 1960s has particularized and delimited discourses of film, violence, and film violence with the consequence of privileging certain meanings and contexts and repressing others.

To paraphrase Townsley, the guiding question here is, What happened to render "the Sixties" such a powerful element in accounts

of historical and contemporary US film violence?[6] Preliminary
answers will emerge from testing the foundations of today's predominant aesthetics, politics, and critical and popular discourses of
film violence, and by challenging the regnant linear history of incre-
mentally more graphic violence onscreen. Concretely, the discussion
will follow Townsley and address three aspects of what is being proposed as a "film violence" trope: (1) the "Sixties" and "New Hollywood" as an *originary moment* for the presentation of, as well as
debate over, film violence; (2) images, standards, and debates from
the period as a *device for normative evaluation* of film and pur-
ported instances of film violence; and (3) "film violence" as an *index*
for connecting and circumscribing narratives of cultural history and
political economy.

This tack resonates with Martin Barker's call, made in this volume,
to return to "specific histories" of the 1950s and 1960s that can be
seen for political reasons to name or to neglect given behaviors as
"violent." While agreeing with that imperative and instructed by
Barker's insightful readings of films, my own claims for unearthing
the emergence of a "film violence" trope go back earlier, to the years
after World War II. Indeed, the importance of examining earlier histories derives from recontextualizing broader if unresolved understandings of "the Sixties" that overdetermine and skew accounts of
film violence. For the present collection, such an examination entails
considering more carefully how knowledge about violence and the
discursive formations affording it meaning have been, and continue
to be, produced.

New Hollywood as originary moment

The trope of "the Sixties," for Townsley, "denotes a break or major
change in American history, after which nothing is the same again."[7]
Her suggestion can be seen as part of a broader critical challenge to
"periodize the Sixties." The seminal expression of this effort is probably Fredric Jameson's reflection on the difficulty of treating "the
Sixties" as a discrete and unified topic of study, and work continues
to appear that problematizes historical periodization generally and,
as with Arthur Marwick's recent history of a "long decade" lasting
roughly from 1958 to 1974, the "Sixties" in particular.[8] As its legacy
continues to be contested, the period itself thus remains a touchstone for organizing contemporary political and cultural narratives.

Historical understandings of the Cold War, the military-industrial complex, Civil Rights, the Great Society and government social programs, and Vietnam can be seen to orient subsequent debates. In structural terms, "the Sixties" becomes a kind of "nucleic function" for linking, catalyzing, and demarcating the beginning and end points of historical narratives.[9]

In the historiography of US cinema, the break inaugurating "the Sixties" appears most canonically (and neatly) at the close of David Bordwell, Janet Staiger, and Kristen Thompson's account of "classical Hollywood cinema" in 1960.[10] The convergence of justifications for that dating – the apparently concurrent breakdown of longstanding aesthetic and narrative norms, changing technologies, industrial structures, and modes of production, and shifting audiences and social contexts – have appeared to many to underscore a major change or break in the history of cinema. As a result, "the Sixties" becomes aligned with the efflorescence of "New Hollywood" as a moment in which various components of classicism are subverted by formal innovation and narrative exploration, alternative modes of production, and institutional participation in the counterculture. Other scholars have taken issue with this model of classicism. One objection has been the downplaying by Bordwell, Staiger, and Thompson of social and cultural contexts in favor of formal and industrial practices. Another, more fundamental concern has been the formulation of a stable, unified, or dominant classicism against which New Hollywood might be defined. While addressing squarely the interdependence of multiple determinants, for instance, Murray Smith questions the historical plausibility of opposing models of stability or equilibrium and change or transition. He then calls for close historical attention to the overlapping factors driving accounts of Hollywood's past – as well as those shaping accounts and analyses of that past.[11] Our understanding of "New Hollywood" may be interwoven with the trope of "the Sixties," Smith suggests, but models privileging beginnings, endings, and classical unities demand greater clarity and historical grounding.

Violence is a topic central to accounts of New Hollywood and the 1960s that demonstrates the problems with clear-cut formulations of classicism. Conventional discussions of film violence during the 1960s characteristically include protracted images of physical brutality and bloodshed, presented spectacularly through the use of special effects and imaginative editing, often with a less serious, even cavalier or mocking tone different from earlier cinematic portrayals of pain and death, and raising questions about what effects they will have on viewers. In Hollywood, the end of the Production Code, the fragmentation of audiences, an increasingly decentralized mode of production and the incorporation of alternative filmmaking practices (including editing techniques and the development of new special effects such as squibs) could be offered as explanation for changes onscreen. Likewise adduced at the time were social contexts such as the controversial war in Vietnam, continuing urban unrest and racial strife, and their coverage on television. Revisiting contemporary responses, J. Hoberman recognizes the efforts to link the carnage and changed attitudes represented in Hollywood productions with broader preoccupations about America as an exceptionally violent society.[12] But the nature of the linkages between cinematic and social violence, between images onscreen and the summary of tumultuous events underway outside the theater, remains circumstantial and speculative. While Hoberman is right to allow "that public attitudes toward violent imagery are historically determined,"[13] the calculus of that determination remains obscure.

Developments on many of these cinematic and social fronts are often seen to converge in 1967 and to shape new films and to generate intense critical and public debates over the seeming explosion of film violence. When tracked specifically, these elements can be seen to have appeared in particular productions during that watershed year: *Bonnie and Clyde* of course (in August), but also the US release of Sergio Leone's *A Fistful of Dollars* (January), Robert Aldrich's wildly successful *The Dirty Dozen* (June), John Boorman's revenge drama *Point Blank* (August), and Richard Brooks' *In Cold Blood* (December). Yet a possible result of such discussions can be a tautological understanding of film violence during the period: specific elements are understood to constitute violence in certain films; meanwhile, particular films are revisited as violent because they exhibit the relevant specific elements. Among possible alternative models would be *both* a complicated conception of classicism that underscores its inherent tensions, longstanding violence, and perhaps lack of unity *and* an expanded appreciation of how violence was represented onscreen and experienced by viewers. Looking more closely at the question of origins can complicate the conventional privileging of 1967 (and after) and destabilize more familiar bases of understanding of "film violence."

Take the shift occurring during the early 1960s in the *tone* employed in presenting increasing (and increasingly sensational) images of brutality and bloodshed. The question was whether such actions were being shown in ways that still had meaning for social interaction and public discourse. Stanley Kubrick's *Dr. Strangelove* (1964) was an unrelenting black comic look at the absurd attitudes and language driving Cold War nuclear politics. Greil Marcus has observed that the challenge of John Frankenheimer's *The Manchurian Candidate* (1962) was the unsettling prospect of "the failure of ordinary languages and images to account for a world that . . . no longer even pretended to make sense."[14] This, too, was a source of controversy about the introduction of the immensely successful James Bond franchise, which undercut cinematic conventions of heroism and official authority with their violent protagonist's cold-bloodedness and consistently sardonic attitudes toward violence and death.[15]

This shift also derived from what were, at the time, innovative images of conflict and production techniques, such as what is arguably Hollywood's first martial-arts fight in Frankenheimer's film or the early, prolonged use of handheld cameras to provide close-ups of hands and feet in the climactic fight in *From Russia With Love* (1963). Such innovations are also suggestive of far-reaching changes in production practices and the filmmaking industry. Bordwell, Staiger, and Thompson rightly attend to changes in industrial practices in their account of the demise of classicism, but the appreciation of ramifications of this for the representation of violence has been limited. Low-budget and independent production, perhaps most conspicuously Roger Corman's work at AIP, expanded at the time, as did foreign and art-house cinema activity. It is also worth remembering that the most galvanizing filmic images of violence during the period were not made in Hollywood at all but by an amateur named Abraham Zapruder when he witnessed the 1963 assassination of President John F. Kennedy. What has amounted to a preoccupation with content too often neglects the shifting industrial and economic practices in Hollywood and other US cinemas.

In 1960, Hitchcock's *Psycho* appeared to mark a rupture with classical forms. What begins as a tale of adultery and the promise of conventional heterosexual desire is abruptly remade into the story of obsessive and murderous psychosis. Yet the film's destabilization of traditional gender categories and identities was not so importantly a thoroughgoing subversion of classical norms as, for Linda

Williams, "the moment when the experience of going to the movies began to be constituted as providing a certain generally transgressive sexualized thrill of promiscuous abandonment to indeterminate, 'other' identities."[16] The production reworked the very process of viewing film, in other words, and remade the pleasures wrought by Hollywood movies. Williams writes,

> *Psycho* needs to be seen as an historical marker of a moment when popular American movies, facing the threat of television, in competition and cooperation with new kinds of amusement parks, began to invent new scopic regimes of visual and visceral "attraction." In this moment visual culture can be seen getting a tighter grip on the visual pleasures of film spectators through the reinstitution of a postmodern cinema of attractions.[17]

Put more simply, Hitchcock's film inaugurates what has been called the "cinema of sensation," in which viewers were more viscerally engaged by new aesthetic forms than they had been by the previously dominant "cinema of sentiment."[18]

Still earlier, mainstream cinema of the 1950s offered increasing visions of bodily violation, injury, and death in narratives that were far more ambivalent about the occurrence or consequence of violence than had previously been the case. These images and narratives bespoke a creative attempt to engage the aesthetic traditions of Hollywood while also addressing new postwar social, political, and psychological realities. Many were personal visions of exceptional individual directors like Hitchcock, Fuller, Ray, and Aldrich; such productions as *Rebel Without A Cause* (1955) and *The Searchers* (1956) self-consciously exploited the tensions their makers understood to be inherent in classical film practice. At the same time, American cinema can be seen to have drawn its dramatic conflicts from those anxieties and fears pervading contemporary society: Cold War paranoia, the influence of consumer culture, post-World War II traumas, and family tensions. Westerns, *film noir*, and domestic melodramas, as well as less easily categorizable films like *In A Lonely Place* (1950) and *Vertigo* (1958), forcefully convey the simmering, often explosive internal, emotional, or psychological violence of familiar characters and everyday situations.

One can go back further, of course, to the widespread and influential visual experience of the battlefront in World War II or to depictions of criminal brutishness in gangster films of the 1930s.[19]

However, the point is that such overlapping historical accounts and criteria for comprehending movie violence make uneasy any stable conceptions of classicism and subversion; that is, of turning points or starting points for a history of onscreen bloodletting. Even as *Bonnie and Clyde* may deserve a privileged place in the history of film – certainly the history of film violence – the matter of *why* warrants thoughtful consideration beyond revisiting public debates at the time or privileging certain critical legacies since. "The idea of historical periodization itself," writes Townsley, "serves as a classification system."[20] Examining that idea and exploring other periods enables one to problematize the prevailing classificatory scheme of film violence grounded in the New Hollywood of "the Sixties."

"The Sixties" as device for normative evaluation[21]

The "film violence" trope circulating today has mostly naturalized the historical rendering of certain events and relations from the 1960s and 1970s such that they are now understood as the given, fundamental terms or frameworks for discourse about the period. The deployment of, and debates over, cinematic bloodletting and carnage from "the Sixties" have become the touchstones of discussions of subsequent movie violence and provide the standards by which such violence is considered – whether in individual film texts or in more wide-ranging accounts of Hollywood as a social institution. Again, this is not to deny the importance and innovations of the period; it is, precisely, to test how characteristic and applicable are the apparently extraordinary productions and contexts of the period in assessing other historical, cultural and institutional forms and contexts of violence. It is also to examine closely the dominant critical field though which the period and given films and problematics of violence are understood.

One reason for questioning the universal or timeless relevance of issues raised by filmmakers and critics in the 1960s and 1970s is the very historical specificity embraced as so fundamental to accounts of Hollywood during these years. The richness and variety of transitions identifiable at the time afford convenient historical referents for changes onscreen: the breakdown and critique of classical economies of vision, new models of social interaction, unprecedented images of corporeal invasion and damage, the collapse of narratives defined by recuperative violence and, again, the familiar social markers of

Vietnam, urban and racial unrest, the political assassinations of JFK and others, and media coverage of them all. For these reasons, "the Sixties" are often seen to reveal allegedly essential attributes, preoccupations, and tensions of American culture and cinema. In this way, the period – and the understanding of "film violence" retrospectively grounded therein – serves as a contested discourse that remains bounded in terms of the questions that might be posed about it. For policymakers, critics, and the public today, the contests over the meaning of "film violence" redound upon their views of the decade, its place in history, and the legacy of the politics that are seen to have defined it. As Townsley writes, "the Sixties" trope "operationalizes a moral standard for liberals and conservatives alike" in their articulation of political, social, and academic positions today.[22] The same might be said of a trope of "film violence" by which are oriented positions on questions of responsibility, effects, and institutional and moral authority.

Illustrating this process is Sam Peckinpah, whose films and ideas about violence in cinema and the actual world have functioned as a central source of subsequent position-taking on "film violence." Never at home in a changing cinema, persistently controversial with the public and tragically fascinated with issues of violence, he has been seen unmistakably as a filmmaker of the 1960s and early 1970s. For Stephen Prince, the probing historian of the director's preoccupation with violence, "Peckinpah's films give articulate shape to the myriad forms of late sixties radical thought and antiestablishment sentiment. His films mirror the national preoccupation with violence that shaped those years and the extent to which violence had infused the inner fantasy life of the culture."[23] In *Savage Cinema*, Prince documents the director's near-obsession with the torporific effects of contemporary media – especially nightly images of television violence – by revealing his adverse reactions to the incident at My Lai and his beliefs in Robert Ardrey's writings on territoriality and the animal origin of human violence.[24] The result is a convincing portrait of the artist as horrified observer of turbulent times.

Peckinpah's stated aim was to undermine viewers' conventional, distanced, and finally safe vantage points for watching movie violence. The director insisted that he wanted neither to celebrate nor to document acts of violence; instead, as in *The Wild Bunch*, he presented stylized renditions of gore in an attempt to upset the complacency he perceived in contemporary consumers of Hollywood films and TV news. By heightening the artifice of violence in his films, he claimed to hope to convey the horrors of the era to viewers inured to society's real violence – as he might put it, to wake viewers up to what violence was really all about. Taking Peckinpah at his word, his attitudes and films reflected the violence in play in contemporary society; it was precisely the large-scale events of the time, of Vietnam and the tumult at home, that gave root to his depictions of horror and pain. Yet once he started making violent films, the responses of viewers made the director rethink the potential of filmgoing as a purgative or illuminating experience and caused him to refashion the images themselves.

Such an approach to cinematic and social violence betrays a more widespread preoccupation of researchers and policymakers (and other filmmakers) at the time with the "effects" of media images on viewers. The search for an empirically demonstrable and unified conception of behavior, which could explain both individual action and the influential force of environmental factors like political propaganda and mass media, had become a priority for social science researchers following World War II. An illustration of this focus is the centrality of "brainwashing" and group thinking to accounts of Hollywood cinema and US society during the 1950s.[25] Yet the consolidation of empirical research on media effects, and the public and institutional debates that occurred around it, took place during the 1960s. Looking back, then, to examine closely the constitution of a discourse of "effects" of film violence in the 1960s also requires evaluating how the predominance of that discourse about film violence is itself an *effect* of "the Sixties."

The discourse of "effects" was consolidated and advanced when communication studies became a discrete academic field of study generating expertise relevant to Cold War-era knowledge production and public policymaking. The institutionalization of this field as a social science and the driving research on propaganda and media effects merit attention in plumbing the intellectual roots of behavioralist approaches to film and media violence.[26] Even a cursory review of research from the 1950s and 1960s on the relation between film and aggression or violence reveals the preponderant attention to behavioral concerns and, particularly, "effects."[27] That attention, for Timothy Glander, was "driven by a mass media system that had redirected its efforts from winning support for World War II to now continuously (and in near unison) warning of the threat of an international communist conspiracy."[28] The priority of much "effects" research was to analyze the instrumentality of media rather than specific cultural, political or ideological concerns engaged by media. Perhaps not surprisingly, the first development of this research was "for the direct, explicit use of broadcasters and advertisers."[29] In part, this was an outgrowth of the radio market research conducted in the 1930s, but it also derived from approaches to individual and group behavior developed for the war effort in the early 1940s. Among these were content analysis, response analysis, individual and group interviews, and participant observation. Linked to other disciplines grounded in empirical inquiry and with a shared interest in the expansion of university research, the "science" of communication's illumination of the operations of mass media fit conceptually into models of society and individual behavior being forged by other social scientists and embraced by government and policy makers.

The major theories underlying these efforts were social learning and behavioralism. Related research thrived during early Cold War years preoccupied with propaganda, persuasion, advertising and mass marketing, and the links between ideology and individual attitudes and behavior. Behavioralism emerged during these years as the authorized form of psychological knowledge by competing with, and triumphing over, models such as psychoanalysis or, in closer relation to media, "direct influence" (which persisted in public discourse despite having been surpassed by many researchers in the 1920s and 1930s). With emphases on attitudinal and behavioral effects of violence, social learning and behavioralism persists in informing and even defining much communication research and policymaking about film and media violence.[30]

Today, the invocation of "film violence" continues to tend strongly toward a critical and public discourse premised on the issue of behavioral "effects" of viewing (putatively) violent movies. In so orienting discourse, the trope of "film violence" effectively delimits the scope and focus of attention to cinematic brutality and bloodletting. It also enables the ready attachment of moral judgments – of Hollywood film being "good" or "bad" for its violence – to these supposedly more objective or scientific evaluations. Such readings of film violence as a matter of effects have become naturalized through repetition and the legitimation accorded by funding, policy debates, and even industry pronouncements, though upon closer inspection they can also be seen to rely directly on formulations that were consolidated in the historically specific conditions of the 1960s. In fact, by identifying the particular political and institutional roots of the "film violence" trope and the discourse of evaluating "effects" it references, we might more critically consider what have evolved as naturalized readings of cinematic violence and the moral judgments attached to them. We might also begin to imagine alternative models of violence and of popular cinema that do not so restrictively or contentiously turn on the fact or morality of behavioral effects.

The politics of history – and of indexing film violence[31]

What might be alternatives to the predominant discourse of "film violence" shaped by research and policymaking attention to behavioral effects? First, the definition of "violence" can be reconsidered to comprise images both of blood and holes, that is, of corporeal transgressions, and of a wider range of injurious social relations. If violence is a function of relations of power, of violations, victimization, oppression, and harm, or of legitimate social and political change, a greater variety of representations – relations between genders, say, or races, or economic classes, or throughout everyday life – can be construed as violent. A second, related approach might involve far-reaching analysis of the corporate media institutions responsible for mainstream cinema; such analysis can proceed from the premise that these corporations are intricately engaged in overarching relations of social power and that the "film violence" they produce is shaped for institutional reasons. Third, the emphasis of research on "film violence" tends to isolate and decontextualize cinema, or the popular culture of which it is part, as discrete and distanced from individual lives or larger social practices. The proliferation and saturation of electronic media can shed more light on the mediation of society – not as cause for lament or nostalgia but as basis for reconceptualizing media and social practices.

These alternatives nevertheless beg a further question: since the 1960s, why has the trope of "film violence" continued chiefly to signify a discourse turning on behavioral effects and mostly excluding alternatives from widespread development? One answer returns to the idea of New Hollywood or, more precisely, whatever break can be discerned between identifiable classical norms and the increasingly self-conscious and subversive moments that followed. Writing of Peckinpah, Prince claims that the filmmaker is "the crucial link between classical and postmodern Hollywood, the figure whose work transforms modern cinema in terms of stylistics for rendering screen violence and in terms of the moral and psychological consequences that ensue."[32] Others, like Christopher Sharrett and Catherine Russell, partly locate such a transformation in changing stylistics and images, while also challenging the integrity of moral, psychological, social, and mythical formations upon which continuities or discontinuities might be based.[33] "Film violence" in this way becomes a shorthand for a contested critical terrain on which are played out arguments about changes in film practice and, much more broadly, the shifting horizons of cultural history and political economy marked by such terms as classicism, modernism, and postmodernism.

The postmodern critical gaze ranges over stylistics and narrative, the status of cultural myths, the role of ideology, and the relations between institutional practices and individuals. A familiar summary definition of postmodernism, from Jean-Francois Lyotard, turns on a refusal of earlier, "modern" claims of grand, unifying narratives or meta-discourse and an embrace of the contingent and the fragmentary.[34] Characterizing contemporary culture are concerns such as a profound exhaustion, disaffection, crisis, and sense of the apocalypse. In cinema, contemporary films employ intertextual references and pastiche appropriate styles and references freely from throughout film and media history, producing historically "depthless" movies whose simulation of, and nostalgia for, the past are based in existing representations rather than any attempt to re-create a "real" past. They signal the collapse of traditional cultural or aesthetic hierarchies and the concomitant exhaustion of given cinematic forms or modes of production.

Among these is perhaps the guiding logic of violence in the American experience, ritual sacrifice, which appears to some postmodern critics as no longer able to redeem individual or community or to restore equilibrium to society. "While scapegoating and the continued persecution of the Other . . . are still paramount in the reunification of a disintegrating social order," Sharrett writes, "such notions have been sufficiently exposed in public discourse as to render them steadily useless as myths reuniting a civilization, yet they are played out, rather desperately, for their own sake."[35] Martin Scorsese's *Taxi Driver*, which concludes with the apparent rewarding of violent action, illustrates how this critique and failure of redemptive cultural myths in society are born from "superficial and

3 Psycho's (1960) rupture with classical forms: "What begins as a tale of adultery and the promise of conventional heterosexual desire is abruptly remade into the story of obsessive and murderous psychosis."

misleading" images "perpetuated by the media" and a "political structure afraid to examine its own bankruptcy."[36] Crucial to Sharrett's critical efforts has been the resituating of sacrifice as a mode of defining and explaining violence in popular culture. Closely reading René Girard's theories, he questions the appropriateness of the structural process of ritual sacrifice to contemporary identity formation and social relations.[37] Sharrett does not question whether contemporary culture continues to feature sacrifice and scapegoating. Instead, his rethinking of Girard's work is driven by the issue of whether the structural employment of these forms and ubiquitous media representations of bloodletting remain connected to shared myths that still shape and define the society and the viewer's place in it – or whether the myths have been destroyed, individuals diminished, and the society depoliticized, leaving narratives of sacrifice empty and defined only by their value as commodities.[38]

Such a failure of traditional discourses of violence, identity formation, and social cohesion also involves the encroachment of media on

the boundaries of individual and collective identities. National myths
or cultural codes of cinematic representation are eroded and other
substantive meanings largely evacuated, leaving only the images
themselves. Even the most graphic instance of filmic violence potentially becomes homogenized and emptied of meaning or seeming
originality. As films become largely self-referential commodities, the
concern is that they are increasingly intended for the spectator's consumption – regardless of "content." This viewpoint casts light on a
contemporary culture of simulated experience, media suffusion, and
symbolic commodification and consumption. It also helps to make
sense of a mainstay of recent Hollywood cinema, the slasher and
serial killer films, which has roots in early productions like
The Texas Chain Saw Massacre (1973) and *Halloween* that directly
link ostensibly depoliticized and commodified images of physical
brutality (ordinarily against women) with discourses of pornography
and exploitation.[39]

The nub of many claims of postmodern violence is their reflexive
critique of institutional, media, and social relations, and the suppo-
sition that the bases of individual identity and social life have been
irremediably changed since the 1960s. To expand a discussion of
"film violence," postmodern critics thus posit different assumptions
concerning cinema, society, psychology, and violence – or, at least, a
greater willingness to interrogate traditional assumptions. Rather
than assuming a coherent contemporary society and cultural order
comparable to that which existed during the period of classical
cinema, critics critique the foundations of the received social contract and mythical compact, and emphasize the fragmentary quality
of social experience. Likewise subject to analysis is the integrity of
individuals with discrete identities shaped by psychologically motivated relations with others and society. Quite obviously, to question
models of psychology and individual action is to challenge the
assumptions underlying behavioral effects models and hence the
widespread public discourse of violence predicated upon them.

The acceptance – or skepticism – of *re*-evaluating traditional
assumptions about identity, psychology, and society determine
responses to much recent film violence and to the historical field one
sees it occupying. Such critiques, in other words, readily assume a
political valence. At least in public policy debates, "film violence"
remains a largely circumscribed topic that does not readily admit
critiques of the inequitable power relations, political economy, or

institutional bases of American society. The historical consolidation
of social authority over the production of knowledge about film violence created "official" approaches to media, media violence, and
their effects. These approaches predominated at universities and
foundations, the social institutions where the production of knowledge was broadly funded and legitimated. They were also embraced
by the government and the public as the basis for policymaking and
debate. Their emphases on social science research on media violence
emerged from discursive formations operating in the early Cold War
years. Put more directly, these social scientists emerged as the stew-
ards of official knowledge that delimited understandings of "film
violence" in research and public policy discussions.

At the same time, other topics of progressive or even radical concern were marginalized from "official" or public debate and con-
signed to particular quarters of the academy or public and
independent media.[40] These have included consideration of a wider
range of violent social and institutional relations, including systemic
oppression and victimization based on social and economic
inequities. They also entail alternatives to prevailing models that
insist US society can no longer (if it ever could) rely on regeneration
through individual or collective violence but that new images and
instances of violence are nevertheless central to reconceptions of
contemporary identity and society. For both traditional and alternative models, in other words, violence serves as a defining referent for
very different guiding assumptions of identity and social life. Similarly, the production of knowledge about "film violence" – whether
functioning to perpetuate or to critique prevailing discourses – tends
to invoke mostly the same basic index of historical, cinematic, and
cultural examples from the 1960s and 1970s.

"Film violence" then (and now)

Images of bodily harm, pain and death, and of the deployment of
rough or injurious physical force – a preliminary baseline definition
of violence – have been presented and then critically approached,
researched, and modeled in specific, bounded ways in public and
especially policymaking discourse. The call here has been to question
assumptions about public authority, institutional roles, media, and
morality that remain grounded in the 1960s and 1970s. As is the case
in a range of historical work, the decade remains a crucible by which

4 A "stylized rendition of gore" in Sam Peckinpah's *The Wild Bunch* (1969)

contemporary politics and society are measured and rearticulated: did the events of the 1960s constitute a revolutionary break from the past whose legacy still irremediably shapes the present, or were they a more ephemeral rupture with few lasting and meaningful consequences?[41] Townsley neatly characterizes the tension as between "conservative narratives of moral decay," quantifiable through research and documentable in challenges to longstanding social relations and institutions, and "liberal accounts of paradise lost," during which structural and historical inequities were addressed and a fuller range of violence (including the systemic and the liberatory) was exposed. That her characterization relies squarely on a moral charge seems especially fitting when considering Hollywood's imaginings of violence, its participation in the counterculture at the time, and their continuing, contested legacy today.

So what are the guiding assumptions or first principles operative in Hollywood representations of violence in the 1960s and 1970s and how are they understood retrospectively? This essay has attempted to contribute to answers by (1) foregrounding the importance of questioning origins and the classification schema used to approach film violence, particularly those of "the Sixties" and "New Hollywood"; (2) tracking the prevailing normative analytics of film violence based in behavioral effects by marking them as historically specific; and (3) illuminating the intellectual and cultural politics in play in either perpetuating or critiquing prevailing analytical models. Throughout, I have proposed that the trope of "film violence" has emerged as a shorthand that circumscribes meaning and authorizes delimited explanations of a wide range of phenomena. It is our responsibility as critics to interrogate that trope and the discursive field in which it operates as fully as possible. Compared to communication scholars and social psychologists, film scholars have indeed been silent and absent. Yet the call should not simply be for them (us) to become participants in existing public debates or contributors to ongoing research; they (we) should not necessarily aspire, as Stephen Prince has urged, to replace their "interpretations" with the approaches undertaken and "findings" produced by social scientists.[42] The challenge today is to expand scholarly as well as public discourse about film and violence so that "interpretations" about the operations and meanings of cinema are as germane to those discourses and debates as the "findings" of social scientists about film and other media's effects on actual behavior. Such an enterprise might constructively proceed with rigorous attention to the histories of these approaches, of periodizations like "New Hollywood" and of critical – and cultural – shorthands like "film violence."

Notes

1 Pauline Kael's Oct. 21, 1967 *New Yorker* magazine review of *Bonnie and Clyde* reads, "The dirty reality of death – not suggestions but blood and holes – is necessary"; rpt. in *Arthur Penn's "Bonnie and Clyde,"* ed. Lester D. Friedman (New York: Cambridge University Press, 2000), 188. See Paul Monaco, "Landmark Movies of the 1960s and the Cinema of Sensation," *The Sixties: 1960–1969, vol. 8: The History of American Cinema* (New York: Charles Scribner's Sons, 2001), 168–97; Stephen Prince, *Savage Cinema: Sam Peckinpah and the Rise of Ultraviolent Movies* (Austin: University of Texas Press, 1998).

2 *Mythologies of Violence in Postmodern Media*, ed. Christopher Sharrett (Detroit: Wayne State University Press, 1999); *Screening Violence*, ed. Stephen Prince (New Brunswick: Rutgers University Press, 2000); Laurent Bouzereau, *Ultraviolent Movies: From Sam Peckinpah to Quentin Tarantino* (Secaucus: Citadel, 1996).

3 Eleanor Townsley, "'The Sixties' Trope," *Theory, Culture & Society* 18.6 (2001): 99–123.

4 *Ibid.*, 100. Among White's seminal writings, see esp. *Tropics of Discourse: Essays in Cultural Criticism* (Baltimore: Johns Hopkins University Press, 1978).

5 Townsley, "'The Sixties'", 112.

6 *Ibid.*, 104.

7 *Ibid.*, 105.

8 Fredric Jameson, "Periodizing the 60s," *The 60s Without Apology*, ed. Sohnya Sayres, *et al.* (Minneapolis: University of Minnesota Press,

1984), 178–209; Andrew Marwick, *The Sixties: Cultural Revolution in Britain, France, Italy, and the United States c. 1958–1974* (New York: Oxford University Press, 1998). See also, Van Gosse and Richard Moser, ed., *The World the 60s Made* (Philadelphia: Temple University Press, 2003).

9 Roland Barthes, "The Structural Analysis of Narratives" (1966), *Image-Music-Text* (New York: Hill & Wang, 1977), 92–7.

10 David Bordwell, Janet Staiger, and Kristen Thompson, *The Classical Hollywood Cinema: Film Style and Mode of Production to 1960* (New York: Columbia University Press, 1987).

11 Murray Smith, "Theses on the Philosophy of Hollywood History," *Contemporary Hollywood Cinema*, ed. Steve Neale and Murray Smith (New York: Routledge, 1998), 3–20.

12 J. Hoberman, "'A Test for the Individual Viewer': *Bonnie and Clyde*'s Violent Reception," *Why We Watch: The Attractions of Violent Entertainment*, ed. Jeffrey Goldstein (New York: Oxford University Press, 1998), 116–43.

13 *Ibid.*, 141.

14 Greil Marcus, *The Manchurian Candidate* (London: BFI, 2002), 26.

15 See James Chapman, *Licence to Thrill: A Cultural History of the James Bond Films* (New York: Columbia University Press, 2000), 65–110.

16 Linda Williams, "Discipline and Fun: *Psycho* and Postmodern Cinema," *Reinventing Film Studies*, ed. Christine Gledhill and Linda Williams (New York: Oxford University Press, 2000), 361–2.

17 *Ibid.*, 367.

18 Monaco, "Landmark Movies", 188–92.

19 In "Film Violence and the Institutionalization of Cinema" (*Social Research* 67.3 [2000]: 649–81), I argue that the evolution across the twentieth century of industry and public discourses about movie violence corresponds with, and contributes to, key moments in the institutionalization of popular cinema. See also, Stephen Prince, *Classical Hollywood Violence: Designing and Regulating Brutality in Hollywood Cinema, 1930–1968* (New Brunswick: Rutgers University Press, 2003).

20 Townsley, "'The Sixties'", 116 n.8.

21 This section reworks material that previously appeared in my review of Prince's *Savage Cinema*, in *Media, Culture, and Society* 22.5 (2000): 692–7.

22 Townsley, "'The Sixties'", 108.

23 Prince, *Savage Cinema*, 42.

24 Ardrey was an anthropologist who contributed to the spirited public debate about the origins of aggression, arguing that culture was merely a sublimation of human animal instinct. His books included *African Genesis* (1961), *The Territorial Imperative* (1966), and *The Social*

Contract (1970). Probably the best-known contribution to the debate overall was Konrad Lorenz's *On Aggression*, which appeared in English translation in 1966.

25   See, for example, Charles Young, "Missing Action: POW Films, Brainwashing and the Korean War, 1954–1968," *Historical Journal of Film, Radio and Television* 18.1 (1998): 49–74; Susan Carruthers, "*The Manchurian Candidate* (1962) and the Cold War Brainwashing Scare," *Historical Journal of Film, Radio and Television* 18.1 (1998): 75–94.

26   Recent histories of the discipline have themselves suggested as much. See, for example, J. D. Peters, "Genealogical Notes on 'the Field'," *Journal of Communication* 43.4 (1993): 132–9; and the essays collected in *American Communication Research: The Remembered History*, ed. Everette Dennis and Ellen Wartella (Mahwah: Lawrence Erlbaum, 1996).

27   Summaries of early research on "effects" include Joseph Klapper, "What We Know About the Effects of Mass Communication," *Public Opinion Quarterly* 21 (1957–58): 453–74; and Steven Chaffee and John Hochheimer, "The Beginnings of Political Communication Research in the United States: Origins of the 'Limited Effects' Model," *The Media Revolution in America and Western Europe*, ed. Everett Rogers and Francis Balle (Norwood: Ablex, 1985), 267–96. On film specifically, see R. S. Albert, "The Role of Mass Media and the Effect of Aggressive Film Content Upon Children's Aggressive Responses and Identification Choices," *Genetic Psychology Monographs* 55 (1957): 221–83; Albert Bandura, *et al.*, "Imitation of Film-Mediated Aggressive Models," *Journal of Abnormal and Social Psychology* 66.1 (1963): 3–11; Leonard Berkowitz and Edna Rawlings, "Effects of Film Violence on Inhibitions against Subsequent Aggression," *Journal of Abnormal and Social Psychology* 66.5 (1963): 405–12; and Leonard Berkowitz and Russell Green, "Film Violence and the Cue Properties of Available Targets," *Journal of Personality and Social Psychology* 3.5 (1966): 525–30.

28   Timothy Glander, *Origins of Mass Communications Research During the American Cold War: Educational Effects and Contemporary Implications* (Mahwah: Lawrence Erlbaum, 2000), 58.

29   Todd Gitlin, "Media Sociology: The Dominant Paradigm," *Theory and Society* 6 (1978): 207.

30   Speaking generally, research into mass communication and behavioral effects prevailed until the development of another (not necessarily incompatible) major theory, of desensitization, in the early 1970s. In the US since then, many communication scholars have attempted to broaden the range of their critical attention to film and media violence. Cecilia von Felitzen observes at least four areas of research today: a continuation of inquiries into effects and the nature of aggression; the

(typically negative) role of media and culture; the variety and activity of audiences; and the economics and political relations that shape and supply context for film and media. Von Felitzen, "Media Violence: Four Research Perspectives," *Approaches to Media: A Reader*, ed. Roger Dickinson, *et al.* (New York: Oxford University Press, 1998), 88–103.

31 This section reworks material that previously appeared in my review of *Mythologies of Violence in Postmodern Media*, ed. Christopher Sharrett, in *Film Quarterly* 54.4 (2001): 58–9.

32 Prince, *Savage Cinema*, 2.

33 See Sharrett, *Mythologies*; and Catherine Russell, "Decadence, Violence, and the Decay of History: Notes on the Spectacular Representation of Death in Narrative Film, 1965–1990," *Crisis Cinema: The Apocalyptic Idea in Postmodern Narrative Film*, ed. Christopher Sharrett (Washington, D.C.: Maisonneuve Press, 1993), 173–201.

34 Jean-Francois Lyotard, *The Postmodern Condition: A Report on Knowledge* (Minneapolis: University of Minnesota Press, 1984).

35 Sharrett, "Introduction," *Mythologies*, 18.

36 Sharrett, "'The American Apocalypse': Scorsese's *Taxi Driver*," *Crisis Cinema*, 233.

37 Sharrett, "Afterword: Sacrificial Violence and Postmodern Ideology," *Mythologies*, 413–34.

38 Sharrett and others have advanced Georges Bataille's alternative model of sacrificial violence as transgression, a way of introducing disequilirium into a society of consumption. Sacrifice for Bataille is a productively disruptive release of excess or irrationality in an ordered economy. See Bataille, *Visions of Excess: Selected Writings, 1927–1939* (Minneapolis: University of Minnesota Press, 1985); Bataille, *The Accursed Share, vol. 1: An Essay on General Economy* (New York: Zone Books, 1988).

39 See, for example, Carol Clover, *Men, Women and Chain Saws: Gender in the Modern Horror Film* (Princeton: Princeton University Press, 1992).

40 The academy has been a central site in the negotiation and privileging of meanings of "film violence" since the 1960s. The very history of Cinema or Film Studies as a discipline since the 1970s can be seen as coinciding with the linguistic, cultural, and theoretical turns and, to an extent, institutionalizing the separations between humanistic studies arguably more willing to critique power relations and political economy *and* social sciences that (with important exceptions) perpetuate prevailing and socially-legitimated modes of media analysis.

41 See, relatedly, Mark Lilla, "A Tale of Two Reactions," *The New York Review of Books* (May 14, 1998).

42 Stephen Prince, "Why Do Film Scholars Ignore Movie Violence?", *The Chronicle of Higher Education* (Aug. 10, 2001): B18–19.

2

Hitchcock and the dramaturgy of screen violence

Murray Pomerance

> Any surface covered with characters turns into something crammed and seething . . . full of lives and objects, of everything to be found in the world. (Henri Michaux)

Two women are subjected onscreen to what viewers can read as extremity of violence. The first is a general practitioner's wife, vacationing with him and their ten-year-old son in a foreign country which is, by their provincial standards, bizarre, dark, even forbidding just so much as it is intoxicating and exotic. One day, the doctor and his wife are called to visit a police station to give account of a murder they have just witnessed, and as they head off, the wife takes the liberty of leaving the boy with some other tourists, a genteel Englishwoman and her well-meaning husband, whom they met the night before at dinner and who promise to take the boy safely back to the hotel so that he isn't exposed to all the unpleasantness. Not long afterward, and completely outside of his wife's ken, the doctor learns that his son has been kidnapped, in fact to prevent the man's giving any details to the police of what the murder victim whispered into his ear just before dying. Stunned, he telephones the hotel and finds that the English couple have not returned. Quickly and tactfully he escorts his wife back, hoping against hope – and with manifest secrecy – that what he has learned isn't true. When they arrive he sends her upstairs and does some checking with the concierge. Sure enough, the tourists have checked out and vanished, with the boy in tow. Now the wife is resting in the hotel room. The doctor enters. Without telling her why, he goes to his kit and withdraws a dose of sedatives, asking her to take them. She protests. He tells her he has something to reveal that involves their son, and that the price of hearing the story is that she take the pills. Resentfully, she complies. When the sedative begins to take effect, he tells her what he knows.

Now, as she is powerlessly dropping off under the drug's influence, her heart cries out pathetically for her lost boy. She curses her husband for having been cruel enough to sedate her before falling into an oblivion that is the quintessence of narrative darkness.

In the second case, a very young mother enters a California convenience store to buy a chocolate bar for her little boy. While she is making the transaction at the counter, a robber with a ski mask on steals up behind her, places a gun to her temple, and fires two shots into her brain. She drops to the floor. Killing the store owner as well, the robber bends to examine the woman and flees the scene, winking insouciantly at the surveillance camera before leaving. Indeed, all of this is seen later on a TV monitor, and from the perspective of that surveillance equipment, by a former FBI agent who has devoted himself to looking for clues to this killing, since, to make a complex story too simple, he has had a heart transplant and has recently learned that the heart in his chest came from the woman he is watching being murdered. Peering at the tape again and again, he ultimately concludes that the motive for the crime was not the robbery of the convenience store but in fact turning the woman into a corpse so that her organs could be harvested. The killing is nothing less than cold-blooded slaughter, and he is the heretofore unwitting beneficiary.

In these two scenes – each in its own way central to the turning of the plot of the film that contains it, yet neither wholly representative of the complexity of the film in which it is a part – it is apparent that a young mother in a vulnerable position has been brutally aggressed upon by a male protagonist with method, motive, and power. Indeed, it could be argued that both scenes centrally depict "an intrusion of the forms of power associated with one field in the functioning of another" – procedures of professional medical practice infiltrating everyday family relations – and therefore fit Pierre Bourdieu's definition of tyranny.[1] Filmed forty-six years apart, Alfred Hitchcock's *The Man Who Knew Too Much* (1956), in which Doris Day is subdued by James Stewart, and Clint Eastwood's *Blood Work* (2002), in which Eastwood observes the murder that makes possible the continuation of his own life, both rely upon very particular stagings (and very different types) of violence to flesh out their stories, even though violence is, in both cases, secondary to what the films are more deeply and more fully about. Though there is considerable violence of many kinds in each, to be sure, the two scenes I have described happen to apotheosize what is violent in those two motion

pictures, and also suggest some lines of approach toward distinguishing violence in film today from violence in the sunset years of
the studio era.

The murder in *Blood Work* – all of the murders in this film look
to be as swift and compulsive as the one I have described – lacks the
preparation, cadence, character, and personal connection one can
expect to find in Hitchcock. The murder is in fact utterly imper-
sonal. It isn't because of who she is but because of her membership
in a group that the woman in *Blood Work* dies: it is a small group,
to be sure, a rare blood type that our protagonist also has (and shares
with yet one more victim – oddly, in the context of the *narrative* the
blood type isn't, and cannot be, so rare), and so it is on the basis of
an exhaustive process of analysis, categorization, comparison, mea-
surement, objectification, even commodification that violence is perpetrated in this film. In the Hitchcock, by contrast, the moves the
doctor makes to lure his wife into readiness for the secret he must
unleash betray his profound knowledge of every aspect of her character, his acquiescence to the bonds of their marriage, his fealty to
the Hippocratic oath, the aggressive nuances of his own character,
and the story's dramatic needs – and *all at once*. In short, the violence is sculpted to serve dramaturgical ends well beyond titillating
the viewer with a safe, detached perspective on pain and suffering.

In numerous recent films, we see hyperobjective, almost abstract
violence perpetrated with no reference to the characterological or
narrative context, rather as though violence has become only a fashionable interior decoration in contemporary blockbuster stories. I will
try to show here that, notwithstanding George Gerbner's observation
that such excessively violent stories "travel best around the world,
since they entertain in the easiest and cheapest way,"[2] there is more to
screen violence than its contribution to profitable production and distribution, the ease with which it can be apprehended, and the jolts it
can offer. Yet the jolts are there. In Kathryn Bigelow's *K-19: The Wid-
owmaker* (2002), for example, a number of handsome young sub-
mariners are forced to enter the reaction chamber of a submarine's
nuclear power supply without adequate protection; after a few minutes, each comes out bleeding, blistered, contaminated, irradiated,
vomiting, and gasping for air, and soon each of them dies. They are
not characters who have been developed roundly, with whom we
have come to feel relation. When they die, we merely count them as
so many festering objects, although their conditions are depicted in

extreme and hideous detail.[3] Nor does the overall story depend radically on what happens to these characters, since none by dying manages to steer the plot, and since it is the survivors who are the film's
stars. In a sanctimonious finale, visiting the graves and toasting the
dead men with vodka, these survivors (among them the tough and
crotchety Harrison Ford and the statuesque Liam Neeson) are given
leave to establish this narrative hegemony, in fact. Yet long sequences
are devoted to showing the incipient victims donning useless rain
gear, opening and then re-sealing heavy protective doors, bravely
climbing into the radioactive area, stumbling around in the cloying
radioactive mist, gagging, coughing, collapsing, stumbling away
again, being dragged to sick bay in a trail of their own regurgitation.

Not all brutal violence is physical. In *Spider Man* (2002), an ego-
tistical, arrogant, and foppish evil scientist (Willem Dafoe) permits
an elderly woman recently widowed (by him, although she doesn't
know it) to cook an elaborate Thanksgiving dinner in his honor. As
soon as the food is brought to the table, however, he allows himself
to be snagged into an argument with his prodigal son, pulls himself
to his feet, and strides out in a smarmy huff, so that the happy party
is broken up and virtually everyone trails off home. The hostess is
left to silently admire her costly meal, which now sits gleaming on
the table and ready to be wasted. But nothing in the scene is vital to
the action: the scientist's arrogance has already been established, as
has the old lady's tenderness and vulnerability, so no overriding dramatic significance attaches to the destruction of her hospitality. Yet
we are asked to revel in a woman's humiliation and in the wanton
deconstruction of a simple testamentary celebration of civic faith.
The shooting down of the Thanksgiving meal is quite as perfunctory
and impulsive as *Blood Work*'s convenience store killing.

Recent Hollywood action and adventure films are by no means
unique in their prominent use of violent content. As Gerbner
implies, the need to amass a global audience and the widely amplified quality of sexuality and violence have combined as forces to
leech superfluity of violent action into even romantic comedy
(*Mickey Blue Eyes* [1999], *Hollywood Ending* [2002]), serious family
drama (*American Beauty* [1999], *Full Frontal* [2002], *Donnie Darko*
[2001]), and children's films (*Small Soldiers* [1998], *Stuart Little*
[1999]). But I do not think we respond to all screen violence in precisely the same way, or that it is as monolithic as moral entrepreneurs
like to make out in campaigning about it – apparatus theorists, for

example, central to whose formulation is "the view that movies are inherently violent."[4] In terms of its structure, we can think of contemporary filmic violence in terms of two discrete variables, which I would call "irony" and "probability." I will give some consideration to these variables by way of exploring the differences between some interesting moments of violence onscreen. I hope this is a way of making some useful distinctions in speaking about contemporary and older film, though my argument will suffice if it only flies in the face of the taken-for-granted assumption that every act of screen violence is indistinguishable from any other in perniciousness and corruptive effect.

By *irony*, I mean to describe the tendency of a particular screen depiction to contradict or subvert received attitudes, impressions, or expectations as to the "normal" or "proper" relationship between any two of the component elements of situated behavior (as itemized by Kenneth Burke): action, actor, scene, agency, and purpose.[5] We would "normally" expect a uniformed police officer wearing a gun in the pursuit of robbers to make use of the gun violently under certain circumstances, for example: the officer and the pursuit taken together establish what Burke would call an actor/purpose ratio. So, for the officer to shoot at the robber would hardly seem ironic. And to return to the example from *Blood Work*, when on a surveillance tape we see a masked man enter a convenience store, we are not shocked to find violence perpetrated by him. I would call "ironic" an instantiation of screen violence which specifically violates or disrupts the elemental ratios commonly accepted and expected in a culture. Clearly, the use of what I am calling irony is a central method filmmakers may use to undermine cultural assumptions, for example, the assumption held by racial profilers that black males are violent. Burke's "grammar of motives" – a heuristic device, and a language, that makes possible a dramaturgical analysis of social and mythic situations by providing a basis for explaining *how we explain that they come about* – is capable of being set up for destruction, transgression, interruption, modification, warping, or interference just as it is capable of being represented straight, as an ideological tool. Any moment of screen violence can therefore be considered as ironic or un-ironic, these labels obviously changing according to the prevailing expectations and attitudes in the cultural and historical setting in which film is watched.

Further, and regardless of irony, rather than hanging independently before the sensitivity of the viewer, filmic moments are set in dramatic contexts of ongoingness, discursive revelation, uncloaking, recall, and increasing probability. Any moment of screen violence, therefore, can be "probable," seeming to flow uninterrupted and untrammeled out of the background action and setting of the film as a whole – as when, in a film about car racing (*Days of Thunder* [1990], *Driven* [2001]), a car-crash occurs; or as when, in a film about a serial murderer (*Se7en* [1995], *The Silence of the Lambs* [1991]), murders occur one after the other. By distinction, an act of violence can seem "improbable," unique and bounded to itself and apparently springing out of a context not otherwise geared to support such an event. The explosion in Fritz Lang's *The Big Heat* (1953) is an example of an improbable moment of screen violence (though not an ironic one, since it occurs in a homicide detective's driveway); so is the introductory explosion in *Touch of Evil* (1958). The murder of Gus (David Duchovny) at the conclusion of *Full Frontal* is yet another. The monstrously casual assault upon his adolescent ego as Bill (Kevin Corrigan) overhears a phone message tape on which he is specifically described as ugly in *Walking and Talking* (1996) is still another. In improbable violence, a film that in general seems pacific and civil in content is suddenly interrupted by a depiction of violence that is generally shocking or alarming even if it is arranged so as to appear particularly apt and exciting at the moment it occurs: it galvanizes momentarily, but more broadly appears not to fit into the structure of the film. The shower scene in *Psycho* (1960) is a nice example. Another particularly vivid one is given by Charles Foster Kane's (Orson Welles) violent foray into his wife's bedroom in *Citizen Kane* (1941): in a film that is generally lucid, rational, intellectual, repressed, and economic there is a sudden explosion of physical violence in which, shot from below with a wide-angle lens, the looming giant, Kane, stiff as a robot gone amok, topples the bookshelves and dismantles the bed of the woman who has walked out on him. François Truffaut's *Fahrenheit 451* (1966) reprises this moment with a flame-thrower and a double-bed; here, the setting of objects on fire is generally structured as an orderly activity – all in the context of the story being what we might regard as ironic. But as the Captain (Cyril Cusack) warns Montag (Oskar Werner) when he sees him moving into the bedroom with the flame thrower, fire is only for entire houses, not for beds. In a film in which whole houses are burned down intentionally, then, one man's venting of rage by firing his marital bed is oddly "improbable."

Given the two variables of *irony* and *probability*, and the possibility in any onscreen instance of violence that each may or may not
contribute to the effect, a fourfold table can be generated giving four
types of screen violence:

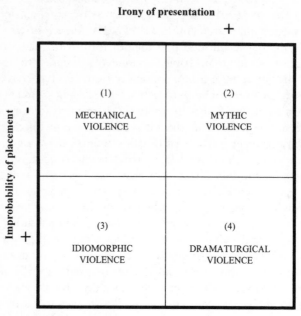

Irony of presentation

	−	+
Improbability of placement −	(1) MECHANICAL VIOLENCE	(2) MYTHIC VIOLENCE
+	(3) IDIOMORPHIC VIOLENCE	(4) DRAMATURGICAL VIOLENCE

5 Four types of screen violence

Let me digress to consider these one by one, with a view to returning afterward to contemporary screen violence in a general way and
to the example of Hitchcockian violence in a particular one. This
will permit some formal examination of screen violence, but also
some specific attention to Hitchcock's techniques – important, I
think, given the anti-auteurist slant of much recent appraisal of his
work. This in turn will allow for a reconsideration of the place of
Hitchcockian narrative structuring in contemporary cinema, which
may explain why Hitchcock holds the place he does in relation to
the makers of the kinds of egregiously violent recent films I have
been mentioning. That Hitchcock's dramaturgy of violence is not a
product of the "New Hollywood" is hardly the ultimate point; more
important is that he was the paradigmatic user of a formal mode
(here labeled "dramaturgical violence") virtually no longer in use

today. It is the dramaturgical violence we find uninteresting in film now, not Hitchcock; Hitchcock exemplifies dramaturgical violence as no other filmmaker ever has.

It is worth noting explicitly here that my analysis and taxonomy are not calculated along traditional historical lines; I do not consider "Old Hollywood violence" and "New Hollywood violence" as inherently different from one another in terms of historically and culturally ascertainable characteristics. But in fact I do hope to show differences – differences generated, to be sure, at different historical moments, but at the same time accessible to our perception through variation in categories (irony and improbability) that are themselves transhistorical.

Mechanical violence: probable and unironic

A moment of screen violence might be considered "mechanical" when it inheres in a narrative itself riddled with violence and established in a setting conducive to, demanding of, even productive of violence (it is probable); and when, also, its performance is framed in utterly conventional terms, fully reflecting expectations and stereotypes (it is unironic). Such violence is probable in context and unironic in manner. In the film which contains it we find, first, that violence is everywhere, often reflected in the setting but homogeneously imbuing the narrative with its fragmenting, brutal essence even if it is not what William Rothman says critics are often looking for, namely "physical violence – killings, beatings, mutilations, and the like."[6] Mechanical violence, then, is done by exactly the sort of doer we would expect and in circumstances already riddled with violence all around. In Henry Jaglom's brilliant *Festival at Cannes* (2002), for example, we have unrelenting extremities of abuse and violence, not a whiff of it physical, and the violence seems to have no imaginable end. In *Star Wars: Episode II – Attack of the Clones* (2002), one clone after another is exploded by people devoted to the explosion of clones in the midst of a great battle in which little else but the explosion of clones is occurring.

Any particular instantiation of violence that might be called "mechanical" involves precisely the sorts of characters, methods, topographies, props, and purposes that we have long accepted as conventional marks of the form. Violence is a normal activity of the social agents we meet in such a story, and these agents are, in and of themselves, stereotypically performed by actors displaying (seeming to embody) the personality types convention has led us to understand as normally associated with violent activity; people whose history is what we expect violent people's history to be, dressed and mannered *comme il faut* and doing violence for exactly the reasons we find intelligible, even proper.

A commando, for example – Arnold Schwarzenegger – blackens his face and dresses in dark clothing by moonlight on a beach, then creeps across an island to a fortress manned by evil villains and uses high-tech weaponry to eradicate all of them, one or two at a time, in seething blasts of gunfire. Doing this, he grimaces obtrusively (shows sharp teeth) and uses exactly the sorts of guns we associate with high-end technology and devastation, big ones that spew fire and make much noise. His victims, for their parts, are the sorts of men who "ought to be" victims, more physically repulsive than he is, hairier, swarthier, more unctuous (literally, their skin is oily), and sadistic. All this is the lack of irony (given the racist attitudes it plays upon). But, too, the movie is called *Commando* (1985) and is altogether about commando activity and the sorts of people who engage in it, so that when Arnold unleashes his power it is only what we have been expecting from him since the film began. Any typical police or military film might be considered as an example of mechanical violence – *The General's Daughter* (1999), *An Officer and a Gentleman* (1982), *No Way Out* (1987), *Q & A* (1990), *L.A. Confidential* (1997) – provided there is little or nothing unconventional about the portrayal of the violent activity contained therein. The same can be said for gang films (*Goodfellas* [1991], *Donnie Brasco* [1997]), spy films (*Behind Enemy Lines* [2001], *Spy Game* [2001]), and panopticon sagas (*Enemy of the State* [1998], *The Bourne Identity* [2002]).

I here borrow the term "mechanical" from Émile Durkheim, whose mechanical solidarity was characterized by uniform and diffuse relationships between parts, and by undiscriminated homogeneous subservience to controlling authority, as could be found in Feudal society.[7] Just as the class of serfs bore a mechanical relationship to the lord and the land, individual members of armies can be seen as undifferentiated actors whose various abilities and powers are combined, first in themselves to produce a single capacity for action, and then mechanically with the abilities of others in their class to help in composing a force which is wholly, substantially and grossly applied. Capitalism develops the mechanical relationship technically, to produce a new and shocking kind of mechanical brutality, a keen cinematic vision of which is the charging, technologically-equipped army (*Starship Troopers* [1997], *The Charge of the Light Brigade* [1968]), an especially entertaining rendition of which is to be found in the various *Star Wars* films, where first the countless Imperial Troopers and ultimately the ineffably plural clones battle against the differentiated, personalized individuals who are the story's apparent protagonists. Our response to mechanical violence – such as when the white-suited troopers attack Princess Leia (Carrie Fisher), Luke Skywalker (Mark Hamill), and their friends to set up the action of *Star Wars* (1977) – is in fact to relax, since we know with a surety that Hollywood cinema is relentlessly individualistic and these heroes must survive. We are cued to attentiveness only when discrete figures emerge from the crowd to challenge or antagonize the indiscriminable ciphers of the army, and we can easily recognize, in a perception grounded entirely in nostalgia for a pre-capitalist era, that an undifferentiated group of ciphers does not threaten but is instead a reflection of the world. Further, the capitalist highlighting of the individual motive in advertising and narrative generally, distracts audiences from imagining that undifferentiated forces might be problematic; and the broader the perspective, the more removed from individual consideration the point of view, the less antagonistic seems the force in our nostalgic imagination. At one point in *Star Wars*, Han Solo (Harrison Ford) and Luke must disguise themselves in the troopers' white suits, and in order for the mise-en-scene to "recognize" their individualities as noteworthy in the overriding context of mechanical sameness, they must behave eccentrically – become comic figures in fact.

The focus on individualism and individual protagonism required by the dramaturgy of capitalism – and our concomitant ability to suspend tension during moments of mechanical violence, to treat them as descriptive, journalistic, topological – is an example of what Wolfgang Schivelbusch has noted as upholstering.[8] Just as in the railway carriage of the nineteenth century (and the airplane of the twentieth) upholstery is used to block both the consumer's perception of the overwhelming physical power implicit in the system of transportation and the consumer's anxious anticipation of death should something go wrong, the view supported in mechanically violent films that exciting, noble, effective, significant, or problematic action is perpetrated by signal individual persons *and not crowds* is an "upholstery" that deflects attention from the actual history of

warfare and violence, causing us to concentrate not on the brute collective capacities and dangers of the machine but on the individual
pleasures it can provide. With the development in early capitalism of
the rudimental coherent army, the precursor to what we see in *Star
Wars*, the dangers are intensive. In fact, writes Schivelbusch (referring to Werner Sombart's *Krieg und Kapitalismus*),

> If the fusion of the energies of horseman and steed into a powerful new
> force behind the lance was the first decisive step towards the develop-
> ment of military shock, the second step occurred with the rise of modern
> armies, at the beginning of the Early Modern era. Sombart . . . gave an
> excellent description of the differences between companies of knights
> on horseback and modern mass armies, demonstrating therein how the
> military shock was no longer executed by the rider-horse unit, but by
> the new mass unit of the army: " . . . When you had a thousand knights
> in the field, they still did not constitute one unified mass: they were a
> thousand individual warriors, fighting together. But a thousand modern
> cavalrymen collaborate to deliver *one blow*, when they charge."[9]

Mechanically-produced actual violence, then, is capable of delivering precisely a debilitating shock, but in cinematic "mechanical"
violence the tendency is to mitigate against the corporate shock
through the use of close-ups revealing individual action and
response – the broken eyeglasses in *October* (1927), intercut shots
of heroic Luke and Han firing back at the identity-less troopers in
Star Wars. In filmed mechanical violence, the attack of the army is
not shocking, just as in Hollywood propaganda more generally it is
the individual who apparently counts.

The Bourne Identity is another interesting case of mechanical violence onscreen. Here, because the plot concerns an amnesiac (Matt
Damon) gradually learning that he used to be a hired hit-man working for the CIA, early in the film our protagonist must seem both
civilized and tranquil enough so that when he discovers himself
reflexively attacking bank guards with extreme capability, or happening to know how to recognize words in many different languages, he can both focus attention on these characteristics – thereby
directing our attentiveness to his attentiveness – and learn from
them, and also find himself sufficiently surprised at himself to cause
us to experience some chills. If, however, Bourne is *too* civilized and
attractive to us, his conversion to a highly sophisticated human
weapon will either be too alarming to be pleasurable or too radical
to induce our engaged belief. Some contrast must background his

early civility, then, to suggest that there is a potentiality for violence present all along, not only in the man but also in the filmic setting where he operates; this is provided by the opening sequence, in which he is fished unconscious from the sea, physically examined by a fishing boat captain and revealed to have not only a pattern of bullet holes in his back but also a surgical incision on his hip. Inside him, as it turns out, is a microcapsule containing the code of a Swiss bank account. Very early on, then, and before Bourne can charm other characters and us with his suavity, we are brought to suspect there is more to him than meets the eye – more than meets his own eye, in fact, since one has to remember how to use one's eye and he has no memory. He is of, and in, a world of brutality, secrecy, and high stakes. It is the opening sequence that stitches the sheath of probability over the film, that frames Bourne and everything he does as appropriate in a world where violence is basic currency. What we may later be surprised to see, then, is not *the fact* that Bourne can be violent but *the degree* to which he has been trained and the extent of the violence he can put into action.

Mythic and idiomorphic violence

In numerous instances of screen violence, we see an extraordinary exhibition of aggression, negativity, destruction, or presumption made exceptionally visible and noteworthy against a violent context precisely by the extremity of the style and manner in which it is executed. The perpetrator becomes mythic by outperforming his context. Schwarzenegger is a well-recognized example, standing out from his context because of his physical size, his prowess, and the staging of his action sequences in such a way as to render him apparently invulnerable to the onslaughts of multitudes of enemy soldiers, agents, mercenaries or henchmen, while single-handedly – either with a limited store of weaponry, or with no weapons at all, or, as in *True Lies* (1994), with a weapon he has no clue how to use – he manages to slay every last one of them. What makes his performance ironic is the veneer of civility and civilization laying just beneath the violent surface; his ability to utter a poignant one-liner, in James Bond fashion; his *gemutlich* Austrian accent;the charming twinkle in his eye; his friendliness to women and children (particularly children); the sense in which he seems generally and adorably clueless.

In "mythic violence," the violent act attains a heightened status by contrast with a background in which violence – at least overt physical violence, oppression, repression, destruction – is not seen. And the act is perpetrated by someone, or in some way, we do not anticipate. In *The Shining* (1980), for instance, the perpetrator turns out to be exactly such an unanticipated someone, and our failure to anticipate is one of the film's kicks. *The Shining*'s improbability lies in a modulating background, which progresses from one which seems pacific – a resort hotel vacated for the winter in an isolated mountain nook of Colorado – to one which seems a perfect setting for what is happening therein. Mythic violence is what we have in mind when we engage in the labeling process that turns some perpetrators into "deviants," and it follows in a long tradition going back to the *Narrenschiffen* of the fifteenth and early sixteenth centuries,[10] in the case of which the isolation and exclusion of the "abnormal" – never a class of beings but always a set of discrete individuals – provided grounding for the community to verify its own moral status. The European witch-craze described by H. R. Trevor-Roper itemizes numerous accounts of "mythic" violence.[11]

What I would call "idiomorphic violence" is the opposite of the mythic type. What we see is a distinct perpetrator, standing out from a ground where we can find no other actor or act of this type; yet so clearly drawn as evil that violence is the only expectable action. The violence is unironic, but wildly improbable. The scene I described above from *Blood Work* is idiomorphic; exactly the sort of event one would expect from such a person in the context of such a setting, and yet completely out of the blue in terms of its placement narratively. A recent archetype of the form is Hannibal Lecter (Anthony Hopkins), who apparently cannot rest with being a cannibal but must extend orality into his every act, speaking with exceptional diction, gobbling up visions of those who come to talk to him with gaping eyes. His excessive orality frames him as a living mouth, the human equivalent of the shark in *Jaws* (1975), whose only thought is eating, eating, and eating again. With Lecter, then, a simple conversation is a setting for serious aggression. He smells people yards away the way a gourmet smells the odors from a chef's kitchen, so that being a passerby in his presence can be life-threatening.

When confronted with idiomorphic violence, we often focus on the perpetrator rather than the circumstance, although it is usually the circumstance that is chilling, the perpetrator very often being a caricature. The motorcycle avenger in *Raising Arizona* (1987) is an archetype of the violent idiomorph. George Lucas' Jabba the Hutt, Darth Vader, Darth Maul, and the Emperor are cases in point; they are stereotypes, in that violence and negativity are all we imagine or expect and virtually all we get, and our ability to focus on these characters depends less on their characterization than on their being isolated from the narrative ground, their being the only source of violence in a scene. Any case of mechanical violence can turn suddenly idiomorphic when one or two agents from the mechanical throng emerge for some reason and occupy the frame as individuals. Similarly, idiomorphic moments can turn mechanical in our imagination, as we conceive of the possibility of multiplication: what if Jabba the Hutt is only one of thousands?

If mechanical violence is relaxing in that individual protagonists do not obtain focus, idiomorphic violence is galvanizing in that they do. What is intriguing structurally about *The Silence of the Lambs*, for instance, is that any scene in which Lecter either appears or is invoked already has a potentiality for excitement regardless of what he does or does not do. This is, of course, a publicity man's fondest dream. It also makes the performance a challenge for Hopkins, since in certain scenes he is in fact called upon to do something hideous but must find a way, mostly using timing, to prepare us and draw our attention *because we are in principle already prepared* and thus, of course, *entirely unprepared*. When near the end of the film he attacks the guard in his cell, for example, the danger is that we may fail completely to notice the moment of the attack, since for us every instant of being in Lecter's presence is already an attack (and we believe that it should be for the too-innocent guard, too).

Marlon Brando's performance in *The Godfather* (1972) is more complex, since there are distinguishable moments with Don Corleone when we can think of him as nothing but a man. In *Se7en*, every call to visit a crime site immediately mobilizes us to readiness for horror, but the criminal behind the sites is absent from the diegesis until the end so the structure does not produce the kinds of performance troubles found in *Lambs*. In the *Batman* films, the tendency is to play the evil villain for laughs, so that the audience's expectation of violence can be confounded by the character turning to comic motive at least as often as he turns to aggression. For the actor – Jack Nicholson as Two-Face, for example – the rhythm and alternation of the performance allows for repose in the tension. It won't be an ironic presentation of the character that galvanizes us for a violent moment; it will be the moment's improbable placement.

As violent filmic scenes and moments are structured as mechanical, idiomorphic, or mythic, a sequence of successive scenes may achieve a particular dynamism through a developing structural rhythm; or, particular modulations of character, feeling, and action can be made possible. A nice example is provided by a trio of contiguous scenes in Renny Harlin's *The Long Kiss Goodnight* (1996). A former US government secret assassin (Geena Davis) has had a severe memory loss and believes herself to be Samantha Caine, a charming if somewhat frumpy live-in girlfriend and schoolteacher in a New Jersey town. In the first scene of the three I have in mind, we find her awkwardly chopping a carrot before dinner one night. Suddenly she finds that, unattended, her hand is using the chef's knife as a professional would, whirring through first one carrot, then two, then three, then a tomato and some peppers and some scallions, all within a matter of seconds. "I'm a chef! Yahoo!' she exclaims, jubilant, with a poster Geena Davis goofy grin. She tosses a tomato in the air and then hurls a knife at it, pinning it to a cupboard door like a marksman and shrugging, "Chefs do that!" In the second scene, an oily and nefarious agent of the dark side has strung a man up by the arms to interrogate him. He uses his knife viciously to slit the man's guts open, cradling his victim malevolently (if also erotically) as he dies. In the third scene, Samantha is teaching her little girl to skate on a pond and the child falls and hurts her wrist. When the child says she wants to go home, Samantha barks at her with exceptional coldness and brutality (perfectly reflected by the brisk winter's day and the snow surrounding the pond), saying, "Life is pain. You're going to skate all the way to the shore."

While the surface action in the three scenes is surely discontinuous, still a continuity of sorts must be structured in order to explain the radical change of sentiment in Samantha from scene I to scene III, since without some kind of fluid logic of transition she might seem to be two different people – not, as the filmmaker would have it, because the character really *is* split for narratological reasons, but because the performance has been corrupted and there appears to be an error in filmic continuity. In (I), we have at the conclusion a moment of mythic violence, as the tomato is skewered brutally by the surprised Samantha. Not only do we see her ability to do this as ironic; she does, too. But the skewering is only a sudden and momentary demonstration of a power that is explicated through the entire scene, so that the only reason the finale of the scene stands out for us is its demonstration of exceptional knife technique by someone who, moments before, could barely cut a carrot. The violence here is ironic but probable, since it's a kitchen scene played for sport and comedy. In (II) we have a neutral scene configured entirely by the focal torture and stabbing, which are heightened with wide-angle lens, frontal lighting, and dramatic business (the death embrace and the calculated malevolence); while there is nothing ironic about the stance of the murderer, the questioning, torture, and stabbing lift the act away from the neutral ground. The violence here is idiomorphic. In (III) we leave the characters in (II) behind and revert to the principal character in (I), yet retaining the feeling structure of scene (II). The harshness Samantha shows to her daughter is woven into the central activity of the scene, but Samantha does not seem ironic in exhibiting it – mothers lose their temper. The instrument of the irony in (I) – the knife, and her skill with it – is echoed in (II), where another knife is used with similar expertise, though without irony. This allows us to imagine in retrospect (while watching II) that Samantha's ability as a chef might mask an ability at brutality, exactly the ability demonstrated, but without the tool, in (III). A successful modulation I→II→III, in which Samantha can be transformed from innocent to self-knowing, from fun-loving to exacting, requires that the idiosyncratically ironic knife/knifing in (I) be transformed (demythologized) into an *unironic* knife/knifing in (II) as preparation for the demythologized verbal knifing in (III). Samantha can make an easy transition from being innocent while being violent (ironic) in (I) to being self-consciously yet notably violent in (III) – the transition, in short, between the two sides of her character, the amnesiac civilian and the brutal professional butcher – because the filmmaker passes through an intermediate scene, or key, to speak musically, only one step away from scene I and one step away from scene III. Scenes I and III are in fact two steps away from one another in the tonal scheme under discussion here: Samantha must change from being ironic to being unironic, and the violent activity must change from being probable to being improbable. A straight edit from (I) to (III) wouldn't work, but instead leave viewers with a disturbing sense of performance discontinuity.

Dramaturgical violence

What happens, however, when the moment of screen violence is notably more complex, when violent performance is ironic and also strongly enunciated against a background of relative tranquility or neutrality? Idiomorphic violence is relatively easy to take in, since it involves only the distantiation and alienation of an act or a perpetrator as extreme and ungrounded, as socio- or psychopathically improbable. Likewise, mythic violence is relatively easy to take in, since it involves little more than the ironizing of the perpetrator or act as being notably unconventional, even if logically grounded. Mechanical violence functions like an atmosphere, and if it is not utterly rejected it is as easy to take in as air. But in "dramaturgical violence," the violent act attains a heightened status by contrast with its background, in which violence – at least overt physical violence, oppression, repression, destruction – is not expressly seen. And the act is perpetrated by someone, or perpetrated in some way, we do not anticipate. There is ironic performance, then, which is also improbable in relation to its context. Since we most typically see violence of this type articulated by an isolated protagonist or group, acting out of what is given as a personal, often psychological, disconnection or warp, it often strikes us as pathological, sociopathic, quaint, bizarre, and therefore especially worth being considered as entertainment.

The explosion of temper is a fairly common example, such as Al Pacino venting to the judge in the concluding diatribe of . . . *And Justice For All* (1979): "YOU'RE out of order, Your Honor. YOU'RE out of order!" In *La Femme Nikita* (1997), the trainer of the assassin who is the "heroine" of the film takes her to dinner in a three-star Parisian restaurant to celebrate the end of her training and give her a break from the arduous training schedule. Around their table in all directions, wealthy people are eating decorously and quietly. The trainer (Tcheky Karyo) hands his pupil (Anne Parillaud) a beautifully-wrapped gift. Her eyes light up. When she opens it, she is dismayed to discover a pistol with silencer, and in a terse voice he tells her she has thirty seconds to kill a man at the table behind them and escape by a route he dictates, before the police, who have already been alerted, arrive. After a split-second hesitation in which she expresses both confusion and deep chagrin, she lunges into an explosion of activity which utterly negates the scene's peacefulness. Though she is surely a violent personality, we believe her to have been disciplined and trained; and now, "graduating from school," she comes to an elegant restaurant dressed to the nines and utterly civilized. But something ferocious must break through this veneer.

In Emir Kusturiça's *Arizona Dream* (1993), after a weeks-long poetic and sexual reverie on a ranch in the Arizona desert, Grace (Lili Taylor) is alone with Axel (Johnny Depp) in her bedroom. Without warning she pulls out a pistol, aims it at her own head, and pulls the trigger. The gun doesn't go off. She spins the cylinder and tries again, Russian roulette-style. Then she encourages Axel to do likewise, but first he must promise her he really will pull the trigger. The reverie, the poetry, the tranquil and transcendent madness, is shattered by the hard reality of the gun, seen in close-up.

In an exceptionally refined vision, dramaturgical violence intrigues and shocks because the irony of performance is delicate. In the case of Pacino in *Justice,* for example, his professional obligations as a lawyer forbid his venting at the judge, and so when finally he does give expression to his rage he is contradicting his professional status ironically; at the same time, however, Pacino has elaborated and transported from film to film a particular persona, that of an ingenious, explosive, emotional, intense hothead. The *role*-performance in *Justice* is therefore ironic to a degree that the *actor*-performance is not, since the casting of Pacino blurs some of the ironic distance in the courtroom explosion. Similarly, having Jack Warden playing the judge allows for an angry riposte which can nudge the diatribe toward a street fight, de-ironizing the performance for the moment.

When we see James Mason's Philip Vandamm smoothly warning Cary Grant that he is going to kill him in *North by Northwest* (1959), by contrast, we have a far more ambiguous and engaging moment of ironic performance and a case of pure dramaturgical violence. The locale is a library in a Long Island estate, the topos of wealth, meditation, retreat, and tranquility. Outside are vast, well-kept lawns. The conversation is civil, even urbane and witty. Vandamm, apparently a diplomat or lawyer but hardly a thug, has a refined, respectable British accent and a very soft, even playful voice. He speaks with meticulous etiquette. Yet he is attempting to enact murder. Hitchcock is so adept at ironizing, in fact, that we may find ourselves chuckling through the scene (in which Ernest Lehman has written some profound and thoroughly witty dialogue) without at all noticing that we are watching violence. As to the scene's context: while it is certainly a kidnapping, Grant's perfect comic performance as

the victim Roger Thornhill betrays such complete disbelief (such sincere engagement with self-image) and also such endearing charm
that we easily identify with him, accepting all his claims that the kidnappers have got the wrong man. In short, this cannot be happening,
and the kidnapping is hardly more than a "kidnapping." Therefore,
the setting only appears to be criminal; in fact it is perfectly peace-
ful, and the politeness and grace of the kidnappers is not a slimy
veneer but, perhaps, genuine. (It is worth noting that at no point in
the film do these agents behave in front of our eyes in such a way as
to unambiguously throw their civility into question.) Given that, so
far, the film is relentlessly social, taking place in such bastions of
well-structured civility as the Plaza Hotel and Madison Avenue, the
scene in question is as improbable as it is ironic. So very ironic and
improbable is the violence, in fact, that – in a fashion entirely credi-
ble to us – even the character who is being victimized cannot believe
it for a moment.

Hitchcock is the master of dramaturgic violence, and to take a
second look at the drugging scene in *The Man Who Knew Too Much*
is to see a striking and profound demonstration of ironic improbability. There is, first, something wildly improbable about a husband
"attacking" his wife in the context of a film where strangers are plot-
ting assassinations, managing a kidnapping, and stabbing a man in
the street. The specific improbability, indeed, is that a violent scene
continues a wave of violence already depicted, when we expect a
sedate respite. Then, too, we can see a high degree of contrast
between the action and its setting, the drugging and the woman resting after a strenuous afternoon in her shadowy hotel room: because
the action, as it occurs, can appear to be a medical administration,
yet Jo McKenna has not complained of being sick. From her point
of view – the point of view with which we are led to identify – something inexplicable is going on.

Further, the irony of performance is so sophisticated that even the
status of the event as a violent one must finally remain open to question, that irony having nothing to do, in this case, with the act/actor
ratio: there is nothing ironic at all in a general practitioner adminis-
tering a sedative. The irony resides in the relationship between the act
and its purpose, in this case, the recipient of the drug *not being distraught* but the doctor believing she very soon will be and therefore
giving the medicine *in advance*. Our affiliation with, or distance from,
his medical status lead us to accept, or reject, both his diagnosis and

6 Dr Ben McKenna (James Stewart) drugs his wife (Doris Day) in Hitchcock's 1956 version of *The Man Who Knew Too Much*

his treatment. What Jo does not know is *not only* that her son has been kidnapped – information enough, to be sure, to throw her out of her mind with anxiety – but also that she has played an instrumental role in the kidnapping by handing him over to the kidnappers. Jo will feel, Ben knows, guilt as well as desperation and it is therefore, arguably, not an act of violence at all for him to sedate her under such circumstances. Hitchcock, of course, has his own purposes: he uses realistic performance style and Jo McKenna is a trained singer – that is to say, a professional at using her voice to express emotion. Without the sedative, she will be over the top vocally – Doris Day will have to be over the top (contrived) or risk seeming artificially restrained (contrived) – and so a technique must be found to dampen her response. Any other mother in this circumstance would merely scream, but Jo's vocality will throw the balance of vocalities that constitutes the voice track out of alignment – unless she suddenly stops behaving like a singer. Suffice it to say, *the one tactic Hitchcock absolutely does not want to use here is to overthrow Jo's professional identity*, since the entire film is in some ways a play upon her ability both to mother and to have a career. Further, much depends on her ability specifically *to sing*. That she may remain the woman with the voice but not distract us by using it here, therefore, drugs are necessary.

What may become evident from this too-abbreviated discussion is the necessity for a dense and involved reading of Hitchcock in order to come to terms with the subtle complexity of violence centering

any one of his violent scenes – in *The Wrong Man* (1956), for example, when we see the *right* man; in *Rear Window* (1954), when we
see flashbulbs being popped on the rooftop across the way and come
to wonder if *everybody in this apartment complex is defending herself against some Lars Thorwald or other*; in *Rebecca* (1940), when
one woman decides to help another woman choose a gown for a ball.
While there are plenty of Hitchcock aficionados who still love doing
this, to be sure, the extremely dramaturgical violence he employed
has by and large fallen out of use in a conglomerate, multi-national,
blockbuster movie culture, having been replaced onscreen by
repeated diegetic settings of mechanical, mythic, and idiomorphic
violence. The mechanical violence, as I have argued, can be used to
extend the scope of a narrative, to present spectacle, and also to provide emotional respite – which is to say, to narrow the range of
response and to make the diegesis simpler. Both mythic and idiomorphic violence stress the individuality of perpetrators and contexts, a
necessary requirement in an age of high capitalism. But compared
with dramaturgical violence, in which it is necessary for the audience
to solve a complex puzzle by contemplating both the nature of an
act and its placement in context, these forms are simple and therefore accessible across cultural barriers to a huge audience with
variant cultural expertise. Increasingly, the magnification of the
audience implies variegation in the demographic and cultural characteristics that describe viewers: educational background, movie-
going experience, professional know-how, etc. The idiomorphic
Hannibal Lecter and Schwarzenegger's legion of mythic tough guys
are far more accessible to audiences around the world than the
dramaturgical Philip Vandamm or Ben McKenna.

Schivelbusch notes that as a new technology ends an original
social relationship the latter also comes, through sentimentality, to
be thought of as having more "soul" and often, also, to be invested
with new content as a kind of "leisure and sports."[12] I would argue
that Hitchcock's dramaturgical violence has been just so invested, in
part by academic scholarly attention and publication, in part by
physical restoration and re-screening, in part by DVD release (with
commentary), in part by public circulation through televised documentary. "Hitchcock," in short, is a new game. Thus, the audience
capable of catching the subtle nuances of his stories at the same time
as enjoying the pleasures of the performances and visions, the viewer
hungry for Hitchcockian irony embedded in an improbable context,

7 Arnold Schwarzenegger exemplifying "mechanical violence" in *Commando* (1985)

is largely gone, replaced by a newly capitalized viewership around the world that requires extremes of irony in performance, extremes of mechanization, or extremes of characterological pathology in order to experience what it has learned to know as "pleasure in the cinema."

That the screen, of all places, should be thought a site of violence of any kind is itself a fact of exceptional interest, since, as we have only recently been coming to see, violence is all around us in the world that contains that screen. What movies contain is, at worst, a reference to that violence. The State has its own storehold of weaponry and its own constitutional logic of violence, as Georges Sorel implied in his commentary on Clemenceau's statement that "Every man or every power whose action consists solely in surrender can only finish by self-annihilation. Everything that lives resists; that which does not resist allows itself to be cut up piecemeal." Sorel wrote, "A social policy founded on middle-class cowardice, which consists in always surrendering before the threat of violence, cannot fail to engender the idea that the middle class is condemned to death, and that its disappearance is only a matter of time."[13] Every critique of "screen violence" that equates fictionalities such as I have been discussing here with waging war, destroying cities, killing civilians, and racially profiling populations is ultimately a defence of the violent powers of the State. Hitchcock's exceptional scenic realism, in its dramaturgic density and with its weave of irony and improbability, incites inspection and reflection and thus affords every opportunity for discerning, slowly and by degrees, the potential for measured and unmeasured violence in our world. That viewing his work has become a preoccupation for theorists and zealots, therefore, rather than the serious activity of the masses, and that our credibility has been more zealously opened and committed to the sorts of presentations high capitalism needs us to see and commit to, may be the real "screen violence" that is our peril.

Notes

1 Pierre Bourdieu, *The State Nobility: Elite Schools in the Field of Power* (Stanford: Stanford University Press, 1996), 389.
2 George Gerbner, "Who Is Shooting Whom? The Content and Context of Media Violence", *Bang Bang, Shoot Shoot! Essays on Guns and Popular Culture*, ed. Murray Pomerance and John Sakeris (Boston: Pearson Education, 2000), 76.
3 See Michael J. Arlen, "The Cold, Bright Charms of Immortality," *The View From Highway 1: Essays on Television* (New York: Farrar, Straus & Giroux, 1969), 108–21.
4 William Rothman, "Violence and Film," *Violence and American Cinema*, ed. J. David Slocum (New York: Routledge, 2001), 37–46.
5 Kenneth Burke, *A Grammar of Motives* (Berkeley: University of California Press, 1969).
6 Rothman, "Violence," 40.
7 Émile Durkheim, *The Division of Labour in Society* (New York: The Free Press, 1964), 70–110.
8 Wolfgang Schivelbusch, *The Railway Journey: The Industrialization of Time and Space in the 19th Century* (Berkeley: University of California Press, 1986), 122.
9 *Ibid.*, 151–2; emphasis added.
10 Michel Foucault, *Madness and Civilization: A History of Insanity in the Age of Reason* (New York: Vintage, 1988).
11 H. R. Trevor-Roper, *The European Witch-Craze of the 16th and 17th Centuries* (New York: Harper Torchbooks, 1969).
12 Schivelbusch, *The Railway Journey*, 13.
13 Georges Sorel, *Reflections on Violence* (London: Allen & Unwin, 1915), 71.

3

Violence redux

Martin Barker

From small beginnings. It was preparing a first-year class on moral crises around films, using Stanley Kubrick's *A Clockwork Orange* (1971), that brought it into focus. The outcome: a plea and an argument for refusing to operate with the category "violence" any longer.

Central assertions of this essay: it isn't possible to say anything very helpful about the issue of "violence in the media" without going back into some very specific histories. Those who research and theorize about the "possible harmful effects of media violence," who repeat mantra-like that it is "obvious" that these are the questions we must ask, insistently drop us out of history. They stop us seeing the most obvious point: that "violence" is not an object which researchers have discovered, in the way that Australopithecus was discovered. "Violence" is an arbitrary re-labeling of behaviors, and then also of representations of those behaviors, which in its very act of naming achieves a number of *political* ends. It excludes many *actually* harmful behaviors by those in power and authority. It turns these into the "solutions" to those it doesn't like. And it dismisses, before they can even be posed, explanations of the re-labeled behaviors in terms of various kinds of conflict. Instead it proffers, sometimes implicitly sometimes explicitly, a wickedly narrow range of possible explanations, all of which rule out by definition the possibility that violence may be rationally conceived. "Violence," in other words, is a social concept with a history – and one into which the very films, television programs, and other materials which are accused of being a potent cause are deeply interwoven.

In this essay I circle between several things: that easily forgotten history of the discourses that produced "violence"; the case of *A Clockwork Orange* as a classic exemplar; and a contemporary illustration of some of the material ways the discourses still operate – the reception of David Cronenberg's *Crash* in Britain in 1996–97.

Lest we forget

If we have learnt anything from cultural theory, it is that a term like "violence" cannot be simply a descriptive collection of naturally-grouping items. Rather, it is a concept, a category, of which we need to ask a number of questions. What is, and isn't, contained under it – and how are the boundaries of the concept policed against intrusions? It is for instance not intuitively obvious that the following things have enough in common to make them worth "labeling" in the same way: a husband hitting his wife for being late with his dinner; crowds of football fans jostling outside a match; playground bullying; threats and punishment in association with an extortion racket – and mediated representations of one and all of these. Even less obvious is that the actions of authorities in response to these aren't counted as the same. What "connotations," then – associations of meaning, implicit explanations – go along with its adoption? In putting these kinds of (inclusive, exclusive) boundaries around the concept, what potential implications are generated? And where, when, and under what conditions did the concept arise? We have well learnt for instance that in the early nineteenth century, under the specific conditions of the medicalization of the human body, the distinct category of "the homosexual" emerged, whereby certain acts were reclassified and rethought as arising from inherent tendencies within the individual.[1] Must we not ask the same of "violence" once we recognize it as a *concept*, rather than as a natural term?

My argument is this: the notion of "violence" as a concept with explanatory force emerged in the late 1950s to early 1960s. Beginning in the US, it took form as a response to social changes and political unrest: from the civil rights movement to the ghetto riots, the rise of student protest movements, the anti-war movements, and certain spin-offs from that range of movements that have variously been called the counter-culture, the permissive society, or sometimes simply "the Sixties." The concept of "violence" increasingly did service as a way of grouping, and thus silently theorizing, these behaviors and forms of action. Then in parallel, and even becoming for some a leading element within this, emerged the idea of "violent media" as possible causal agent: a case of one arbitrarily constructed semiotic unit explaining another.

Of course there had been earlier uses and discussions of "violence," not least claims that US history may have an exceptional interest in the issue because of the role of violence in the formation of the American polity; or – in parallel – through the impact of Gunnar Myrdal's arguments about the dilemmas of American democracy.[2] But an array of new definitions began to emerge in the 1960s, and then – rather like the concept of "mugging" a few years later – were exported to a number of other countries, including Britain. Unlike the earlier arguments which, for all their ambiguous attribution of praise or blame, focused on the *exceptional* nature of American history, now there was a trend towards a generalized, ahistorical, desocialized account – one indeed, as I will show, which could become in some variants a putative account of evolved human nature.

An interesting test-case in this respect is the report of the National Commission on the Causes and Prevention of Violence.[3] Produced in the aftermath of the assassinations of Robert Kennedy and Martin Luther King, this fascinating document attempted to account for the paradox that America was, in their words, the world's leading democratic nation, the archetypical "free society"; yet it was also world leader in crime, political violence, assassinations, and so on. It should be noted straightaway that the Report guarded its borders very strictly. Whilst civil disobedience over the Vietnam War was part of the problem of "violence" needing discussion, the Vietnam War itself was *not*. But beyond this, the report is interesting because it exists in all kinds of tension with itself, which reveals symptomatically the uneasy co-existence of three tendencies.

First, there was a residue of that older, exceptionalist account of American history, which saw a distinctive, if sometimes problematic, special "American character."[4] But now exceptionalism gained a definitely pessimistic thrust. American society had been founded upon the expropriation of native American lands, on the vicious system of slavery, on the refusal of union rights to workers, etc. Perhaps these had left a "brutalizing" and "callous imprint"[5] on class, racial, and sexual relations. Exceptionalism here almost gives way to a potentially radical account that understood destructive behavior in terms of an opposition between exploitation and repression, and angry responses to the resultant appalling conditions of life – hence the reference to "justice" in the title, and the (risky) admission that you can't expect violent acts to cease if you don't provide people with a decent life.

From the end of the 1960s, the idea of exceptionalism gave way, if that is the right term, to a critique of the frontier myth. That critique took place in many media. New Hollywood productions such as *The Wild Bunch* (1969) and *Little Big Man* (1970), and the heavily-censored *Soldier Blue* (1970), offered counter-narratives of the frontier – and ironically, were often attacked for displaying the very qualities they were critiquing. But for our purposes, the most telling moment is the publication of Richard Slotkin's revisionist account of American mythologies, *Regeneration Through Violence.*[6] Interestingly, Slotkin slid in a sidesweeping reference to the "voluminous reports of presidential commissions on violence, racism and civil disorder"[7] as just saying what others had said before, without addressing the central issues: the role of foundation myths in justifying unparalleled violence. The vast, 650-page book went on to re-examine the history of American literature, from the earliest days to the 1860s, for the ways it embodied dangerous dreams of a special destiny – dreams which became, in Slotkin's words, a horrifying "pyramid of skulls" of both humans and animals, as their warranty for cleansing through violence found expression.

But there is a fundamental ambivalence in Slotkin's account. Myths, he argues, are essential to us – "Man is essentially a myth-making animal."[8] But *these particular* myths have turned against us: "A people unaware of its myths is likely to continue living by them, though the world around that people may change and demand changes in their psychology, their world-view, their ethics, and their institutions."[9] Once upon a time, it seems, American frontier mythologies were necessary, even if murderous. Now, the time has arrived to name them for what they are: justifications of "violence." Bringing these mythic concepts into full consciousness, then, is a political task. But once achieved, there is no escape – "we" will need to find new ones, new stories to tell about ourselves which will ground, make sense of and permit the American "body politic" to be what it must and do what it has to. How telling that the idea of "mythologies of violence" should crystallize for Slotkin this bridge between old and new myth-forms.

For in the Commission Report there is an awkward third, and emergent, view of "violence" as a generic social problem, in which frame the issue of "television violence" was posed. After all the reviewing of evidence on the historical circumstances which have promoted different kinds of violence, gears suddenly shift markedly when, in Chapter 8, the Report addresses "violence in the media." Here the talk is not of, say, the media's role in marginalizing or besmirching disaffected groups, in stereotyping minorities – accounts which would have sat tidily with the emphasis on injustice. Alternatively, a radical account of media violence (as opposed to just "violence") would have particularly examined the complicated role that images of the Vietnam war played in public consciousness. Neither of these is present, even as a hint. Instead, another account is already dominant: "we are deeply troubled by the television's constant portrayal of violence, not in any genuine attempt to focus artistic expression on the human condition, but rather in pandering to a public preoccupation with violence that television itself has helped to generate."[10] Here are allowed no distinctions of kind, genre, or function. Straightaway we are off into content analyses of the "amounts" of violence, and their putative cumulative "effects."

This disjunction is so marked as to require explanation. Is this just because by this time the communications model was so dominant in American academia that it simply operated here as a default? Possibly – but perhaps not entirely. The chapter following this one on the media concerned campus unrest. Here again a new conceptualization showed its head, one that could, under the right conditions, congeal with the "media violence" account. This chapter opens with a statement of the "deep concern" at the "violence and disorder that has swept the nation's campuses." What is striking is that this is instantly expressed as a problem of an opposition between "power" v. "truth," "passion" v. "reason," "confrontation" v. "rational discourse."[11] It is not conceivable that an *alternative* mode of reasoning, a different critique, was at work, e.g., in the escalating resistance to the Draft and the Vietnam War. No, campus radicals were giving way to a pre-rational mode of behavior – and that permits the classification of everything that worries our authors as "violence." Thus it becomes cognate with the emergent language. Thus it becomes obvious to ask what might have *stimulated* such emotional excess (look back at that word "pandering"). Thus "the media" become logical targets.

Turning attention to the media as likely sources/causes was, of course, not new. Historians have traced this tendency back at least a century and a half – to long before there was even a nascent "science" of media effects. But a change was beginning in the terms of reference of the complaint. As late at the 1950s, the dominant mode of expression of fears was "delinquency." This has the force of limiting the issue to a troublesome minority – and even admitting that it may only be a part of their behavior. It was thus easily possible for arch-moralist Fredric Wertham to fit his critique of delinquency-inducing tendencies in comics into a general account of goodness in young people, and then to celebrate, elsewhere, the subversive cultural qualities of comic fanzines.[12]

The turning point was around 1960, when a definitional shift seems to have taken place. Leonard Berkowitz's *Aggression* is one of the first embodiments of the new style. In a 1962 book set securely within American-style behavioral psychology – a style which has great trouble finding space for the role of perceptions and under-standings of the world, except as entirely dependent variables – Berkowitz comes late to a chapter on the media and "violence." For him, some things are just givens: content analysis provides us with legitimate guides to media content; laboratory experiments are valid grounds for weighing their impact; and "violence" is a thing-in-itself, whether it be a drive or a conditioned response. Perhaps the key that marks the book's transitional nature is one sentence in his Summary to this chapter, where he writes: "There is a good deal of controversy and greater uncertainty as to the possible effects of the heavy concentration of crime and violence in the mass media."[13] It is worth pausing over this virtual elision between crime and violence. First, "crime" now excludes a host of actually illegal activities: fraud, smuggling, burglary, you name it. Second, "violence" takes on almost synonymity with criminality: if it's legal, it can't be violence. So, State actions couldn't possibly be addressed, or even be part of the syndrome – because they are by definition not illegal (who makes the laws?).

A proper history of the emergence of the concept of "violence" would of course find that it has been around and used for much longer than I have indicated above. And that would be right. But I am here interested in two things in particular: the emergence of a syndrome of assumptions about what "it" may be, and how "it" may be provoked, which has persisted at the public and policy levels, even when it has been repeatedly shown to be both nonsensical and untrue. And the impact of this persistence on those who feel them-selves to be *potentially included* under these definitional regimes. My argument is that the concept of "violence" has to be re-examined much more widely, leading to rethinking its quite central position as an ideological category.

It is worth revisiting in this respect Stuart Hall, *et al.*'s *Policing The Crisis*, for its broad-sweeping interrogation of the discourses which preceded and prepared for the rise of "Thatcherism" in Britain. Although their book is centrally interested in the "mugging" controversy around the turn of 1970 as a focal point to the storms of reaction, as their investigation and argument proceeds, the category "violence" unequivocally rears its head. Importantly, their analysis shows the emergent *levels* at which the concept works. Early on, they show well how newspapers in particular deployed ideas about "violence" as rhetorical terms. So, calling "muggings" "apparently senseless attacks"[14] nicely disables any sense that there might be explanations. Developing this into a theme of "Wild Boys"[15] grounds it in a social location, requiring control.

But the crucial move, the one that authorizes not simply policing actions, but a wholesale political and ideological response, was the depiction of a Violent Society. They exemplify this through a feature in the *Sunday Express* (February 6, 1972) where its author manages a move from blaming the victims of the Bloody Sunday massacre as "loud-mouthed lunatic hooligans" to asserting that their kinds of behavior are now to be found "festering all over the country."[16] It then compiles an ideological hit-list of quite unassociated phenomena, ranging from advocates of strike action, through playground threats, to an attack on an elderly woman in her home, to construct its account of "violent Britain." Hall *et al.* capture the main point brilliantly:

> The fact is that the things being used here as a peg to hang a thesis on are not "connected" in any tangible or concrete way at all, except *rhetorically*, ideologically. They may be part of the same nightmare: they are only in the most metaphorical manner part of the same historical phenomenon. It is not the similarity of the events, but the similarity of the underlying sense of panic in the mind of the beholder which provides the real connection.[17]

The authors are right, I suspect, to see this as the limit within which the concept of "violence" functions in this article. But it is important to recognize that other things were also in play. Strongly present among those was the debate over "instinctual determinants." If it might be "in the nature of the beast" to be violent, if those "Wild Ones" might be precisely that – by nature wild – then the solutions will have to be different. The debate was fierce and real. It is here that Stanley Kubrick re-enters.

From emotions to instincts

Re-reading various people's accounts of Kubrick's life, and the controversy around *A Clockwork Orange*, reminds just how fiercely a new set of discourses around "violence" took shape in that period – discourses which may have shifted ground and confidence but, I would argue, are still largely operative. Kubrick's film was of course itself accused, especially in Britain, of causing all kinds of mayhem. Along with *Straw Dogs*, *Macbeth*, *Dirty Harry* (all 1971), and *The Wild Bunch*, among others, it signaled to an emergent moralist movement a new climate of "permissiveness" (another key concept) and a new "gratuitous glorification of violence."

Vincent Lobrutto, writing about Kubrick's life at this point, gets half the point: "As [the Kubricks] were leaving the United States, the country was torn by the war in Vietnam, racial tension, unrest on the nation's campuses, and the assassinations of Robert Kennedy and Martin Luther King."[18] Of course all this was true, but to see this is to miss the more important truth: this period saw a rising tide of *talk* about these. And Kubrick's film was to be one of the vehicles for carrying abroad, both in itself and through the debates it aroused, those very American-sourced conceptualizations of "violence."

Not innocently, either. The film took a position, in many respects, on the nature of the problem. Kubrick was a considerable fan of the crudely speculative ideas of Robert Ardrey, whose 1966 book, *The Territorial Imperative*, theorized "aggression" in proto-sociobiological terms. Ardrey's work was complemented by the similar ideas of Desmond Morris, Konrad Lorenz, and, within a few years, E. O. Wilson, Richard Dawkins, and others – each of whom posited originary impulses.[19] All these were becoming sources of popularized discourse about the nature of society. Quite contradictorily, it must be said: their work is premised on the essential unchangeability of human behavior, yet it was promoted as a means to understand the large *changes* perceived to be taking place. Kubrick bought heavily into this, and gave expression to this kind of view, for example in the following: "Man isn't a noble savage. He is irrational, brutal, weak, unable to be objective about anything where his own interests are involved . . . and any attempt to create social institutions to a false view of the nature of man is probably doomed to failure."[20] Beyond simple pessimism, this is a half-articulated ideology of human nature – one whose supposed "opposite" and only alternative was Skinnerian behaviorism (which

Kubrick researched extensively as he was preparing to make *A Clockwork Orange*), an equally crude account of human behavior in terms of operant conditioning: we are what we have been conditioned to be. *A Clockwork Orange* mounts an imaginative debate between the two approaches, in terms of their capacity to account for human "violence" and how the State can manage this.

The debate prompted various critical responses. Some feminist accounts, for instance, simply relocated the problem to "men" as an almost distinct species. Erich Fromm, drawing on a fading conjunction of psychoanalysis and New Left optimism, re-explained "violence" as the response of distorted souls to inhuman conditions. But all these broadly accepted that it made sense to gather up and label a diverse set of behaviors, group and individual, as signs of "violence." If ever there was a case of a hegemonic concept (in Gramsci's sense), this was it. It seemed so *obvious* to talk of playground bullying, drunken brawls, rapes, confrontations with the police – even bad thoughts about the state of the world – as the epiphenomena of one vast problem: the problem of "violence."

The point is this: not simply the debates around the film, but the film itself, were constituted within the crucible of this emerging category, concept and incipient theorization, "violence." It is as clear a modern example as it would be possible to find of exactly the processes which Annette Kuhn has described in relation to early cinema and the regulation of sexuality. As she shows very well with regard to *Maisie's Marriage* (1923), for example, the discourses around women and the control of reproduction were not simply external limits on what films were allowed to do, but permeated the films themselves, at the levels of script, address and marketing.[21]

The debate was not one-sided, or indeed ever closed – and of course that is the point. Apart from those who stood wholly outside the terrain (I am thinking of some who entered the fray against socio-biological accounts of human nature from the late 1970s, and attacked the whole debate from an ideological point of view),[22] the debate about the nature and sources of aggression in human beings rolled back and forth between the instinctivists and the behaviorists/culturalists during this period. The anthropologist Ashley Montagu was a principal critic of the ethologists, in particular for the implications of their views for thinking about "race"; in this, he sat in line with the work produced by UNESCO from the early 1950s, which sought to undercut the presumed legitimacy of "race-talk" and race-theorization. But Montagu also assaulted the "litany of innate depravity" which he identified as coming from the ethologists.[23] By the mid-1970s the terrain crucially included the work of Stanley Milgram, whose studies of obedience to authority occasioned a long debate, far outside academia. Milgram explicitly challenged "aggression" models of explanation, arguing – in a way that had chill resonances with the politics of the time – that soldiers' willingness to behave brutally resulted from a kind of conditioning:

> Although aggressive tendencies are part and parcel of human nature, they have hardly anything to do with the behavior observed in the experiment. Nor do they have much to do with the destructive obedience of soldiers in war, of bombardiers killing thousands on a single mission, or enveloping a Vietnamese village in searing napalm. The typical soldier kills because he is told to kill and he regards it as his duty to obey orders.[24]

This was dangerous stuff because it redefined what would count as the "problem," including within its domain the otherwise excluded actions of State functionaries. Now the concept of "violence" embraced also the actions of the war-makers – and its excesses were blamed on those at the top. Since Milgram's book opened on the question of how German annihilation of the Jews had been possible, to make this equation was even more provocative – and the debate was indeed intense.

By the late 1970s, a deep fissure was opening up. On the one hand, traditionalists such as Hans Eysenck and David Nias were still presenting arguments that "violence," and indeed "sex," could be understood as primitive forces within humans, too easily activated by the powerful and cumulative imagery of film or television – where "violence" (if we judge by their opening list of anecdotal horror stories to be explained) exists entirely in the sphere of the private and the criminal, as opposed to the State-instrumental and the political.[25] On the other hand, a new set of discourses, both political and academic, were fracturing the very notion of a unitary condition or problem called "violence." In the same year as Eysenck and Nias' book, there appeared Fromm's denunciation of this entire tradition – both instinctivist and behaviorist – from a neo-Marxist position.[26] Feminist critics began to emphasize the extent to which violence is a problem of *male* behavior, and how much of it indeed is directed at women. And more academic researchers increasingly demonstrated the multiplicity of *kinds* of aggression and violence, while simultaneously denouncing those who proposed, for instance, evolutionary "explanations."[27]

Only in relation to the mass media did the category linger on. Here, the myth of a singular force survives, even prospers. The alliance of a blind version of behavioral psychology with the worst kinds of moralizing politics, liaising in strange ways with the narrower interests of certain broadcasters,[28] has somehow allowed the claim that cumulative, contextually-dissociated, generically-unbedded "images" may have the power either to *stimulate* some kind of imitative behavior, or to *desensitize* viewers to the wrongness of what they are seeing.

How bizarre. How effective. Even good researchers seem unable to escape the taint. Here, for instance, is James Lull, excellent ethnologist, who has demonstrated repeatedly that it is impossible to understand the role and meaning of the media except in the context of everyday routines and practices, still conceding the territory:

> Only the truly cynical, massively uninformed, or profoundly compromised person could deny that this body of research cumulatively reveals that violent programming helps stir up aggressive behavior. By studying the short-term and long-term consequences of violent TV, social scientists have documented just what parents feared all along. Despite the unusually clear experimental and survey research evidence, broadcasters have typically stonewalled the issue or denied culpability.[29]

The effects of "effects" discourses

My argument is that the category "violence" has sedimented around the media. It has become a *concept* in the rich sense of the term, with claims and implicit theories attached to it. It has also come to carry a substantial moral loading, made very evident every time (in the UK at any rate) research is done to ask viewers "What do you think about the amount of violence on television?" This deliciously loaded question permits few answers. To respond "Too much" is to position oneself among the righteous. To respond "About right" is almost to duck the question. To respond "Too little" is to say of yourself that you are a worrying, possibly rather sick individual.

But the moral loading of "violence" operates far beyond the rarities of public opinion polling. It accompanies any and every film which, upon release, is greeted with the serious moral suspicions of opinion-leaders: the Press, moral politicians, spokespeople of various kinds who readily gain the ear of media gatekeepers. A very clear, and instructive, example of this happened in the UK with Cronenberg's *Crash*. For a full year, between June 1996–97, the ground of *Crash*'s release was tilled by an extraordinary campaign. Led and fronted by the *Daily Mail*, the campaign came close to preventing the film's release in Britain.

Interestingly, the concept of "violence" was never central to that campaign. Instead, a series of morally-loaded terms was invoked, such as "debased," "depraved," "sick," and "degrading." From time to time, though, as part of invoking associated figures of a sick/vulnerable audience who might be perverted by the film, claims verging on "violence" showed themselves. For instance, one regional newspaper editorialized about *Crash* as follows:

> Ram-raiding and reckless driving by youngsters for the fun of it are already endemic throughout the country, with a particular West country favorite being a game of chicken in which the drivers of stolen cars signal they are going in one direction before going in the other. When it is a fact that scenes of violence or depravity from other films have produced real-life copycats it is not being sensational to suggest this one's lethally reckless driving for sexual thrills, fetishism, voyeurism and sadomasochism could prove the latest game for some lunatic West thrill-seekers.[30]

"Violence" and "depravity" run hand in glove here and in many other reports, often in association with this kind of mock-explanatory framework. The "violence" framework is a resource that may be summoned up, a mental map of dangerous territories. More than a label, it is the toe-end of a wider conceptualization.

What impact on ordinary viewers of the film did this have? How did the idea of "violence" feature within their feelings about the film? During 1996–97, with two colleagues, I conducted a year-long research project into the campaign against *Crash*.[31] One crucial part of this involved mounting a special screening of the film and researching audience responses. We were not just interested in judgments and responses, however, but also in how people had experienced the campaign against *Crash*, and with what kinds of expectations they had approached it. All 167 participants completed a questionnaire before seeing the film, part of which aimed to tap into viewers' expectations, and their sources. These were supplemented by a questionnaire completed immediately after viewing the film, and then – following a categorization of audience responses according to their like/dislike and approval/disapproval of the film – detailed small-group interviews with 40 per cent of our audience.

Without question, the idea of "violence" played a significant role for a large part of our audience. The following was one fairly typical response from two people in an interview:

> *Deborah:* I had expected it to be controversial because of the reviews I'd read, and that was . . . that was my expectation . . . Really. And I knew it had sex and violence . . . well I thought it had violence in it, although I didn't think that when I saw it, but I was told it had lots of sex in it, and it was depraved, and so that's what I expected.
>
> *Int.:* So, it was unexpected in that you didn't ex . . . that wasn't part of what you expected? That was a surprise?
>
> *Sunny:* That was a surprise, yeah, I think. I don't think it's a straight-forward sex and violence movie.

A "straightforward sex and violence movie": the invoking of this *kind* (which was, for many, a kind for which there are not even many clear exemplars) has a number of consequences. At the very least, it promises low enjoyment. At worst, extreme discomfort, perhaps running into feeling threatened, morally worried. If something is a "straightforward sex and violence movie," it is to be avoided – and indeed many people did tell us that they had avoided seeing *Crash* for just this reason. They came to our screening *expecting to be miserable*, perhaps even affronted by it.

Something more of this can be seen in the following:

> *Int.:* When you actually saw the film was it like what you'd expected?
>
> *Helen:* No. No because I was expecting something violent and porno-graphic, and I didn't think it was either. I thought . . . I thought it was a very calm film in that respect . . . although quite intense at the same time, and I thought that the sex . . . I thought . . . I was expect-ing the sex thing to be more [pause] pornographic. I'm not sure exactly what . . . it's a dodgy one, but . . . I was expecting the vio-lence to be perhaps a bit gorier, but I didn't think that either of those sort of issues . . . I thought [laughs] uh – what's all this about?

The expectation of "violence" had a powerful interruptive capacity for Helen, and others. It disabled for a while their ability to make any other kind of meaning out of the film. And to associate "violent" and "pornographic" is to make clear how far "violence" is beyond being a descriptive term – it is already implicitly theorized. This shows particularly clearly in a third response: Tim – "I'd heard . . .

I'd read about the film, just read about car crashes and people getting off on the violence basically." To speak of "getting off on violence" is to presume its having a *mode of effect*, a capacity to reach and arouse (certain kinds of) people. And it is interesting to note that here, at least, it isn't easy to tell whether Tim is speaking 'of the *characters* or the *audience*. An elision seems possible, once the term "violence" is in play.

It would be wrong to suggest that everyone who hears that a film is "violent" is such a tender plant that they run away, or indeed that if they are attracted to see it, there is the proof of their degradation. For a number of our viewers, the point precisely was that the controversy stimulated an interest to *see if the complaints were correct*. Sometimes, but not always, this went with a distrust of those who claimed the authority to make those judgments. (*Mary:* "At the time I was saying, you know, look, you haven't seen it, I haven't seen it, who are we to judge? And now I'm saying, look, I've seen it, you haven't seen it, how dare you judge?") Most commonly, it went with an attitude of demanding the right to judge for oneself, as here:

> *David:* Umm, personally I didn't know much about it at all apart from
> . . . I'd read about it in the papers and I'd been watching film, Barry
> Norman on TV. Umm. And, and I was interested in seeing it. I think
> that was it, I don't think I would have been so interested in seeing
> it, if it hadn't caused all the controversy actually. Because I wanted
> to decide for myself.
> *Int.:* Right. So based on what you did know, was the film as you had
> imagined it would be?
> *David:* Partly. Umm . . . I didn't think it was shocking at all. I thought
> it was an interesting film, I didn't find it shocking.

But all the people so far quoted were those who, on seeing the film, found a disjunction between their expectations and their experiences.

Some (for example, Helen and Tim) became positive advocates for *Crash* once having seen it. Others (for example, David and Stephen) were less enthusiastic and more ambivalent, but still aware that, for them, the film just didn't match the implicit claims of being "violent":

> *Stephen:* Yeah I'd heard about it through word of mouth really and I
> saw a review by Barry Norman, talking about it and . . . the controversy around it made me sit up and take notice and want to see it,
> but I never actually got round to seeing it actually at the time. But
> then I saw your project, I thought I'd like to see the film 'cause I

hadn't seen it and then, but I didn't, I didn't really know how explicit it was, you know sexually or how, how, how bad the violence and the drug-taking or whether it was just a combination of the two, I had no idea, I was going to it pretty blind.

"Violence" is that which will shock; if the film has not shocked, it cannot be "violent." The force of this syllogism again reveals the extent to which people *experience* the accusation of "violence" as an emergent social explanation.

Some, however, did want to call *Crash* "violent." It is important to see how the category worked in their thought, as well. First, they too evidenced that "bleeding" between film and life, as in the following interview:

> *Horst:* No, for me that was it, and as I said before, I'm . . . it repels me and simply because of the violence. The senseless violence from my perspective. I do not think that . . . you can be as err . . . ruthless to other human beings by simply saying OK, we kill them . . . we kill them just for the heck of it. That is just totally alien to me, and . . . that's what I rejected in the film.

The equation of "violence" with "senselessness" (think also: "pointless," "gratuitous") is close to, albeit not quite identical with, the kinds of account that talk of "mindless" violence. But Horst is doing more than this: he "reads" the film for a meaning (that ruthlessness is acceptable), parallels that with a world beyond and finds the parallel too uncomfortable to live with. But that can have a number of motives and dimensions. Logically, it is quite possible for someone to acknowledge that *for them personally* seeing, hearing, or reading about something that causes discomfort leads to avoidance behavior. But at the back of the complaints about "violence" is that, while I avoid, you are attracted. While I see the horror, you are attracted to it. While I see the danger, you *become* dangerous. Again, "violence" as an implicit, emergent social theory.

But of real importance is to see how those who wished to condemn *Crash* responded to queries about their calling it "violent." One particularly revealing interview brought together two men who rejected the film on very different grounds. Both, however, wanted – at least at first – to call it "violent." Graham, for instance, early on stated: "I found absolutely minimal storyline. It just seemed a . . . a succession of err, violence and . . . and sexual activities, which just didn't hang together in any sort of meaningful way. So I got no satisfaction out of it at all." That hesitation later came back to bite him.

Later he talked of the film as "pandering to that taste in violence, car accidents and sex." But Graham's main objection to *Crash* was that it was badly made, dull, and boring. So when questioned on the sense in which he was using "violence" to describe *Crash*, he shifted:

> Well, for me the violence is in the road accidents and the fact that people are getting injured. But I fully accept that errm . . . there is no person-to-person violence, all the activities of the film are engaged in by consenting adults [laughs] if that's the right word. And you know that all the cars are driven by stunt men, there was about twenty of them listed at the end [laughing/indistinct]. That's what I mean when I say it could have been much worse. Therefore I personally would have no objection to that film being seen, presumably it had an . . . an over 18 . . . ?

Faced with the direct question, Graham admits that in no literal sense is *Crash* violent – and that has to be a limit to his objections. His co-interviewee Derek was far more confident. With a religiously-based objection to the film, he saw it as not simply perverted, but even worse – it symbolized a return to the "animal" in us, a retreat down the Great Chain of Being. It was an *embodiment* of the pre-human, a desertion of morals, something which "even primitive tribes" would shun. The force of the category "violence" for him showed on two occasions. In the first, he was responding to a question about how he felt about those who did enjoy *Crash*: "The thing is that this type of violence, promiscuous violence really, unnecessary violence, is errm . . . is err . . . particularly directed now towards ever younger children." The hesitations in here indicated nicely the difficulties he was experiencing in managing the move from a wide, to him quite philosophically-based category, to the particular case of *Crash* – which was never going to be directed at children. When asked directly about why he insisted on calling *Crash* "violent," his response is revealing precisely because at first it *appears* totally irrelevant to the question:

> Let us take just two examples. One is the emphasis on the prosthesis, the artificial limb . . . Quite unnecessary. . . . OK, there's plenty of people with artificial limbs, they come to some of our lectures actually. We don't comment on it, nor are we . . . disturbed by it. They just get on with it, we get on with it, they get on with it . . . But the other thing was this focusing on the lesion . . . it was a very severe lesion which had only just healed I should say. I know quite a bit about this, and errr . . . this seemed to me, again, quite unnecessary. Perhaps one shot to

convey the severity of the injury, but that wasn't the purpose. The purpose was to draw attention to the prosthesis and the difficulty of getting into the car.

For Derek, anything which demeans people's "dignity" is "violence." "Dignity" was a rich personal term for him, found often in his answers. It signified rising above the body, achieving a humanity in which anything purely physical is overcome. Albeit differently from the main public assaults on the film, a generalized philosophical position undergirded his insistence that *Crash* was "violent."

And that precisely is the point of this essay. I am arguing that we must challenge the very notion of "violence-talk." My objection is not simply to the strength or otherwise of the evidence, or to the reliability of the research that has been done. The very concept and category of "violence" is the problem. It has become a central repository for a set of fears about social change, which at the same time proffers an understanding of those changes in an ideologically-skewed way. The concept and its associated discourses make their presence felt, and press their point, in a continuous stream of small but effective ways – as indeed we found with *Crash*. The reporting of *Crash* was beset with puns, as is the Press's wont. It was a "crash course in perversions," "tearing through the barriers," and on a "collision course" with ordinary folks' morality. Or it was simply the "sex and wrecks" movie, by far the most common phrase in the Press coverage. It is tempting to see this last simply as a neat and cynical label. But it is actually more. It is, first, reductive. The film becomes narrativeless, purposeless, a set of incidents just waiting to be counted in a content analysis ("This movie is morally vacuous, nasty, violent, and little more than an excuse to string together one scene after another of sexual intercourse. I totted up sixteen such scenes ... before I stopped counting.")[32] Second, it becomes nigh-on impossible to understand how someone might *enjoy* such a movie except as something perverse, gratuitous, and possibly harmful ("Oh yeah, I am seriously into sex and wrecks ... ").

Also striking, of course, is the way the term "violent" is slipped into "descriptions" of the film. Now, to call *Crash* violent is distinctly odd. With one partial exception, every action in the narrative is clearly and overtly consensual. The car crashes are filmed in real time, evidently avoiding the cinematic highlighting which slow motion, for instance, would contribute. The one ambiguous moment

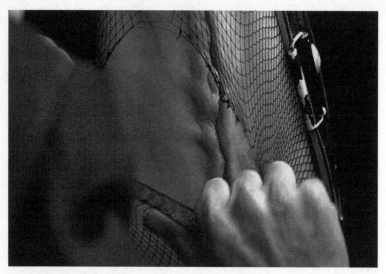

8 "Tearing through the barriers ..." One of the popular press's punning, cynical, and ultimately reductive misrepresentations of Cronenberg's film

is a sex scene two-thirds through the film, in which Catherine Ballard (Deborah Unger) invites the sexual attentions of Vaughan (Elias Koteas), but emerges from the resultant sex bruised and shaken. It isn't clear exactly how far she wanted or perhaps even enjoyed the rough sex. This aside, simply descriptively, it is very difficult to warrant attributing the word "violent" to *Crash*. This didn't prevent it happening – and that is perhaps itself an important testimony to how far the word has sedimented into public debates.

Ordinary, even non-condemnatory press coverage granted the point. One newspaper, for instance, while welcoming a decision by Kirkless councillors to reverse their decision to ban the film from their area, still conceded they had a point: they were in "a no-win situation when called upon to view a film which had aroused attention because of its violent or sexual content."[33] Other commentary strode deeper into the discourse, summoning the ghost of its "scientific" credentials. Again reporting a local move to bar the film, another newspaper reported: "Addressing the film's content, Councillor Barkworth said: "Violent and perverted screen images can influence very susceptible people"."[34] The persistent reduction of *Crash* to a sequence of "gratuitous," "pointless" episodes of sex and violence moves far beyond simple distortion. It marks something far more telling: the imprint of a vernacular film genre, derived from a general philosophical position.[35] In this light, Sunny's (above) acknowledgment of a generic label "ordinary sex and violence movie" takes on a new aspect. The application of generic labels can from time to time be a site for conflicts over general philosophies.

Of course the whole point is that the films themselves are not innocent outsiders – they are caught up within the very debates which lead to their labeling. But the case of *Crash* is a complicated one. There is effectively no "violence" in even ordinary meanings of the term within the film. The sex is consensual. The car crashes are anything but glamorized. It is not in the actions or events of the film, but in a confrontation between film and audience, that its power may lie. One of our research devices was the construction of a semantic table of people's chosen epithets to characterize *Crash*; these ranged from "thrilling," "invigorating," and "liberating" for those who responded positively, to "appalling," "disgusting," and "degrading" for those who responded negatively. But revealingly, our research uncovered one term held in common by both positive and negative viewers: "disturbing." For those who loved *Crash*, to be disturbed was an exhilarating experience, a challenge to their sense of themselves they were delighted to be taken through. For those who loathed *Crash*, disturbance evoked dismay – a sense of personal discomfort not to be located in any specific *events* of the film but in the blunt manner of their representation.

Cronenberg himself, in an interview for the magazine *Dazed & Confused*, named this rather well, but in a way that provokes many new questions:

> *D&C: Crash* has already been slated in certain quarters as being violently pornographic. How do you respond to your critics?
> *DC:* Well, if you compare it to what we would all consider a normal action film, it is not that violent. There are no guns, no heads being blown off, no knives, but people feel that it has done violence to them. If that is true then that is the art of the film and it is a conceptual violence: it attacks some basic concepts that people cling to, so that is where the violence is, but, to me, that's art, not pornography.[36]

If this implication from our evidence is right, it suggests that our understanding of how film genres work needs to be adjusted, to take further into account not just the way generic definitions may be powerfully derived from wider censorious, philosophical concerns. We also need to consider how, in particular, vernacular genres may

9 Whence the violence, exactly? In *Crash* (1996) the sex is largely consensual, and the automobile accidents themselves are anything but glamorized.

owe their shape less to narrative concerns or filmic conventions, and more to the kind of experiential encounter they seek to label. In which case, the problem with *Crash* was surely not that it was "violent," but that labeling the to-some-uncomfortable experience it provoked as "violence" provided legitimate grounds for refusing to consider why it might have had this effect. The play of the concept "violence" in these processes is yet more complicated. No longer a para-descriptive term at all, it has become a barrier against discomforting thoughts and feelings.

A modest proposal

We badly need a complete change of direction. I have sketched a very particular kind of history. If correct, its implications are that the concept "violence" is irredeemably ideological and that no valid research can take place under its aegis. But my history remains just that, a thin sketch. Who else out there can extend and expand my sketch, take it in new directions? What parallel histories might inform and enrich this one? What may explain its weird circumscription around the media and, even more, visual media? And crucially, *whose* interests precisely are embodied in this all-conquering concept?

Notes

1   See, for example, Jeffrey Weeks, *Against Nature: Essays on History, Sexuality and Identity* (London: Rivers Oram, 1991).

2   Gunnar Myrdal, *An American Dilemma: The Negro Problem and Modern Democracy* (New York: Harper, 1944).

3   *To Establish Justice: To Insure Domestic Tranquillity*, Final Report of the National Commission on the Causes and Prevention of Violence (New York: Bantam Books, 1970).

4   For a general account of the rise and decline of this mode of thinking, see David Wrobel, *The End of American Exceptionalism: Frontier Anxiety from the Old West to the New Deal* (Lawrence: University of Kansas Press, 2000). The survival of it as a habit of thought, of course, extends far beyond the motive forces which originated it.

5   *To Establish Justice*, 12.

6   Richard Slotkin, *Regeneration Through Violence: the Mythology of the American Frontier* (Middletown: Wesleyan University Press, 1973).

7   Slotkin, *Regeneration Through Violence*, 5.

8   *Ibid.*, 7.

9   *Ibid.*, 4–5.

10 *To Establish Justice*, 160.

11 *Ibid.*, 177.

12 On Fredric Wertham, see James Gilbert, *A Cycle of Outrage* (New York: Oxford University Press, 1986). See also Martin Barker, "Fredric Wertham – the sad case of the unhappy humanist," *Pulp Demons: International Dimensions of the Postwar Anti-Comics Campaign*, ed. John Lent (Madison: Fairleigh Dickinson University Press, 1999), 215–33.

13 Leonard Berkowitz, *Aggression: A Social Psychological Analysis* (New York: McGraw-Hill, 1962), 254.

14 Stuart Hall, *et al.*, *Policing The Crisis: Mugging, the State and Law and Order* (Basingstoke: Macmillan Press, 1978), 51 (from the *Daily Telegraph*, Aug. 25, 1971).

15 *Ibid.*, 275 (from the *Sunday Express*, Feb. 22, 1970).

16 *Ibid.*, 300.

17 *Ibid.* They point to an identical rhetorical strategy in other press accounts, e.g., a *Sunday Times* editorial which talked of three murders separated by thousands of miles. But "in death they acquired a terrible unity," linked by "the barbarism that characterises our age" (301; from the *Sunday Times*, April 2, 1972).

18 Vincent LaBrutto, *Stanley Kubrick* (London: Faber, 1997), 334–45.

19 See, for example, Robert Ardrey, *The Territorial Imperative: A Personal Inquiry into the Animal Origins of Property and Nations* (New York: Dell Publishing Co., 1967); Robert Ardrey, *The Social Contract: A*

Personal Inquiry into the Evolutionary Sources of Order and Disorder (New York: Dell Publishing Co., 1970); Konrad Lorenz, *On Aggression*, trans. Marjorie Kerr Wilson (New York: Bantam, 1967); Desmond Morris, *The Naked Ape: A Zoologist's Study of the Human Animal* (New York: McGraw-Hill, 1967); Desmond Morris, *The Human Zoo* (New York: McGraw-Hill, 1969); Niko Tinbergen, "On War and Peace in Animals and Men," *Science* 160 (1968): 1411–18.

20 Quoted. in Laurent Bouzereau, *Ultraviolent Movies: From Sam Peckinpah to Quentin Tarantino* (New York: Citadel, 2000), 35.

21 Annette Kuhn, *Cinema, Censorship and Sexuality, 1909–1925* (London: Routledge, 1988).

22 See, for example, Marshall Sahlins, *The Use and Abuse of Biology: An Anthropological Critique of Sociobiology* (London: Tavistock, 1977).

23 *Man and Aggression* (New York: Oxford University Press, 1968), ed. Ahley Montagu. The title of Montagu's first chapter is "The new litany of 'innate depravity'."

24 Stanley Milgram, *Obedience to Authority: An Experimental View* (London: Tavistock, 1974), 166.

25 H. J. Eysenck and D. B. Nias, *Sex, Violence and the Media* (London: Maurice Temple Smith, 1978).

26 Erich Fromm, *The Anatomy of Human Destructiveness* (Harmondsworth: Penguin, 1977; originally published 1973).

27 See, for example, *Aggression and War: their Biological and Social Bases*, ed. Jo Groebel and Robert Hinde (Cambridge: Cambridge University Press, 1989).

28 On this last, see Willard Rowland, Jr., *The Politics of TV Violence: Policy Uses of Communication Research* (Beverly Hills: Sage, 1983) and Rowland's contribution to *Ill Effects: The Media-Violence Debate*, ed. Martin Barker and Julian Petley (London: Routledge, 1997).

29 James Lull, *Media, Communication, Culture: A Global Approach* (Cambridge: Polity Press 2000), 88.

30 Editorial, *Western Daily Press* (Nov. 23, 1996).

31 Martin Barker, Jane Arthurs, and Ramaswami Harindranath, *The Crash Controversy: Censorship Campaigns and Film Reception* (London: Wallflower Press, 2001).

32 Nigel Reynolds, "Violent, Nasty and Morally Vacuous," *Daily Telegraph* (Nov. 9, 1996).

33 "Comment," *Huddersfield Daily Examiner* (Aug. 11, 1997).

34 "Crash Control," *Scunthorpe Evening Telegraph* (Nov. 12, 1996).

35 Rick Altman's remarkable study *Film/Genre* (London: BFI, 1999) reminds us of the need to examine the historical processes whereby film genres are constructed, and the definitional competition between the

industry (studios, stars, marketing regimes), publicity and reviewing agencies, and even academics.

36 "Interview with David Cronenberg," *Dazed & Confused* (Nov. 1996): 116–17.

4

The big impossible: action-adventure's appeal to adolescent boys

Theresa Webb and Nick Browne

One of New Hollywood's most successful line of products is the action-adventure film. Resembling the folktale in numerous ways, this genre magnetically attracts teenage boys, offering them instructive lessons relevant to their lives, but discretely, cloaked under the mantle of fantasy. Both the mantle, woven out of colorful but violent action, and the lessons it veils have made this genre hugely profitable. In what follows, we will examine the interaction between the virtual culture of the action-adventure genre (its violence content, narrative structure, characters, and ideas), and the "culture of cruelty" inhabited by most American adolescent boys. The 1994 big-budget action-adventure films Hollywood retailed to its targeted consumers, along with recent writings on the emotional life of male adolescents, will form the basis of our analysis.

What makes the relationship between these two distinct "cultures" worth exploring is their common link to violence. Our exploration of the dynamics of the action-adventure genre and its appeal to teenage boys will be both cultural and psychological. Learning is often imitative of available social models. Conditioning by modeling is particularly effective under certain circumstances: when the role model has something in common with the observer; when the role model is shown to have social power; when the actions of the role model are reinforced in a manner the viewer can experience vicariously; and when the role model receives rewards the observer envies.[1] American society has reason to be interested in movie violence when young viewers come to perceive connections between themselves and the heroes and villains of action-adventure films but not for the reasons that cultural critics think.

Underlying the relation between the fictional worlds designed in the action-adventure mode and violence in our real existing social world is a deeply-rooted problem in American society and to some degree in all post-industrial capitalist societies. This problem, often obscured as such, has to do with the social oppression (discipline and regimentation) of men. How boys and men are systematically (mis)treated by their society has everything to do with the fact that interpersonal and public violence is a problem almost entirely unique to them. Two aspects of this oppression are relevant to our analysis here. First is the widely held, but largely unexamined, assumption that males are by nature aggressive and therefore violent. So far as we know, males are no more naturally inclined to aggression than their female counterparts, yet they are subject to societal conditioning which encourages violent behavior. Second is the fact that boys are conditioned against all emotions except anger. Emotionally expressive boys and men are commonly ostracized by their peers and labeled "sissies" and "queers." Given the conditioning boys receive and the cultural biases and expectations imposed upon them, it is no surprise that the action-adventure genre, which celebrates successful manhood and violence, is so appealing to them.

The action genre

The action-adventure genre as we know it today emerged in the early 1980s. For many critics the exact year was 1982, when *Rambo: First Blood* was released. The genre's dominant structural codes include brilliant mise-en-scene, hyperbolic action, and fast-moving stories accelerated by rapid editing. Accentuated, hard-edged dramaturgy and fast-paced editing generate action's characteristic dramatic tension and discourage any sort of reflection during the viewing experience. The genre's narrative stripes are further shown in a nearly obligatory set of story elements: the heroes are largely invulnerable and embody Herculean strength; the stories are Manichean, laying out the forces of good and evil in simple, broad brushstrokes; the hero usually has to work outside the protection of the law, often becoming an outlaw in order to do the work of the good; the villain's violation of the laws of humanity justifies his eventual extermination by the hero; the stories are strictly fictional and always have a happy ending.

In *The Uses of Enchantment*, Bruno Bettelheim tells us that fairy-tales characteristically state an existential dilemma briefly and pointedly; that they simplify all situations; that characters are typical rather than unique; that evil is as omnipresent as virtue; that evil is not without its attractions and often temporarily gains in power or authority; that evil always loses out in the end; and that the ending is always happy.[2] Bettelheim also argues that fairytales are *functional* – they are oriented to the future and serve to guide children and adolescents toward adult ways.[3] We found that the action-adventure genre as a narrative format embodies in a graphically delineated mode all these features.

In action-adventure, as in the fairytale, the most common scheme is the overcoming of difficulties. In both modes, the initial narrative situation is defined by a lack or problem which is then transformed or overcome. Perhaps more to the point, like fairytales, action-adventure films contain certain features which "fantastically exaggerate real life"[4] and commonly transgress the boundaries of reality. What is important about this, however, is that there is no requirement in either genre that their fantastic elements be believed, nor any sanction for transgression of the boundaries of narrative plausibility. "Although possible and impossible occurrences recklessly mingle and the laws of causality often seem forgotten, certain causal relationships survive. The coexistence of fantasy and reality represents an important feature of the fairytale."[5] It would be hard to name a New Hollywood action movie that does not overstep the boundaries of reality, or one that does not commingle reality with fantasy. In such films the fantasy elements are consistently situated at the level of the plot, where the violent action takes place, and the dimension of reality (generally tinged with the magic of simplicity) is situated at the level of subplot, where relationships unfold.

At the plot level, idealized models of fully-realized men (heroes) engage in elaborate games of hide-and-seek with other powerful, but deeply flawed, male characters (villains) who in the end lose everything. The discourse at this level supports and ratifies the assumption that men are by nature violent and the societal expectation that they be so. At the subplot level, the genre addresses from the perspective of the hero some of the most essential human problems that the members of the audience must inevitably face over the course of their lives. On this plane, the heroes deal with real, even everyday, conflicts and challenges and display contemporary methods of resolving them.

Below we will examine the action genre in terms of its two distinct tracks of representation. While books have been written on the subject of the male film hero engaged in violent action, for example, Yvonne Tasker's *Spectacular Bodies*, none that we know of have analyzed the work he does at the interpersonal relationship level. First, however, we lay out the contours of our sample of films, our methods, and the results of our study.

Our sample

Because action-adventure films are so highly formulaic along the lines just described, we could have chosen any random grouping from this genre to make our case. We are focusing on those released in 1994, however, because we have in our possession a rich set of data on them. That year the genre was composed of the following films and actors: *Blown Away* (Jeff Bridges, Tommy Lee Jones), *Clear and Present Danger* (Harrison Ford, Willem Dafoe), *Drop Zone* (Wesley Snipes, Gary Busey), *On Deadly Ground* (Steven Seagal, John McGinley), *Speed* (Keanu Reeves, Denis Hopper), *Street Fighter* (Jean-Claude Van Damme, Raul Julia), *Terminal Velocity* (Charlie Sheen, Nastassja Kinski), *The Getaway* (Alec Baldwin, Kim Bassinger, Michael Madsen), *The River Wild* (Meryl Streep, Kevin Bacon), *The Shadow* (Alec Baldwin, John Lone), *The Specialist* (Sylvester Stallone, Sharon Stone, James Woods), *Three Ninjas Kick Back* (Victor Wong), *Timecop* (Jean-Claude Van Damme, Ron Silver), and *True Lies* (Arnold Schwarzenegger, Jamie Lee Curtis, Art Malik).

Methods

The empirical data for our analysis of these fourteen action-adventure films was collected as part of a large-scale study on film violence. The sample in its entirety was made up of the 100 top-grossing pictures of 1994 as identified by *The Hollywood Reporter*'s annual summary of American films. An analytic instrument was designed to capture the violence content and its contextualization in these films. The instrument reflected the schematization of filmic violence and progressed from scene to episode to violent act to consequences in a way that allowed for the progressive logic of each film to unfold. To garner information about each film as a whole, a four-part inventory of attributes was designed to cover such things as cinematic style, narrative, language, and the role of violence as an element of their social worlds. Most importantly, a character index composed of fifty-one questions was applied to each character. It included a categorization of the character's attitude toward the social world he inhabited, whether or not the character reflected on his violent conduct, and whether or not his self-image was affirmed by it. In this essay, we draw on data drawn from each of these three components of our analytic instrument.

For the purposes of our study, we defined violence very narrowly as any aggressive physical gesture made by an initiator against one or more recipients or against any kind of inanimate object. A slap to the face, for instance, would qualify as a violent action, as would blowing up a building. Verbal and non-verbal threats and other types of abusive language were excluded from our definition of violence but were taken into consideration as contextual variables.

Action's violence content

The sheer quantity of violent actions against characters and property in the fourteen films of our sample was very high. The total number counted was 778. The bulk of the violence was directed at characters, with a total of 658 discrete acts counted. More than half of this violence was expressed in one-on-one exchanges (337). The other half was made up of various combinations of ensemble fighting, often involving numerous characters of undetermined quantities (275). There were four acts of sexual violence accounting for a tiny fraction of the total for the genre. Of the 658 violent actions against characters in this genre, almost half were coded as involving aggression levels of fatal or potentially fatal force (317 acts, 48.2 per cent). In spite of this, only fifty-seven bodily injury consequences were counted, involving only twenty-seven representations of critical injury. Of course, the deaths of incidental characters was quite high.

In terms of property violence, our fourteen films represented eighty-two acts of willful destruction, nineteen of which were of spectacular magnitude (involving large-scale pyrotechnics). Additionally, twelve acts of theft and twenty-two acts of trespassing were counted.

Timecop was the most violent film of 1994. It contained 110 violent acts against characters, forty-four of which involved ensembles of more than two people, and four large-scale acts of violence against property. *True Lies* ranked second with ninety-one discrete acts of violence against characters, including eighteen huge ensemble fights and eleven acts of spectacular property destruction – including an entire island destroyed with a nuclear weapon. The third most violent film was *Drop Zone*. With sixty-six violent actions against characters involving fifteen ensemble brawls and only two violent acts against property, the film was significantly less violent than *Timecop* and *True Lies*. Still it was one of the most violent movies of 1994. Six other films in the genre that year had between forty and fifty acts of violence against characters: *The Specialist*, *The River Wild*, *Terminal Velocity*, *Street Fighter*, *On Deadly Ground*, and *Three Ninjas Strike Back*. *Clear and Present Danger* was the genre's least violent film, with nineteen acts of violence against characters and five against property.

Action's heroes

In 1994 the action heroes were all male, with one exception: Streep in *The River Wild*. They were also all white with one exception: Snipes in *Drop Zone*. All were shown to have power and executive authority within their milieus. All but two fell somewhere in the middle class, with one being very rich: Baldwin's Lamont Cranston in *The Shadow*. All but one character was clearly and fixedly on one side of the law or the other. Van Damme's Agent Walker in *Timecop* was the exception. While more than half the heroes "excelled at violence" – that is, showed special competence – one was strictly nonviolent: Ford's Jack Ryan in *Clear and Present Danger*. As agents carrying out violence and as recipients receiving it, most remained "cool and composed."

In terms of image, all but one hero was presented as "cool," and only two stood in opposition to mainstream culture (Seagal's Forrest Taft in *On Deadly Ground* and Baldwin's Doc McCoy in *The Getaway*). Jack Ryan in *Clear and Present Danger* was the genre's only "square" protagonist. More than half the heroes were "heroized" by the society of the film due to their willingness to engage in violent conduct. While the heroes rarely (just twice) showed restraint in the exercise of violence, their intentions remained consistent, meaning their actions were neither irrational nor arbitrary. Most of the heroes experienced some kind of personal loss and most were at one point or another injured in the commission of violence. However, in almost every case the violence the heroes enacted was related to their survival or the survival of others close to them. Almost all the heroes were satisfied with their enactment of violence, and for all the blows they sustained there was very little suffering; none of them died.

10 Howard Payne (Dennis Hopper), the revenge-obsessed villain in *Speed* (1994)

Action-adventure heroes are very often warriors of one sort or another. In our sample of thirteen (male) heroes, nine fell into this category.[6] Schwarzenegger's Harry Tasker in *True Lies* is based on the comic book character Clark Kent/Superman and is a national security spy. Like Harry, Lamont Cranston in *The Shadow* is also based on a comic book hero and is a masked warrior against evil in Manhattan. Van Damme's two characters in the sample are also both warriors. Agent Walker in *Timecop* is responsible for policing time and Colonel Guile in *Street Fighter* is the leader of a national military in "Shadaloo," a fictional Southeast Asian country, who has the responsibility of defeating a political and military tyrant. Forrest in *On Deadly Ground* plays a noble savage who single-handedly takes on an oil baron and his army of thugs to reclaim Alaskan land and its resources for the Native Americans. Bridges' Jimmy Dove in *Blown Away*, a film with a mere twenty-seven acts of violence against characters, plays an ex-IRA terrorist now a bomb specialist for the Boston police department. Reeves' Jack Traven in *Speed* is a highly-trained police officer who rescues a bus full of people and does away with the villain who would kill them all to serve his revenge plot against the LA Police Department. Stallone's Ray Quick in *The Specialist* is an ex-CIA agent, a loner-"do-gooder" who assists a woman in avenging her parents' murder. Finally, Snipe's Pete Nessip in *Drop Zone* is a federal marshal who alone takes on a vicious gang of corporate pirates.

Schwarzenegger, Stallone, Snipes, Van Damme, and Seagal come to their respective roles as Harry, Ray, Pete, Walker, Guile, and Forrest as action stars. Tasker points out that they are all well-built and muscle-bound, and that their films are written and structured specifically to showcase their bodies and display their fighting abilities.[7] While the first three action stars on this list usually use weapons (large and exotic guns and explosives), the latter two engage in a lot of hand-to-hand fighting, showing off their martial-arts and kick-boxing prowess. But beyond being strong, highly-trained warriors, the characters these stars play are likeable and fit the bill of the classic boy scout. That is, in addition to being strong, they are also brave, courageous, and nice, and express concern for those in need of their help. This is not to say that the violent acts these characters commit are not gruesome. For example, in one violent scene in *True Lies*, Harry throws a knife-like object into the eye of one of his captors, impales another with a large fishhook, then breaks a couple of necks as he and wife escape from the shack in which they are being held hostage.

The other dominant type of hero in our sample was the naive "Everyman" who accidentally stumbles into a trap and has to figure his/her way out. Gale (Streep) in *The River Wild* just happened to be at the wrong place at the wrong time and ended up saddled with two dangerous thieves. Jack in *Clear and Present Danger* becomes acting Deputy-Director of CIA intelligence when his boss is diagnosed with pancreatic cancer and soon thereafter gets ambushed by a Colombian drug cartel. Sheen's character in *Terminal Velocity* gets himself embroiled in a Russian Mafia/KGB escapade taking place on American soil by sheer chance and bad luck. And lastly, Doc McCoy, *The Getaway*'s good guy/bad guy character, has to defend his wife and himself against a malicious gang he involved himself with to pull off a heist earlier.

While this group of heroes is similar to the warriors in terms of disposition and comportment, they are neither muscle-bound nor trained fighters. Like the warrior characters, each of these heroes exhibit in their attitudes and conduct the basic cardinal virtues of justice, prudence, fortitude, temperance, and magnanimity, and the violence they engage in is defensive and/or restorative in nature. The difference, however, is that while the warrior heroes engage in violence with cavalier ease, the Everyman heroes do not. Sheen, who plays an Olympic-level swimmer and expert skydiver, is dumbfounded by the violence he encounters, exhibits fear the first time he fires a gun, and stumbles through the entire film in the dark about what's happening to him. Ford plays an intellectual, bureaucratic type who is also baffled and overwhelmed by the violence he encounters in his work. And Streep, who plays a former college rower, exhibits moments of terror and grief, all the while managing a large canoe in treacherous waters and sparring with Wade (Bacon) – the film's "real-man" villain – until she finally kills him with a bullet to the head.

Action's villains

A composite profile of the thirteen major action-adventure villains obviously looks quite different than that of the heroes'. All were male, nine were white, two were Asian, one was Persian, and one was Latino. Seven villains were foreigners. All were involved in criminal activity. They were warlords, drug dealers, hit-men, terrorists, one was a weapons dealers, and one a corporate criminal. Like the heroes, most were shown to have executive power and authority in their milieus. While eight of them fell somewhere in the middle class, two were rich, and with two it was impossible to determine. In two cases the character's relationship to the law was ambiguous: in one the character appeared to be lawful (McGinley's MacGruder in *On Deadly Ground*), and in the other there was oscillation between lawful and unlawful conduct (Silver's Senator McComb in *Timecop*). As agents of violence most villains remained composed, but as recipients only four consistently remained so.

In terms of image, only two villains were presented as "cool": Madsen's Rudy in *The Getaway* and Dafoe's Clark in *Clear and Present Danger*. Half the villains stood in opposition to mainstream culture. The majority of them had an aggressively defensive attitude toward others, and in most cases the character's prestige within an outlaw group was defined by his willingness to enact violence. Violence was committed by most of the villains in order to remove perceived obstacles in obtaining their goals. Villains almost always expressed enthusiasm in the exercise of violence and many were ecstatic about it. Almost none of them reflected on their use of violence. For all the villains there was personal cost associated with their activities and all of them were injured in the commission of violence. In the end, they all died a violent death.

All the villains in our sample share a certain number of character flaws: arrogance, stupidity, selfishness, and egomania being the most common. All were small-minded, petty, vulgar, condescending, tyrannical, and brutal. All were classic schoolyard bullies: mean-spirited and vicious. They were all also autistic in that they were unable to bond with anyone else and were indifferent to the pain and suffering their reckless behavior inflicted on others. In fact, many of the villains sadistically received pleasure from this behavior. While greed for money and/or power were the most common operative vices motivating our sample's villains, desire for revenge also played a role.

Hopper's psychotic Howard Payne in *Speed*, one of the two villains not motivated by greed, is a retired police officer. Having been injured in the line of duty years earlier and never rewarded a pension, he becomes obsessed with taking revenge on his department. The other vengeful character is *Blown Away*'s Ryan Gaerity (Jones), a terrorist who specializes in bombs. This character is as equally obsessed with revenge as Payne, but for different reasons. Having spent many years in a Northern Ireland prison for acts of terrorism, he comes to America to inflict vengeance on his former patriot Jimmy, now a bomb specialist for the Boston Police Department. When Gaerity first contacts Jimmy, he declares: "I'm bringing you the gift of pain . . . I'm a creator . . . I've come to create a new country for you called Chaos and a new government called Anarchy. All for you! . . . You betrayed the cause . . . " Gaerity's deranged plan is to kill everyone around Jimmy before doing away with him. Jimmy, of course, stops him before he completes his psychotic mission, but before doing so, Gaerity kills quite a few people in massive explosions around Boston.

The greed for power side of the coin involves characters from all over the globe. *The Shadow*'s Shi Wan Khan (Lone), a descendent of Ghengis Khan, comes to the US from China entertaining the delusional idea of conquering the world and establishing himself as the emperor of mankind. Shi Wan Khan is a brutal character whose mind-control powers enable him to, among other things, force people to commit suicide. Needless to say, he uses this power indiscriminately and for personal gain. The other power monger is Azis (Malik) in *True Lies*. This character is coded as an Arab terrorist who plans to bomb America with nuclear weapons if the government does not cooperate with him.

Greed for money was a slightly more common motivation for villainy than that of power in our sample. The bad guys in *Clear and Present Danger*, *Terminal Velocity*, *The River Wild*, *On Deadly Ground*, and *The Getaway* were all twisted into psychotic killers out of obsession for money. The two villains coded as "cool" fall into this category. Rudy in *The Getaway* is a brutal, unscrupulous criminal bent on recovering stolen money. Over the course of the narrative he betrays one of his partners in crime, murders another one, and attempts to kill a third so he won't have to share the booty from a heist. In a disturbing turn of events, he seduces the woman he is holding captive and the two become lovers in her husband's presence. As a result of this aberrant coupling, the husband commits suicide in a motel bathroom while Rudy and his wife are having sex in the next room.

Clark, the "cool" antagonist in *Clear and Present Danger*, is an American expatriate living in Panama and an unscrupulous mercenary willing to kill for money. He is introduced in the story doing business with one of the American president's corrupt advisors. Then midway through the job of wiping out cocaine production laboratories and everyone in them – when the money dries up and some of his "discretionary" warriors are killed – he changes sides and works with the film's hero.

Action's narrativization of violence

As we have just tried to show, violence in the action-adventure genre has two faces. One is righteous, enacted to promote the right and the good, while the other is malfeasant, enacted to meet the often-psychotic needs of an evil fiend. The narrative structuring of violence reflects this distinction in a formulaic, and thus largely unambiguous, manner. With few exceptions, films in this genre open and close with a bang. That is, they begin with a destructive violent event initiated by the villain(s), which, in turn, engages the protagonist-hero both personally and professionally. This event or its after-effects then poses a simple, straightforward existential dilemma situated inside the larger conundrum the hero is commissioned to solve. Final resolution of the problem always involves a violent exchange between the forces of good and evil, during which time the hero unleashes a wrath of restorative violence bringing about the bang before the calm at the film's conclusion. While the plot is usually structured around the larger issue to be resolved, the subplot carries the weight of the hero's personal engagement in it. Because all the films in our sample reflected this narrativization, one example each of opening and closing violent events will suffice to make our point.

Timecop, a futuristic film, will illustrate the initial structuring of violence in the plot. The opening scene is staged to look like a Western.

A title on the screen reads "1863." It is common knowledge that during that year America was at war with itself. A posse of men traveling by horseback is shown being held up by a man in a confederate uniform. He demands their money, they refuse to hand it over, and he opens fire on them. The hitch is that he uses machine guns – a weapon not yet invented in 1863. The machine guns in this context create the strange incongruity which establishes the film's peculiar predicament – that of the ravaging of history by a greedy American senator in order to support his evil and tyrannical plot to become president.

The next scene brings us back to the contemporary world where we are introduced to Agent Walker, the man hired to solve this problem. The story quickly conveys the affection he shares with his wife in a lovemaking scene, and then immediately shows Walker getting ambushed by a group of thugs as he walks out the front door to go to work. After he is beaten up and left for dead on the front lawn, the history pirates enter the house and murder his wife. Temporarily crippled by pain, Walker is unable to move fast enough to intervene before the house blows up and his wife dies. The moral dilemma Walker thus faces is whether or not he too can go back in time and change the circumstances leading to the brutal death of his pregnant wife and the destruction of his personal life. Of course, by the story's end he has reversed the devastation wrought upon his family, done away with the bad guys, and destroyed the technology enabling the ransacking of history's wealth.

The finale of action-adventure films, during which the hero metes out the villain's punishment, is almost always an elaborately choreographed dance of violence and bloodshed. The destruction of the villain is usually Dante-esque in nature, which is to say that the punishment received reflects the very old maxim of justice, "I do unto you as you do unto me." Thus, how the villain meets his end is a direct reflection of his own evildoing in the story. The thirteen films in our sample were no exception. To take just one example, in the finale of *The Shadow*, Shi Wan Khan and the Shadow (Baldwin) fight a war of willpower and concentration mediated by an anthropomorphized knife after the trigger on an atom bomb's timer has been tricked. When the Shadow finally regains full power of his mind he shatters a wall of mirrors and sends a shard into Shi Wan Khan's head, simultaneously killing him and breaking the evil villain's spell over Manhattan.

11 "Real man" Wade (Kevin Bacon) temporarily displaces young Rourke's (Joseph Mazzello) negligant and effeminized father in *The River Wild* (1994)

The subplot: action's lessons

Woven in at the level of the subplot, action-adventure films, like fairytales, imaginatively address some of the most essential human problems. In our sample we witnessed such issues as fear of infidelity, jealousy, and anxiety about monogamy in sexual relationships (*True Lies*, *The Getaway*), extreme marital tension (*The River Wild*), the loss of a sibling in one case (*Drop Zone*) and that of a wife in another (*Timecop*) due to violence, the loss of an older friend and mentor to cancer (*Clear and Present Danger*), the politics of revenge and the devastating effects it has on the individual who embraces it (*Speed*, *Blown Away*), the politics of identity and environmental destruction as motivational forces (*On Deadly Ground*), budding romance (*Blown Away*, *The Specialist*, *Terminal Velocity*, *Speed*), and friend-ship (*True Lies*, *Clear and Present Danger*). The instructive value of these films lies in the various ways their heroes conduct themselves in relation to such personal, professional, and political challenges.

Two subplots in our sample deal with the moral imperatives of hon-esty, fairness, and doing what is right within the context of the family: *True Lies* and *The River Wild*. Both films focused critical attention on a component of men's oppression that effects the lives of everyone in conventional nuclear families. The problem, experienced one way by women and children and another by men, has to do with the way men (in all classes) devote themselves to their jobs or careers, often to the exclusion of everything else. This is a problem with deep roots in American economy and society where men have historically worked themselves to death (or, at any rate, early death) to provide for their families. In this regard, the ideological imperatives that form the ideals of American masculinity are part and parcel of the discipline that supports and sustains the American way of life.

In both films, the husband/father characters are shown to be completely driven in this way, and thus out of touch with their children's lives and emotionally and sexually cut off from their wives. At the beginning of *The River Wild*, husband/father Tom (David Strathairn) has so little respect or authority that even the family dog ignores his commands. In this film, the conflict between the three family members – Tom, Gale, and their son Roarke (Joseph Mazzello) – unfolds during a whitewater canoe trip besieged by two killer thieves. The family falls in with the villains indirectly because of Tom. Being an absent and negligent father, he has left a void in his son's life. When the family arrives at the river, Roarke meets Wade, the main villain, and, impressed with his "real man" style, sees a role model to take his father's place. The shrewd Wade quickly realizes that the boy is manipulable and works him in order to penetrate the family circle.

Over the course of their bizarre journey down the river with the two thugs (whom the family witnesses murdering a river patrolman and an old friend of Gale's), the mother and son confront Tom about his negligence, and by the end of story, when they have reached land and safety, Tom has changed. There is one scene in particular in which Tom directly reveals how overburdened with responsibility he feels towards his family. When Gale says to him, "I think that you spend so much time at work because you don't like being around me anymore," he responds, "Gale, it's not about that. You set such high standards for yourself and everybody around you. I'm just trying to live up to your expectations of me. I'm trying to make you proud of me again." In this he conveys the belief that his value to his family has everything to do with attaining professional success. After escaping the captivity of the thieves, Tom, who is a sedentary middle-aged architect, must push himself physically to the limit to help rescue his wife and son. To do so he lays an architectural rescue plan and executes it with the help and cooperation of the family dog. His method of rescue, and the fact that the dog assists, functions symbolically to reveal his efforts at integrating work and family life. In the end, this character has modeled the difficult work of self-overcoming and the rebuilding of broken bridges in an instructive way.

Harry Tasker, the Clark Kent/Superman hero of *True Lies*, is at
the center of a number of different types of relationships: some successful, some not so successful. Harry is a national security agent in
such deep cover that even his wife is in the dark about his real profession. Early on in the film, we learn that Harry is emotionally cut
off from both his wife and his daughter and vice-versa. Harry's
daughter, like Tom's son, has nothing but contempt for her father,
whom she feels has no interest in her. It is Harry's troubled relationship with his wife Helen (Curtis), however, that becomes the
main personal problem he confronts and resolves. After learning
that his wife's desire is drifting and that she is being seduced by a
used-car salesman posing as an undercover spy, he works obsessively
to reconnect with her. Eventually, Harry comes clean with Helen
about his real profession, deals with her wrath about the deception,
brings her into his world (a much more interesting one than hers –
she's a legal secretary), and reconnects with her sexually. In the end,
they live happily ever after. But the point is that Harry does the
work necessary to save his relationship and builds a foundation
upon which it can grow.

Action's appeal to adolescent boys

In an essentialist sort of way the action-adventure genre appeals
powerfully to adolescent boys because it solicits and capitalizes on
certain natural qualities common to their demographic: high physical energy, boldness, unanchored imagination, and an action orientation, all of which translates into a kind of psychological boldness.[8]
Dan Kindlon and Michael Thompson, two psychologists who have
spent many years studying boys within the context of school, argue
that male adolescents are naturally inclined to want to *do* things, and
that much of what they talk about is "wide-eyed and unrealistic,"
that is, fantasy-driven and experimental in nature – a "necessary
calibration of an unfolding identity."[9]

The peer culture adolescent boys create, or more accurately
inherit, Thompson and Kindlon call the "culture of cruelty," the
operative dynamic of which is a transference of the disrespect and
distrust they intuit from the adult culture on to each other. Beginning around puberty, boys begin the process of separating from their
parents and establishing their independence. During this period
friendships and peer groups become more significant in their lives,

informally offering them the support of comradery. In exchange for "peer support," loyalty, and conformity are required.

Of the millions of adolescent male peer groups within the culture of cruelty there are two common features. One is that all rely on a pecking order for structure, with the strongest alpha male(s) at the top. The other is that cruel teasing is the main mode of communication and discipline. In this hierarchical culture, older boys dominate younger boys by virtue of their greater size and younger boys imitate their older peers, "creating an environment that pits the strong against the weak, the conformity-driven 'boy pack' against the boy who fails in any way to conform to pack expectations."[10] Being an insider in the culture of cruelty is exacting as boys are under constant pressure to assert "power" and remain in synch with the alpha males in order to avoid being the target of a cruel joke or prank, or worse, harassment, humiliation, or rejection. Kindlon and Thompson claim that the emotional damage done to male adolescents during this cruel interlude in their lives is extensive. In recent school shootings perpetrated by teenage boys, revenge for felt disrespect by the peer community has been one of the reported motives.

Normal adolescent cognitive development makes boys more self-consciously aware of themselves. Given their developing gender identity they are looking for models of successful masculinity. It is for this reason that the action-adventure genre, with its representations of idealized versions of manhood, is so appealing to them. Heroes in the action mode powerfully portray the physical and moral embodiment of manhood in a manner unlike other film heroes. Identification with appropriate social role models assists in transcending adolescence, and action heroes play a part in this process by modeling power, autonomy, and sovereignty in a distinctly different manner than that offered by family and school in everyday life.

While there are numerous cultural expectations surrounding manhood in American society, there is one which exceeds all others in the lives of adolescent boys and young men. It is the test of manhood: in the private sphere, the fight, in the public sphere, combat. Though the test may not occur, the boy must be ready nevertheless. Fighting a war is without a doubt the most serious responsibility of young American manhood. While not every generation has had to fight one, each is coached in preparation for its eventuality. The New Hollywood action-adventure film speaks directly to this particular cultural expectation in a way that no other popular film genre does.

This is partly because the genre is a synthesis of the two classical film genres which have historically dealt with the cultural expectation of conquest: the Western and the war film. In the popular media, heroes are almost always men with guns. Reflecting this martial legacy, nine of the thirteen heroes in our sample were warrior cops of one stripe or another and eight of the thirteen villains were trained warriors gone bad.

Action-adventure characters and the stories they enact play a complicated role in the socialization process of boys. Based on the genre's polarization of good (hero) and evil (villain), identification should be a simple and straightforward matter. In action films as in fairytales, however, identification vacillates between the two competing poles right up to the end. This is so in part because evil has its attractions. The villain's cunning, norm-transgressing, and powerful, ego-gratifying cruelty is a compelling option. There is no limit to the scope of his willful destruction and malevolence. Moreover, like the heroes, the villains are powerful and often highly-accomplished figures with all the trappings of successful manhood – attractive women, wealth, autonomy – thus enviable to the adolescent struggling with his nascent sexual desire, on the lowest rung of the economic ladder, and at the mercy of parental whim.

How the heroes react to situations on the main track of action speaks to boys directly about what society expects and requires of them. Boys are aware that many struggles lay ahead, and what the films tell them is that all conflicts are resolvable, but frequently demand violence. The invincible warrior organized around the dictum "Kill or be killed!" sends a message to boys and young men who may be obliged to fight. Heroes of this sort keep alive the reality of war but reassure boys that fighting against evil is necessary and can be done successfully.

Though ultimately the one-on-one confrontation of the hero and villain offers the most dramatic resolution of the founding conflict, this combat takes place within a network of social relationships that reveals what ultimately is at stake in their opposition. It is a premise of these films that the two principals have equal powers and the seesaw plots show that when the villain gains the upper hand, the balance of power is up for grabs. The principal characters differ, however, in their attitudes toward their partners and associates. Ultimately, the villains are tyrannical, opportunistic egoists whose helpers distrust one another, often betray each other, and are treated by the villain as expendable. By contrast, the hero maintains a loyal affiliation with partner or family. In a number of cases (*Blown Away, True Lies, Time Cop, The River Wild*) the family is indirectly implicated or put at risk by the hero's work. In such instances, he often suffers the anxiety of loss, if rarely the loss itself, and when suffering bodily harm or pain he consistently and heroically overcomes it. Further, he knows the importance of the social order and when in his professional life he is called to stand, he rises bravely to the occasion. The action hero, however, occupies a professionally uncertain condition. He is typically an employee of a public institution (police, military), subscribes to its creed, and though he may be of it, he does not follow its procedures. In other words, he operates outside its bureaucratic strictures, demands independence in his choice of strategies and operations, and necessarily improvises in novel situations (e.g., defusing a bomb on a runaway bus). In his solitary, resourceful, yet militaristic ways, he is the prototypical guerrilla entrepreneur. He enjoys a public trust and acts on behalf of the family, the city, or the state, using methods that are unique and personal to him.

The appeal of the action-adventure genre to adolescent boys, most of whom are situated inside an adversarial culture of their own making, is due largely to the type of role models it offers its targeted audience. The genre presents a real choice in its models of identification, and the villain is one of them. Indeed the villain may well be the instinctively preferred choice of male adolescents, frustrated by social discipline or its lack, and only a well-constructed story can solicit, consolidate, and maintain audience identification with the hero for this population in the process of socialization.

The action film works to bring its young audience to adhere to a certain picture of society and justice. The villain does offer the vicarious thrill of playing God with the lives of others, but viewers soon see that the support of weaker friends or associates – the very condition of the teenage boy – is an easily abandoned pragmatic convenience. Identification with the hero, we might say, is a matter of entertaining, *but ultimately refusing*, identification with the villain or, more accurately, of maintaining, up to the end, an ambivalent relationship to him. The villain's cruelty is a vehicle for the unrestrained, pleasurable release of anti-social instincts, for expressing resentment for ordinary humiliations associated with the adolescent's less-than-adult status, and for supporting the audience's vicarious enjoyment in the sadistic destruction of social norms. But

attachment, by the weak, to the villain ultimately means annihilation. In this way, the genre moves the audience to accept a positive
identification with the other killer, the hero. These reasons are situated on the second track of the narrative, the one on which the hero
maintains and cultivates life-preserving relations with those around
him. In every film in our sample, the hero enjoys a special relationship with the public, which he helps to maintain, and when a family
member (the metonymic figure for the public) is threatened, injured,
or killed, the social fabric is torn and the hero suffers.

In effect, the law in this genre is figured as a function of social self-
preservation. The hero's violent action, even if it involves vengeance,
or the taking of life, must not be either capricious or motivated principally by personal gain. Action answers to and dramatizes a sense of
justice that recognizes the protections due the weak, and celebrates
the power of the strong to do the right thing. As such, the audience
who identifies with the hero can safely project its own life into the
future. The genre also provides a testing ground for arbitrating
the terms of popular justice. The villain's defeat and death at the
hands of the hero allows the young viewer both the security of self-
preservation and the pleasures of juvenile nihilism.

The action-adventure genre is both a tutorial justifying the military
demands of the state to the population which could soon (at eighteen) be called upon to enlist, and a recruitment poster outlining the
gratifications that service offers. The genre in other words serves a
socializing function by aligning the anarchic and destructive intensi-
ties of the adolescent male to the jobs required in the modern war
machine, jobs which require not only bold, inventive action but
respect for proper authority and loyalty to brothers – all in the service of a righteous cause. But along with this glamorized and gratify-
ing indoctrination goes the lesson about self-sacrifice as well. In this
way, popular culture installs the civic virtue required by the modern
military state. But none of these lessons are too clearly spelled out in
the sound and fury which gives the genre its spectacular life.[11]

Notes

1   Dave Grossman, *On Killing: The Psychological Cost of Learning to Kill
    in War and Society* (Boston: Little, Brown & Co., 1996), 317–18.
2   Bruno Bettelheim, *The Uses of Enchantment: The Meaning and Impor-
    tance of Fairytales* (New York: Vintage, 1989), 8–9.
3   *Ibid.*, 11.

4 Lutz Rohrich, *Folktales and Reality* (Bloomington: Indiana University Press, 1991), xx.
5 *Ibid.*
6 Since *Three Ninjas Kick Back* is more a family film than an action-adventure film, we will not be discussing it here.
7 Yvonne Tasker, *Spectacular Bodies: Gender, Genre and the Action Cinema* (London: Routledge, 1993).
8 Dan Kindlon and Michael Thompson, *Raising Cain: Protecting the Emotional Life of Boys* (New York: Ballantine, 1999), 30.
9 *Ibid.*, 106.
10 *Ibid.*, 73.
11 Support for this research was provided by the Southern California Injury Prevention Research Center, which is funded by a grant from the Centers for Disease Control and Prevention (#CCR 903622).

II

Spectacle and style

5

Aristotle v. the action film

Thomas Leitch

Though he is no threat to Bakhtin, Baudrillard, or Stuart Hall, Aristotle has found a surprisingly cordial reception among commentators on popular culture. Apart from a collection of essays on feminist responses to his ethical and scientific texts,[1] his analysis of tragedy in the *Poetics* has been invoked as a model for twentieth-century discussions of comedy, the detective story, and the horror film.[2] As far as I know, however, there has been no work from a neo-Aristotelian perspective on the action film – a situation as ironic as it is surprising, since the very name given to the Hollywood genre stretching from *The Mark of Zorro* (1920) to *The Fast and the Furious* (2001) suggests that it would have been Aristotle's favorite.

Yet, the most cursory survey of recent action films shows how profoundly *anti*-Aristotelian they are. It is true, of course, that they follow to a fault Aristotle's well-known prescription for tragedy in Chapter Six of the *Poetics*:

> Tragedy is an imitation, not of men, but of an action and of life, and life consists in action, and its end is a mode of action, not a quality. Now character determines men's qualities, but it is by their actions that they are happy or the reverse. Dramatic action, therefore, is not with a view to the representation of character: character comes in as subsidiary to the actions. Hence the incidents and the plot are the end of tragedy; and the end is the chief thing of all.[3]

Not even Syd Field, whose screenwriting textbooks seek to codify rather than improve Hollywood practice,[4] could have summarized the matter more cogently: since action is more important than character, movies should exclude all characters, and all characterization, beyond whatever is necessary to motivate the incidents of the plot. Not all Hollywood genres assign such wholehearted priority to action, but the action film does so by definition, and action films that betray too sociological or psychological an interest in character, from *The Public Enemy* (1931) to *The Silence of the Lambs* (1991), may lose their claim to action film status.

What makes recent action films so anti-Aristotelian is not any dearth of represented action – for they are extraordinarily generous and increasingly explicit in representing certain trademark actions – but the narrow range of actions they represent and the attitudes they adopt, and encourage their viewers to adopt, toward the represented actions and action in general. In this essay, I would like to consider just how remote is Hollywood's idea of action from Aristotle's, to look in some detail at the ways it came to differ from its model, and to explore the implications of this shift for the philosophy of action generally.

My speculations about these questions stem from two apparently contrary remarks students of mine made recently. One student who had been working on a video project entitled "Destrucumentary" deflected a question at its premiere about the paradoxical relationship between the multiple scenes of destruction (of a series of objects hacked, bashed, burned, or dropped from a rooftop) that were its subject and the construction of a new text to record these acts of destruction by assuring his interlocutor, "I just wanted to show myself destroying a lot of stuff." Against this remark, another student enrolled in a course I was teaching on action films complained when I showed John Woo's *Face/Off* (1997) that the movie was "boring – it's nothing but action."

All action, all the time

Violent destruction is inseparable from the action film's idea of action, and from my students' criteria for what counts *as* an action. After only a few meetings, the students in my action-film course compiled a menu of three quintessential movie actions – gunplay, explosions, and car chases – which they saw no reason to revise or expand for the rest of the term. No film devoid of gunplay, explosions, or car chases could hope to succeed as an action film, even though a film like *Face/Off* ran into the opposite hazard: by excluding everything but such noisy, violent, destructive actions, it ran the risk of monotony even among its target audience (the student who complained about *Face/Off* claimed to have seen it six times already).

This emphasis on action as violent destruction is remote from Aristotle's conception of tragic action, and not merely because the films involved are not tragedies. Apart from distinguishing between simple and complex plots and noting the importance of reversals of fortune, Aristotle says nothing about the *kinds* of actions that are appropriate to tragedy; his definition instead is one of his most frustratingly oracular passages:

> Tragedy is an imitation of an action that is complete, and whole, and of a certain magnitude; for there may be a whole that is wanting in magnitude. A whole is that which has a beginning, a middle, and an end. A beginning is that which does not itself follow anything by causal necessity, but after which something naturally is or comes to be. An end, on the contrary, is that which itself naturally follows some other thing, either by necessity, or as a rule, but has nothing following it. A middle is that which follows something as some other thing follows it. A well constructed plot, therefore, must neither begin or end at haphazard, but conform to these principles.[5]

The emphasis here on beginnings, middles, and ends is meant not only to encourage aesthetic unity but to mark off a tragic action from the endless chain of situations which might be seen as preceding and following it. Aristotle sees a tragic action as distinct from other events, freely chosen, logically consequential, but ultimately limited by a final end. Hence Sophocles (in Aristotle's most famous example) chooses as his subject not the life of Oedipus, blasted by an inescapable prophecy of doom, but his freely-chosen decision, when a plague afflicts the land he has come to rule as king, to discover the regicide who has provoked the plague. The play moves from the immediate circumstances explaining why he made this decision (though not forcing him to make it) to the decision's unavoidably fatal, but still limited, consequences. Behind Aristotelian tragedy is a belief – amounting to an article of faith – that actions like Oedipus's decision can be defined by a chain of logical and ethical causality that prevents them from being swallowed in the vast network of states-of-being surrounding them. To complain that such a tragedy was "nothing but action" would mark not a paradox but a rejection of Aristotelian dramaturgy, which defines action precisely as distinct from what is nothing but a chaos of fathomless mutation.

Although the contemporary action film preserves Aristotle's dramatic unity of action, it is no longer what makes the action an action. If he were considering *Face/Off*, Aristotle would doubtless dismiss most of its action as "spectacle," the "least artistic" of the six parts of tragedy headed by action.[6] Indeed, all of Woo's work in Hong Kong and Hollywood would be subject to the same stricture because its most memorable moments, from the hospital siege in *Hard Boiled* (1992) to the martial-arts duel between Tom Cruise and Dougray Scott that ends *Mission: Impossible II* (2000), are spectacular set-pieces which, as Aristotle presciently notes, depend "more on the art of the stage machinist than on that of the poet."[7]

More generally, every viewer who sits patiently through James Bond's adventures awaiting the next gunfight, car chase, or explosion is attesting to the belief that in any action film, some actions seem more active than others. Linda Williams has pointed out that hardcore pornography's alternation between graphic sex scenes and perfunctory bridges or exposition, which gives the genre its distinctively "episodic structure,"[8] echoes the dialectic between production numbers and narrative continuity in the Hollywood musical, a genre which uses the continuity to motivate the numbers which have presumably brought viewers into the theater. Cynthia Freeland, expanding on Williams's parallel, notes the importance of analogous production numbers in the realist horror film, which "showcases the spectacular nature of monstrous violence," so that "plots in realist horror, like stories in the nightly news, are dominated by the three r's: random, reductive, repetitious."[9] In the same way, contemporary action films, though they may borrow from Athenian tragedy the structuring reversal of fortune from happiness to woe or from initial failure to final success, make money by displaying the spectacular set-pieces by which this reversal is effected.

Just as most of the running time of a typical Hollywood musical is given over to the continuity, most scenes in a typical action film are not action sequences. In order to carry any dramatic weight beyond the spectacle of a Destrucumentary, actions must be set up by expository scenes that give the audience a rooting interest in the central conflict by establishing the principals' ethical disposition. They must be interspersed with scenes that will provide comic or romantic or sentimental relief. Suspense must be ratcheted up, as in *Gunga Din* (1939), by reports of mounting casualties, diminishing supplies, or impending threats of greater catastrophe. Climactic victories must be celebrated with due pomp, as in the final scene of *Star Wars* (1977). But all these scenes, like the continuity parceled out between a musical's song-and-dance numbers, are created and shaped to increase the effectiveness of these privileged sequences, not vice versa.

The distinctiveness of Woo's films is that they come closer than any previous mainstream action films to paring away low-energy exposition altogether, so that *every* scene becomes an action scene. In *Mission: Impossible II*, for example, the obligatory scenes – the hero's learning of his new assignment, his first meeting with the heroine and the moment, cribbed from *Notorious* (1946), when, having insinuated herself into the villain's bed, the heroine betrays him by pinching and passing the hero a telltale object (a key in Hitchcock, a digital memory card in Woo) – are all inflated so far beyond their models by rapid cutting, swish-pans, amplified sound effects, and techno music that they become action sequences themselves. In the even more stylized world of *Face/Off*, anything worth doing is worth doing over and over again, in sublimely ethereal slow motion, with masks and mirrors, before a backdrop of doves and church architecture. The narrative trajectory of this film is provided not so much by John Travolta's exchange of identities with Nicolas Cage or by the confrontation between these two opposing figures – since they do nothing throughout the story but confront variously mediated images of each other – as by the operatic expressiveness, the increasing resourcefulness, and the mounting volume of each successive clash. If Hitchcock could claim that his idea of drama was "life with the dull bits cut out,"[10] Woo might fairly claim to make action films that are wall-to-wall action.

Woo can achieve extraordinary concentration and intensity through a particular image, as in the frozen moment in *Face/Off* when his antagonists square off on opposite sides of a pair of mirrors, each one pointing a gun at his own reflection – thereby showing him the face he has literally stolen from his enemy. But this visual epitome of the film's conflict, though prolonged as usual by the trick (borrowed from grand opera and Sam Peckinpah) of slowing time to inflate moments of privileged emotional energy, passes without resolution, and the two enemies go right on shooting at each other in a wildly extended motorboat chase sequence which ends with a mock cruci-fixion on a sandy beach. Each individual clash, however striking, eventually loses its leading Aristotelian associations – the narrative potency and cognitive content specific to its particular place in a chain of events – through ceaseless repetition, and remains memorable only as spectacle.

12 Infusing violence with stillness: John Woo's *The Killer* (1989)

An action film that consists of nothing but action sequences will inevitably suffer from a lack of dramatic variety that alienates viewers who are not attuned to its visual stylization. But Woo's operatically inflated handling of individual set-pieces suggests a paradoxical discovery. At the heart of the most violent scenes from *A Better Tomorrow* (1986) to *The Killer* (1989) to *Mission: Impossible II* is an extraordinary stillness – as if by excluding every non-active element from his stories in order to present action undiluted by exposition, Woo had succeeded in penetrating to a uniquely ritualized view of action purged of such excrescencies as psychology, plausibility, or ethical disposition as well. But this well-nigh mystical handling of action has the potential to polarize audiences sharply, since the more tightly the films are organized around action sequences, the less conventionally active, even inert, they seem, even to those viewers willing to sit through them six times.

How did the action film evolve from its distant models in Aristotelian tragedy to a wholehearted embrace of spectacle that not only elevates violent destruction over the hallmarks of Aristotelian action – a freely-chosen origin, logical and ethical causality, a definitive ending – but that turns action itself into such a curiously inert ritual? It is tempting to claim that Woo's spectacle-driven films exemplify a distinctively Eastern aesthetic alternative to the dramaturgy Western storytellers have inherited from Aristotle. In fact, however, as David Bordwell notes, Woo's films – "a glossy synthesis of Italian Westerns, swordplay, *film noir*, and romantic melodrama"

– present a hyperstylized aesthetic "new to both Hong Kong and the West."[11] It is no coincidence that Woo, of all Hong Kong action filmmakers, has, along with Jackie Chan, enjoyed the greatest US success, since Woo himself, who has identified Martin Scorsese as his idol, acknowledges that "I'm not very Chinese. My techniques, my themes, my film language are not traditionally Chinese."[12] Moreover, Bordwell's observation that "in Hong Kong, the musical comedy has been box-office poison for years"[13] suggests that the continued enormous popularity in Hong Kong of Woo's spectacular treatment of violence must have less to do with its aesthetic stylization than with its violent content.

No regular moviegoer, however, is likely to see Woo's stylized violence as an isolated failure to live up to Aristotle's ideal of action as a privileged trope for human experience. Woo's staging of action as violently ritualized spectacle does not so much represent a logical alternative to the dramatic action Aristotle valorizes as a climactic transformation toward which the action film has been moving since its beginning. Action can be conceived not only by philosophers of action but by popular entertainers in many different ways. From its inception, the action film's Aristotelian ties have steadily broken down in favor of an aesthetics of spectacle, one which has crucial implications for the philosophy of action. While action films continue to retain such vestigial Aristotelian associations as their generic label, the nature of their represented actions has been so profoundly recast that the films have lost all their investment in action but its name. The roots of the action film remain in Aristotelian dramaturgy; what twentieth-century cinema adds is a change in emphasis that substitutes spectacular elements – not only of action as such, but of many particular associations of action – for the teleological, ethically consequential associations central to Aristotle. What was peripheral in Aristotelian action has become central, what was central has become vestigial.

The Aristotelianism of Howard Hawks

These changes have been decisive even though Aristotelian dramaturgy survived well into the twentieth century. Francis Fergusson, the most Aristotelian of all commentators on modern drama in his acceptance of the theater as essentially a mimetic representation of "human life and action," argued fifty years ago that the leading

Western plays through the time of Chekhov, Pirandello, and Eliot could still be recuperated under a broadly Aristotelian rubric by noting the ways different theaters as well as different playwrights have each in their own way "focused . . . the complementary insights of the whole culture."[14] Hence *Hamlet* recasts action as playacting, *Bérénice* as rational public discourse, *Tristan and Isolde* as the expression of absolute emotional passion, *The Cherry Orchard* as the systematic frustration of the characters' plans to maintain a fragile status quo, all in order to engage their culture's larger concerns about the valence of action in general.

Despite its undoubted fascination with spectacle – a fascination coeval with the rise of cinema – Hollywood did not turn its back on Aristotle either. The films of Howard Hawks, which span the entire gamut of action subgenres from gangster films to Westerns, are deeply Aristotelian in their emphasis on freely-chosen beginnings (Tony Camonte's [Paul Muni] assassination of Big Louie Costello [Harry Vejar] in *Scarface* [1932]; the killing that leads John T. Chance [John Wayne] to arrest Joe Burdette [Claude Akins] in *Rio Bravo* [1959]), apparently chaotic middles (the mind-boggling intrigues of *Bringing Up Baby* [1938] and *The Big Sleep* [1946]), and decisive endings which validate the heroic potential of individual human action to resolve cultural anxieties (Alvin York's [Gary Cooper] triumphant homecoming in *Sergeant York* [1941]; the street fight that ends the Oedipal rivalry in *Red River* [1948]). The exception that proves the rule is *Twentieth Century* (1934), whose circular ending mocks actress Lily Garland's (Carole Lombard) attempt to escape her Svengali, megalomaniac Broadway producer Oscar Jaffe (John Barrymore), at the same time confirming the difference between her incessantly histrionic brand of stage acting and truly decisive action.

Aristotelian as they are in the ways they conceive action, however, Hawks' films portend the future of the action film in many ways, most obviously through the problems they pose for its definition. Most viewers, however they define action movies, consider them a relatively discrete genre. But the genre is difficult to define because what counts as an action for one kind of protagonist (the pursuit of eligible male romantic partners in *Gentlemen Prefer Blondes* [1953]) will barely register for another (the crewmen's determination to keep the *Mary Ann* flying in *Air Force* [1943]). One reason the genre has been relatively neglected by theorists is that it is impossible to separate it from the many other more easily recognized Hollywood genres with which it has been entangled: Westerns, war films, crime films (especially gangster films), pirate films, adventure films, exploration films, science fiction, visions of Empire, quest romances, and films involving stunt flying, race-car driving, and other dangerous occupations. Lacking a distinctive *mise-en-scène* or overriding moral problem of its own, the action film is typically upstaged by these smaller, more self-contained genres. But if *The Thing* (1951) is not an action film because it is a science-fiction film, and *Hatari!* (1962) is not an action film because it is a film about big-game hunting, it is hard to imagine how the Hollywood action genre might be defined at all, and easy to see why it is so often tacitly defined as a collection of films containing the requisite number of action sequences in order to prevent every movie ever made from qualifying as an action movie.

It is hardly surprising, then, that action films are widely, albeit informally, defined in terms of the violent spectacles that are their most obvious common feature, even though these spectacles often mitigate one of the most vital Aristotelian associations of action. Kenneth Burke, following Aristotle, observes that action is irreducibly a moral category which distinguishes a human being from, for example, a billiard ball, which "is neither moral nor immoral, for it cannot act, it can only move, or be moved."[15] Burke argues that materialist philosophers like Hobbes reduce action to motion as a function of the material laws they consider axiomatic, whereas idealistic philosophers like Kant, taking human agency as primary, project a world more amenable to action. Hollywood's staging of human conflicts against a photographed physical reality emphasizes both continuities and distinctions between motion (waves crash against the shore of a tropical island) and action (Tom Hanks, cast away on the island, builds a raft he hopes will carry him beyond the waves). Except perhaps for Ken Burns' historical documentaries and Chris Marker's *La Jetée* (1964), all movies present motion, but Burke would presumably reserve the name of action films for those focusing on the *moral* conflicts arising from human agency.

Even the most spectacular action films retain the association Aristotle, Burke, and Fergusson establish between represented action and the purposive, morally consequential human agency of characters and audiences. Hence even the most action-oriented action movies include scenes showing the hero's motivation, establishing the stakes of the conflict, and encouraging viewers to choose sides;

if they did not, then action films would be structurally and morally indistinguishable from a Destrucumentary, or indeed from their own trailers. But the analyses of Fergusson and Burke fail to describe contemporary action films in two especially revealing ways. First, they are too general, since virtually all classical Hollywood narratives revolve around a conflict shaped by human agency. As Bordwell has observed, "character-centered . . . causality is the armature of the classical story";[16] even when the antagonists are monsters like the Terminator or natural forces like the Perfect Storm, freely-chosen human responses to these forces remain the films' focal point. Fergusson's analysis of the mimetic perception of action, and Burke's distinction between action and motion, would cast every classical Hollywood narrative as an action film.

In addition to being too general, Fergusson and Burke are too specific, for neither of them distinguishes between actions like car chases, gunfights, and explosions central to action films and the less violent actions most devotees would consider unworthy of the name. For better or worse, a very wide range of human activities is specifically excluded from the action sequences of action films. Not only the three pivotal moments Burke identifies as the dialectic of Aristotelian tragedy – *poiema*, *pathema*, and *mathema*, which Fergusson translates as purpose, passion, and perception[17] – but more specific activities like debating, building, changing, developing, and maturing are remote from the interests of action cinema. Since viewers and filmmakers agree that dialogue scenes can never be action scenes, it follows that persuasion and accord cannot produce action on screen; only disagreement or coercion can, and then only if they lead to physical conflict, because action films are more invested in the staging of conflict as spectacle than in its resolution.

Here Hawks' work is pivotal. In Hawks, the scenes contemporary audiences would most likely call action sequences – the rare moments in *Rio Bravo* when gunshots are fired, for example –are normally reserved for crucial points in the plot, especially the ending, whereas the tendency in more recent filmmakers like Woo is to devise plots that make room for such moments as often as possible. The richest of Hawks' personal associations with action – the masculine action hero, a man who does heroic things most audience members could only dream of, a performer whose corporal presence becomes a locus for physical and ethical actions recorded in a simulacrum of real time and space – is again symptomatic of a more general readjustment of the elements and associations of action, looking back to Aristotle even as it looks forward to the contemporary action film.

What makes an action an action?

The recasting of action as violent spectacle does not, of course, begin with Hawks. Even in Aristotle's reading of tragedy, the notion of action as a freely-chosen, purposive, ethically consequential expression of human agency is complicated by other factors. Action involves *doing something*, effecting a change in one's personal circumstances and one's world (as Oedipus's search for Laius's killer topples him from power and kills his wife and mother but saves his city from a crippling plague). The examples of Oedipus and Ajax suggest that Aristotelian action also involves *areté* or *skill*; heroes establish their heroism by doing things they are particularly good at, from detective work to feats of strength, even if the consequences of these skillful actions are disastrous. Action in Aristotle's examples is always shaped by and expressed through *conflict*, the dramatic element action films are more likely to borrow from Athenian tragedy than any other. Walking across a deserted battlefield is not an Aristotelian action, but advancing against an enemy is. At the same time, the theater of Athens staged even the most violent action as reassuring *ritual*, recycling familiar stories from the revenge of Orestes and Electra to the origin of the Athenian patron gods. Finally, the nature of Aristotle's theater depends on the intimacy between *acting* and action, between staged action and the putatively real thing.

Hollywood movies begin translating these affinities into spectacle as far back as the Edison actualité, *Railroad Smashup* (1904), which records the popular pastime of staging a collision between two railroad trains for the amusement of onlookers. The typical action hero who arrives onscreen soon thereafter is active in the sense of being always busy, always thirsting for action. In *The Mark of Zorro*, Douglas Fairbanks endures enforced periods of inaction as the milksop Don Diego with barely concealed impatience. Diego's alter-ego, the dashing avenger Zorro, is an assumed role that harnesses his apparently natural bent for action and useful gift for swordplay more effectively than the identity he was born with, despite its being a masquerade. Although Zorro's heroic actions have the effect of freeing his people from oppression, what establishes Fairbanks as an action hero is that he *looks* and *acts* active from moment to moment;

13 Last action hero: formerly meek accountant Oscar Wallace (Charles Martin Smith) falls in love with the shotgun in *The Untouchables* (1987)

if he plotted to free his people by discovering a legal flaw in the laws that encumber them – just as consequential an action for Aristotle – his film might still be effective, but not as an action film. Hawks follows this pattern by repeatedly casting such action-ready heroes as James Cagney, Humphrey Bogart, and John Wayne. More recent action films recast purposive action as violent physical conflict ever more decisively, as in the scene in *The Untouchables* (1987) in which mild-mannered accountant Oscar Wallace (Charles Martin Smith) suddenly graduates to action-hero status by firing a shotgun.

Douglas Fairbanks' status as an action hero suggests another dimension of action more familiar to Hollywood than to Aristotle: the conflation of the performer with the active figure he plays, as if playing an active figure established one as an active figure. This histrionic notion of action, explored in detail in *Hamlet* and *North by Northwest* (1959), emphasizes the intimacy between action and acting, or between acting and *staging* or *playing*. Like Prince Hamlet, the initially unheroic advertising executive Roger Thornhill (Cary Grant) learns to be a hero by playing a variety of roles and gradually becoming so convincing in them that he masters and internalizes acting as a mode of action. Most of the action scenes in *The Adventures of Robin Hood* (1938), from Robin's (Errol Flynn) first meeting with Little John (Alan Hale) to his entry at the archery contest that will lead to his capture, contain a strong element of play, as if the film were trying to erase the distinction between acting and playing at acting. More generally, Flynn's genially self-mocking persona, like that of Fairbanks, consistently deflates the seriousness of his characters and reveals the nature of his acting as performance rather than impersonation without diminishing their status, or his own, as action heroes. This sort of play with stars' personas, a particular hallmark of the Hawks films starring Cary Grant – *Bringing Up Baby, Only Angels Have Wings* (1939), *His Girl Friday* (1940), *I Was a Male War Bride* (1949), *Monkey Business* (1952) – gives even these comic star performances an action-hero edge.

The trajectory of performance toward spectacle is clearest in the principal Hollywood incarnations of James Bond. Sean Connery, the screen's first Bond, was widely remarked as playing the role with one eye winking, maintaining an amused, ironic aloofness from his character. But his replacement, the good-natured Roger Moore, played the role so broadly and jestingly that reviewers noted he seemed to be winking with both eyes. When MGM/United Artists replaced Moore with the more intense Timothy Dalton, audiences refused to accept such a self-serious Bond, and Dalton was himself replaced after two films with the more lightweight Pierce Brosnan, who has demonstrated his ability to go through all the motions of the action hero licensed to kill in order to save the world without communicating any distracting intensity.

The conflation of performer and hero not only equates acting with action but emphasizes the physical status of action as *a natural extension of bodily movement as a way of controlling the immediately contiguous space*, an affinity which places martial-arts masters like Bruce Lee and Jackie Chan in a tradition going back to Fairbanks, Cagney, and Wayne, and indeed to such masters of theatrical space as Phèdre and Clytemnestra, both of whom advance their plots by withdrawing their bodies from public view. It may seem self-evident to think of the body as the natural vehicle for the expression of active impulses, especially in the closed environment of the theatrical stage, but in fact it has become highly tendentious in ways that mark a crucial turn in the action film. The clearest of these ways is the gendering of the active body as male and the staging of action as *a test of masculinity*, as in virtually all of Hawks' films, whether their heroes are Cagney (*Ceiling Zero* [1935]) or Danny Kaye (*A Song Is Born* [1948]). Sylvester Stallone's more recent action films define machismo in terms of an equally masculine masochism, and the two are neatly balanced in *Die Hard* (1988), in which Bruce Willis – standing alone and barefoot against ten murderous thieves armed to the teeth and capable of inflicting real damage on his battered body – is challenged to confirm his status as husband, father and manly man by killing them all, one by one, before his energy level, like that of a computer-game hero, reaches zero.

The action film's spectacular imperative tends to depart from Aristotelian dramaturgy by balancing the limited space the human body can command with a journey into the vast unknown spaces that bespeak *adventure*. The exotic settings possible in contemporary big-budget filmmaking provide a spatial answer to the call for novelty dating back to the gruesome accounts of offstage deaths Euripides loved. At the same time, these settings transform the cathartic reversal characteristic of Aristotelian tragedy into melioristic *melodrama*, celebrating the coming of civilization to what Joseph Conrad, in *Heart of Darkness*, ironically called "the dark places of the earth."[18] At the same time, such spaces challenge both the body's ability to control its immediate surroundings and an imperialistic culture's ability to work its will on a hostile environment.

Although some theorists draw a line between action fantasies and adventure films,[19] the *Indiana Jones* films illustrate the close affinities between action and adventure by succeeding in both genres at once. In outline the films are latter-day quest romances along the lines of medieval searches for the Holy Grail, although that particular talisman does not turn up until Steven Spielberg's third installment. But the screenplays are so jammed with swashbuckling incident that they become action films as well, films whose archeologist-hero (Harrison Ford) constantly succeeds in eluding the infernal serpents (Indy's well-established anathema) and breaking out of the enclosed spaces – caves, excavation sites, secret passages whose ceilings suddenly begin to close in on him – in which his enemies have confined him. Indy's obvious imperialism is abated by substituting even more imperialistic Nazis for the native antagonists he would otherwise face. Though his signature weapon, a bullwhip, marks a classic extension of corporal power into the immediately surrounding space, he is always ready to forego it for the more effective revolver he uses to execute the unwisely showoff native swordsman who threatens him in a Cairo marketplace. By staging his adventures as a nonstop series of conflicts with the Nazis and their third-world lackeys, the films translate Indy's imperialistic imperative to sack foreign lands for treasures that will be stored in British or American museums into the terms of a more comfortable political dualism.

The one trace of imperialism left intact in Indy is his masterful attitude toward women – another legacy from Hawks, whose films groom female stars like Jean Arthur and Lauren Bacall to be exactly as powerful as their men can handle. (If *Gentlemen Prefer Blondes* suggests that the perquisites of the male Hawks hero are equally available to adventurous females, Hawks' next film, *Land of the Pharaohs* [1955], shows just how catastrophically destructive a powerful woman can be.) *Raiders of the Lost Ark* (1981) is especially critical of Indy's seduction and abandonment of Marion Ravenwood (Karen Allen), daughter of his late partner, whom he treats as just one more treasure to be excavated and appreciated before moving on. This last bastion of Indy's imperialism – a male sexuality directed against a sympathetic woman – is an imbalance that will be duly redressed by the predatory Elsa Schneider's (Alison Doody) appearance in *Indiana Jones and the Last Crusade* (1989).

Virtually all contemporary action heroes are male, and most female exceptions succeed precisely to the extent that they manage to become more masculine. The pumped-up heroines played by Linda Hamilton in *Terminator 2* (1991) and Demi Moore in *G.I. Jane* (1997), both surrounded by males whose lacerating skepticism casts a stigma on their sense of themselves, retaliate by self-consciously hardening their bodies along militaristic male models. The heroines played by Geena Davis in *Cutthroat Island* (1995) and *The Long Kiss Goodnight* (1996) are again women in a man's world, forced to succeed on men's terms or not at all. In *The Long Kiss Goodnight*, Davis, on the run from mysterious killers, discovers the pieces of a high-powered rifle in a secret compartment in her suitcase, and proceeds to put it together in a robotic daze. Her unwitting, unwilling recovery of her long-buried skills as a CIA assassin, complete with male-gendered habits of swearing and shooting that unnerve her hypermasculine companion (Samuel L. Jackson), suggests that her past, a secret even to her, is more authentic than her present hypnotically-supported cover as a suburban schoolteacher. Since, as in John Ford's Westerns, "woman" is an identity that must be mastered through acculturation, "man" through action, you can often scratch a woman and find a man underneath.

The most thoroughgoing challenge so far to the masculinity of the action hero, *Aliens* (1986), complicates this pattern with respect to the heroine's personal identity without disturbing the male gendering of action. The film is distinctive because the villains as well as the hero are female; because the threat underlying its outbreaks of violence is specifically female (the uncontrolled procreation of the

aliens Sigourney Weaver's Ripley is battling); and because the heroine triumphs by exhibiting specifically female virtues (caution about
the technology the rest of the gung-ho crew relies on; skepticism
about the male-dominated capitalism of her greedy parent company;
nurturing the frightened girl she rescues; evoking the sensitive side
of the one surviving crew member and the demasculinized cyborg).
Even as it explores the contradictions of motherhood in the super-
mom era, however, the film certifies both its villains' power and its
hero's bravery by staging its leading actions as an escalating curve of
violence which allows Ripley to demonstrate that she is fully the
equal of the destructive "bitch" – another mother fighting to protect
her young – against whom she is paired. Although both antagonists
maintain their female integrity, their clashes are staged as stereotypical explosions of testosterone that develop what Yvonne Tasker
calls the heroine's "musculinity."[20]

A far more serious challenge than female hormones to the
centrality of the male body as a locus of action is the rise of post-
Aristotelian technology. In *The Terminator* (1984), Arnold Schwarzenegger brings an awe-inspiring physical presence to the title role
that effectively suggests the Terminator's apparently unlimited
power. Yet what makes the Terminator powerful is not his matchless
physique but his cyborg construction, which allows him to take bullets and emerge from fires and explosions with no more lasting
damage than Wile E. Coyote. *Terminator 2* drives this point home
by matching Schwarzenegger against the more cybernetically
advanced, hence more powerful and implacable, T-1000 (played by
Robert Patrick). Since the T-1000, unlike Schwarzenegger's T-101,
can shape-shift to any role he likes, his relative slightness through
most of the film emphasizes the arbitrary, even if visually striking,
use of bodily strength and an imposing physique as credentials for
an action hero whose real power depends on technology.

The transition from physicality to technology as the locus of action,
figured most often in Hollywood by the use of guns as technological
extensions of the body, is well underway as early as the Hawks flying
films *The Dawn Patrol* (1930) and *Ceiling Zero*, in which aviators
prove their manhood by the way they handle their planes; in *The
Adventures of Robin Hood*, in which Prince John's swordsmen are no
match for Robin Hood's expert archers; and in *The Crimson Pirate*
(1952), in which Burt Lancaster's joyously acrobatic physical prowess
as the eighteenth-century Captain Vallo establishes his action-hero

credentials without winning him success. Vallo defeats his enemies by hooking up with Professor Prudence (James Hayter), who for the climactic battle develops three variously anachronistic technologies: an enormous hot-air balloon, a submarine, and some amazing new-fangled explosive compounded from "nitrogen and glycerine." A decade later, in *From Russia with Love* (1963), Connery's James Bond – who survived his first film appearance in *Dr. No* (1962) largely by his native wiles – is given the first of many obligatory meetings with the peevish engineer later films will identify as "Q" (Desmond Llewelyn) and outfitted with a briefcase that includes a knife, fifty sovereigns, and a charge of gas that will play a crucial role in his turning the tables on the assassin who is about to kill him. Bond's status as the physically magnetic superspy who is also the bearer of the latest technological perks will help to maintain his heroic status even when Connery is replaced in the role by the less physically imposing Roger Moore. By the time of *Rocky* (1976) and *First Blood* (1982), which inaugurate Stallone's trademark Rocky and Rambo franchises, the nominal opposition between active body and miracles of technology will produce a new reversal: the spectacle of the *technologized body*, engineered by the increasingly self-alienated person who inhabits it only to absorb pain and destroy enemies.

However, the opposition between state-of-the-art technology and the more old-fashioned technology of the body continues to animate contemporary action films. In the high-tech age of James Cameron, Jackie Chan's resourceful dependence on his body and the physical props within immediate reach seems positively nostalgic, even though Chan the performer has engineered his own body more purposefully than John Rambo ever did. In the same way, Luke Skywalker's (Mark Hamill) determination in *Star Wars* to listen to the voice of Obi-Wan Kenobi (Alec Guinness) and "trust the force" by using intuition instead of his spaceship's computerized guidance system during the climactic bomb run against the Death Star comes across as a return to a simpler, more direct mode of action, even though Luke expends exactly the same amount of physical action (he pushes a button), and his knockout punch, however reminiscent of World War II's glory days, is still a bomb. When Keanu Reeves' Neo finally succeeds in *The Matrix* (1999) in mastering such paranormal skills as leaping from skyscrapers or stopping bullets in their tracks, his victory of mind over body is presented as a defeat of alien technology rather than what it really is – a Rambo-esque technologizing of oneself.

The rise of technologies of action has had a decisive impact not only on the action hero's construction but on his place within the world of the film. Action films before James Bond are performer-centered. They present the adventures of an action hero like Fairbanks, Cagney, Flynn, Lancaster, or Wayne whose capacity for action is intimately bound up with both a masculine physical presence and an ethical disposition. The Bond films starring Connery begin with this premise but gradually replace it with a conception of action as technologically-centered spectacle, as the performer's body is first supplemented, then displaced, by an exteriorized, detached view of action as a function of spectacularly violent narrative. The strong hero remains in his (occasionally her) ethical motivation, but now he is a shell, a receptive vessel for the nonstop wisecracks put into the mouth of Brosnan's Bond, or for the impossible martial-arts prowess conferred on Cruise's Ethan Hunt in *Mission: Impossible II* through the power of digital effects, which turn personal agency into fully exteriorized action. Writing of the cattle crossing sequence in *Red River*, Gerald Mast notes that since there was no way to shoot the sequence without staging a crossing to be shot, "the act of shooting this event becomes as strenuous, as demanding, indeed the same as the event itself."[21] But Cruise can succeed as an action hero without performing the specific actions Woo depicts – even without being especially fit.

An even more anti-Aristotelian twist to this peculiarly late twentieth-century view of action is its staging as *reaction*, an unwilling but inevitable response to threats demanding violent countermeasures. This pattern, rare among Hawks' adventurous heroes, emerges most clearly in Humphrey Bogart's Harry Morgan. The fishing-boat captain of *To Have and Have Not* (1945) is only gradually and reluctantly drawn into local and international intrigue before he finally turns on the bullying Captain Renard (Dan Seymour) in the film's understated climax. Harry's turning worm is a thinly-disguised variant of Bogart's Richard Blaine in *Casablanca* (1942), drawn into World War II despite his earlier assertion that "I stick my neck out for nobody." American audiences are always ready to ignore their status as citizens of the most powerful nation on earth and identify with the underdog, and Hollywood has obliged with heroes from Harry Morgan to mousy David Sumner (Dustin Hoffman) in *Straw Dogs* (1972), goaded into a long-overdue but horrifyingly grisly response to the British roughnecks who have raped his wife and now plan to kill them. The initially peace-seeking but heroically reactive heroes of *Die Hard* and *Straw Dogs* are both motivated by revenge, a personal animus which naturally strengthens their heroic status and the audience's commitment to them.

Between the extremes of *Die Hard*, which gives its hero only a few quiet moments before he is forced to take arms against the murderous thugs threatening his estranged wife, and *Straw Dogs*, which is almost over before Hoffman's embattled mathematician finally stands up to the bullying locals, comes Spielberg's *Jaws* (1975), whose neat division into two equal parts cuts to the heart of the action film's philosophical reconfiguration of action. In the first half, Roy Scheider's police-chief hero is purely reactive, doing his best to mediate between the monstrous shark wreaking havoc on his Cape Cod town and the pusillanimous town leaders who refuse to give him the powers to combat the threat. In the second half, Chief Brody, encouraged by oceanographer Matt Hooper (Richard Dreyfuss), goes on the offensive, steaming out with Hooper and the old seadog Quint (Robert Shaw) to find and kill the shark. Now it is the shark who is on the defensive; only in the film's final sequence, when the shark swamps their boat miles from land, do the men share the position in which they have put the shark of fighting for their very lives.

For Aristotle and Burke, action and reaction are essentially opposed: it makes all the difference in the world whether the shark is attacking the citizens or the citizens are attacking the shark. In the world of the action film, however, action and reaction might seem interchangeable, for they are equally capable of producing the spectacularly violent set-pieces the audience has come to see. But this apparent equivalence is qualified by one last vestige of Aristotelian dramaturgy: the hero's reaction leads to action, not the other way around. Just as the spectacular set-pieces in *The Rock* (1996) follow a rising curve of violence, scale and volume, their narrative trajectory runs from the heroes' baffled passivity to their triumphant activity. In one sense, Woo's films consist of nonstop action; in another, their defining action is only the final term in a series of spectacles that have portended this action from the beginning. Savvy viewers wait in pleasurable frustration for the action hero – as often as not someone who, like the messianic newscaster Howard Beale (Peter Finch) in *Network* (1976), is madder than hell and who's not going to take it anymore – to earn his title through a display of violent reprisal even more spectacular than anything he has endured.

Acting, reacting, watching

This philosophical inconsistency – all violent spectacle is equally deserving of the name of action, but reacting to such spectacles by striking back with your own spectacular violence is more active than reacting by cowering or suffering, indeed more active than the provocations behind them – is not a flaw in the action film but its defining problem. Viewers of action films go to the movies expressly to see two things: a melodramatic victory of good over evil, and the maximum number of maximally destructive set-pieces along the way. Since destructiveness is not obviously an admirable quality, action heroes from Robin Hood to Rambo must be goaded to action by provocative acts of violence whose patent injustice licenses their status as heroic avengers and earns them the title "action heroes" instead of the more ignominious alternative "reaction heroes." Their films work to confer on them all the power for violence originally figured as destructive while uniting it with a sense of moral consequence. Instead of an anatomy of action along the lines of *Hamlet* or *Oedipus the King*, these films amount to an *apology* for action, an indulgence of viewers' fantasies of untrammeled destructive power by cloaking them in moral justification.

Action heroes from James Bond to Ethan Hunt continue to pose as moral agents. What is most distinctive, and most disturbing, about the contemporary action film is not its problematic justifications of their ultimate power but its staging of that power as violent spectacle. Just as the target audiences for musicals or hard-core pornography look forward to the song-and-dance numbers or the sex scenes their genres distinctively feature, action viewers are less interested in each new story as the Aristotelian *imitation of an action* than in a *collection of actions* of the sort Aristotle called spectacles. The recasting of action films toward violent spectacle is only the most obvious symptom of contemporary moviegoers' growing taste for spectacle over Aristotelian action in all genres of popular entertainment. The appetite for action films bespeaks at once a longing for the agency to effect decisive actions and a profound suspicion of action. Unlike the Athenian theater that staged dramatic action as an invitation to its audience to contemplate the problematic nature of action itself, Hollywood has turned action into a spectacle at once frightening and entertaining. Their target audience is too intimidated by the power they crave to dream of coming any closer to power than fantasies of Robin Hood, James Bond, or the Terminator.

Yet this consumption, in one final paradox, may take a uniquely active form. Fergusson, seeking a common denominator among all the different theaters that drew on Aristotelian dramaturgy, found it in "the histrionic sensibility" which expressed itself in "the mimetic perception of action": learning and perceiving and understanding actions by imitating rather than analyzing them.[22] This capacity, represented in different ways by the films in which groups of Hawks heroes (like the befuddled linguists in *Ball of Fire* [1941] or the *Mary Ann*'s crew in *Air Force*) become a cohesive unit, or the films in which Jackie Chan emerges from his initial status as a gifted but limited apprentice to assume the mantle of martial-arts hero, has become narrowed in more recent action films into what Aaron Anderson has called "metakinesis" or "muscular sympathy" – audiences' kinesthetic responses of physical strain and release to car chases and hand-to-hand battles.[23] What makes fictional imitations of action dramatic, Anderson contends, is not only that they constitute ethically consequential expressions of human agency that audiences hungry for wisdom can use as models for their own moral actions, but that they provoke a physiological simulacrum of urgent activity in their viewers, at least until they leave the theater. The effect of contemporary action films, as of Aristotelian tragedy, is to make audiences more active. But now the notion of what it means to be active has changed from the ability to imagine and execute a single, freely-chosen, morally consequential, definitive course of behavior to the kinesthetic unleashing of fantasies of unchecked violence cloaked in the moral justification of reaction.

This power of Hollywood's ferocious apology for action reaches far beyond the movies. American audiences watching the horrifying images of the terrorist attacks against the Pentagon and the World Trade Center as if they were a movie, unable to accept the intolerable proposition that these attacks constituted a complete Aristotelian action, cast them instead as the opening act in a revenge drama in which the nation's resolve would be tested by whether it "did something" (i.e., counterattacked with condign force) or "did nothing" (temporized, negotiated, investigated the roots of terrorism, asked why anyone would want to attack the US, etc.). Even in Hawks' day, the script would have demanded that America strike back, the models of action Hollywood has favored since the rise of James

Bond making the violent reprisals Aristotelian dramaturgy would once have deemed reaction into the very essence of action. Yet US citizens seemed to anticipate a completely different relation to this violent national reprisal than the active participation which has already spawned historic numbers of blood donors and charitable gifts of cash; when America responded this time, they expected to be in the audience, watching televised images of more therapeutic violence, rather than among the participants. In a culture that defines action in terms of escalating scenes of spectacular violence rather than in terms of rationally chosen, morally consequential behavior, and that stipulates an audience whose sole contribution to the onscreen violence is a kinesthetic desire to see images of a decisive counterstrike, it is profoundly disturbing to imagine how this story will turn out.

Notes

1   *Feminist Interpretations of Aristotle*, ed. Cynthia Freeland (University Park: Penn State University Press, 1998).
2   See, for example, Duane Berquist, "A Definition of Comedy," *Philosophia Perennis* 1.1 (1994): 3–47; Dorothy Sayers, "Aristotle on Detective Fiction," *Unpopular Opinions: Twenty-One Essays* (New York: Harcourt, Brace, 1947), 222–36; Noël Carroll, *The Philosophy of Horror; or Paradoxes of the Heart* (New York: Routledge, 1990). The standard neo-Aristotelian discussion of comedy remains Elder Olson, *A Theory of Comedy* (Bloomington: Indiana University Press, 1968).
3   *Aristotle's Theory of Poetry and Fine Art*, trans. S. H. Butcher (New York: Dover, 1951), 27.
4   See, for example, Syd Field, *Screenplay: The Foundations of Screenwriting* (New York: Dell, 1994): "When you think subject, think action and character" (23).
5   Aristotle, *Theory of Poetry*, ch. 7, 31.
6   *Ibid.*, ch. 6, 29.
7   *Ibid.*, 31.
8   Linda Williams, *Hard Core: Power, Pleasure, and the "Frenzy of the Visible"* (Berkeley: University of California Press, 1989), 134.
9   Cynthia Freeland, "Realist Horror," *Philosophy and Film*, ed. Cynthia Freeland and Thomas Wartenberg (New York: Routledge, 1995), 132; 134.
10 François Truffaut, *Hitchcock*, rev. edn (New York: Simon & Schuster, 1984), 103.

11 David Bordell, *Planet Hong Kong: Popular Cinema and the Art of Entertainment* (Cambridge: Harvard University Press, 2000), 100.

12 Bérénice Reynaud, "Woo in Interview," *Sight and Sound* 3.5 (1993): 25.

13 Bordwell, *Planet Hong Kong*, 150.

14 Francis Fergusson, *The Idea of a Theater: A Study of Ten Plays; The Art of Drama in Changing Perspective* (Princeton: Princeton University Press, 1949), 10; 9.

15 Kenneth Burke, *A Grammar of Motives* (Englewood Cliffs: Prentice-Hall, 1945), 136.

16 David Bordwell, Janet Staiger and Kristin Thompson, *The Classical Hollywood Cinema: Film Style and Mode of Production to 1960* (New York: Columbia University Press, 1985), 13.

17 Burke, *A Grammar*, 39–41; Fergusson, *The Idea*, 18.

18 Joseph Conrad, *Works, Vol. 5* (London: Heinemann, 1921), 57.

19 See, for example, Brian Taves, *The Romance of Adventure: The Genre of Historical Adventure Movies* (Jackson: University Press of Mississippi, 1993): "The basic traits of action are not specific enough for a generic approach that will sort out the films that appropriately belong to adventure" (5).

20 Yvonne Tasker, *Spectacular Bodies: Gender, Genre and the Action Cinema* (London: Routledge, 1993), 149.

21 Gerald Mast, *Howard Hawks, Storyteller* (New York: Oxford University Press, 1982), 319.

22 Fergusson, *The Idea*, 236.

23 Aaron Anderson, "Action in Motion: Kinesthesia in Martial Arts Films," *Jump Cut* 42 (1998): 4, 6.

6

"Killingly funny": mixing modalities in New Hollywood's comedy-with-violence

Geoff King

What happens when explicit, graphic, or potentially disturbing representations of physical violence are mixed with comedy? Violence has always been a feature of screen comedy, from the silent slapstick tradition onwards. In the case of broad comic forms such as slapstick or farce, an overwhelmingly comic modality usually insulates against any sense of the violence having "real" implications within the diegetic universe. One significant feature of some New Hollywood comedy-with-violence, however, is that the balance between comic distance/ insulation and violence-with-consequences is more uncertain and uncomfortable. Comedy often plays an important role in helping to "legitimate" – or enable filmmakers to "get away with" and/or make pleasurable – representations of violence that might otherwise be more contentious. This causes problems of its own, however, as it is usually deemed "inappropriate," and is sometimes disturbing, for comedy to be mixed up with graphic violence. Satire – comedy with a critical-social edge – is sometimes used as a legitimating framework, making a claim to "seriousness" that seeks to absolve the text from accusations that its violence is merely "gratuitous." But how far this really explains the location of comedy-with-violence in some of New Hollywood's darker productions remains open to question.

Mixing comedy and "real-seeming" or graphic violence can be seen as a distinctively New Hollywood phenomenon, especially in the broader definition of "New Hollywood" that includes the products of the Hollywood Renaissance period, from the mid-to-late 1960s to the mid-to-late 1970s.[1] Space for more overt and sometimes challenging blending of tones was created by the gradual demise of the old Production Code and its replacement by the ratings system in 1968. *Bonnie and Clyde* (1967) is a landmark film in this, as in other, aspects of New Hollywood violence, much of its impact deriving from sudden shifts between comedy and violence. Comedy is often used as a way of reducing the impact of violence. In some cases, however, comedy and violence coexist more uncomfortably, recent examples including *American Psycho* (2000) and *Series 7: The Contenders* (2001).

My interest here is in seeking to understand one of the contexts in which New Hollywood violence is often presented, rather than to engage in "moralistic" debates about its merits or alleged "effects," either in this context or more generally. The combination of comedy and violence is examined in this essay primarily at the formal level, through close analysis of moments of mixed modality in a number of recent examples. More strategically, comedy-with-violence is understood as an approach adopted within New Hollywood to offer qualities expected to attract particular audience groups. An important starting point is some suggestion of what explicit (or explicit-seeming) physical violence offers to Hollywood and its viewers. The appeal of violence can be understood in the dimensions of both narrative and spectacle, for example. Violence can serve as a convenient narrative device. Its existence or threat provides the motivation for many a Hollywood plot. Violent events often provide the disruption of equilibrium so basic to the establishment of the classical-style narrative trajectory, a shift out of "routine" or "ordinary" life into the heightened register of the world we usually experience vicariously on screen. Violent events, confrontations, or climaxes are handy ways of rendering conflict into a form that is clearly manifest, visible, and audible. Some would argue that violence is a "lazy" narrative device for this reason, an easy alternative to the exploration of more complexly shaded areas of experience.

If violence is conflict made manifest, explicit and (melo)dramatic, its manifest *forms* also have appeals of their own, in the realm of audiovisual spectacle. Violence is convenient as a source of the kinds of kinaesthetic thrills that have always been offered by cinema, as Leo Charney argues, drawing on Tom Gunning's description of early film as a "cinema of attractions" designed to offer an experience based on audiovisual sensation more than the logic of narrative.[2] The orchestration of striking sequences of violence is also a useful means by which young or emerging directors can showcase their formal skills, as Devin McKinney suggests,[3] lending itself to a variety of stylistic flourishes and audiovisual pyrotechnics.

Violence in New Hollywood cinema offers compressed bursts of intense action and spectacle that can be understood in this broader context and in terms of specific developments in more recent decades. Hollywood has always offered a blend of appeals, rooted partly in narrative and partly in the cinema of attractions. This takes on particular forms in particular periods. The New Hollywood era is one in which spectacular attraction has often been foregrounded, especially in large-scale blockbuster franchise production. In many cases, explicit violence is avoided or toned-down in an attempt to attract the broadly-based or "family" audience on which the greatest profits can, potentially, be built. A contrary logic, however, has produced a dynamic that favors the depiction of increasingly graphic or hyperbolically-staged violence in films targeted primarily more specifically at an audience of young adult males. This is the outcome, in part at least, of the advent of the ratings system. Ratings permitted Hollywood to sell more explicit violent and sexual material as one of its key points of differentiation – along with the "big-screen experience" more generally – from television. The success of early examples, including *Bonnie and Clyde* and *Dirty Harry* (1971), encouraged the pursuit of this strategy, in a strain of production that continues today. Once this was established, for specific reasons locatable in a particular context, a logic of upping-the-ante was more or less inevitable.

To maintain the same level of intensity, over time, a continual increasing of the degree of spectacular effect is often required. This is the same in the arena of screen violence as it is in the special-effects-heavy world of the blockbuster franchise. As Charney puts it, the effect "wanes by definition,"[4] creating a pressure towards the orchestration of an increased intensity of screen violence in films targeted at audiences attracted by this particular form of cinematic spectacle. In some cases, the violence is broad and comic-book in nature: escalation might involve more protracted and destructive car chases, larger numbers of noisier automatic weapons, or more and increasingly ferocious enemies to combat. In others, it is potentially more disturbing and explicit in terms such as the context in which it occurs or its impact on the human body (depicted, implied or shown primarily in terms of its aftermath). Increased intensity is often as much a function of cinematic technique as it is of literal "explicitness" in the depiction of violent acts. Rapid montage editing is an especially favored technique, often combined with other devices, to increase the sense of violent "impact" offered to the viewer.[5] The above argument is not quite the same as the conventional formulation in which audiences are said to have become increasingly "desensitized" to the impact of violence. The latter implies some kind of vague, general, negative, unspecified, and unsubstantiated "cultural effect," rather than an argument grounded in the specific and more limited context of a particular form of spectacular production.

Screen violence is never presented in anything like a "pure" and "immediate" form. It is always "contained," one way or another: given context and, especially in the light of pressure from censorship bodies, some kind of implicit or explicit legitimation. This is often the work of narrative: to place and situate violence, which usually entails a reduction of its potential impact. A balance is usually found between the intense orchestration of violence and legitimating frameworks that make it palatable for both audiences and regulatory authorities. The intensity of violence is located to a large extent in the degree to which it is presented as immediate and impactful on the viewer. *Too much* immediacy is likely to be too disturbing for enjoyment, however. To render the spectacle of violence as a source of pleasure – for some audiences, at least – distancing frameworks are necessary. These can take a number of forms, including familiar genre or subgenre conventions such as those of horror or of the serial-killer format, in which "disturbing" violence is part of the expected and anticipated repertoire. Comedy is another device that can be used to this effect, along with other and sometimes allied strategies such as the exaggeration and/or heavily-stylized aestheticization of violence. If the intensity of screen violence is intensified in some formats, the logical corollary might be a heightening of the use of such devices to ameliorate its impact.

Mixing modalities

The production of comedy and the production of graphic or graphic-seeming violence that has painful consequences in the fictional world of the film involve the operation of potentially very different modalities. I am using the term "modality" here in the sense in which it is used by Robert Hodge and David Tripp in their study of the relationship between children and television. A modality, for Hodge and Tripp, is a way of "situating messages in relation to an ostensible reality."[6] Some texts are coded in a manner that suggests that the events they depict are to be taken as "real," for example, news and documentary footage. Others use a range of devices to mark out their status as fantasy. In between, many shadings and relative degrees of apparent "reality" – or approximate relation with likely events of the external world – can be indicated within fictional works.

Broad forms of comedy, such as slapstick and farce, establish a modality in which we are not meant to take events too seriously, in relation to either the "real" world or to the fictional world constructed onscreen. The methodical, slow-burning violence found in Laurel and Hardy's films, for example, does not have any real consequences in their own world. A sharp poke in the eye, or the setting of the seat-of-the-pants on fire, creates a momentary yelp, but no sense of lasting damage to the fictional character. Comedy of this kind offers, as many commentators have suggested, a form of insulation, a safety-net, an underpinning guarantee that the violence is only a form a play, not in any way real.[7] The establishment of a comic modality can permit the viewer to remain detached, to enjoy the spectacle of violent antics or violent destruction without any feeling of implication, of having to "care" very much about the consequences, even if only within the world of the fiction.

This is, clearly, a feature of a great deal of New Hollywood violence as well. If we ask how filmmakers, producers, or distributors are able to "get away with" the inclusion of some scenes of graphic violence on screen – in terms of regulatory/censorship regimes or the likely acceptability of such sequences to a sufficient number of viewers – the answer might often be: through the use of the distancing effect created by the inclusion of a comic dimension. The presence of comedy can have an effect similar to, and reinforcing, the aestheticization of screen violence achieved through the use of techniques such as rapid montage editing, slow motion, and other special effects that have become ubiquitous in New Hollywood. Such effects offer one way of heightening intensity, of increasing the kinaesthetic impact of violence on the viewer. But, at the same time, they act as markers of modality, underlining, as Stephen Prince suggests, the extent to which the violence is not "real" but "staged for the cameras and filtered through the various effects and techniques employed by the filmmakers."[8] An implicitly comic and distanced effect is created in some cases through the sheer exuberance and excessive nature of stylized sequences of physical violence.[9] That representations of violence of a heavily-stylized variety are more likely to be defined as "safe" and therefore "entertaining," rather than disturbing, is confirmed by audience research interviews conducted by Annette Hill with viewers of some of the films examined in this chapter.[10]

A close combination of comedy and aestheticization is characteristic of many of the most celebrated/notorious examples of New Hollywood violence in recent years, including films such as *Pulp Fiction* (1994), *Natural Born Killers* (1994), and *American Psycho*. Moments of violence in these films are often coded as "witty" and stylized and, therefore, more detached from potentially "real" implications than might otherwise be the case. Notable examples include the opening sequence of mayhem in *Natural Born Killers*, in which Mickey (Woody Harrelson) and Mallory Knox (Juliette Lewis) dispatch the occupants of a roadside bar amid a mixture of over-the-top and sometimes comically stylized effects (canted angles, shifts between color and black and white footage, cartoon-like effects such as a knife- and bullet's-eye-view of their trajectory towards victims, to mention just a few) and comic one-liners. The overall effect is one of great intensity and cinematic impact but also an encouragement of awareness that this is an operatically confected, *staged*, and exaggerated attraction, a veritable production-number of violence.[11] The comic dimension of comedy-with-violence is sometimes rooted in incongruity, a major source of comedy more generally.[12] In some cases motivation for murder is absurd, wildly incommensurate with the act and thus clearly – and safely/enjoyably – unreal. The axe-murder of a character in *American Psycho*, for example, is sparked by envy of the quality of his business card and his ability to secure reservations at an exclusive restaurant. In *Serial Mom* (1994), the eponymous perfect-housewife/crazed-killer Beverly Sutphin (Kathleen Turner) is tipped over the edge by progressively more absurd "provocations," including the failure of one victim to rewind a rental videotape and, for another, the heinous sin of "wearing white shoes after Labor Day." (The term "killingly funny," used in the title of this chapter, comes from a quotation used prominently on the film's video cover.)

The modality of these films is not always so clear-cut, however. Stylized though it may be, the violence is still designed to provide a frisson of shock for the viewer. The axe attack by Patrick Bateman (Christian Bale) is frenzied and sustained. The first blow produces a spray of blood onto his face; more flows from the body as he pulls out the blade. Another six blows follow, during which the camera holds on a chest-to-head shot of Bateman. The two attacks by Sutphin cited above are shot in a similar style, powerful in their impression despite an oblique approach that avoids direct focus on the actual bodily impact (in one case, death by numerous blows to the head with a leg of lamb – reinforcing the sense of blackly comic incongruity – which produce a splat of blood onto a television set; in the other, forceful blows to the head with a telephone handset). The violence here retains an ability to disturb greater than that found in the routine "comic book" style of violence found in the more mainstream Hollywood action film (the latter also tends to be accompanied by a dose of comedy, the standard comic quip that strongly disavows any serious implications or consequences amid the trails of destruction left by action-spectacle set pieces such as extended car chases or shoot-outs with enemies).

The balance of operative modalities is rather different in cases where comedy is used with violence that maintains its ability to disturb because of either its explicitness, its implied force, its mode of presentation, or its narratively-situated context. In some cases, a real uncertainty of modality can be generated, which might go a long way to explaining the controversy that often surrounds such films: a discomfort, and debate, about precisely how the violence of such films is to be situated. An uncertain modality can increase the impact of potentially disturbing material such as sudden or graphic outbursts of violence, by leaving viewers in the awkward position of not being able clearly to determine how seriously or otherwise it is meant to be taken. As Hodge and Tripp suggest, modality is not a fixed property. It can shift, from moment to moment, within individual texts, as well as between one text and another (the operative modality also depends to a significant extent on the perspective of the viewer and is liable to be shaped or influenced by intermediary forms such as publicity, reviews, or other forms of media coverage).

Affective distance and comic or stylistic (or comically stylistic) insulation is not always maintained in the examples given above. The axe-murder in *American Psycho* starts out with the emphasis on its darkly comic qualities, Bateman's preparations for the attack being accompanied, incongruously, by an earnest disquisition on the merits of the band Huey Lewis and the News. The balance seems to shift towards a more "serious" modality, however, as the attack is sustained and in its immediate aftermath. The viewer is obliged to stay in the scene longer than might be comfortable or than might be expected if the emphasis remained on the sharply witty stylization with which the act began, as Bateman re-gathers himself, sits blankly and lights a cigar, a profile shot briefly obscuring the blood-spattered side of his face and inviting consideration of his Janus-faced persona.

Dark comedy verging on farce is the operative modality throughout *Serial Mom*, in which sympathy is rarely solicited for any of the victims. *American Psycho* is different in its overall balance. Some of Bateman's killings occur very elliptically, in a witty and distanced manner, off-screen, in the gap between one shot or scene and another (he picks up a blonde model one night; cut to what we assume to be the following day, Bateman at his desk fondling a blonde lock of hair; that night, a blonde head sits in his fridge). A rather different investment on the part of the viewer is encouraged in the extended sequence in which he manages to pull back from killing his secretary Jean (Chloe Sevigny) after inviting her to his apartment (a sequence interlaced with the previous one: it is while fondling the lock that Bateman is disturbed by Jean – also blonde – and invites her to dinner; it is while he takes sorbet from his fridge for Jean that we glimpse the head). There is plenty of deadpan, distancing irony in her inability to appreciate how literally he is speaking when he says he might "hurt" her, after standing behind her with a nail-gun at her head. The sequence is characterized by a real tension, however, based in both its staging and the extent to which the film solicits the viewer's sympathy for the vulnerable and innocent-seeming Jean, one of the few "likeable" characters encountered in the movie.

American Psycho sets out to be a distinctly chilling and disturbing account, rather than simply a work of black comedy in which the comic dimension remains dominant. The end is unsettling, partly ameliorative in the suggestion that the preceding mayhem might have been restricted to the world of Bateman's fantasy, but not allowing the viewer any certainty on this point. His final voice-over speech is disturbing, offering no prospect of resolution, redemption, or retribution. Even after admitting his pain to himself, and his desire to inflict it on others, he says, "there is no catharsis. My punishment continues to elude me and I gain no deeper knowledge of myself. No new knowledge can be extracted from my telling. This confession has meant nothing." Over these words, an edgy, insistent high string note is held. The camera closes in on Bateman's blank visage, coming to rest in extreme close-up on the eyes. Cut to black;

a moment's silence, then the closing credits. Signifiers of blankness, irresolution, and disturbance that constitute a "seriousness" of operative modality.

The violence of *Pulp Fiction*, in contrast, is not meant to disturb. Any potentially unsettling implications are subordinated to the use of violence as stylish flourish, an effect underpinned to a large extent by the use of deadpan comedy. Incongruity is, again, a source of much of the comic effect, as in the apparent disjuncture between the engaged trivial discourse of the hit-men Vincent (John Travolta) and Jules (Samuel L. Jackson) and the off-hand manner in which the latter dispatches one of a group of young men during a sequence in which they retrieve a briefcase belonging to their employer. Comedy emerges, as in *American Psycho*, in the gap between the level of the discourse and the life-and-death nature of the events within which it is situated.[13] It creates distance, reducing the impact of the assault, although not entirely; we are still invited to "feel," to some extent, for the victim, in his state of panicked-hysterical paralysis.

Genre frameworks play a large part in the motivation/legitimation and distancing of the violence of films such as *American Psycho* and *Pulp Fiction*. A rather different location of comedy-with-violence is found in *Very Bad Things* (1998), in which violent events are situated within a fictional terrain closer to that of relatively "normal" life. Violence, initially, is accidental, the death of a prostitute impaled on a bathroom hook in an over-enthusiastic sexual encounter during a bachelor-party trip to Las Vegas. A downward spiral into mayhem is triggered when the somewhat unhinged Boyle (Christian Slater) convinces the other members of the party to cover up the incident. By the end of the film, all are either dead or maimed in sequences that blend impactful violence with various forms of comic and stylized detachment. The prostitute's death is followed by Boyle's "shocking" murder of a hotel security guard. Moments such as the discovery of the prostitute's fate and the killing of the guard are coded as "real" and impactful within the fiction. The four members of the party accompanying Boyle are themselves shocked and stunned at this intrusion of bloody violence into their lives. The guard is stabbed with a corkscrew and left to die, screaming, disturbingly, like a dying animal, after being shut into the bathroom. The resulting scene is one of carnage, a bathroom that has been blood-streaked in a manner that appears designed to give an impression of authenticity.

The subsequent "clean-up" scenes, however, are highly stylized and more distanced. Boyd advises the others to follow his orders: cut to a series of shots of the group walking in slowed motion towards the camera, in a store where they are buying the buckets, mops and saw necessary to do the job – a reference to the iconic title sequence of *Reservoir Dogs* (1992) that is comic-parodic both in itself, as a reference to a landmark example of comedy-with-violence, and through the incongruity of the juxtaposition of the "cool" walk with the purchase of domestic cleaning products. The clean-up operation itself is conveyed through a montage sequence played to music, including overhead shots and time-lapse effects. The impression of carnage-awfulness is maintained – we see some shots of the sawing of bodies, the wrapping and packing into suit-cases of body-parts – but also rendered into a stylized sequence that, in itself, creates a blackly comic effect. Blood there is, aplenty, as a reminder of the "reality" of what happened, but that, too, can be a source of comedy, if only in passing, as one of the party has a pratfall slip on the bloody floor during the operation.

A sense of grim hysteria that bubbles over into dark comedy is the dominant tone of the film, nowhere more clearly than in the sequence in which the cut-up bodies are taken to the desert to be buried. The very "straight" family-man Adam (Daniel Stern) insists that the body parts of each victim be sorted out and buried together, for reason of religious propriety. The process of compiling two complete sets of parts that ensues is inflected comically – "Do you have any of him?" one enquires; "Heads-up," quips Adam's brother Michael (Jeremy Piven) as he tosses one of the heads – but also conveys a mood of increasing hysteria. In another example of shifting modality, Michael prepares to ram Adam's minivan after a confrontation between the two, at a point where Adam is cracking up under the pressure of fear and guilt. The fact that Michael targets the minivan, and Adam's precious attitude towards his vehicle, is comic. Adam stands in front of the van, protectively, foolishly. A discomforting and abrupt shift of tone occurs, however, as Michael accelerates and slams his vehicle into his brother-and-van, crushing Adam in a sudden and shocking moment of impact: another example in which the viewer is encouraged to share more immediately the shock experienced by the occupants of the fiction.

Such moments of violence in *Very Bad Things* are potentially more disturbing than similar events that occur in the world of professional hoodlums or confirmed psychos (the main qualification necessary here is the presence of Boyd, a figure of somewhat demonic detachment whose existence sets off the nightmare sequence of events and thus distances it from the world of the other more "normal"-seeming characters). Similar strategies of darkly comic stylization are used, however, to create a sense of protective distance, and to locate the violence-and-its-consequences in something more like a generic – and therefore "unreal" – territory in which its very black humor, which has some allegiances to the "gross-out" tradition, can become an object of enjoyment.[14]

Another striking mixture of modalities is found in Daniel Minahan's *Series 7: The Contenders*, a dark-spoof "reality TV" contest: *Survivor*, but played literally and for the ultimate stakes, the aim of the contenders being to kill one another. The formal strategy adopted here is very different from that used in sequences of montage-impact violence, or the glossy stylization of *American Psycho*, although it has some similarly ambivalent results. If comedy-with-violence often serves to provide distance and insulation, it is mixed in *Series 7* with formal procedures associated with opposite qualities of directness and immediacy: those of extended game-shows sold on the basis of the "realness" of the experiences faced by participants within the constraints of the particular format involved. The use of documentary/reality-style handheld video-quality footage and available light lends a particular form of impact to moments of violence such as the opening sequence in which a woman, later identified as reigning contender Dawn (Brooke Smith), enters a food store, walks up behind a man standing at the counter, and summarily shoots him in the back. A downplaying of overtly aesthetic or stylized qualities creates an impression of immediacy, of events being captured as if happening "for real." That a comic modality is also in play is rapidly indicated, however. Dawn, clearly in an advanced stage of pregnancy (incongruous enough in itself), puts two more shots into the man's body before enquiring of the clerk: "Hey, do you have any bean dip?"

Series 7 is filled with sequences in which the normal, often banal and occasionally melodramatic stuff of "reality" TV is mixed, incongruously, with matters of violent life-and-death. Student contender Lindsay (Merritt Wever), preparing for and engaging in a shootout with one rival, is egged on and harangued by her father, as if it were a normal situation of a pushy parent at a sporting event. Unemployed Tony (Michael Kaycheck) is told that the baby he thought his own is not: the stuff of domestic-melodramatic-revelation, except for the fact that Dawn lurks threateningly with her gun outside the house. Dawn is about to dispatch Connie (Marylouise Burke), a nurse, when her waters break and she has to plead for her would-be victim's help as she goes into labor. The film's texture mimics closely that of the reality-TV/game-show hybrid. This is developed to a point at which indicators of immediacy and of stylized distance begin to overlap, however. Undemonstrative, documentary-style footage is cut and mixed into what becomes a highly-stylized, American-TV-show blend of seemingly current, ongoing proceedings, brief capsule reca-pitulations and teaser flashforwards, accompanied by the seductive tones of two different voice-over commentators. This is parody, which offers comic distance, yet a version of parody that remains deadpan and very close to the original form: exaggeration is offered of *content* (the fact that the contestants are to kill each other) rather than of the stylistic devices themselves.

Series 7 is a good example of the process, termed "remediation" by Jay David Bolter and Richard Grusin, through which one medium often takes up and uses conventions associated with another.[15] Reme-diation, in Bolter and Grusin's account, involves two apparently contradictory but often complementary components: immediacy and hypermediacy. One medium, or form, often uses conventions associated with another in order to create an impression of direct-ness, immediacy, access to the real. *Series 7* is one of a number of recent fiction films to have used handheld, documentary-reality con-ventions to create this impression, other examples ranging from *Saving Private Ryan* (1998) to *The Blair Witch Project* (1999). Hyper-mediacy results when attention is drawn to this process; when the conventions become visible as such, as *signifiers* of "reality," rather than as a source of seemingly "transparent" access to the real itself. The logic of hypermediacy, for Bolter and Grusin, "multiplies the signs of mediation,"[16] which is exactly what happens in the textural weave of *Series 7*. The introduction of comedy, or other forms of stylization, is likely to contribute to an awareness of mediation, and thus to reduce the potential impact of screen violence.

This can be a complex issue, however. Our senses of immediacy and hypermediacy are often difficult to separate. It is the very aware-ness of the formal conventions of *Series 7* that gives the violence its impact, because the conventions are usually associated with access to a certain kind of reality. The more these devices are adopted in the

14 Coding violence as "witty" and stylized: the opening sequence of *Natural Born Killers* (1994)

realm of fiction, however, the less this might eventually become the case. Immediacy is, here and in all forms of representation, a construct, based on the associations carried at any particular time by particular formal devices. What appear to be overtly hypermediated forms can also claim to create a sense of access to the real. As Bolter and Grusin put it, "hypermedia seek the real by multiplying mediation so as to create a feeling of fullness, a satiety of experience, which can be taken as reality."[17] Apparently distancing and stylized forms of representation, including hypermediated assemblages of comedy-with-violence such as those found in *Natural Born Killers*, can also make claims to "getting past" conventional forms of mediation to give a more immediate impact.

For Leo Charney, the depiction of intense violence offers a impression of immediacy and presence that attempts to satisfy a hunger for presence characteristic of the experience of modernity. Other accounts might locate the particular examples discussed in this chapter in the context of postmodernity, in which the illusion of presence is offered as something that breaks through an environment of encompassing (and, by implication, corrupting) mass-mediation and simulation. This kind of discourse is also found within some of the films analyzed above, in which acts of violent transgression are sometimes cast as existential moments of purity or presence. Boyle, in *Very Bad Things*, encourages the speaking of usually-unspoken home truths between the brothers Adam and Michael, after the burial of bodies in the desert, on the basis that "this is real time . . . we're in the moment." As the self-justifying Mickey Knox opines to the broadcaster Wayne Gayle (Robert Downey, Jr.) in *Natural Born Killers*: "Was an instant of my purity worth a lifetime of your lies? [. . .] Media's like a web, only it's a man-made web. Murder? It's pure." What the films themselves offer is, and only can ever be, a fabrication of a *sense* of presence, however, which can be conveyed through a variety of mediated or hypermediated formal techniques, and is usually reduced and made "safer," less exposing, through the distancing effect of comedy.

Satire?

Comedy can be mixed with violence in ways that both reduce and, in some cases, heighten the potential of violence to disturb. Either way, the combination is one that is often criticized. The argument usually goes something like this: to mix comedy with violence is to risk trivializing the latter, using it as a source of pleasure during which we do not have to face up to the real consequences of violence as something that exists in the real, external world, as well as that on screen.[18] One way out of this difficulty, in terms of the legitimating strategies available to filmmakers (whether deployed consciously/ deliberately for this reason or not), is to make claims to the status of satire. If comedy as a mode is usually underpinned by claims that, ultimately, it is not to be taken seriously, satire suggests otherwise. Satirical comedy usually implies a more substantial relationship with "serious" matters in the real world; comedy with a critical edge, of some kind, usually directed towards social, cultural, or political phenomena. In its satirical form, comedy has implications and purpose that might protect it from accusations of gratuitousness.

Four of the films examined in this chapter make claims to the status of satire, although these are sometimes contested. In the case of *Natural Born Killers* this was a live issue in the reception of the film, described in the press pack – issued to journalists and designed to shape the framework within which it was received in the media – as "a satire on our culture of violence and the media's ratings-driven exploitation of that culture."[19] The general assumption is that the film was intended that way by the director, Oliver Stone. A recurrent suggestion in media coverage, amid the furor that greeted the release of *Natural Born Killers*, was that the film failed to achieve this critically

15 Patrick Bateman's (Christian Bale) blank visage in *American Psycho* (2000): a serious ending to a darkly humorous serial killer film

distanced status: that it remained a *manifestation* rather than an *analysis* of problems related to media portrayals of violence; that it "glorified" acts of violence rather than using them as the basis for a critique.[20] This is the ground on which it was condemned by many commentators, which demonstrates the extent to which the claim to satire can be used – or rejected – as a defence for films that produce graphic or hyperbolic images of violence.

It seems to be no accident that three of the four films that make claims to the status of satire direct much of their critique at *other* forms of media, principally television. One of the key targets in *Natural Born Killers* is Wayne Gayle, manically larger-than-life presenter of the exploitative *American Maniacs* show. The satirical portrait of "normal" suburban America in *Serial Mom* also singles out the media, on a similar basis, for its transformation of serial killer into cultural icon and hero. The entire fabric of *Series 7* suggests more than just parody of the reality-TV/game-show format. Also implied is satirical critique of the lengths to which television might be imagined to go in the search for sensational material to improve ratings. Attacking *other* media, explicitly or implicitly, is a way films such as these can take up the theme of violence-and-supposed-media-irresponsibility, laying claim to some critical thrust on this issue, while continuing to produce a largely unquestioned pleasurable spectacle of violence of their own.

How far the heart of these films is invested in their status as satire remains open to debate. Certain key ingredients of satire are present, including a sense of critical distance from the central protagonists, a notable feature of *Natural Born Killers* and, especially, *American Psycho*. As a legitimating strategy satire might perform largely as "cover" in many cases, as an available defense for films the appeal of which for some key audience groups is located elsewhere. It might be argued that what films such as *Natural Born Killers*, *American Psycho*, and *Series 7* offer – along with *Pulp Fiction* and *Very Bad Things* – is a pleasurable spectacle of transgressively violent action; a frisson of intensity that is both heightened, in some respects, and made palatable, in others, through distancing strategies such as the introduction of dark comedy.

Violence is a convenient source of the intensity of audiovisual experience sought by some viewers and sold by Hollywood as part of the essence of the cinematic experience (even when transferred onto home video). A cooler, deadpan, blackly-comic or hyperbolically black-comically-excessive mobilization of sequences of explicit violence might, however, be a formula of particular appeal to media-savvy young-adult or late-teenage males, one of the key target audiences for such films. The violence tends to be off-hand, its purveyors under-invested emotionally, "cool," and "in charge": qualities that might be expected to appeal to adolescent and post-adolescent male viewers, given the prevailing cultural constructions of gender in the US and other target territories.

Films such as these offer some of the appeals associated with cult films, especially the "midnight movie" that often sets out deliberately to attract a particular niche audience with material that transgresses certain expectations usually associated with the mainstream. As J. P. Telotte suggests, the transgressions offered by such films often include territorial "violations" at the level of genre, such as the darker mixtures of comedy and violence explored in this chapter.[21] Those who kill, often coldly, are vivid and heightened representations of the kind of alienated rebellion likely to appeal especially to some sectors of the adolescent or younger-adult audience, the notoriety gained by some such films only adding to their lure as signifiers of transgressive-escapist experience. Mixing comedy with otherwise potentially disturbing violence is one way to up-the-ante, to increase the overall frisson, without taking representation of violence itself to a point at which disgust might outweigh pleasurable vicarious impact-sensation.[22] As films that offer this kind of appeal, the examples examined in this chapter might appear to be located somewhat on the margins of Hollywood. This is a terrain that is distinctly "New Hollywood," however, in its commercial strategy of offering qualities associated with more marginal spheres of production and distribution on a larger, potentially very profitable, and high-profile scale.[23]

Notes

1   For more on definitions of "New Hollywood," including the "Hollywood Renaissance," see my *New Hollywood Cinema: An Introduction* (London: I. B. Tauris, 2002).

2   Leo Charney, "The Violence of a Perfect Moment," *Violence and American Cinema*, ed. J. David Slocum (New York: Routledge, 2001), 47–62. See Tom Gunning, "The Cinema of Attractions: Early Film, its Spectator and the Avant-Garde," *Early Cinema: Space, Frame, Narrative*, ed. Thomas Elsaesser (London: BFI, 1990), 56–62.

3   Devin McKinney, "Violence: The Strong and the Weak," *Screening Violence*, ed. Stephen Prince (London: Athlone Press, 2000), 99–109.

4   Charney, "Violence," 48.

5   See Stephen Prince, *Savage Cinema: Sam Peckinpah and the Rise of Ultraviolent Movies* (Austin: University of Texas Press, 1998).

6   Robert Hodge and David Tripp, *Children and Television: A Semiotic Approach* (Cambridge: Polity Press, 1986), 43.

7   For more discussion in detail, see my *Film Comedy* (London: Wallflower Press, 2002). This is not to say that there was no concern about the presence of violence in the earlier slapstick era, however; see Peter Kramer, "'Clean, Dependable Slapstick': Comic Violence and the Emergence of Classical Hollywood Cinema," in Slocum, *Violence and American Cinema*, 103–16.

8   Stephen Prince, "Graphic Violence in the Cinema: Origins, Aesthetic Design, and Social Effects," in Prince, *Savage Cinema*, 29.

9   A point made by Marsha Kinder, "Violence American Style: The Narrative Orchestration of Violent Attractions," in Slocum, *Violence and American Cinema*, 68.

10 Annette Hill, *Shocking Entertainment: Viewer Response to Violent Movies* (Luton: University of Luton Press, 1997), 85.

11 For more on the staging of violence as akin to the production numbers of musicals and other attractions, see Kinder, "Violence American Style".

12 For more detailed discussion of approaches to comedy based on incongruity, see King, *Film Comedy*, especially "Introduction: Taking Comedy Seriously."

13 See King, *Film Comedy*.

14 For more on gross-out comedy, see King, *Film Comedy*, ch. 2.

15 Jay David Bolter and Richard Grusin, *Remediation: Understanding New Media* (Cambridge: MIT Press, 1999).

16 *Ibid.*, 34.

17 *Ibid.*, 53.
18 A similar argument, in terms of the stylization of violence, is found in McKinney, "Violence".
19 Quoted. in Thomas Austin, *Hollywood, Hype and Audiences: Selling and watching popular film in the 1990s* (Manchester: Manchester University Press, 2002), 154.
20 See Austin, *Hollywood*, 152–87.
21 J. P. Telotte, "Beyond All Reason: The Nature of the Cult," *The Cult Film Experience: Beyond All Reason*, ed. J. P. Telotte (Austin: University of Texas Press, 1991), 5–17.
22 As studies cited by Stephen Prince (*Savage Cinema*, 28–9) suggest, scenes of overly "raw" or actual violence tend not to be pleasurable for viewers.
23 Both the Hollywood Renaissance and the blockbuster-franchise strategy were founded in part on key lessons learned from the independent/exploitation sector, as I argue in *New Hollywood Cinema*.

Killing in style: the aestheticization of violence in Donald Cammell's *White of the Eye*

Steven Jay Schneider

> Everything in this world has two handles. Murder, for instance, may be laid hold of by its moral handle ... and *that*, I confess, is its weak side; or it may also be treated *aesthetically*, as the Germans call it – that is, in relation to good taste. —— Thomas De Quincey

> If any human act evokes the aesthetic experience of the sublime, certainly it is the act of murder. And if murder can be experienced aesthetically, the murderer can in turn be regarded as a kind of artist – a performance artist or anti-artist whose specialty is not creation but destruction. —— Joel Black

> Donald looked upon violence as an artist might look on paint. What are its components? What's its nature? Its glamour? —— James Fox

Death imitates art

APRIL 24, 1996. 9:45PM. LOS ANGELES, CALIFORNIA. Local police receive word that 62-year-old British filmmaker Donald Cammell has shot himself in the head with a handgun. "Because the shot went through his forehead rather than through the roof of his mouth," reported Tom Dewe Matthews in London's *The Guardian* one week later, "he lived for another 45 minutes."[1] According to Cammell's widow, China Kong, who was with him at the time of his death, the writer-director had been studying the art of suicide for some time, reading about where you should aim the bullet in order to obtain not just a painless death, but a pleasurable one.[2] In her deposition, Kong recalled that Cammell asked for a pillow before he died, because he didn't want the carpet to be "fucked up" by his blood. He also asked for a mirror in the hopes of observing his own death.[3] Among the last things Cammell said was: "Can you see the picture of Borges now?"[4]

Immensely talented, but perennially frustrated by the limitations placed on him by Hollywood's conservative studio system, Donald Cammell directed just four feature films in his lifetime: *Performance* (1970, with Nicholas Roeg), *Demon Seed* (1977), *White of the Eye* (1988), and *Wild Side* (1995). Except for *Demon Seed*, Cammell also wrote or co-wrote the screenplay for all of these productions.

FACT: At the end of *Performance*, psychosexually traumatized gangster Chas (James Fox) shoots polymorphously perverse ex-rock star Turner (Mick Jagger) in the head. The camera follows the bullet as it penetrates Turner's brain, where, inexplicably, a portrait of Argentinian author Jorge Luis Borges appears and is shattered. Because *Performance* is far and away Cammell's most commercially and critically successful work – screenwriter David Pirie has called it "a colossus in postwar British cinema"[5] – reporters jumped on the similarities between the film and Cammell's suicide. Mick Brown has gone so far as to claim that Cammell's favorite Borges story was "Theme of the Traitor and the Hero," about a disgraced conspirator who agrees to a scheme which would provide him "the occasion to redeem himself ... and for which his death would provide the final flourish":[6] the staging of his own assassination, based on elements from *Macbeth* and *Julius Caesar*.[7]

FACT: About halfway through *White of the Eye*, as-yet-unidentified psychopath Paul White (David Keith) bursts into a woman's bathroom, ties up the terrified occupant with stereo wire, and drowns her in the tub. Taking, or perhaps stealing, a page from Michael Powell's *Peeping Tom* (1960), the killer holds a mirror up to the woman's face, thereby forcing her to watch herself die. In large part because *White of the Eye*, like *Peeping Tom* before it, flopped miserably at the box office (total gross: $225,000) even while garnering lofty praise from critics, the relevance of this scene to Cammell's death was never commented upon.

Despite the privileged status accorded to *Performance*, as well as its own lack of recognition, *White of the Eye* may stand as Cammell's most profound meditation on the aesthetics of violence, something that fascinated him throughout his life at both the personal and professional levels. Kevin Macdonald, co-director of the 1998 documentary *Donald Cammell: The Ultimate Performance*, believes that "Cammell's suicide was the culmination of a life-long obsession with the strange territory where violence and death intermingle with pleasure."[8] The first time we see Cammell in this film, he is being interviewed on a previously-recorded television show wearing a black t-shirt with white lettering on the front that reads "MURDER IS A WORK OF ART." Elsewhere, Macdonald states that "Cammell didn't kill himself because of years of failure. He killed himself because he had always wanted to kill himself."[9]

In what follows, I seek to identify via close analysis of a few key scenes the cinematic means by which Cammell sought to aestheticize both the *act* and the *product* of murder in *White of the Eye*. Not only is it the case that particular shots in this film ask to be "extracted" from their narrative context and viewed as paintings of a highly disturbing and challenging nature; a cinematic metaphor is effected whereby the killer gets equated with a kind of artist, and the carnage he leaves behind with works of art.[10] I will also be arguing for a restricted version of auteurism, insofar as I claim that Cammell took full advantage of the subject matter and conventions he was working with so as to create an identification of sorts between himself as director and the diegetic killer, perhaps in order to explore/experience in a virtual or secondhand manner the possibilities of artistic murder. Preparation, one might say, for his own carefully planned, even staged (*à la* Fergus Kilpatrick, Borges' traitor-hero in the above-mentioned story) suicide eight years later.

The art of murder

To the extent that *White of the Eye* warrants classification as a genre picture, it falls under the hybrid heading of "horror-thriller-suspense." As Leonard Klady notes, "calling … *White of the Eye* … a thriller is rather like saying that Van Gogh's *The Potato Eaters* is a painting. Both descriptions are unquestionably correct and immeasurably insufficient."[11] There are no supernatural occurrences in this tale of an on-the-loose serial killer, loosely adapted from a 1983 novel, *Mrs. White*, by Andrew Klaven (writing under the pseudonym Margaret Tracy).[12] According to Kong, whose husband gave her a co-screenwriter credit, Cammell did not like *Ms. White* at all, viewing it as just another slasher-type exploitation yarn. Canon Films offered him the chance to direct after yet another of his ambitious projects was shelved, and he only agreed when Kong informed him, "you can just throw out the story."[13] In an interview published shortly after his death, Cammell is only slightly more generous, calling *Mrs. White* a "strange little novel," and describing how he "rethought the plot":

Basically, her novel [apparently Cammell was so uninterested in his source material as to neglect performing even a superficial inquiry into its author's history] explored this woman's feelings as she discovers that her husband is insane and yet she is completely dominated by him. Well, I ... decided that it was more interesting to have her deeply in love, so that when she discovers that he's a serial killer, she has to make that decision to leave him or confront him and continue to love him. Even to the point where he degenerates into bestiality.[14]

Despite his effort at reconceiving Klavan's novel as first and foremost a love story – albeit a particularly perverse one – Cammell still makes use of numerous horror conventions, including a steady diet of PoV camerawork and sudden explosions into the frame from off-screen space. The combination of dark subject matter and graphic violence actually resulted in the film's initially receiving an X rating from the MPAA. It took a letter from none other than Cammell's occasional chum, Marlon Brando, one which "analyz[ed] sequences in the film in great detail ... praising it for its originality and its artistry," to get the X changed to an R, with only a "couple of nominal cuts" made to the original print.[15]

Charming, handsome, happily married father of an adorable if tomboyish little girl, Paul White – a gifted stereo technician from a small town outside Tucson, Arizona[16] – becomes prime suspect in a series of gruesome murders when it is determined that the killer's vehicle has the same rare brand of tires as his own. Though it soon becomes clear that Paul is not quite the faithful husband he appears, as the film's charismatic protagonist with whom we can hardly help sympathizing, we are encouraged to believe his protestations of innocence despite the mounting evidence against him.

About two-thirds of the way through, the film's existing hermeneutic code is shattered, as Paul's devoted wife Joan (Cathy Moriarity) makes a gruesome discovery: human body parts, wrapped up neatly in translucent plastic bags, hidden in a hollow space underneath the bathtub. From this point on, events are focalized primarily through Joan rather than Paul. What follows is an extended denouement in which Paul elaborates his demented and horrifyingly misogynistic motivation.[17] After taking potshots at his daughter with a rifle, Paul – now wearing blue Indian war paint and with a massive amount of dynamite strapped to his chest (a seeming allusion to the finale of Godard's *Pierrot La Fou* [1965]) – chases Joan to an abandoned construction site, where in a clichéd moment her ex-lover suddenly arrives to play hero, only to be blown up along with Paul. Joan avoids the explosion by diving into a nearby lake, and in the epilogue a new, "healthy" family is constituted between Mrs. White, her daughter, and the detective previously assigned to the case, Charles Mendoza (Art Evans).

A mere retelling of *White of the Eye*'s serial killer narrative does little justice to the picture's haunting power and strikingly original construction. What has led reviewers such as David Thomson to champion the film as "one of the great secret works in cinema"?[18] Here is one answer: through the creative employment of a host of audiovisual devices, including montage and overlapping editing, slow-motion camerawork, mise-en-scene, and an eclectic sound-track, Cammell forsakes the codes of "realism" (for example, tempo-ral linearity, motivational cues, a clear demarcation between diegetic and non-diegetic material) in favor of a highly-stylized presentation of violence.[19] This in turn produces a complex psychological and emotional response in viewers, who have little choice but to analyze, reflect upon, even *appreciate* what they would normally despise, disavow, or deny. In a book on Sam Peckinpah, director of the con-troversial New Hollywood classic *The Wild Bunch* (1969), Stephen Prince argues that "most films do not hold viewers accountable for, or implicate them in, the violent spectacles they witness. Peckinpah's films do, and this is one reason for their controversial nature."[20] The same can be said of *White of the Eye*, with the added exceptions that Cammell implicates his viewers by means of violent tableaux as well as violent spectacles, and that the person he implicates first and foremost is *himself*.

The first of *White of the Eye*'s two elaborate murder scenes occurs just a few minutes into the picture, before any of the main characters have been introduced. I want to take a close look at how this scene, which incorporates approximately 55 cuts in a mere 140-second interval, is constructed.[21] Rather than go through it shot-by-shot, however, I will analyze the scene into three distinct segments. But first, some remarks on the film's opening sequence are warranted.

White of the Eye opens with a long shot of a beat-up car driving towards us on a dusty road in the middle of the Arizona desert. This is a film largely concerned with the collapsing or conjoining of oppo-sites, and right away we get our first examples: a pair of motorcycles pass the car going the other way. Among the differences brought to bear and momentarily united here are size, number, visibility (the driver of the car can't be seen, the bikers themselves are pretty much all we see), direction, and social identity. The fact that neither the vehicles nor their respective drivers play any role in what follows can be taken as support for the claim that Cammell's concern here is with providing an economical image that at once instantiates and exemplifies the narrative-proper's central "argument."

The credits, which initially appear in white against an all-blue background, are intercut with shots of a hawk in flight. First we get an extreme close-up of one of the bird's staring, straining eyes; next we watch quasi-documentary footage of it killing some defenseless prey; finally we see it gracefully circle the sky in slow motion. The camera then begins cutting back and forth between the gliding hawk and the Arizona cityscape. It soon becomes apparent, from the cinematography as well as the editing, that the shots of the city are actually to be understood as POV shots from the hawk's own perspective.

What is so striking about this credit sequence is the way it successfully alerts us to the film's central theme while simultaneously mirroring in formal terms the murder scene to follow. Cammell's interest in problematizing certain key oppositions of modern Western, and especially American, culture can be seen in his association of archetypal images of violence (the hawk killing its prey) and beauty (the hawk in flight). Mediating between these two traditionally-contrasted notions is a third one: nature. If we interpret the extreme close-ups of the hawk's eye (soon to be substituted by the killer's eye) surveying its prey, surveying *us*, with a fearful yet amoral intensity, as signifying the potency of pure, untempered natural instinct – the question of sexual desire does not arise here – we may conclude that, for Cammell, violence and beauty are in fact capable of co-existing. In this case, the killing and the flying both involve a performance, without reflection or hesitation, of what comes naturally. In the subsequent murder scene, Cammell takes this idea a giant step further, transforming a plausible assertion about the co-existence of cultural contraries (the vicious killer is *also* a graceful animal) into a radical identity claim (murder *is* art, art *is* murder).

The complicated use of PoV camerawork in the opening also warrants comment. When we initially cut from a shot of the bird in flight to a smooth mobile crane shot of the cityscape, we are not apt to attribute the latter viewpoint to the hawk's own perspective. It is only through repeated intercutting and the sweeping motion of what

we probably thought at first was non-focalized or "objective" camerawork that we realize we have been looking at Tucson from a
literal bird's-eye view. This somewhat manipulative ploy anticipates
Cammell's self-conscious association of himself as director with the
film's killer (as prefigured by the hawk), achieved through a conflation of objective and subjective vision. This conflation becomes
manifest, however, only *after* we correct our original assumption
regarding the source of the images presented; the awkwardness
entailed by such a retroactive ascription of visual authority is precisely what encourages viewers to reflect upon its meaning. What we
initially take for granted as the omniscient director narrating with
his camera from a safe and secure position outside the diegesis, guilt-
less insofar as he is merely the teller of the tale and not the agent
of death within it, turns out to share the perspective – visual *and*
aesthetic – of the latter.

The contrast between *White of the Eye*'s complex opening sequence
(comprising as it does the vehicles, credits, hawk, and cityscape) and
the scene that follows is registered both formally and thematically.
This next scene opens with a slow pan across the side of a beige building, where the name of a department store, "Goldwaters," can be seen
in huge white letters. Besides linguistically foreshadowing a key image
present in the coming murder scene, this pan alerts us to the fact that,
despite the desert backdrop, we are no longer in a world of nature but
rather one of culture, commerce, and consumption. This shift is reinforced by the cheesy electric guitar music blaring on the soundtrack,
strikingly different from the New Age, possibly Native American-
influenced melody heard in the preceding scene. Through a tinted-
mirror reflection, a medium long shot shows a woman coming out of
Goldwaters, wearing a tacky leather jacket and high-heeled snakeskin
shoes. She is followed by a young male employee who struggles to prevent a pile of boxes from falling to the ground. The comical excess of
this latter image, which represents the woman's daily haul, positions
her in opposition to the hawk, who kills exactly what it needs in order
to survive and requires no assistance in doing so.

As the pair proceed towards a car in the mall parking lot, the
camera cuts back and forth between the young man's face and eyeline matches to the woman's legs. As opposed to the previous scene,
with its naturalistic backdrop and documentary inserts, this one is
highly artificial. The reflected images invest the couple with a less-
than-authentic ontological status; and the absence of dialogue,

amped-up guitar music, the young man's objectifying looks, and the woman's self-conscious strut (which ends with her turning towards the camera, smiling, and putting on her sunglasses) all results in the odd but unmistakable impression that we are watching a by-now-dated rock music video.[22]

Despite the obvious differences between this scene and the ones preceding it, the editing, *mise-en-scène*, and soundtrack of the former all contain elements which problematize any too-simple conclusions regarding essential difference or mutual exclusivity. This is in keeping with Cammell's desire to call into question the status of certain culturally-enforced oppositions. For example, although we are now positioned directly outside a mall – that locus of post-industrial capitalism – the Arizona desert can still be clearly seen in the background. As he explained later, "My main set piece is [in] a run-down mining town called Globe, which is on the edge of an Apache reservation, where a crumbling civilization has this uneasy coexistence with violence – *pagan* violence."[23] In addition, the New Age music accompanying the credits possesses a noticeable electronic component which connects it to the electric guitar music here. Most obviously, the young man with his leering eyes is set up as a less threatening but still potentially violent analogue of the hawk, and the woman – with her snakeskin shoes and the black, snake-like pattern on her jacket – his prey. Snakes, of course, are a favorite delicacy of hawks. And considering that the boy's eyeline matches to the woman's legs are intercut with seemingly "objective" shots of the woman taken from just over his shoulder, we have here another closing of the gap between director as external narrator and diegetic killer. The latter is here seen in the guise of the young man, hunting his prey like the hawk before him, focusing his attention on specific body parts like Paul White after him.

I turn now to *White of the Eye*'s first murder scene. My aim here is to further reveal Cammell's interest in problematizing (by collapsing, through cinematic means) a number of traditional dichotomies, and to support the claim that the director variously aligns himself with the film's killer. Perhaps this association served to provide Cammell with a more direct experience of aestheticized violence, predating his own aesthetically-motivated suicide in 1996.

I. ESTABLISHING SEGMENT (SHOTS 1–9): The scene opens with a high-angled shot of a goldfish swimming in a bowl (shades of

"Goldwaters") that is sitting on a table in the center of the frame. Some pink and green objects float in the bowl alongside the fish. The camera pulls back slowly to reveal a set of kitchen knives in a holder positioned a foot or so in front of the bowl; what we have here is an early juxtaposition of (contained) beauty and (potential) violence. The camera continues its deliberate retreat backwards and to the left, finally resting on a counter upon which lies a bottle of red wine, a half-filled wineglass, a lemon, an eggplant, and some lettuce on a cutting board. The *mise-en-scène* here is so balanced in terms of color, shape, relative position of objects, and background – the extreme whiteness of the countertop serves as a virtual canvas – that it begs to be viewed as a kind of portrait. More accurately, a cinematic still life, eliciting a measure of aesthetic acknowledgment, if not appreciation, from the viewer.

The camera now cuts, first to an overhead close-up of some brown meat in a glass dish (ribs to be precise, promising nourishment even while conjuring thoughts of emaciation), then to a collection of shiny pots hanging above the counter, and finally to a close-up of the refrigerator door. A slow tilt up the door reveals some conventional signs of domesticity: a photo of a child, some fruit magnets, a post-card. Suddenly the camera jerks back, then cuts to an establishing shot of the house as a car pulls in the driveway.

II. HUNTING SEGMENT (SHOTS 10–31): The next cut, to a PoV shot from above of a pair of gloved hands removing the lid from the bowl of meat, is significant. For here, as in the credit sequence, we are encouraged to reinterpret the previous segment in such a way that the director's seemingly objective camerawork – achieved via Steadicam shooting, smooth cutting, and the seeming absence of human presence in the *mise-en-scène* – gets conflated with the killer's subjective vision. Why else would the camera have pulled back so abruptly from its methodical inspection of the refrigerator door (shot 8), unless the killer/director suddenly heard the car approaching (seen in shot 9)? In the modern horror film, first-person camerawork is often employed as a means of effecting a measure of epistemological identification between viewer and monster, or alternatively, between viewer and victim. In *White of the Eye*, such camerawork evokes a *three-way* identification of sorts, between viewer, killer, and director. Not only do the PoV shots force us to share the perspective of the soon-to-be murderer; we are given reason to interpret these actions as expressions of Cammell's own, "personal" aesthetic choices. And lest I be accused of advocating a naïve, because too literal-minded, auteurism here, it is important to emphasize the extent to which, even before we see the killer's gloved hands from his own perspective (shot 10), the previous segment's methodical, probing, apparently objective cinematography evokes the idea of a cautious, curious, and surely up-to-no-good intruder.

Next come a series of shots alternating between the killer's PoV of the interior, non-focalized shots from behind of the woman from the previous scene entering the house, and extreme close-ups of a bulging eye, presumably the killer's. Immediately upon entering her living room, the woman stops, freezes, and cocks her head slightly: precisely the reaction of a squirrel or rabbit when it senses a predator lurking nearby. The phone rings, breaking the woman's spell – really her survival instinct – and she goes to the kitchen to answer it. Once again in PoV mode, the camera catches a glimpse of the woman, moving quickly up a short flight of stairs so as to keep her in view. One also hears a sniffing noise coming from the foreground where the camera is positioned, furthering the association between human and animal stalker. Keeping its distance, the camera follows the woman around a table, stopping with only her midsection in view (her face and legs are obstructed by cabinets); as in the previous scene, we get a visual dissection of the woman into (body) parts.

There is certainly room here, and throughout *White of the Eye* – a film which registers its interest in and prioritization of the unblinking gaze through its very title – for post-Mulveyan feminist film theorists to criticize such sequences on the grounds that they promote a sexualized objectification of the female form, whether fetishistic-scopophilic (woman displayed as erotic spectacle, rendered unthreatening by the controlling male look) or sadistic-voyeuristic (woman investigated, demystified, and eventually controlled through punishment) in nature.[24] However, I would suggest an alternative interpretation. Just as the hawk, whose relentless stare signifies the drive of natural instinct rather than perverse, even if pervasive, sexual impulse, so the sequences in question are guilty of objectification primarily in their reduction of the woman to a mere source of sustenance, not unlike the ribs. (Cammell was reported to be especially fond of the line appearing on *White of the Eye*'s poster art: "The only difference between a hunter and a killer is his prey.")[25] The disturbing question never adequately answered by the film is what exactly is being "sustained" by the murder of these women;

after all, Paul is no cannibal, and the "explanation" he eventually offers of his behavior is both untrustworthy and unsatisfying.

The claim here is that female bodies provide Paul with the raw material he requires in order to satisfy his overwhelming artistic urges. Of course, such a view does nothing to counter the charges of misogyny capable of being directed against either Paul White or Donald Cammell, but it does help to explain why the film seems to go out of its way so as *not* to satisfy the heterosexual male spectator's presumed desire for either gratuitous female nudity (the fetishistic-scopophilic preference) or sexualized violence against women (the sadistic-voyeuristic preference).

After another brief insert of the killer's eye – a great way to tease the viewer, by simultaneously revealing him/her and keeping his/her identity a secret[26] – the camera edges right up behind the woman, who is busy telling a friend on the phone how her hairdresser, "*butchered* ... just *butchered*, my hair." (Cammell's dialogue clearly lacks the subtlety of his camerawork, a fact pointed out by more than one reviewer.) The woman says goodbye to her friend, hangs up the phone, and reacts as she catches sight of something on the table. Cut to a close-up of the ribs, on top of which lies the goldfish gasping for water. After one final insert of the killer's eye, all hell breaks loose.

Of this segment, we may note the following: 1) first-person camerawork is employed somewhat confusingly here, as Cammell cuts from a shot of the killer's PoV directly to one of the woman's, right before she gets attacked; 2) the contents of the glass dish serve not only to warn the woman of a malevolent presence in her home, but to once again conflate traditional aesthetic opposites (the uncooked ribs are skeletal, revolting, and evocative of death, while the goldfish is shimmering, beautiful, and still fighting for life); and 3) the soundtrack, composed by Pink Floyd percussionist Nick Mason, serves to reinforce the three-way identification between viewer/listener, killer, and director discussed above. Throughout this segment, an electronic bass note sounds rhythmically such that we can hardly help interpreting it as a non-diegetic analogue of the killer's heartbeat: something we could hear only if we were positioned "inside" his body. It is precisely because Cammell (via Mason) chooses *not* to use the sound of an actual heart beating, opting instead for a stylized treatment that is at once objective *and* subjective – it isn't *literally* the killer's heartbeat, though in a virtual or metaphorical sense it is

– that the distinction between killer and director is elided, and the scene's artificiality foregrounded.

III. ATTACKING SEGMENT (SHOTS 32–55): The next cut is to a PoV shot of the woman, who wheels around to face the camera/killer. A gloved hand reaches out from the position of the camera and grabs the woman's face as she starts to scream. Whose hand is it? Paul White's? Donald Cammell's? The cameraman's? From the visual material presented to us, there is no way of deciding between these options ... which may be the whole point. After another shot of the dying goldfish, we cut to the killer grappling with the woman; this latter shot is "objective" insofar as the camera remains static and there is no one else around to claim it, but "subjective" insofar as the camera is positioned exactly where the killer was standing in the previous segment, when he was staring at the woman's torso from behind the kitchen cabinets. In other words, what was previously a shot from the killer's PoV now gets taken up by the director, once again in the guise of non-diegetic narrator, thereby strengthening the visual and psychological link between them. Unable to overpower her right away, or perhaps choosing not to, the killer spins around the room with his victim in a manner reminiscent of a cat playing with a wounded mouse – or a hawk toying with a defenseless rabbit – before finally ending its life.

What follows is a bit of highly-stylized camerawork reminiscent of Italian horror auteur Dario Argento, as we cut to the woman's head slamming into and shattering the glass door of a microwave, all in excruciatingly slow motion. Still in slow-mo mode, the camera next cuts to a butcher's knife slamming down on the bowl of meat; the impact jolts the dying goldfish up in the air and the scene's locus of symbolic meaning explodes in our faces. Another cut shows the bloody, detrital meat sauce spilling from screen right onto the white countertop. Like a mini-avalanche, it knocks over the glasses of wine, which proceed to empty their own red contents onto the counter. These last two shots serve to conjoin, and thereby call into question, such familiar oppositions as violence and beauty, civility and wildness, nature and culture – especially when contrasted with the earlier cinematic still-life of the wine bottle, glasses, etc. The cutting and use of slow motion here only adds to the poetic effect.

Writing about Peckinpah's *The Wild Bunch*, Prince observes that "The editing reconfigures, stylistically transforms, the deaths ... The cutaways and the use of slow motion impose a marked distortion upon the time and space of the represented action ... Their design foregrounds the hyperkinetic spectacle so that it becomes a detachable part of the film."[27] But more than just a detachable "hyperkinetic spectacle," easy enough to produce in today's big-budget, f/x-happy New Hollywood cinema, this segment from *White of the Eye* offers viewers at least a modicum of experiential awareness – subjective, psychological, temporal, aesthetic – concerning what it is like to commit murder. Consider this quotation from Jack Katz, who uses phenomenological language to describe even the "common" killer's experience when performing the ultimate act of violence:

> Like the promise of an erotic drive, rage moves toward the experience of time suspended; it blows up the present moment so the situation becomes a portentous, potentially an endless present, possibly the occasion for a destruction that will become an eternally significant creativity. This is the spiritual beauty of rage.[28]

The shots now come in rapid succession: we see the woman's legs splattered with blood; the microwave shatter once again; the killer's back as he finishes his murderous work; another wineglass as it gets kicked off the table and crashes on the floor. Upon its release, one critic declared *White of the Eye* "a complex, Cubist kaleidoscope of images";[29] from this segment, it is easy to see why. As a child, Cammell exhibited immense talent at drawing, later attending the Royal Academy of Art. Before turning to film in the mid-1960s he worked as a popular and respected portrait painter in London. The turning point in Cammell's career came when he "discovered" that figurative painting was dead, and that to continue on as an artist he would have to fragment the image. "He realized," said his brother in a 1996 interview, "that the mental process involved in observing objects shouldn't necessarily be linear, that what you are actually observing is a whole series of events at the same time. It's like a Picasso – you have to include several viewpoints, all within one frame."[30] If we substitute "sequence" for "frame" in this last sentence, then the attacking segment of *White of the Eye*'s first murder scene – with its overlapping edits and several viewpoints of "the same series of events at the same time" – stands as a Cubist-like moment in cinema. "I am a painter who happens to make films,"[31] Cammell was fond of saying, not without justification.

But Cubism is not the only artistic movement to find echoes in *White of the Eye*. In a 1987 review, Nigel Andrews wrote that

16 *White of the Eye* (1987): Donald Cammell's "most profound meditation on the aesthetics of violence."

"Cammell ... has taken a novel ... and wreathed its story in busily expressionist visuals."[32] We have already seen how Cammell, through the creative use of first-person cinematography and sound design, conflates the killer's PoV, even his physiological reactions, with his own. Montage editing allows him to further express his aesthetic sensibilities through the poetic juxtaposition of images. Returning to Segment III: from the wineglass crashing on the floor, we cut to a pair of extreme close-ups of broken glass mixed with blood. Next we cut to the goldfish dying on the floor; yet another insert of the killer's eye; and another shot of the victim's blood spilling out onto the countertop. What we have here is a kind of cinematic *haiku* constructed by the director, one which follows an emotional rather than logical progression in order to demonstrate at the level of symbolism the awful beauty of violent crime. As Cammell himself once stated, "any film, like any story, forms an elaborate pattern. It is not a statement of truth, it's a design, a mandala; it's a construct whose virtues lies in its harmonies and its paradoxes and its evocations."[33]

But beyond this, and throughout the entire scene, we have what Theodore Ziolkowski describes as "a projection of the artist's own subjectivity."[34] Besides employing the various audiovisual techniques detailed above, Cammell, by endowing Paul White's violent actions with an undeniable aesthetic quality, "implies his identification with the criminal, his self-glorification as a transgressor."[35] It is not simply that the killer in *White of the Eye* gets fashioned an artist; the artist behind the film fashions himself a killer. As Cammell himself stated in an interview, "The killer has a painter's eye, which I suppose *is* mine."[36] Eight years later, Cammell would take such self-glorifying transgression to the ultimate extreme: the artist who believed there was beauty to be found in the inherently violent act of murder took *himself* as subject of a terminal artistic statement.[37]

Murder as art

Not long after *White of the Eye*'s initial murder sequence, Detective Mendoza and a crew of police officers arrive at the dead woman's apartment to survey the damage. Although a relatively brief scene, consisting of only ten shots and lasting just a couple of minutes, it is nevertheless worth going over in some detail. For what we find here is a continuation and furthering of the murderer-as-artist theme, not so much through first-person camerawork, montage editing, and sound effects as through mise-en-scene and dialogue.

The scene begins with a shot of Mendoza walking into the apartment, the victim's body having already been removed. We then cut to a shot, presumably from Mendoza's PoV, of the interior. At first glance, it looks like utter chaos. But as the camera slowly proceeds inside, we notice that various items have been arranged quite self-consciously (again, whether by the killer or the director is a moot point). The now-empty goldfish bowl and one high-heeled shoe have been positioned carefully atop a white blouse which is resting on the smashed microwave, itself sitting on a table in the middle of the room. This collection of items is more sculpture or pop-art than still life, and it forces the detective – now standing in for the viewer – into the role of art interpreter and critic. In much the same fashion as *Manhunter* (1987), *The Silence of the Lambs* (1991), *Se7en* (1996), and *The Apostate* (1998), the detective/spectator must attempt to determine the meaning of, or message in, the crime scene.[38] Former FBI serial killer profiler Robert Ressler explains that "a disorganized crime scene displays the confusion of the killer's mind, and has spontaneous and symbolic qualities that are commensurate with his delusions."[39] In *White of the Eye*, it is obvious that the crime scene has "spontaneous and symbolic qualities" that are to be understood as somehow commensurate with the killer's delusions; what remains open is the extent to which the scene is "disorganized" or (what amounts to the same thing) whether it is indeed accurate to describe Paul White's mind as confused. For the possibility exists – one that is never completely eliminated – that his mind is quite clear, at least in some sense. And that is a far more sinister and disturbing conclusion at which to arrive.[40]

Next we cut to a high-angle shot of Mendoza reaching down to pull a plastic covering off a bizarre arrangement of objects (cf. shot #10 in the murder scene discussed above). A pot with something unidentifiable in it, possibly an internal organ, is surrounded by four kitchen knives with their blades turned outwards. The pot is sitting on a white table – another canvas – and what appears to be the victim's blood is smeared off to the left. It is in reference to this constellation of objects that Mendoza remarks to no one in particular, "I know a goddamn work of art when I see one." Nowhere in his oeuvre does Cammell make a more direct appeal to his viewers' aesthetic sensibilities. The camera lingers on the pot and knives, then moves in for a closer look. But what makes Mendoza so sure this is a "work of art"? After all, it is not something most of us would be inclined to call beautiful.

Cammell's response to this might well be that beauty is in the eye of the beholder, and moreover, that a work does not have to be "beautiful" in the traditional (i.e., culturally-sanctioned) sense of the term to be art. Aesthetic experience comes in a wide variety of

17 The association of violence, beauty, and nature extends to *White of the Eye*'s (1987) poster art

forms, some a great deal less pleasant, or pleasurable, than others. According to cultural theorist Joel Black, "Violent acts compel an aesthetic response in the viewer of awe, admiration, or bafflement. If an action evokes an aesthetic response, then it is logical to assume that this action – even if it is a murder – must have been the work of an artist."[41] Since certainly not *all* violent acts "compel an aesthetic response in the viewer of awe, admiration, or bafflement," however, the question remains as to just where the difference lies. Cammell's description of Paul White as a "serial killer [who] happens to be a psychotic with an aesthetic imagination"[42] can be taken as the beginning of an answer.

In his life, as in his films, Donald Cammell stylized violence so as to produce a rift between the aesthetic and the ethical. The murderer-as-artist, by taking it upon himself to violate the physical and psychological boundaries of his victims, is free to express himself and leave his mark in any way he desires. "Didn't you ever look at a Picasso?", Mendoza asks his partner, referring to the self-conscious arrangement of pot and knives left behind by the killer at the crime scene. "Picasso, my ass" is the cynical, naïve reply. But Mendoza is not to be deterred: "We're talking post-Cubist Picasso ... or maybe even later." Some viewers may be inclined to laugh at this exchange, thinking it pretentious at best, totally inappropriate at worst. But in Cammell's defense, it is clear that he is less interested in comparing Paul White's work with that of post-Cubist Picasso at the level of technical skill than of visceral impact. In this context, it may be worth calling to mind *Guernica*, Picasso's 1937 testimony to the horrors of the Spanish Civil War – a painting of terrible beauty, replete with symbolic archetypes and encoded meaning.[43]

Notes

1 Tom Dewe Matthews, "Shoot to Kill," *Guardian* (May 1, 1996): 4.
2 Kevin Macdonald, "Donald Cammell: When He Shot Himself, Did He Set the Scene For His Finest Show?", *Observer* (May 3, 1998): 9.
3 Matthews, "Shoot to Kill."
4 Macdonald, "Donald Cammell."
5 *Ibid.*
6 Jorge Luis Borges, "Theme of the Traitor and the Hero," in *Labyrinths: Selected Stories and Other Writings*, ed. James Irby and Donald Yates (New York: New Directions, 1964), 74–5.
7 Mick Brown, "The Final Cut," *Telegraph Magazine* (May 9, 1998).
8 Macdonald, "Donald Cammell."
9 Geoffrey Macnab, "What a Great Performance," *Independent* (May 1, 1998): 8.
10 See Steven Jay Schneider, "Murder as Art/The Art of Murder: Aetheticizing Violence in Modern Cinematic Horror," *Dark Thoughts: Philosophic Reflections on Cinematic Horror*, ed. Steven Jay Schneider and Daniel Shaw (Lanham, MD: Scarecrow Press, 2003): 174–97.
11 Leonard Klady, "*White of the Eye* Peers Inside Horror's Disturbing Territories," *LA Times* (June 3, 1988), pt. 6: 6.
12 Margaret Tracey, *Mrs. White* (New York: Dell, 1983).
13 China Kong qtd. in the 1998 BBC documentary, *Donald Cammell: The Ultimate Performance* (dir. Kevin Macdonald and Chris Rodley).

14 David Del Valle, "Memo From Cammell," *Video Watchdog* 35 (1996): 33.
15 *Ibid.*
16 Shades of *Psycho* here. Actually, *White of the Eye*'s opening scene (discussed in detail above), which includes a bird's-eye view of an Arizona cityscape, is reminiscent of *Psycho*'s opening. By way of contrast, Klaven's novel takes place in small-town New England.
17 In *Donald Cammell: The Ultimate Performance*, Kong remarks on the difficulty she and Cammell had writing Paul's dialogue in this scene, since they wanted to depict a man who was insane but who nevertheless "made a kind of sense" and had "a religious point of view."
18 David Thomson, "The Sunday Movie," *Independent* (May 17, 1998): 3.
19 One may be tempted to conclude that Cammell is engaged in a distinctly "postmodern" experiment here. But despite the non-linear violent set-pieces and the homages to Hitchcock, Godard, and Argento, the complete absence of self-reflexivity in *White of the Eye* – the characters never evince any awareness of their fictional status, for example – as well as the film's relative lack of intertexual generic references, renders postmodernism a less than ideal axis upon which to analyze it. For more on postmodern horror, see, for example, Tania Modleski, "The Terrors of Pleasure: The Contemporary Horror Film and Postmodern Theory," in *Studies in Entertainment: Critical Approaches to Mass Culture*, ed. Tania Modleski (Bloomington: Indiana UP, 1986), 155–66; and Steven Jay Schneider, "Kevin Williamson and the Rise of the Neo-Stalker, *Post Script: Essays in Film and the Humanities* 19.2 (2000): 73–87.
20 Stephen Prince, *Savage Cinema: Sam Peckinpah and the Rise of Ultra-violent Movies* (Austin: University of Texas Press, 1998), 48.
21 By way of comparison, *Psycho*'s famous shower scene employs somewhere between 65 and 78 cuts in about a three-minute time interval.
22 In his interview with Del Valle, Cammell proudly notes that he "directed several rock videos" in the years just prior to *White of the Eye*'s release. In his own estimation, the "Memo from Turner" sequence in *Performance* "is probably the first rock video." He also points out that he "did a bit of editing on *Gimme Shelter* for the Maysles Brothers" (33).
23 *Ibid.*
24 See Laura Mulvey, "Visual Pleasure and Narrative Cinema" (1975), in *Film Theory and Criticism: Introductory Readings* (5th edn), ed. Leo Braudy and Marshall Cohen (New York: Oxford University Press, 1999), 833–44.
25 Del Valle, "Memo From Cammell," 34.
26 In effect, the numerous shots from the killer's perspective constitute

unclaimed PoV's. Carol Clover argues that this convention is part of the "gender-identity game" played by the slasher film subgenre: "we are invited, by conventional expectation and by glimpses of 'our' own bodily parts – a heavily-booted foot, a roughly-gloved hand – to suppose that 'we' are male, but 'we' [may be] revealed, at film's end, as a woman." Carol Clover, *Men, Women, and Chainsaws: Gender in the Modern Horror Film* (Princeton: Princeton University Press, 1992), 56.

27 Prince, *Savage Cinema*, 72.

28 Jack Katz, *Seductions of Crime: Moral & Sensual Attractions in Doing Evil* (New York: Basic Books, 1988), 31.

29 Geoff Andrew, quoted. in Kevin Jackson, "A Final Memo From Turner," *Guardian* (May 9, 1996): T2.

30 Matthews, "Shoot to Kill."

31 Del Valle, "Memo From Cammell," 33.

32 Nigel Andrews, "Psychedelic View of a Schizophrenic Killer," *Financial Times* (June 19, 1987): 19.

33 Macdonald: 9. Cf. Cammell's reply to Del Valle, who observes that, in another of *White of the Eye*'s violent set pieces, "your painter's eye seems to be at work": "Well yes, I painted it as best I can, and if art is to be involved at all, you hope that some kind of energy or sincerity will result in some kind of revelation" (33–4).

34 Theodore Ziolkowski, "A Portrait of the Artist as a Criminal," in *Dimensions of the Modern Novel: German Texts and European Contexts* (Princeton: Princeton University Press, 1969), 290–1.

35 Joel Black, *The Aesthetics of Murder: A Study in Romantic Literature and Contemporary Culture* (Baltimore: Johns Hopkins University Press, 1991), 38.

36 Del Valle, "Memo From Cammell," 34.

37 Colin Wilson writes of the similarities between murderers and artists: "[Outsiders who become killers] share certain characteristics of the artist; they know they are unlike other men, they experience drives and tensions that alienate them from the rest of society, they possess the courage to satisfy those drives in defiance of society. But while the artist releases his tensions in an act of imaginative creation, the Outsider-criminal releases his in an act of violence." Qtd. in Brian Masters, *Killing for Company: The Case of Denis Nilsen* (London: Cape, 1985), 283.

38 See Schneider, "Murder as Art."

39 Robert Ressler and Tom Shachtman, *Whoever Fights Monsters* (New York: St. Martin's, 1992), 135.

40 See *n.*16 above. According to Cammell, "I suppose I'm really asking [in *White of the Eye*] if we really know the people we love. Do we really understand their motives?" (Del Valle, "Memo From Cammell," 34).

41 Black, *The Aesthetics of Murder*, 39.

42 Del Valle, "Memo From Cammell," 34.
43 My thanks to Richard Allen, Joel Black, Noël Carroll, Thomas
    Elsaesser, Peter Playdon, Stephen Prince, Sam Umland, Rebecca
    Umland, and the anonymous referees at *Scope* for helpful feedback on
    earlier versions of this essay.

8

Terrence Malick's war film sutra: meditating on *The Thin Red Line*

Fred Pfeil

The title, white over black, fades out and a two-note organ chord emerges from the ensuing darkness and silence. As this chord's slow crescendo levels off, the image fades in of a crocodile on a bank, seen straight on at first in a medium shot which follows via a smooth pan as the animal slides into a body of water whose bright green algae'd surface its dark green glide gently cleaves. The camera zooms in on the crocodile's head; the chord, having shifted towards resolution, abates; the crocodile submerges and the chord continues to fade, as the image of the algae-frosted water purling over its vanished head gives way in an equivalently slow dissolve to a medium-long shot, at near-ground level, of a banyan tree amidst rainforest, its moist morning haze transmuted by sunlight into rays of radiant smoke. A few seconds more, the chord still fading; and a straight cut to what we might well be tempted to read as a reverse shot from ground-level by the banyan to the sunlight speckling or streaming down in smoking silver-blue rays through the sky of leaves above, panning and swiveling across that green irradiated sky as the last of the chord is replaced by a human voice, the drawling tones of an American Southerner unhurriedly posing (whose voice? from where? to whom?) a series of queries: *"What's this war in the heart of nature? Why does nature vie with itself . . . the land contend with the sea?"*

Thus the first minute of the film called *The Thin Red Line*, written and directed by Terrence Malick, and released by Twentieth-Century Fox in December 1998 with considerable hoopla as the director's return to filmmaking after two decades of self-imposed silence. But despite the publicity surrounding its release, *The Thin Red Line* fared rather poorly, both at the box office and at the hands of many if not most critics. The latter, indeed, might well have reflected larger audience misgivings about Malick's new film, in the two lines to which they tended to hew. Mainstream notices, like the brief that ran in *People* or the review that Roger Ebert wrote for the Chicago papers, were wont to criticize the film for failing to offer its viewers stable and secure points of identification – a clear protagonist, that is, and a story line in which to become absorbed.[1] Meanwhile, however, and conversely, critics outside and to the left of mainstream media – Stuart Klawans in *The Nation*, Colin McCabe in *Sight and Sound* – excoriated the same film for its failure to ground its characters and actions within any specific historico-political context, and subsequent forfeiture of any opportunity for political or ideological critique.[2]

As any viewer of *The Thin Red Line* must admit, both these sorts of complaints are amply justified. Indeed, my sense is that the best way to introduce you to the kind of film *The Thin Red Line* is and the sort of attention it invites and rewards is precisely by comparison with the sorts of war films these two sets of critics and audiences prefer and expect to see. How, then, do those other types of films – say, for example, the Spielberg smash *Saving Private Ryan* (1998), and, alternatively, Stanley Kubrick's critically acclaimed *Full Metal Jacket* (1987) – induct their audiences into the kinds of viewing they require?

Spielberg and Kubrick: conventions of war

Let us take *Saving Private Ryan* (1998) first, since its solicitations and satisfactions are surely more familiar to most of us. And let us set aside, at least for the moment, the ideological implications of the fact that the film opens (and concludes!) with a shot of the American flag, accompanied by a Coplandesque trumpet call. For what is more important for our present purposes than the film's thematic conservatism is the conservative nature of its very narrativity, which following these opening flourishes quickly draws our attention to a particular character – the old paterfamilias who is first followed, then framed by his surrounding family as he leads them through the vet's cemetery to the gravesite at which, overwhelmed, he falls to his knees. Here the camera moves in to an extreme close-up as his gaze quickens and blurs, intensely drawn back, we feel, following the internalized conventions of our own Hollywood-habituated viewing, to what the slow dissolve now reveals . . . long shots of a fortified coast and choppy sea with many landing craft approaching, seen behind a title announcing "Omaha

Beach, June 7, 1944." This is followed by a straight cut to a close-up of hands, dirty and trembling, on board one of the landing crafts, the hands of – now the shot opens up – Tom Hanks! So *that's* who the old man was in that introductory scene, and *this* is what and where and when that old man's remembering!

Actually, by the time the film is done we'll realize we've been misled; for that old man back at the beginning turns out to be not Tom Hanks, owner of the trembling hands to which the dissolve led us, but the Private Ryan Hanks' Captain Miller and his men follow special humane orders from the top to find and save. By then, though, we will be inclined to forgive the miscue. For the film's moments of suture between its main and framing narratives – between Tom Hanks telling Matt Damon with his dying breath he has to "earn it," i.e., make himself worthy of the lives that have been spent to rescue him, and the old man in the frame narrative who plaintively asks the loyal wife standing dutifully behind him if he has really been "a good man" – help us understand that such a trick has been played on us only in the service of the vision of a nation-blessed, righteous line of hierarchical-masculinist descent, from Abraham Lincoln to General George Marshall to Hanks' Captain Miller to Matt Damon's Private Ryan, now grown into a good old American father himself.

Thus this deceptive employment of the familiar codes of classical Hollywood style only reinforces the film's otherwise total faithfulness to those codes, and the type of story they were designed to deliver. Scenes composing such a story thus typically begin with a long shot or two, to situate Hanks/Miller and his men in their present milieu, then break down that space into closer shots of the characters as the action proceeds, albeit, in battle scenes especially, alternating between long shot and mid- or even close-up, to knit together the subjective experience of the characters with more objective views of what is going on. Likewise, the framing and composition of the shots themselves within such editing patterns tend to center on Hanks/Miller, who thereby "naturally" becomes, by virtue of these visual practices plus Hanks' star power, the one we come to know best and care for most. In these ways, *Saving Private Ryan*'s visual style and syntax are well-suited to deliver a plot which conforms to those norms described and summarized by David Bordwell as follows:

> The classical Hollywood film presents psychologically defined individuals who struggle to solve a clear-cut problem or to attain specific

goals. In the course of this struggle, the characters enter into conflicts with others or with external circumstances. The story ends with a decisive victory or defeat, a resolution of the problem and a clear achievement or non-achievement of the goal. The principal causal agency is thus the character, a discriminated individual endowed with a consistent batch of evident traits, qualities, and behaviors . . . The most "specified" character is usually the protagonist, who becomes the principal causal agent, the target of any narrational restriction, and the chief object of audience identification. . . . [T]he reliance upon character-centered causality and the definition of the action as the attempt to achieve a goal are both salient features of the canonic format.[3]

The contrast here is already obvious: for even the first minute of *The Thin Red Line* cues us that it has something else in mind besides such a story. So, continuing on from that opening, we are treated to nearly another minute-and-a-half-long montage of dreamily dissolve-connected images of Melanesian people and their natural surroundings before the first available (i.e., white, male, American) candidate for the owner of that querying voice appears – after which another minute yet will pass before we both see and hear him speak, and so are more or less definitely able to assign that voice to this face. Even then, moreover, our habituated inclination to think this guy might turn out to be the film's protagonist, center and focus of the storyline to come, is likely to be somewhat mitigated by the fact that the actor playing the role, James Cavaziel, brings little if any star power from past films to this one. And a good thing, too, given the limited and qualified extent to which he does fill a protagonist's role in the shots, scenes and actions to come. How, then, we might well ask, do the style, effects, and apparent intentions of Malick's film differ from those of another movie also held together only weakly at best by its nominal protagonist, Kubrick's *Full Metal Jacket*? Aside from their different settings, are they really the same sort of film?

It is a reasonable question, since Kubrick's film is fueled by its refusal to be a classical Hollywood war movie. For starters, rather than offering us a linear story line, it is split down the middle into two distinct settings and stories, the first in Parris Island during Basic Training, the second in Vietnam, just before, then during, the 1968 Tet Offensive – the separateness of each emphasized by the pro-longed fade halfway through the film separating the first from the second. And *Full Metal Jacket* takes its time selecting and settling

18 *"What's this war in the heart of nature?"* The unconventional opening of
The Thin Red Line (1998)

itself down around a protagonist as well. We are past the film's
credit-sequence montage of the new inductees getting their hair
sheared away, and well into its subsequent opening scene, in which
the brutal drill instructor Sergeant Hartman (R. Lee Ermey) delivers
his first harangue to the newest group of "pukes" under his command, before there is any direct interaction between Hartman and
the recruit we come to know only as "Joker" (Matthew Modine) –
and that interaction itself is no more than equivalent to the equally
nasty brow-beatings the Sergeant deals out within the same scene to
two other men. This opening scene, moreover, is followed by an
episodic montage of Basic Training in which such narrative energy
and visual focus as there are fall largely not upon Joker but upon the
character Hartman christens "Pyle" (Vincent D'Onofrio). Only gradually, almost desultorily, will Joker come to play an important role in
an episodic, come-and-go plot centered mainly on the accumulated
humiliations and punishments meted out, first by Hartman, then by
the whole platoon, on poor, flabby Pyle, leading up to the patently
psychotic state in which Pyle shoots first Hartman then himself.

To be sure, just before the moment of his first face-to-face
encounter with Hartman in that opening scene, we have heard the
voiceover of the character soon to be dubbed "Joker" breaking
through the film's ominous stillness to announce where we are. But
here and throughout the film, diegetically and in voiceover, the very

flatness of Joker's wisecracking voice, like the studied, ironic impassivity of Modine (an actor devoid, then and now, of a classical star's attracting aura), militates against our investment in his character or concern for his destiny. So, too, with the camerawork and editing throughout each of the film's two halves, which eschew the security and satisfaction of the classical style's typical intrascenic movement between objective establishment shots and those closer and more subjective framings that take us into the scene's action. Instead, Kubrick's camerawork in a given scene is apt to begin with a long shot in motion, capturing some movement which often is already underway – as when, at the beginning of the film's second half, it follows along behind a Vietnamese hooker strolling from the camera's initial vantage point up to the streetcorner café at which Joker and his buddy Raptor (Kevyn Major) are lounging around, or, later, tracks a squad of men some thirty or forty yards away through the ruins of the bombed out Vietnamese city they are entering on patrol. And the film's most extensive deployment of close-ups renders them a far cry from anything like a privileged glimpse into a subjectivity meant to touch or merge with our own: instead, close-ups serve as the building blocks of two montage sequences in which various soldiers in the combat unit Joker has momentarily hooked up with in the Tet Offensive testify to their various canned and coldly detached attitudes towards war and death – in the first sequence, to a military reporter; in the second, around a fresh corpse.

However *Full Metal Jacket* provides two signal exceptions to these self-imposed rules of the game, in the form of one crucial medium-close-up at the climax of each of its two unsutured halves; but these close-ups themselves, precisely in their horrifying power, do no more than prove the rule. The first gives us the leering, gaping face of Pyle, sitting on the toilet with his eyes rolled back in his head, just before killing Hartman and himself; the second, Joker as he forces himself to shoot at point-blank range the wounded female Vietnamese sniper who has just picked off most of the unit he has joined, including his old buddy from Basic, the guy Hartman nicknamed "Cowboy" (Arliss Howard). Each of these close-ups thus takes us straight to the subjectivity of a character at a moment when his defenses have been eroded and destroyed by the violence to which he has been subject, a moment when he is about to render violence back in turn. And each, likewise, provides a sudden, shocking suspension of that kinetic detachment which otherwise characterizes the film's visual style. For *Full Metal Jacket* is quite clearly a film about the brutal and brutalizing depersonalization its very style attempts to imitate and underscore, in its relentless refusal to allow its audience the canonical blandishments of absorption in a gripping linear story, character, identification with a protagonist portrayed by an auratic star, and a safe and secure viewing position from which we can feel and enjoy just as we conventionally please.

The sight of death

How different the quite different styles and projects of these two films are from those of *The Thin Red Line* might best be glimpsed via a simple comparison. Since war films are, by definition, concerned with killing and dying, let us take a death scene from each of our three films, and examine how each stages, shoots, and edits such a scene to produce its particular meanings and effects. Furthermore, to keep our comparison that much more on the level, let us make sure each respective death occurs to a secondary character – yet one for whose death the film slows or suspends its forward movement even so.

In *Saving Private Ryan*, the death I am thinking of is that of the medical corpsman who accompanies Miller and his squad in search of the eponymous private, only to be cut down in an assault on a machine-gun nest the squad encounters on its way. We have only shortly beforehand been given a special glimpse into this character's individual subjectivity, as with his fellows during a brief moment of rest he lapsed into a remorseful and loving memory of his mother back home. Accordingly, when in this subsequent scene what seems to be a hand-held camera first discovers, then closes in on his bleeding self, what we feel first and foremost is the possibility of losing a character we have only just gotten to know; and so, too, when his last words are a cry for "Momma" we feel we have a special connection with his particular, individual dying self. Meanwhile, in this scene's master shot of the corpsman surrounded by his unit, as well as in the rapid cutaways back and forth from these crowded three-, four-, and five-shots to close-ups of the various men and their reactions to his suffering and death, we are given a touching sense of their individual and collective care for him. But those group shots and close-ups alike are framed and edited in such a way as to return our attention most often to Miller's experience; and it is Hanks'

Miller whose exit from the camera's frame tells us that this death scene is through.

   In Kubrick's film there is only one character whose death qualifies for comparison to this young corpsman's: the one named "Cowboy," the only character aside from Joker to appear in both halves of the film. Yet in neither half are we given any glimpse of this character's individuality. Rather, both in Basic and in Vietnam, Cowboy is nothing more nor less than a secondary site of the same defensively ironic patter that so minimally defines Joker himself. Even his last words, uttered as he is centered within a tight five-shot at least roughly similar to the master shot of *Ryan*'s corpsman's death scene, are stunningly defensive and clichéd: "I can hack it," he says, then dies in the arms of Joker, the buddy from Basic who said just a minute ago, to reassure him, "I wouldn't shit you, man, you're my favorite turd." The film holds the same shot through the moment just after Cowboy dies wide-eyed, when Joker bends over from the kneeling position in which he has been holding his – should we say "friend"? – embracing him more closely even as he eases his body to the ground, thereby assuming a somewhat awkward, even goony doubled-over posture with his butt sticking out, from which the film cuts away to a long shot in which the group appears at one with the gray rubble of the battlefield. Only then do we get a closer shot of anyone – and the one we get it of, via another straight cut, is the film's most vicious character, the one whose nickname in the unit is "Animal Mother" (Adam Baldwin), as, in mid-shot, he rounds the corner and says to Joker and the rest of the guys, "Let's go get some payback." And Joker, in a reverse mid-shot that prominently features the peace-sign button on his jacket, says "Okay."

   Against both the ironized flatness of this scene from Kubrick's film, then, and the careful guidance of our prioritized sympathies and identifications in the scene from Spielberg's, let us now juxtapose a death scene from *The Thin Red Line*. The one I have in mind comes from little short of halfway through the film, in the midst of the long stretch devoted to the company's attempt to take a hill on top of which the Japanese are well dug in, and just after a dramatically crucial scene in which the company commander, Lieutenant Staros (Elias Koteas), has refused to obey an order from his superior officer to keep throwing his men directly into the maw of this suicidal assault. With this interpersonal conflict between Staros on the hill and Colonel Tall (Nick Nolte) down below, on which in turn this battle's outcome itself may hang, the film comes as close as it ever gets to focusing our interest on something we could experience and consume as a plot. Yet what follows the scene of Staros' confrontation with Tall is hard to take in as a link in any such focused storyline.

Here is what we are shown, from the moment Staros puts down the field telephone on which he was just talking with Tall, and moves out of the shot. First a straight-cut to an overhead shot some six-to-eight seconds long of some portion of the battlefield, just as something strikes and detonates, so that as the camera backs up from the explosion we are looking down in long shot on a soldier's body in upper screen right; then a cut to someplace else which might or might not be the same partly grassy, partly-wooded gully where Staros just was; and a ten- or twelve-second medium-close up of another soldier, presumably a sergeant, urging the men around him to move on out. Another straight cut, then, and we are gazing at a near-ground level medium-long two-shot of another soldier bracing up a young man we have seen off and on from early in the film, when we first glimpsed him below deck on the troopship, an unnamed soldier we recall primarily by virtue of his startlingly child-like appearance – that, and his particular palefaced, staring, shivering way of manifesting his pre-battle fear. Neither then nor since have we learned his name, nor heard him say a word; nor, for that matter, do we know now the site or circumstances of his wounding.

Someone enters the shot from screen right: Staros, we soon see, though after how much time since his last scene or from how far away we cannot tell. The sun streams through the trees and foliage behind them, as we saw it doing from above in some of the film's opening shots; there are trails of blood coming from both of the young man's ears. He calls in a weak, trembling voice for someone named Fife (Adrien Brody), who shows up, in anguished and terrified close-up, on the other side of him from Staros, but who can say nothing; nor can we make out anything the gasping, whimpering young man murmurs to him other than his name. Viewed more closely from front on, the dying boy looks up; and the film cuts to a long shot from below of some treetops, with light radiating down in thick streams, again as in the film's opening montage. Cut to another close-up of Staros; then two very quick, quite disparate shots, each between three and six seconds long, under eight beautiful bars of the soundtrack music we've been hearing off and on since the battle and the killing began. The first begins as an otherwise soundless close-up from behind an unknown soldier who is struck and falls over as the camera moves up over and past him; the second is a stationary medium close-up of another, equally unknown man in the tall grass clutching his head and writhing in torment, the sound of his screams replaced by the same stately soundtrack hymn which rises and resolves, rises and resolves, four bars at a time. Now, still riding on that soundtrack, we are back via yet another straight cut to the medium close-up from front on of the dying boy; another close-up of Staros; a close-up of three leaves, speckled with holes, through which the light shines radiantly through. Another close-up of Staros; and the sequence closes with another medium close-up of the anonymous boy, who is now dying, slumping, dead, and from the final sight of whom the film dissolves to a long shot of the smoking field on which the next scene or shot sequence will begin.

The death scene I have just described exhibits several features that both resemble yet depart from both Spielberg's and Kubrick's opposed modes of cinematic narrative. For Malick is up to something that is, in a sense, in between the two, yet in another sense altogether different from those other films' respective meanings and effects: something that derives from the fact that we have seen the young man here and there throughout the film thus far, as one among others similarly distinguished yet unidentified: on the ship, on patrol, running forward or pinned down in his own particular version of terror in the hill's long grass; just as in this scene, in the terrible specificity of his mumbled words, his sweaty hair, tossing head, and brokenhearted frightened gaze, he is now become the event of this one ineluctably, heartbreakingly particular death. In effect, Malick depicts this not as the death of an individual self, defined in the conventionalized bourgeois sense as both a "discrete, isolate, unique" and a "constant stable thing,"[4] but as the passing away of one of an infinite, and infinitely precious, number of *singularities* – a term whose meaning with regard to characterization in *The Thin Red Line* may now be further specified by connecting what we have just seen with the film's overall perverse deployment of such star power and aura as it contains.

After all – to make the same point from the opposite direction – this is a war flick with George Clooney, Nick Nolte, John Travolta, Woody Harrelson, Sean Penn, and John Cusack in it: but where are they at the moment of this moving death scene, or for that matter, through most of the rest of the film? Surely, if any of them appeared in a scene like this one, he would bring with him some traits and associations from his previous films; and surely, then, that star image would contribute to our sense of the kind of more or less "constant stable thing" his particular character is in this film as well. But Clooney and Travolta appear only briefly, playing officers whose thoughts and words are scarcely relevant to the company of named and unnamed men we follow through the film; Harrelson, shockingly, shows up only long enough to make a mistake with a grenade that gets him killed; Cusack plays a somewhat larger part, that of a captain attached to Colonel Tall, who volunteers to lead the small squad of men who succeed in taking out a lethal Japanese machine-gun nest. Only Nick Nolte as Tall has something like a fully individualized characterization, complete with occasional voiceover, as a middle-aged career officer pitted out with self-loathing for what his disappointed ambitions have led him to; but his role in the film ends just past its halfway mark. Likewise, of all these stars, only Sean Penn, as Sergeant Welsh, the hostile yet helpful interlocutor of the film's demi-protagonist Witt, plays a role that comes and goes throughout the film and is central to it – but he plays a character, like Nolte's Tall, and perhaps even more like *Full Metal Jacket*'s Joker, hard at work armoring up against any hope or openness through which he might be hurt.

In effect, then, the actors with star power to their names mainly portray peripheral characters who are typically shut down against any opening to what the film is most deeply about; conversely, it is left to other actors without star power to appear most often and attract the greater part of our interest and involvement. Yet when it comes to even these characters – Witt or Bell or Staros, say – the film has several ways of modifying our investment habits. We have already noted how long it takes, at the beginning of the film, for us to feel at all confident that the nondiegetic voice we have been hearing belongs to Witt; so, too, it will be with Bell as well, whose voiceovers expressing his yearning and commitment to his wife feature a drawl that sounds, quite deliberately I should think, a lot like Witt's. Sometimes the voiceover is clearly assignable to one of them, or to some other, more briefly yet still quite vividly seen character. At other times, and especially when, as at the beginning, some voiceover utters some *koan*-like questions, it is less as though individualized characters were posing the questions than as if the questions spoke themselves through the voices available to them. Such queries arrive, then, from the outer edge of what we are accustomed to regard *as* character; indeed, one especially startling conjuncture of sight and sound suggests that one such series of questions reaches us via the now-stilled voice and extinct mind of a dead Japanese.

Carried by the voices articulating them, such queries drift over the picture in a haze of mild indeterminacy, of personal impersonality, as they do one last time in the film's final few moments:

> Where is it that we were together? Who were you that I lived with – walked with? The brother. The friend. Darkness and light. Strife and love. Are they the workings of one mind, the features of the same face? O my soul, let me be in you now. Look out through my eyes – look out at the things you made. All things shining.

Is it the now-dead Witt who makes these remarks from beyond the grave, over a shot sequence depicting the remaining members of the company getting back onto a troop carrier and moving out – some of the many singularities we have, however briefly, lived through in the course of the film looking one way, some another, some gazing straight ahead, some back at the boat's seething wake? Probably so, I suppose, but just maybe not, as in the film's beginning; and just as in the beginning but now in reverse, the film moves back to a montage of undisturbed nature – a small group of islanders in long shot, paddling in green water next to a coast; a pair of parrots in close-up grooming one another on a branch; another close-up, this one at ground-level, of a new palm sprouting on a beach, surrounded by the world but all by itself – as it draws to a close.

And as with the film's floating, not-quite-individualized voiceovers, so it is with the film's diegesis, both on a shot-by-shot level and structurally. Returning one last time to our death scene, for example, consider first the relationship between the mid-close-up of the young soldier as he turns his head and gaze upwards, and the long shot from below of the light streaming down through the trees. Surely, given our conventionalized habits, we will be tempted to read this latter shot's relation to its predecessor as an eyeline match or point-look, merging our view, and thereby our subjectivity, with the dying boy's. But what then happens to our confidence in this reading when it comes up against those two quick shots of disparate, suffering soldiers that follow the close-up of Staros that comes next – or when, after another return to the dying boy and Staros, we are given that close-up of the sun streaming through those three hole-speckled leaves? The Holly-

19 The passing away of one of an infinite number of "singularities" in *The Thin Red Line* (1998)

wood film style to which we are all accustomed customarily offers us only two ways of viewing or interpreting a given shot or shot squence: as a subjectively motivated view, assignable to a particular character, or as an objective view whose function is to keep us grounded in a particular time and bounded space. Yet the shots given us at these two moments resist any effort to read them either subjectively – as, say, the involuntary recall of either Staros or the dying boy – or objectively, as object or occurrence within this scene's exterior space.

How then should we view and interpret such shots and their ilk, which appear in the midst of any number of otherwise bounded and grounded scenes in *The Thin Red Line*? Within the scene we are examining, it seems to me the interjection of those shots of one soldier falling and another screaming stretches our awareness out towards the whole field of subjective human singularities – exhausted or exultant, furiously anguished or stilly withdrawn – within which the scene's two principals are having their particular experiences and interactions. And likewise, the shot of the leaves, like many others of light and landscape, flora and fauna, dispersed throughout the film, returns us to the much wider stream of processual activity within which human actions and experience of no greater and no less import are also always taking place.

In both cases, then, these shots and others like them function to soften what would otherwise be the clearly-defined edges of our conventional sense of both character and scene, and, in so doing, to enfold both within a much larger webwork. And some analogous sense of "enfoldment within" might also be used to describe the place of conventionally linear plot within *The Thin Red Line*'s wider field of eventfulness as well. For the very shape of the film colludes with its visual texture in resisting reduction to any such dramatically cumulative, plot-driven, character-centered narrative. To start off, as we have seen, it takes a good while even to get clearly around to Witt, the character we are most likely to bet on as the protagonist. Then, without explanation or transition, the film cuts abruptly from his first sight of the patrol boat from the island on which he is apparently AWOL to the troopship from which, back together with his company, he is about to embark on a new campaign. And from then on, through the boat's approach and landing and well into the awful campaign to take that grassy hill, he and his voiceover are basically absent from the film, displaced, in effect, by a slew of other characters, some seen and/or heard only briefly, though always memorably; others, like Staros, Welch, and Bell, showing up for longer stretches of time. Witt himself, like these others, comes and goes throughout *The Thin Red Line*, until he dies; and that death takes place somewhere else, and sometime later, well after the battle for the hill – which is itself concluded and left behind somewhere around halfway through the film.

Some critics, and no doubt some regular viewers as well, have chastised Malick for not making that battle his film's climactic event. But his decision not to do so seems to me the equivalent, on the level of emplotment, of what I have tried to argue he is up to stylistically as well. By placing this section of the film somewhere around its halfway point, and following it up with another, much more desultory section depicting the company's time of rest behind the lines, and then by yet another stretch of action, he achieves a structural effect quite different from that cold detachment which the broken-backed dual structure of Kubrick's film encourages us to adopt. What the elongated structuration and measured pacing of *The Thin Red Line* suggests, by contrast, is that Malick is less concerned with refusing and rebelling against the norms of conventional cinematic narrative than with decathecting and diffusing that narrative's bottled-up energy by positioning such crucial "plot points" on a much wider and more dispersed field in which every moment and each stretch of action is as singularly distinct and important as any and all others. There is, in other words, a plot enfolded *within The Thin Red*

Line; but the film's structure and pace seem designed to deliver something other, and more, than just a plot.

Abiding nowhere

But just what is that "something more"? If *The Thin Red Line* distributes our attention and cultivates our caring across a much broader field and wider bandwidth than those delineated for us either by a conventional Hollywood film like *Saving Private Ryan* or an anti-humanist arthouse feature like *Full Metal Jacket*, how to say what that field is?

I cannot claim the right to affix some once-and-for-all label to *The Thin Red Line*'s uncentered and ultimately unnarrativizable network of punctual moments and singular experiences. But I *can* say what that field or network seems to me to resemble, and what giving Malick's picture the kind of attention it solicits and rewards reminds me of out here beyond the film. For the more I have given myself over to where and how it moves and what it shows, the more vibrantly comprehensible, even exemplary, it has come to seem to me from a Buddhist perspective – or, if you will, as a Buddhist film. *"What's this war in the heart of nature?"* You'll recall that question, posed by a Witt-like voice, and floating over those images of nature, and humans in nature, from this film's opening. Consider, then, *The Thin Red Line* as a response to that question – a response that is not so much solution or answer as a representation of a group of men in battle *within* a nature that includes all its subjectivities, experiences, and events within itself. Putting the same point in yet more explicitly Buddhist terms, we might say that by placing and re-placing the war it depicts within a non-human nature that precedes and succeeds it, Malick's film depicts the limited, deluded world of *samsara* – the conventional, narrowly purposeful reality of most but not all its characters, most but not all of the time – within a perspective which, like that of *nirvana* or enlightenment, neither critiques nor affirms that limited world but rather absorbs and encompasses it.

"Each moment," said Zen master Dogen centuries ago, "is all being, is the entire world."[5] And I hope to have provided some evidence of how the enactments, shots, and arrangements that compose Malick's film encourage us to view it in just such an open-minded way. It is a way very like what happens via meditative practice: as when, for example, one has seriously brought the most elemental *koan* of all, *What* is *this?* to bear on one's immediate, instant-by-instant experience for some considerable length of time, until the question begins to ask itself; or has simply begun to register the coming and going of all kinds of events – thoughts, feelings, sensations, memories, whatever – via a bare awareness that neither seizes hold of those events nor pushes them away. The meditator at such times does not so much construct such bare awareness as discover the "mind that abides nowhere"[6] – that no-mind field of awareness, that is, which subtends and pre-exists the clinging and/or aversive operation of conventional mind in the latter's endless restless project of sorting through each moment's range of choices for whatever can be used to re-construct and defend an illusory sense-of-self. The relationship of this "no-mind" awareness to our customarily deluded self-centered experience is thus neither detached nor identificatory: awareness simply allows even such experience to be taken in and to pass on through – just as *The Thin Red Line* takes in the self-experience of its characters with a benign, hospitable, non-attached regard that invites our compassionate awareness for the singularity of each experiential moment, and the causes and conditions that have given rise to it, while enfolding all – subjective experience, external circumstances, causes, and conditions alike – within its wider field and broader flow.

To view, and invite us to view, the complex and terrible knot of pride and will, hope and suffering, pain and fear and violence we call "war" with the non-attached yet compassionate regard of a "mind that abides nowhere" is surely an extraordinary achievement, given the fervor with which self-centeredness is celebrated, pursued, and worshipped as an article of faith within the culture we inhabit today. Nor, conversely, given its centrality, should it surprise us to have found such self-centeredness at the heart of *Saving Private Ryan*, which both stylistically and thematically clings to it for dear life, and at the cold core of *Full Metal Jacket*'s aversive rage at the brutal processes by which such selfhood is stunted and destroyed. By contrast, in the ways *The Thin Red Line* both literally and figuratively "sees *through* the self," it invites us to contemplate the possibility and prospect of a realm of insight not transcendentally above such "self-ing" operations but around and within them, even in battle and death enfolding that sense-of-self to which we cling. For as the ancient sutra has it: "to the extent that one does not take hold of things and does not settle down in them, to that extent can one conceive of the absence of I- and mine-making."[7]

If Malick's film, while rejecting no experience contained within it, models nonetheless what it means not to "settle down in things," and thereby allows us a sight of "all things shining" (as the last not-quite attributable words we hear within it put it), perhaps we may regard it too as a sutra or meditation, helping us to let go of the "I- and mine-making" by which we are imprisoned, and imprison our-selves. At least so I hope the film may be viewed, even and especially here in the country of its origin and the one from which I write, where the tendencies of greed, hatred, and delusion that give rise to such selfishness presently hold such undisputed sway over our public and private lives alike. But just here, too, logically speaking, resides the contradiction with which both Malick's film and this essay have had to struggle all along: for only insofar as we suspend our Holly-wood- (and Washington-) supported habit of viewing our separate lives as so many movies, each with its own individualized protago-nist/director as star, will we become able to receive what this film – and perhaps life itself – have to show and to give.[8]

Notes

1   Roger Ebert, "Review: The Thin Red Line (1998)," *Chicago Sun-Times* (July 3, 1999). Ebert tells his readers *The Thin Red Line* would have been better "filmed by Spielberg in the style of *Saving Private Ryan*," while the uncredited review in *People Weekly* 51.2 (Jan. 11, 1999) likewise opines that "Malick too often sacrifices characters and plot for flora and fauna" and reaches the same conclusion: "It's no *Saving Private Ryan*" (35).

2   From Stuart Klawans' review of *The Thin Red Line*, for *The Nation* 268.1 (Jan. 4, 1999): "Say what you like against that movie [*Saving Pri-vate Ryan* again!], it's about a specific war, fought for specific reasons in a specific time and place" (43). And so, too, with Colin McCabe in "Bayonets in Paradise," *Sight and Sound* 9.2 (1999): "Malick is not concerned with the citizen army and its political conflicts representing the class and ethnic diversity of the nation; indeed, he has no interest in World War II" (13).

3   David Bordwell, *Narration in the Fiction Film* (Madison: University of Wisconsin Press, 1985), 157.

4   W. J. Harvey, *Character in the Novel*, qtd. in Richard Dyer, *Stars* (London: BFI, 1979), 107.

5 *Moon in a Dewdrop: Writings of Zen Master Dogen*, ed. Kazuaki Tana-hashi (New York: Farrar, Straus & Giroux, 1995), 77.

6 *The Zen Teaching of Hui Hai*, ed. and trans. John Blofield (London: Rider, 1969), 56.

7 *The Perfection of Wisdom in Eight Thousand Lines and Its Verse Sum-mary*, ed. and trans. Edward Conze (Bolinas: Four Seasons Foundation, 1973), sec. 22, ll. 399–400, 237–8.

8 Special thanks to Elli Findly, Steven Schneider, Todd Vogel, and Brian Waddell for their helpful comments and suggestions.

III

Race and gender

9

From homeboy to *Baby Boy*: masculinity and violence in the films of John Singleton

Paula J. Massood

Violence is not new to American film, nor is it new to the African American cinematic image, which from almost its very beginnings has been characterized either by its potential for violence or for the atrocities experienced by black people on screen. We have only to examine D. W. Griffith's *Birth of a Nation* (1915) to see this duality exemplified, for in Gus (Walter Long), the sexually rapacious black brute who drove innocent Flora Cameron (Mae Marsh) to her death, a specific form of historical violence was enacted. Gus was driven by a lust for white flesh, and his attempted rape of Flora defined African American cinematic masculinity for decades. In the diegesis, Gus's actions were punished (thus alleviating distress among members of the film's white audiences), and his lynching and castration was a graphic warning against black male transgression in a white patriarchal world.

The African American community responded to the dual filmic characterizations of black men as brutish and as deserving of the brutalities they received in a variety of ways. Race film production companies such as the Lincoln Motion Picture Company produced films focusing on black achievement, hoping that their models of bourgeois masculinity would counteract the plethora of Guses on screen. Other filmmakers, such as Oscar Micheaux, directly confronted this cinematic legacy by making films that responded to both filmic and actual atrocities against black people. In *Within Our Gates* (1920), for example, Micheaux suggests the history of the rape of female slaves by white plantation owners, thus providing an alternative version of *Birth*'s rape scenario. Furthermore, in the wrongful punishment of a family at the hands of an angry white mob, Micheaux graphically depicts lynching's savagery and identifies the suspect circumstances surrounding it. Notably, the lynch mob is filled with a collection of men, women, and children, eliminating the chivalrous mythology surrounding the act (protection of white womanhood) and placing the responsibility for white violence equally on the shoulders of men and women.

In a curious interconnectedness of effects, *Birth of a Nation* and *Within Our Gates* – both explorations of similar acts of racial violence from differing points of view – enacted a "violence discourse" based upon a fundamental terror of the inciteful potential of images.[1] Each film met either actual or imagined acts of violence prior to or during screenings, fueling a number of censorship battles across the country. With *Birth of a Nation*, for example, white and black audience members in New York and Boston, respectively, jeered the film and threw eggs at the screen during the "Gus Chase" scene.[2] Micheaux's *Within Our Gates* initiated a different discourse based upon the belief that "'violence on screen' is . . . given the same discursive weight as the real historical events to which the screen image refers."[3] In cities like Chicago, still reeling from the effects of a deadly racial uprising the summer before, the film's opening prompted fears of additional unrest. Each director was required to make multiple cuts, contributing another level of violence to the films (if we are to believe that making cuts in a film or its forced restructuring/rewriting is a form of aggression towards the text).[4]

A discussion of early film production might seem out of place in an essay focusing on John Singleton's films, but it has two purposes. First, it is intended to expand the historical parameters of violence studies beyond the blaxploitation period, the most common reference point for discussions of violence in contemporary black film.[5] Like discussions of American cinema as a whole, which have tended to cite the dissolution of the Production Code as the formative period for American screen violence, films like *Boyz N the Hood* (1991) are most commonly linked back to *Shaft* (1971) and *Superfly* (1972). In blaxploitation film audiences saw, for the first time, empowered black male (and some female) characters on screen. But periodizing in such a manner suggests that brutality did not exist prior to this time. In understanding that African Americans have always had a fraught relationship to American cinema, this discussion argues that what has been increasingly referred to as "new violence" to "characterize a range of films and other media productions, including rap music and popular fiction," is not all that new.[6] American cinema has always been violent, and even more so when focusing on African American subject matter. Often, as the legacy of cinematic lynchings suggests, this violence has been related to gender.

Since the early 1970s, African American directors have pursued a project of self-definition. Filmmakers have engaged in theoretical and stylistic attempts at defining a cohesive black film aesthetic, whether it is associated with dominant industrial practices or produced from within an independent sector. These projects have manifested themselves socially and politically in attempts to identify and differentiate cultural characteristics specific to African American life, an impetus that can best be seen in the influence of the Black Arts Movement, the Los Angeles School of filmmakers and, in different ways, in the blaxploitation narratives produced by Hollywood. What is also complexly imbricated in these endeavors is an attempt to both reclaim and to redefine African American gender roles, especially those related to black men, who, along with black women, had been maligned in the 1960s by policymakers such as Daniel Patrick Moynihan, whose *The Negro Family* (1965) described impoverished inner cities populated by single welfare mothers and absent (and therefore ineffectual) fathers. The result was the hyper-masculine myths and images associated with the Black Panthers, and with their fictional equivalents, Sweetback (Melvin Van Peebles in *Sweet Sweetback's Baadasssss Song*, 1971), John Shaft (Richard Roundtree), and Priest (Ron O'Neal in *Superfly*, 1972). From the 1970s forward, therefore, black masculinity has been representationally associated with either a fist or a gun, thereby "defining the politics of race within a metaphor of phallic power as a counter to cultural articulations of black male inferiority."[7]

Like these earlier images, which were attuned to, and in many ways refracted, the Civil Rights, Black Power, and sociological and political discourses of the time, the hood genre established by John Singleton (by way of Spike Lee's *Do The Right Thing* [1989] and Matty Rich's *Straight Out of Brooklyn* [1991]) and manifesting itself in rap and hip-hop in the early 1990s continued the attempt at self-definition, especially in its endeavor to outline the parameters of a young, black masculinity. Like the preceding blaxploitation and Lee films, Singleton's *Boyz N the Hood* specifically links masculinity to violence by referencing sociological discourses focusing on black youth, inner-city crime, and urban poverty. Unlike the earlier films, however, Singleton's film posits the self-destructive side to the

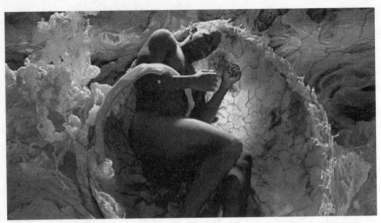

20 A fully-grown Jody (Tyrese Gibson) in utero in John Singleton's *Baby Boy* (2001)

gender/violence linkage first celebrated as empowering in films like Van Peebles' *Sweet Sweetback's Baadassss Song*.

The remainder of this essay will examine the links between masculinity and violence in three films by John Singleton, *Boyz N the Hood*, *Shaft* (2000), and *Baby Boy* (2001). The films offer a perfect opportunity to trace the continuities and ruptures in Singleton's filmmaking style and thematic *foci* over the last decade and they illuminate the tensions faced by many young black filmmakers between making "message" films and making money. The films differ in some ways; for example, *Shaft* is an "action-adventure blockbuster," whereas *Boyz* and *Baby Boy* are low-budget films which combine "action-adventure violence and political or historicized theme[s]," and which are respectively the first and third installments in Singleton's homeboy trilogy.[8] *Shaft* is a generic hybrid, combining the elements of action, blaxploitation, and hood films. *Boyz* and *Baby Boy* are strictly hood films. Despite these differences, each film focuses on interconnected themes first introduced in *Boyz*: violence, family issues, criminality, and constructions of masculinity. Each film defines, to varying degrees, manhood, and this project is often related to characters' attitudes towards violence. The difference, however, is that *Baby Boy* and *Shaft* argue, unlike *Boyz*, for the affectivity of vigilante action as a politically viable form of justice in African American communities, as if suggesting that "revolutionary commitment" is the "image of an armed Black man."[9]

Introducing the new boyz on the block: *Boyz N the Hood*

Boyz N the Hood, Singleton's first film, introduced many of the thematic and stylistic elements that now define his filmmaking. The film is set in South Central Los Angeles, and its coming-of-age narrative details the pressures and constraints of inner-city living experienced by young black men. Stylistically, the film utilizes an aesthetics of immediacy similar to that first seen in African American filmmaking in the 1970s: location shooting in recognizable city spaces (associated with large black communities), contemporary costumes, dialogue inflected with up-to-date urban speech idioms, and a soundtrack featuring contemporary rap and R&B.[10] This sense of temporal immediacy is supported by the performance of rapper Ice Cube as Doughboy, his presence helping Singleton "seize symbolic capital from a real-life rap icon" by adding both diegetic and extra-diegetic authority to the film's homeboy narrative.[11] Singleton has continued this sort of casting in the performances of rap personalities Tupac Shakur in *Poetic Justice* (1993), Busta Rhymes and Bonz Malone in *Shaft*, and Tyrese Gibson and Snoop Dogg in *Baby Boy*.

In addition to its vérité style and the performances of actual rap personalities, *Boyz'* diegesis references its social, political, and industrial context via the narrative. The opening shots introduce the film's major thematic concern – violence – prior to introducing character or setting. In a reflexive inversion of the conventional establishing shot, *Boyz'* opening frames focus on the results of violence in the African American community through text (white words on a black screen) rather than image:

> shot one: "One out of every twenty-one Black American males will be murdered in their lifetime."
> shot two: "Most will die at the hands of another Black male."

The opening titles contribute a sociological authority almost in keeping with the dystopian constructions of inner-city African American life depicted by Moynihan in the 1960s and expanded upon in the 1980s by sociologists and policy-makers such as William Julius Wilson, who argued that inner cities had become populated by an entire generation of minorities to whom poverty, crime, and dysfunction was the norm, not the exception.[12] Unlike Moynihan or Wilson, however, Singleton's intention is to suggest the effects of violence and to agitate against them by extending the negative influences on the community to governmental policies, policing strategies, and unemployment. This approach shifts some (though not all) of the responsibility for urban conditions away from a dys-functional black family and onto social policy.

In its focus on Tre's (Cuba Gooding, Jr.) maturation, *Boyz*'s narrative explores the themes of violence, masculinity, and family/generational issues. The film is split into two parts, an earlier section explaining Tre's move from his mother's to his father's house and establishing the relationship between father and son, and a longer later section focusing on Tre's experiences as a young man in South Central. While separated by a period of several years, the two sections ask a similar question: what does it take to be a man in light of the eco-nomic, political, and social pressures in the hood? The answer is related to the tensions between two options: the maintenance of family and community, and criminality and violence. In *Boyz*, the answer is the former and it appears in the form of Furious (Laurence Fishburne), the metonymic father of the community.

After an incident of misdirected aggression results in Tre's sus-pension from school, his mother Reva (Angela Bassett) surrenders Tre's care to Furious because she "can't teach him how to be a man." The remainder of the film focuses on Furious' lessons, shown in both the earlier and later sections, which include instilling Tre with a work ethic, a sense of history and identity, and a notion of sexual responsibility ("Anyone with a dick can make a baby, it takes a man to take care of his children"). Furious even provides Tre with a knowledge of the potentially destructive power of violence: when their house is burgled early in the film, Furious shoots at the intruder. Later, when Tre expresses his wish that Furious had hit his target, Furious chastises him for wishing for the death of another black man.

In the film's latter half, an almost-grown Tre encounters many of the pressures and tests endured by young black men in South Central. *Boyz* identifies the area as a neighborhood that in the 1980s resembled a war zone, the result of the combined forces of deindustrialization, increased unemployment, the appearance of crack cocaine, the rising influence of gangs, and the heightened civil rights abuses of the LAPD. In these references, combined with its rap intertext, *Boyz* suggests that criminality and gang member-ship is the predominant model of masculinity for black men in the area, as exemplified by Tre's childhood friend Doughboy and his compatriots. Tre avoids gangs and crime, instead excelling at school and work, and *Boyz* suggests that this is due to his father's example.

Furious is a tremendous influence on Tre, and in this way *Boyz* refracts a larger sociological debate about the effects of absent fathers in African American urban communities (a theme that returns in *Baby Boy*). The film stresses the importance of strong father figures as enabling factors in the survival of young black men, and suggests that fathers are essential to the continuing existence of the community. This is apparent when Tre's fate is compared to Ricky (Morris Chestnut) and Doughboy, half-brothers with different but equally absent fathers. Near the end of the film, for example, Ricky is gunned down in a drive-by shooting. A distraught Tre joins Doughboy and his friends in search of the killers. Since we have seen Furious instill a sense of self and an understanding of the destructive power of violence in Tre, it is no surprise that he chooses to leave before additional lives are taken. Both Ricky and Doughboy die violent deaths while Tre survives and escapes the neighborhood, a fact already foreshadowed in Furious' earlier lesson to Tre about avoiding violent acts towards other men.

In Furious, *Boyz* argues for community-building strategies, such as property ownership and family responsibilities, that discourage violence. Its preferred model of masculinity, fully developed in Furious and nascent in Tre throughout most of the narrative, includes a "politics of caring" for the community,[13] including an understanding of the historical and economic factors contributing to the circumstances in urban African American neighborhoods. What this proposal for community-building excludes is an effective model of black womanhood; *Boyz* not only vilifies single black mothers, but suggests that they are just as responsible for the violence in the neighborhood as poverty, unemployment, gangs, and drugs because they cannot teach their sons how to be men.[14] While, as I have mentioned, violence is not particularly new to African American filmic subject matter, it is linked specifically to black men. Hood films, like blaxploitation films, are engaged in a dialogue with an emasculating political, social, economic, and industrial context. The resulting model of masculinity equates violence with manliness. There is little room for women in this model.[15]

From homeboy to *Baby Boy*: Tre grows up

The construction of a specific model of masculinity, and the vilifica-
tion of black women in general, single mothers in particular, continues in Singleton's *Baby Boy*, the third in what he has called his
"hood trilogy" (the second is *Poetic Justice*).[16] *Baby Boy*, even more
than *Poetic Justice*, returns to many of the issues first introduced by
Boyz. *Poetic Justice* is more a road movie than it is a hood film, and
its split focus both on a female and a male lead shifts the genre's
emphasis away from an exclusively male point of view. *Baby Boy*,
on the other hand, is linked to the trilogy's first film in its focus on
violence in African American urban communities and the connections it makes between these outrages, the construction of the black
family, and the endangered black male. Like *Boyz*, *Baby Boy* (and
Shaft) is engaged in an exploration of masculinity and its links
to violence and criminality. The film explores the tensions raised
by a definition of masculinity which is shored up by violent action,
and Jody's (Tyrese Gibson) rite of passage, like Tre's, involves the
decision to murder another man.

Jody, a young man in his early twenties with two children by different women, still lives at home with his mother, Juanita (A. J.
Johnson). Jody is satisfied with this situation until it is upset by two
factors; the presence of Juanita's new boyfriend, Melvin (Ving
Rhames), and his rivalry with Rodney (Snoop Dogg), ex-boyfriend
of Yvette (Taraji Hanson), his main love interest. Melvin, a tattooed,
"OG" (old-school gangsta), upsets the equilibrium in the house by
taking Juanita's attention away from Jody. Rodney upsets Jody's
faux household with Yvette by moving in with her upon his release
from prison. Jody's interactions with Melvin and Rodney are the
most basic conflicts in the film. More deeply, however, the film
posits that Jody's main problem is that he does not know how (or
refuses) to be a man and Melvin and Rodney are presented as the
two models from which he has to choose.

Like the opening shots in *Boyz*, *Baby Boy*'s first scene references a
particular context. The film opens on a shot of a fully-grown Jody,
in utero, as his voice-over declares that a "system of racism" in
America has resulted in a population of young black men who have
remained babies or boys (therefore, not men), and who have failed
to reach their full potential. This scene is granted authority through
its sociological mode of address, which cites *The Isis Papers: The*

Keys to the Colors (1991), by Dr Frances Cress Welsing as proof. While anchored in a specific text, the scene, as well as the film to follow, echoes popular psychological and sociological discourses focusing on the development of black boys. Many have argued for special programs geared towards guiding boys into manhood through an adult male influence, thus averting the "arrested development" experienced by so many young black men (including Jody) who have no male role models.[17]

In addition to the Welsing citation and these other references, the discourses surrounding the film (and being manufactured by the press, the production company, and the director himself) contributed to its assertions of sociological authority. This was especially the case with statements from Singleton, who has consistently claimed experiential authenticity of subject matter. (*Boyz*, for example, was marketed as an authentic rendition of South Central life.) As Singleton suggests, the "movie is like watching the soul of a black man on screen . . . [I]t may be dysfunctional, but it's real. I'm not celebrating something that is not reality; I'm just being honest to a story I'm familiar with."[18] The sociological allusions and claims of verisimilitude provide Jody's subsequent actions with a plausibility that is based on unspecified racism and family dysfunction.

For Singleton, *Baby Boy*'s narrative was not only real, but it also detailed a significant rite of passage for young men in the hood; the choice between committing acts of violence or walking away. Near the end of the film Jody learns that Yvette has been nearly raped by Rodney, who stops his attack, surprisingly, because Yvette and Jody's young son is present (earlier in the film Rodney claims that he has no interest in being the child's father). Rodney has already questioned Jody's manhood on multiple occasions and his attack on Yvette is the ultimate emasculation of Jody. Once Yvette rejects Rodney, he decides to kill Jody in response. When Jody hears of Rodney's attack he is forced to prove his manhood and he, along with his gangsta friend Sweetpea (Omar Gooding), prepare to shoot Rodney by saying a prayer. In a last-minute act of conscience, however, Jody decides that "he is a lover, not a killer." At this point Rodney unsuccessfully shoots at Jody, and the stage is set for Jody's revenge – meted out later when Jody shoots Rodney in the legs and Sweetpea finishes him off.

In this narrative trajectory, *Baby Boy* closely follows *Boyz*. In the latter film, Tre's decision first to take part in a revenge killing and then to leave before any acts of violence are performed is his test, and he becomes a man when he refuses to kill. In *Baby Boy*, however, the significance of this rite of manhood has changed. According to Singleton, "you're not a man unless you're a killer and who're you talking about killing? Your brother. Jail has become a rite of passage now. Like the Masai kill a lion or an Indian kill a bear, our rite of passage is you're going to jail."[19] While Singleton's words, in context, are critical of such a worldview, Jody's involvement in Rodney's murder is his defining moment as a man: he not only avoids jail for the murder; he's a better man because of it (for example, he settles down with Yvette and his son).

The fact that Jody, unlike Tre, actually takes part in a murder of another black man is the strongest indication of the ruptures between *Boyz* and *Baby Boy*, and yet, these differences have been foreshadowed throughout the text. The first and perhaps most significant (in what it says about the changes in the hood genre) difference between the films is that *Baby Boy* lacks references to the outside forces bearing down on Jody. In *Boyz*, close-ups of a re-election poster for the Reagan administration, punctuated by sounds of gunshots, follow the film's opening titles and immediately precede shots of a murder scene. The juxtaposition of text, image, and sound place responsibility for inner-city violence on the shoulders of governmental policies like Reagan's "War on Drugs." *Baby Boy* only references the situation of the black family vis-à-vis *The Isis Papers* and a reference to generalized and unidentified racism. Besides some asides regarding Jody's and Sweetpea's inability to get jobs, no specific reference is made to economics or politics.

Indeed, the forces infantilizing Jody are squarely identified as his mother and his "babies" mammas. Jody verbally alludes to the possibility of being murdered on the streets, but there is no indication of actual threats on his life until Rodney enters the narrative. Until then Jody's life has been almost completely sealed off from the rest of South Central, and he childishly uses his potential death as a threat when his mother wants him to move out. Additionally, a number of dream and fantasy sequences enact Jody's death and funeral. Socio-political causes, whether identified as rival gangs or the LAPD (both are notably absent from the narrative), are never identified in these examples. Yet, the flashbacks and dream sequences, and a later moment when Jody imagines himself in Rodney's place during the murder, successfully and repeatedly "murder" Jody. This last sequence suggests a situation in which "black men-in-the-making aim real guns, not at the 'police' . . . but at mirrors of themselves, caught in a perilous stage of development."[20] Unlike *Boyz*, however, *Baby Boy* fails to explore this notion of self-destruction, nor is Jody's death linked to specific institutionalized racism. As a result, Jody's death sequences do little more than contribute to the film's otherwise quite minimal violence.

Singleton's change in focus is manifested in the film's style. While *Baby Boy* capitalizes on recognizable South Central iconography (including landmarks such as the Liquor Bank and the Crenshaw Car Wash), the film's *mise-en-scène* is characterized by an overall myopia. There are very few long shots integrating characters into their surroundings. Jody, for example, is mostly shot in the interiors of his mother's or Yvette's houses. When he is set in exterior settings, he is again placed within "feminine" spaces: his mother's garden, outside Yvette's apartment, and in Sweetpea's girlfriend's backyard. While the domestic settings could be compelling environments within which to construct Jody's masculinity, they effectively remove him from the surrounding urban space (and spatially support the sociological message from the opening scene). Additionally, whether he is driving a car or riding his bike, Jody is tightly framed in medium shots and close-ups, showing little surrounding space. Such a compositional strategy, combined with Jody's social isolation (he has no friends besides Sweetpea), removes the story from the city rather than placing it within its borders. The film focuses on the effects of racism on urban African American men, yet Jody rarely interacts with his surrounding context.

Boyz was effective in outlining the traumatic effects of the violence surrounding young African American men living in city spaces. Tre's abuse at the hands of the LAPD and his near involvement in a drive-by shooting were vivid indicators of the pressures he faced – it was the trauma of violence that led Tre to pick up a gun, and it was Furious' guidance that helped him put it down again. This interpretation of trauma, violence, and fatherhood is transformed in *Baby Boy*. After Rodney's murder, Jody returns to his mother's house (he had previously been kicked out after an altercation with Melvin). In a scene closely mirroring Tre's return home after leaving the shooting, Jody collapses with the gun in his hand and Melvin coaxes it away from him just as Furious took the gun from Tre. The difference is that Jody actually used his gun and Melvin presumably gets rid of it (his OG experience is useful after all).

This, more than the previous murder scene, becomes the seminal moment in *Baby Boy*, and the one which most strongly suggests its rupture with *Boyz*. Throughout the film there has been a growing rancor between Jody and Melvin, as Melvin replaces Jody in Juanita's affections. Melvin, a reformed ex-con (whose "187" tattoo suggests his crimes include homicide), attempts to mentor Jody, whom he sees as a mamma's boy (and typical of his generation in his lack of respect for his elders).[21] Jody rejects Melvin's paternal advances, and his animosity towards Melvin finally culminates in a physical altercation between the two which results in Jody leaving the house. It isn't until after Rodney's murder that Jody accepts Melvin's assistance in destroying evidence. Despite all Melvin's help trying to set Jody straight, his warnings against violence and the example he's set as a gainfully self-employed black man, his only significance for Jody comes through the knowledge he gained as a murderer.

With *Baby Boy*, Singleton "wanted to make a movie about the dysfunctional relationships and the dysfunctional rites of passage within the black community, where people say 'you're not a man unless you're a killer' . . . I wanted to make a comment on that."[22] This commentary is located in Jody's words and actions, which are extended via intertextual references to extradiegetic figures such as Tupac Shakur, whose face looms over Jody's bedroom from a wall mural, symbolizing the loss of male lives through gun violence.[23] But while the *mise-en-scène* comments on violence in one way, the narrative takes another trajectory, with Jody becoming a man *because* he has killed; not, like Tre in *Boyz*, because he has managed to *avoid* killing. Following the murder and Jody's short-lived trauma, he makes up with his mother and moves in with Yvette and his son. The film ends with Jody and Yvette enacting a fairy-tale version of a now "naturalized" black family, with Jody and a pregnant and engaged Yvette playing cards in a beautiful park setting. The cycle of violence stops with Rodney's death, and in the combination of the film's ending and its narrative emphasis on Jody, *Baby Boy* asserts that violence may be bad, but it is nevertheless sometimes justified.

One of the main reasons for the differences between the two films connects to *Baby Boy*'s dearth of references to its socio-political context. *Boyz* appeared at a very specific moment and catalogued (and capitalized on) the destruction of city spaces like South Central following the increased influence of a poverty/drugs/police cycle in the area in the 1980s. *Baby Boy*, released in 2001, was set in a different historical time-frame, one which experienced an overall economic growth in the country (albeit, a smaller growth for inner-city residents), a decrease in gang activity, an overall decline in violent crime in most urban areas, a reduction, due to events like the 1992 Los Angeles riots, in police infractions, and an increased consciousness of policing strategies like racial profiling. The inner city was no longer a top media story.

The second reason for the differences between the two films is related to genre. *Baby Boy* appeared, rather belatedly, at the end of a long run of hood films initiated by *Boyz*. The hood genre had reached its pinnacle in Albert and Allen Hughes's *Menace II Society* (1993), had been critically revised in Spike Lee's *Clockers* (1995), and had been parodied in Paris Barclay's *Don't Be a Menace to South Central While Drinking Your Juice in The Hood* (1996).[24] *Baby Boy*, a late addition to the genre, is outdated in comparison to the Hugheses and Lee films because it has the overall look and tone of a hood film from the early 1990s (perhaps because the screenplay was actually written years before the film was made). The film's references are more generic than contextual, with Singleton's *Boyz* serving as the central intertext and gangsta rap mythology fueling its interpretations of genre. Additionally, the profitability of hood films declined at the turn of the century as black filmmakers began to diversify narratives, styles, and genres.

Shaft: still the man

While Singleton built his career establishing many conventions of the hood film, he has also ventured into other genres such as the historical drama (*Rosewood*, 1997) and the action/blaxploitation film with his update of *Shaft*. The latter production is a very loose revision of the blaxploitation series of the same name, and it combines elements of the blaxploitation formula with those of the action and the hood film. Unlike all of Singleton's other films, *Shaft* is a big-budget blockbuster ($46 million compared to *Baby Boy*'s $16 million budget), released during the summer for maximum box-office impact. Its eponymous protagonist, John Shaft (Samuel L. Jackson), is an empowered action hero, fully armed and willing to do whatever it takes to fight evil-doers (most egregiously, a wealthy white murderer).

Unlike *Boyz* and *Baby Boy*, *Shaft* is not a hood film because it focuses on a middle-aged New York police detective, not a South

Central teen. There are ways, however, in which the film connects
to the concerns of the hood film. First, while John Shaft is a combination blaxploitation/action hero, his acknowledgment of generational differences among black men link him to Melvin in *Baby Boy*.
Like Melvin, Shaft has the swagger of an OG (albeit with an NYPD
badge), which arises from a shared vernacular tradition of the "bad
nigger," so influential to blaxploitation heroes and Black Power
masculinity from the 1970s (modeled on Sweetback).[25] Singleton's
Shaft, like *Baby Boy*, also posits violent action as an effective
response to injustice and crime in African American communities.
All three films are concerned with community building, but *Shaft*
and *Baby Boy* suggest that aggression is a viable strategy for change,
and this is the most significant development in Singleton's decade-
long exploration of violence.

   In its very existence, *Shaft* already references generational issues
and tensions. For many young African American male filmmakers,
blaxploitation films were seminal models – as seen in the Hughes
Brothers' acknowledgment of blaxploitation style and form in an
early scene in *Menace II Society* and in their documentary *American
Pimp* (2000), in Keenan Ivory Wayans' *I'm Gonna Git You Sucka*
(1988), in Malcolm D. Lee's *Undercover Brother* (2002), and in Singleton's long desire to return to the *Shaft* series. In most cases, contemporary filmmakers have celebrated the blaxploitation formula,
especially its construction of an empowered, performative black
masculinity. This masculinity is also clearly referenced in the film's
promotional materials, including the tag-line, "Still the Man. Any
Questions?", which concurrently suggests the original film, *Shaft*'s
age, and his preeminence among bad-guy heroes.

   In an update on the series, *Shaft* features John Shaft, nephew of
the original protagonist. The original Shaft (Uncle Shaft in Singleton's film), played by Richard Roundtree, appears in the film and
often acts as a cynical sounding board for his nephew's struggles as a
black representative of a racist legal system who is trying to solve the
murder of a young black man named Trey (Mekhi Phifer). A significant development in the film is that Shaft is a member of the NYPD,
and therefore has at least a provisional belief in the legal and justice
systems. Roundtree's Uncle Shaft, still the private investigator he was
in the original films, maintains his liminal relationship to the law, and
his doubts help convince his nephew of the inability of the justice
system to prosecute a wealthy white man for Trey's murder.

21 John Shaft's (Samuel L. Jackson) "almost approving" glance at the African American woman who kills a white killer in *Shaft* (2000)

While Shaft and his uncle have a respectful, mentoring relationship, similar to that between Furious and Tre in *Boyz*, Shaft fails to extend that model of guidance to the younger individuals around him. In fact, most of Shaft's interactions with young African American or Hispanic men in the neighborhoods he polices are based upon the relationship between cop and criminal (besides Shaft's non-cop sidekick, Rasaan [Busta Rhymes], and the murdered Trey, all young black men are gang members and drug dealers). Shaft's experiences with younger men, all of whom are presented as a gangstas, are characterized by violent intimidation (the level of force and physical abuse does not change, regardless of whether Shaft has quit the NYPD or not). In one scene in particular, Shaft tries to collect testimony from an eyewitness to Trey's murder. The witness responds that she'll only provide information if Shaft will rid her neighborhood of the drug dealers on the corner who are trying to enlist her young son. Shaft responds by savagely beating the young man in charge, Malik (Bonz Malone), on the street, in broad daylight.

Much of the violence in the film, like Singleton's other films, is based upon a lack of trust in conventional forms of justice, which have historically either brutalized or ignored black urban communities. In *Boyz*, for example, an African American cop menaces Tre on two occasions; first, as a child and then more maliciously when Tre is a teen and is perceived to be a gang member because of the car he's driving. Shaft's beating of Malik aligns him with the LAPD officer in *Boyz*, criminalizing and violently abusing a younger generation of urban-dwelling men (what is absent is the self-hatred suggested in the LAPD officer's response to Tre). Because we are asked to follow

Shaft's point of view in this scene (and in the entire film), his actions seem appropriate, or at least laudable, for ridding the city of crime. Yet we cannot overlook the fact that he is still aligned with the NYPD, and therefore his actions are all the more brutal because he's supposed "to protect and to serve." This point is emphasized when a police cruiser drives by during the beating, Shaft and the white officer exchange glances, and the cop fails to intervene. Like *Baby Boy*'s omission of most political and economic factors, *Shaft* overlooks context: the film was released following highly publicized incidents of police brutality in New York City, including the sodomy of Abner Louima and the murder of Amadou Diallo.[26] In this context, Shaft is more rogue cop than action hero.

Near the end of the film, Shaft shares a similar exchange of glances with Carla Howard (Lynn Thigpen), mother of the murdered Trey. Once it becomes clear that Walter Wade (Christian Bale), her son's wealthy white murderer, is receiving preferential treatment from the court, Howard shoots Wade on the steps of the courthouse rather than risk seeing his acquittal. Like the earlier exchange of glances between Shaft and the cop, Shaft and Howard trade ambiguous, through almost approving looks before she is arrested and led away. Howard takes the law into her own hands, and in this act the film posits that the only possible path to justice is murder. Like the earlier scene in which point of view, camera angle, and composition all ask the audience to identify with Shaft while he beats Malik, in this scene the audience is prompted to applaud Howard's actions because they are supported by Shaft (and are presented as justified under the circumstances).

Conclusion: violence, as American as apple pie

Many big-budget action films, like hood films, incorporate violence into their narratives, and *Shaft* is no different. In some ways it is difficult to read too much into the film's violence – it is a product of a specific genre and, unlike some of his other films (including *Boyz* and *Baby Boy*), Singleton had relatively limited control over *Shaft*, which was produced by Scott Rudin and written by Richard Price.[27] And yet, choosing to focus on a police detective who belongs to a unit very similar to the NYPD's notorious (and now defunct) Street Crimes Unit provides *Shaft* with an interesting twist on violence that has audiences cheering the highly-stylized brutality rather than agitating against it. Furthermore, the film opens with the violent beating of a young black man, Trey, who is killed by Wade because he is in the wrong place (a downtown bar with all-white patrons) with the wrong girl (his white girlfriend). Trey's beating, rendered by a phallic-looking metal rod wielded by Wade, initiates a narrative in which the body count for Latinos and African American men vastly outnumbers that of whites. More significantly, Trey's brutal death metaphorically reenacts lynching scenarios that have haunted African American representation since *Birth of a Nation*, again reminding us that racial violence in contemporary film is not new.

African American filmmakers have struggled for almost a century to undo and respond to the cinematic brutalities meted out on and by black Americans in *Birth of a Nation*. For black men in particular, film has provided an arena for an exploration of the constitution of the self.[28] Many times, as in the case of John Singleton's films, explorations of black masculinity have been intertwined with the trauma of violence and brutality. Singleton's first film, *Boyz N the Hood*, highlighted the links between socio-political factors and the construction of African American urban life, especially for black men. His latest films explore similar ground but, perhaps due to their overall reliance on generic conventions, they elicit different attitudes towards screen violence. In *Baby Boy*, the historical and traumatic links between violence and masculinity are overshadowed by specious sociology, generic concessions, and a seemingly justified act of murder. In *Shaft*, the fetishization of the original series, combined with the generic demands of the action film, overshadows the problematics of inner city police brutality and vigilante violence. *Boyz* refracts political and social realities. *Baby Boy* and *Shaft*, perhaps because of their changed political and industrial contexts, replace those refractions with the pleasure of fulfilled generic expectations, the spectacular thrills of stylized violence, and the empowerment of revenge fantasies.

Notes

1 Jane Gaines, *Fire and Desire: Mixed-Race Movies in the Silent Era* (Chicago: University of Chicago Press, 2001), 220–1.

2 The New York and Boston events occurred in close succession, with the one in Boston thought to be a "copycat action" (Gaines, *Fire and Desire*, 220). The white man arrested for egging the screen in New York identified himself as a Southerner, thereby complicating the regional

bias often implied in race politics. See Egg Negro Scenes in Liberty Film Play," *New York Times* (April 15, 1915): 1, col. 2.

3   Gaines, *Fire and Desire*, 221.

4   Gaines offers the most detailed discussion of the ideological and textual implications of the censorship battles concerning both films in chapters 5 and 7 of *Fire and Desire*.

5   See, for example, Ed Guerrero, "Black Violence as Cinema: From Cheap Thrills to Historical Agonies," *Violence in American Cinema*, ed. J. David Slocum (New York: Routledge, 2001), 213. Besides Guerrero, there are very few studies of violence in African American film. Rather, violence is often discussed in relationship to gender (masculinity). Cf. Phillip Brian Harper, *Are We Not Men? Masculine Anxiety and the Problem of African-American Identity* (New York: Oxford University Press, 1996); *Race and the Subject of Masculinities*, ed. Harry Stecopoulos and Michael Uebel (Durham: Duke University Press, 1997); and Hazel V. Carby, *Race Men* (Cambridge: Harvard University Press, 1998).

6   J. David Slocum, "Violence and American Cinema: Notes for an Investigation," Slocum, *Violence*, 1. In the same anthology, William Rothman ("Violence and Film," 37–46) offers a discussion which traces filmic violence to Griffith, but he does not analyze the specifically *racial* acts of vilence in the director's work. More often, discussions of screen violence focus on films from the late twentieth century. See, for example, *Mythologies of Violence in Postmodern Media*, ed. Christopher Sharrett (Detroit: Wayne State University Press, 1997).

7   Robyn Wiegman, "Feminism, 'The Boyz,' and Other Matters Regarding the Male," *Screening the Male: Exploring Masculinities in Hollywood Cinema*, ed. Steven Cohan and Ina Rae Hark (New York: Routledge, 1993), 181.

8   Guerrero, "Black Violence", 212–13.

9   Angela Davis qtd. in Deborah McDowell, "Pecs and Reps: Muscling in on Race and the Subject of Masculinities," in *Race and the Subject of Masculinities*, ed. Harry Stecopoulos and Michael Uebel (Durham: Duke University Press, 1997), 379.

10 For more on the film's aesthetics, along with an extended discussion of *Boyz* in relation to the representation of city space, see Paula J. Massood, *Black City Cinema: Visualizing African American Urban Experiences in Film* (Philadelphia: Temple University Press, 2003).

11 Michael Eric Dyson, *Reflecting Black: African-American Cultural Criticism* (Minneapolis: University of Minnesota Press, 1993), 93.

12 Thomas Doherty and Jacquie Jones, "Two Takes on *Boyz N the Hood*." *Cineaste* 18.4 (1991): 17. See also William Julius Wilson, *The Truly Disadvantaged: The Inner City, the Underclass, and Public Policy* (Chicago: University of Chicago Press, 1987).

13   Manthia Diawara, "Black American Cinema: The New Realism," *Black American Cinema*, ed. Manthia Diawara (New York: Routledge, 1993), 24.

14   There have been many discussions focusing on the problematics of Singleton's, along with the genre's, gender politics. See, for example, Weigman, "Feminism"; Jacquie Jones, "The New Ghetto Aesthetic," *Wide Angle* 13.3–4 (1991): 32–43; bell hooks, *Outlaw Culture: Resisting Representations* (New York: Routledge, 1994); Michele Wallace, "*Boyz N the Hood* and *Jungle Fever*," *Black Popular Culture*, ed. Gina Dent (Seattle: Bay Press, 1992); Robin D.G. Kelley, *Yo' Mama's Disfunktional! Fighting the Culture Wars in Urban America* (Boston: Beacon, 1997).

15   Very few films have been made by African American directors that focus on young black women in urban settings. Of the few, the most exceptional are *Just Another Girl on the IRT* (Leslie Harris, 1991), *I Like It Like That* (Darnell Martin, 1994), *Set It Off* (F. Gary Gray, 1996), *Drylongso* (Cauleen Smith, 1999), and *Our Song* (Jim McKay, 2000). The city has remained a masculine space and, with few exceptions, black urban women are solely defined through their reproductive or sexual roles (even in some of the films listed here). The reason for this is partially generic (hood films, like gangster films, are a masculine genre) and partially sociological and political (black women have been constructed by policymakers and the media as single mothers and welfare queens).

16   *Baby Boy* press packet, 3. Clippings file, Billy Rose Theater Collection, New York Public Library for the Performing Arts.

17   McDowell, "Pecs and Reps", 370–1.

18   *Baby Boy* press packet, 3. Singleton might also be alluding to the fact that, at the time of *Baby Boy*'s release, he had fathered five children with four different women.

19   Qtd. in Greg Tate, "Sex and Negrocity: John Singleton on Shtupping, Shaft, and Spike," *Village Voice* (July 3, 2001): 51.

20   McDowell, "Pecs and Reps", 380.

21   Earlier in the film Jody and Sweetpea try mentoring a group of younger boys who have stolen Jody's alcohol outside the Liquor Bank. Their pedagogical approach is to punch each boy, excluding one who doesn't flinch, in the face.

22   Qtd. in Dimitri Ehrlich, "Growing Pains: John Singleton's *Baby Boy* Probes Black Youths' Struggle to Reach Manhood," *Daily News* (June 24, 2001): 5 (Showtime).

23   *Baby Boy* was originally written for Shakur, star of *Poetic Justice*. The project was shelved after Shakur's death in 1996.

24   *Clockers* is a much more effective comment on violence in the African American community, and in the hood genre, than *Baby Boy*. For more

on this, see Paula J. Massood, "Which Way to the Promised Land? *Clockers* and the Legacy of the African American City," *African American Review* 32.2 (2001): 263–79.

25 Mel Watkins, *On The Real Side: Laughing, Lying, and Signifying – The Underground Tradition of African-American Humor That Transformed American Culture, From Slavery to Richard Pryor* (New York: Touchstone, 1994), 462.

26 This interpretation is supported when Shaft, at one point in the film, shouts, "It's Guiliani time," a quote that was (incorrectly) attributed to one of the officers in the Louima assault.

27 Singleton's and Samuel L. Jackson's problems with both Rudin and Price, whom Jackson described as "that white man," were much publicized during production.

28 African American men, while vastly underrepresented in American filmmaking, far outnumber the number of black women working in the industry.

10

"Once upon a time there were three little girls ...": girls, violence, and *Charlie's Angels*

Jacinda Read

> Once upon a time there were three very different little girls who grew up to be three very different women. But they have three things in common: they're brilliant, they're beautiful and they work for me. My name is Charlie. (Charles Townsend [voice of John Forsythe] in *Charlie's Angels* [2000])

Discussing the "post-feminist girly" of films such as *Working Girl* (1988) and *Pretty Woman* (1990), Charlotte Brunsdon suggests that "feminist critics have tended to be attracted by less girly characters such as Thelma and Louise."[1] As the reference to the ubiquitous *Thelma and Louise* (1990) here implies, what really seems to have attracted feminist critics in recent years is the violent woman or action heroine: from "the monstrous-feminine" of the horror film,[2] through the "final girls" of the slasher subgenre,[3] to the numerous discussions of *Terminator 2*'s (1991) Sarah Connor (Linda Hamilton), the *Alien* series' Ripley (Sigourney Weaver), and, of course, the eponymous Thelma (Geena Davis) and Louise (Susan Sarandon).[4] Despite the characterization of these figures both as "feminine" and as "girls," however, they are, as Elizabeth Hills observes, "often described within feminist film theory as 'pseudo-males' or as being not 'really' women."[5] Thus, as Clover argues with reference to the final girl, "to the extent she means 'girl' at all, it is only for purposes of signifying male lack, and even that meaning is nullified in the final scenes . . . The discourse is wholly masculine, and females figure into it only insofar as they 'read' some aspect of male experience."[6] These figures are not simply "less girly," then; they are, in Hills' words, "figurative males."

This tendency to read cinema's violent women as "figurative males" can largely be traced to the binary logic on which such discussions rely. As Hills observes, from a binary perspective that associates masculinity with activity and femininity with passivity, "active and aggressive women in the cinema can only be seen as phallic, unnatural or 'figuratively male'."[7] Clover, for example, argues that both the slasher film's final girl and the rape-revenge film's female avenger undergo a process of "masculinization" in order to provide a point of (cross-gender) identification, rather than objectification, for the male spectator. As my own work on the rape-revenge cycle has shown, however, the female avenger frequently undergoes a process of eroticization rather than masculinization.[8] In this context, binary logic would decree that we read the female avenger, like Weaver's Ripley, either "as phallic, and therefore figuratively male, or as eroticized, and therefore regressive rather than transgressive."[9]

It is her desire to read the female avenger as a feminist-inspired figure who "transgresses both cinematic genre codes and cultural gender codes which position female characters as the passive, immobile and peripheral characters of Hollywood action cinema,"[10] rather than as a regressive figure who "is recuperated into a more traditional feminine role as sexualized object,"[11] then, that causes Clover to overlook her quite obvious eroticization. Here we come up against another binary, that between *feminism* and *femininity*, which informs work on violent women in less direct but equally important ways. While my own work has attempted to offer ways of thinking beyond this binary in relation to the (erotic) female avenger of the rape-revenge cycle,[12] and Hills' work offers ways of thinking beyond the active male/passive female binary in relation to the action heroine of films such as *Alien* (1979), a more recent coupling of girls and violence in film, television, and popular culture more generally has yet to be adequately explored.

As a film of a television show made by a director of music videos, Joseph McGinty Nichols' (a/k/a McG) *Charlie's Angels* (2000) blurs the boundaries of at least three different mediums and thus represents a privileged site for thinking through this recent coupling of girls and violence in film, TV, and popular culture. Indeed, as Yvonne Tasker has argued in her discussion of New Hollywood, "The number of film images available and the different forms of entertainment and cultural commodities with which they interact propose a challenge to the consideration of film as a distinct medium."[13] In what follows, I explore this interaction with reference to *Charlie's Angels* as a means of explicating and problematizing the relationship between girls and violence.

"Another movie from an old TV show": film, television, and New Hollywood

Until recently, the (post-feminist) girlie as described by Brunsdon – a figure who, in Joanne Hollows' succinct explanation, is "not feminist, but informed by feminism"[14] – was almost solely confined to romantic comedies such as *Working Girl*, *Pretty Woman*, and, of late, *My Best Friend's Wedding* (1997) and *Bridget Jones's Diary* (2001). While she could also be found on television, this was largely in traditionally feminine genres such as sitcoms (*Absolutely Fabulous*), chat shows (*The Girlie Show*), and the kind of "television for women" found on the US cable network *Lifetime*. However, if the development of cable narrowcasting has enabled a network dedicated solely to more traditional "women's genres," more recently it can also be seen as responsible for the development of newer generic forms epitomized by the eponymous "tough girls"[15] of female-centered action series such as *Buffy the Vampire Slayer* and *Xena: Warrior Princess*. Of course, the female-centered action series is not exactly new. What *is* new is the current resurgence of interest in the genre and its origins.[16]

The action heroine's television roots can be traced back as far as 1966, when *Batman* and *The Avengers* first aired in the US. Figures such as Batgirl, Catwoman, and Emma Peel, however, always appeared alongside a male hero, and perhaps with the exception of Batgirl, were constructed through costume, particularly the preponderance of leather, as fetish objects for male spectators. It was not until the mid-1970s that the television action heroine really came into her own with *Wonder Woman*, *The Bionic Woman* (both 1975), and *Charlie's Angels* (1976). Unlike the leather-clad heroines of the TV shows that preceded them, or the hard-bodied heroines of the action movies that superseded them, the heroines of all three of these shows were clearly constructed – as *Charlie's Angels'* opening voiceover indicates – as girls, equally concerned with the accoutrements and pleasures of normative femininity (fashion, beauty, romance) as with crime-fighting (Lynda Carter, star of *Wonder Woman*, was a former Miss America). As Susan Douglas observes, it is precisely in this combination that the particular appeal of these programs for their female audiences laid.[17]

The resurgence of interest in such "kickass Barbies"[18] is clearly indicated not only in programs such as *Xena* and *Buffy*, but in New

Hollywood's recent plundering of this televisual past. First up was Michelle Pfeiffer's Catwoman in *Batman Returns* (1992), followed by Alicia Silverstone's Batgirl in *Batman and Robin* and Uma Thurman's Emma Peel in *The Avengers* (both 1997). More recently, following the success of *Charlie's Angels* in 2000, there has been a film version of the 1970s television cartoon *Josie and the Pussycats* (2001), and rumors that a *Wonder Woman* movie is about to go into production. While these figures clearly differ in significant ways, what unites them is the emphasis on their femininity – whether the fetishized femininity of Catwoman and Peel or the fashion-conscious femininity of the Angels – marking them out as distinct from the "Rambolinas" (as Sigourney Weaver reportedly dubbed her Ripley character) of the 1980s and early 1990s. Indeed, it could be argued that the emphasis on these figures' femininity is, in fact, a product of their shared televisual past, in the sense that they reference periods in which representations of women were somehow less progressive. Certainly, the original *Charlie's Angels* TV show was the subject of unfavorable feminist analyses both at the time it was originally broadcast[19] and more recently.[20]

The combination of femininity and violence in texts such as *Charlie's Angels*, for example, has been read by critics such as Sherrie Inness as indicating that these "tough girls," at least in their 1970s incarnations, are simply "pseudo tough."[21] In other words, relying on the traditional binary logic discussed above, critics like Inness construct essentialist analyses in which femininity and violence are seen as mutually exclusive by their very nature. Here, then, the construction of these figures as feminized, as "tough girls," functions as one of the ways in which their toughness is recuperated. Thus, while Inness's, Charlie's Angels, Emma Peel, and the Bionic Woman represented women "who could be just as tough as men," they "also helped support stereotypes about women."[22] In Inness's view, these shows employed a variety of strategies to undermine the tough girl's toughness. For example, Inness claims that the use of masquerade and disguise functions to imply that toughness is simply another disguise, while the often sexual nature of these disguises and the use of clothing which "revealed . . . every curve" functions to confirm the stereotype that "women must be sexually attractive to men."[23]

Inness concludes her discussion of tough girls, however, with an analysis of *Xena: Warrior Princess* and, in so doing, constructs a narrative of progression in which Xena "is a far tougher image of

22 Even in her pre-Angel mode, the "grungey" Dylan (Drew Barrymore) "embraces notions of female empowerment in a way which exceeds ... traditional ... feminist identities."

womanhood than we would have seen on television even ten years ago."[24] Conversely, writing about such recent examples of tough girls in the media, Elyce Rae Helford constructs a narrative of regression in which she argues that we are witnessing a return to the past's stereotypical representations:

> Increased emphasis on traditional femininity in looks and behavior (in various combinations and to various degrees) have again become a significant part of the media's normative image of the empowered woman. Ripley has been replaced by butch but sexily clad Xena; Connor is outdone by increasingly blonde teen heartthrob Buffy the Vampire Slayer.[25]

What I think Helford overlooks here is the way "traditional femininity" is rendered "campy" or excessive in these programs. Indeed, although she goes on to identify moments of "self-conscious feminist representation of feminine excess"[26] in her primary text, *Tank Girl* (1995), this kind of analysis is not extended to the examples cited above. Furthermore, she argues that these moments are ultimately compromised by the heroine's childishly irresponsible behavior. Inness, on the other hand, does identify moments of "high camp" in *Xena* but argues, in contrast to Helford, that these moments are recuperating rather than recuperated, i.e., that Xena remains a tough character *despite* the way in which the show's "campy nature diminishes the threat posed by the tough woman."[27]

I will return to this issue of campiness below. For now, I think neither the narrative of progression suggested by Inness nor the narrative of regression suggested by Helford offer particularly useful ways of understanding representations of femininity in contemporary cultural texts. As Hollows has argued, for example, the problem with the narratives of "progress" found in some recent feminist analyses of femininity is their tendency to depend on an opposition between "new" femininity and "old" femininity according to which the latter "continues to operate as the incontestably bad 'other'."[28] Instead, I think we need to attend to the ways in which such texts frequently muddle the distinction between past and present (note, for example, *Charlie's Angels'* use of pop music from different periods), "old" and "new" femininities, progressive and regressive, and, of course, girls and violence. For instance, although the opening voiceover cited at the beginning of this essay ostensibly sets *Charlie's Angels* up as a narrative of progress by signaling that the contemporary Angels are "very different" from the "three little girls" of the original show (partly, as I will argue, because they are also "very different" from each other), it is simultaneously dependent on the generic conventions of the fairytale and the identities associated with them which framed the original television series in ways that are not necessarily regressive.

In analyzing the relationship between the film and TV versions of *Charlie's Angels* within the context of New Hollywood, therefore, we need to be alert to the fact that, as John Storey (following Jim Collins) observes, "part of what is postmodern about Western societies is the fact that the old is not simply replaced by the new, but is recycled for circulation together with the new."[29] Consequently, we must attend to the way in which the television show circulates in the *present* through re-runs, repeats, and video releases, and thus to the way in which both the show and the film exist *simultaneously* (a video box-set of episodes from the original television show released in Britain in October 2000, for example, featured a trailer for the recent movie). As Jane Feuer has argued, "the recycling of television programs can be a form of re-writing and can even be of historical significance."[30] This "re-writing" frequently manifests itself in the way re-runs are rendered campy, and Feuer argues that "it is often the historical and aesthetic *raison d'etre* of the cable TV services to frame old programs in this way."[31]

This is certainly true of the way in which *Charlie's Angels* repeats are currently framed on Channel 5, a British terrestrial channel with a cable aesthetic, which broadcast repeats of the show each weekday morning during Summer 2001. Indeed, Channel 5 is known for programming such as *Sunset Beach* and *The Bold and the Beautiful* which, consciously or not, can be read as parodying soap opera conventions. Such a reading is clearly encouraged, on this channel at least, by the announcer's ironic commentary over the closing credits. During Summer 2001, *Charlie's Angels* was broadcast directly after *The Bold and the Beautiful*. In this way, the scheduling of repeats in Britain explicitly encourages ironic/campy readings of the show and, by extension, the film itself, making it hard to read the show or the film's self-conscious referencing of its conventions "straight." Anna Gough-Yates, for example, argues that the TV Angels' use of clothes and make-up as disguise represents a subversive performance of femininity, one that exemplifies "Judith Butler's notion of gender as 'corporeal style' . . . fabricated and sustained through a set of performative acts and 'a ritualized repetition of conventions'."[32] But it is only the TV show's insertion into the contemporary cultural context that renders its 1970s femininity campy in this way; the recent film can thus be analyzed as a response to the manner in which the original show circulates and is understood at present.

In this respect – and despite the implicit comparison to the T. J. Hooker movie playing in the film's opening sequence – *Charlie's Angels* is clearly more than just "another movie from an old TV show." Rather, it constitutes a "distinctive [response] to the changed media landscape within which [it is] produced,"[33] and in which the original television show is currently circulating and understood. Thus, as I suggested earlier, to fully understand the relationship between girls and violence in *Charlie's Angels* one must look beyond the confines of the film itself to a contemporary media landscape in which not only is the figure of the "girl" increasingly ubiquitous, particularly in terms of youth culture and pop music (Riot Grrls and the Spice Girls are obvious examples here), but in which the term "girl" itself is increasingly associated with ideas of power and violence. One of the privileged sites for the working through of this rapprochement between girls and power in contemporary popular culture has been the teenage female witch, as she is represented in films and TV programs such as *Charmed*, *The Craft* (1996), *Practical Magic* (1998), and *Sabrina the Teenage Witch*.[34] These representations, however, exist within a wider media landscape which explicitly and apparently unproblematically couples the identity "girl" with power or violence – "Girl Power," Riot Grrls, Bad Girls, and *Tank Girl* – a combination which perhaps finds its clearest articulation in an episode of *Buffy* in which our heroine proclaims: "I want to date, and shop, and hang out, and go to school, and save the world from unspeakable demons. You know . . . I wanna do girly stuff."[35]

Post-feminism and "girlie culture": excess and parody

The late 1990s witnessed a distinct culture or movement emerging from this media landscape. Championed in the US by two former journalists, Jennifer Baumgardner and Amy Richards, and in the UK by academics such as Angela McRobbie, "Girlie Culture" has been described as "a phenomenon of female self-empowerment that emerged in the 1990s with movies like *Buffy the Vampire Slayer*, activist groups like Riot Grrrl, and books like Elizabeth Wurtzel's *Bitch*."[36] In America, girlie culture finds expression in the figure of the "riot grrl," while in Britain it finds expression in the figure of the "ladette" or, as McRobbie puts it, "girls 'behaving badly'"[37] – a reference to one of the key televisual representations of lad culture in the UK, *Men Behaving Badly*. These figures are personified by celebrities like Denise Van Outen and Sara Cox in Britain and, in their "wild child" phases, by American stars like Drew Barrymore and Courtney Love.

Despite appearing to set us back onto the terrain of woman as "figurative male," it is not enough, according to McRobbie, "to write this off as girls simply becoming like boys." Instead, she argues that the "spunky, vulgar or aggressive" behavior of today's girls "can be seen as a riposte to an older generation of feminists whom younger women now see as weary, white and middle-class, academic and professional."[38] In this way, girlie culture can be viewed as marking a generational shift in understandings of feminism and femininity; it does not simply reproduce traditional feminine identity but instead often renders it campy or excessive. For McRobbie, girlie culture "does gender" in "an exaggerated and ironic way."[39]

Similarly, the addition of an "-ie" to the stem "girl" should alert us to the hyperbolic and parodic nature of the girlie identity, to the way in which it depends upon yet exceeds the more traditional identity "girl." Thus, as Martina Ladendorf observes in her discussion of "grrlzines" (webzines created for a young, feminist audience), while "riot grrl" denotes "subversive punk rock and young feminism," the word "riot" connotes "both disturbance and uproar, but also excess and extravagance . . . traits or activities that are not appropriate for a girl."[40] At the same time, in appropriating feminized symbols and artefacts,

> the riot grrrls celebrate what is cute, pink and "feminine" in a way that is analog [sic] to the use of "girls" instead of "women" when they refer to themselves. The feminists of the sixties and seventies felt that the label "girl" was degrading, and insisted on being called women. The tactics of the Riot grrrls is to reclaim the word "girl," and everything associated with it. In the same way, some of the grrlzines use older images of women, that could be labeled sexist, but put them into new contexts.[41]

Thus, while girlie culture embraces the pink things of stereotypical girlhood (such as "Hello Kitty" merchandise)[42] by recontextualizing them within an overall identity that embraces notions of female empowerment, it does so in a way which exceeds both traditional feminine and feminist identities. In this respect, the girlie is both a post-modern and a post-feminist figure:

> The post-feminist woman has a different relation to femininity than either the pre-feminist or the feminist woman . . . Precisely because this postmodern girl is a figure partly constructed through a relation to consumption, the positionality is more available. She is in this sense much more like the postmodern feminist, for she is neither trapped in femininity (pre-feminist), nor rejecting of it (feminist). She can use it. However, although this may mean apparently inhabiting a very similar terrain to the pre-feminist woman, who manipulates her appearance to get her man, the post-feminist woman also has ideas about her life and being in control which clearly come from feminism. She may manipulate her appearance, but she doesn't just do it to get a man on the old terms. She wants it all.[43]

From the "grungey" identity of Dylan (Drew Barrymore) to the girl band "pop video" of the closing credits, the contemporary Angels are clearly informed by this girlie figure. As such, and as their construction in the opening credits suggests, they are simultaneously formed by and disavowing of the original Angels' feminine identities. Consequently, while the contemporary Angels are "three *very different* little girls," they remain "little girls," since the girlie identity is predicated precisely on a resistance to the "grown up" feminine and feminist identities inscribed in the term "woman."

While the phrase "three very different little girls" can be interpreted in two different ways – that the contemporary Angels are "very
different" from the "three little girls" of the original show, or that
they are very different from each other – I think the film actually pref-
erences a third interpretation: that the contemporary Angels are "very
different" from the "three little girls" of the original show *precisely
because* they are "very different" from each other. The film thus shuns
essentialist notions of gender inscribed in the term "girl" in favor of a
construction of femininity as performance, as both mutable and multiple.[44] And so Natalie (Cameron Diaz) is transformed from a geeky
student driver to a beautiful game-show contestant, Alex (Lucy Liu)
from a spoilt little rich kid to an astronaut, and Dylan from riot grrl
to, albeit still rebellious, police academy trainee.

Like the Spice Girls, the contemporary Angels each perform very
different versions of femininity.[45] In this way, girlieness is shown to
exceed the identity "girl" insofar as it offers *different* ways of being
a girl, thereby acknowledging this subject position's contradictions
(in a sense, then, the riot grrl and the ladette are simply key figures
within a repertoire of girlie identities). If the opening credits reference contemporary girlie identities, however, they also reference the
original Angels. Alongside explicit references to specific episodes
such as "Angels in Chains" (1976–77), for example, there are more
implicit references to the representation of the Angels themselves. In
particular, the moment in the original show's credits where Jaclyn
Smith's Kelly removes her motorcycle helmet and shakes her hair
out becomes the subject of parody. When Liu's Alex reprises this
moment in the film, the additional use of slow-motion camerawork
marks the action as excessive and exaggerated, suggesting that the
contemporary Angels' feminine identities depend on, yet exceed and
caricature, the more traditional femininities associated with their
1970s counterparts in ways which acknowledge both the pleasures
and the problems of this subject position.

Our introduction to Alex, for example, carries all the promise of
sexual spectacle; as her voiceover proclaims, "I want to get one thing
straight between us . . . This is going to be long, hard, and rough."
But as the scene cuts from an establishing shot of a Western landscape and huge silver trailer to a close-up two-shot of Alex and her
boyfriend Jason (Matt Le Blanc), then to a mid-shot of the couple
standing inside the trailer, we come to realize that Alex is simply
helping Jason practice his lines. The beginning of the scene is thus

explicitly marked out as a performance. Indeed, should we need any confirmation about Jason's identity as an actor – as literally performative – it is reinforced by the large-bulbed mirror behind him.

This performance, however, continues in less explicit ways throughout the rest of the scene, suggesting that we should also read *Alex*'s identity as performative. In a gender reversal of the narrative scenario of James Cameron's *True Lies* (1994), Jason is unaware that Alex is a private investigator, believing instead that she is a bikini-waxer. Moreover, the *mise-en-scène* of cluttered, cozy domesticity contrasts with Alex's fetishistic clothing of strapless, tight-fitting black basque and tight black trousers to construct a contradictory and ambiguous identity, one that is further reinforced by her unisex name. While the latter is suggestive of the slasher film's masculinized final girls and is reinforced by Alex's masculine "competence in mechanical and other practical matters"[46] – i.e., her jargon-filled explanation of why Jason's fictional character would not just "yank the wires" – this explanation is still delivered while she is mixing cake, and is quickly joined by a hyperbolic display of girlieness as she embraces Jason and purrs: "Isn't it amazing how much information you can learn off of the *in-ter-net?*" Clearly, this show of girlieness, combined with Alex's culinary ineptitude and the incongruous excess of her fetishized appearance and masculine competence, marks her identity out as performative and parodic. However, her culinary failures cause Alex genuine distress, suggesting that even while the film parodies traditional feminine identities, it also seeks to address the problem of how to combine traditional feminine desires for romance and domesticity with feminist desires for career and independence. Indeed, this conflict is set up in the next scene, where we learn that Alex is "having trouble with her secret identity" and the "façade" it requires her to maintain with Jason.

"Never send a man to do a woman's job": *Charlie's Angels* and the action movie

As this scene reveals, however, it is not simply traditional feminine identities which are the subject of parody here, but traditional *masculine* identities too. This is most clearly signaled in the casting of Le Blanc – most famous for his role as the dumb and gullible soap actor, Joey Tribbiani, in the hit television series *Friends* – as that bastion of traditional masculinity, the male action star. The figure of Jason thus functions to ensure that we read the film's referencing of male-centered action movies, such as the *Mission Impossible* and James Bond series, and the masculine identities associated with them, as parody rather than pastiche. And this in turn serves to distance the Angels from the figurative males or "Rambolinas" of earlier female-centered action films. Indeed, the trope of a fictional-action-movie-within-an action-movie highlights *Charlie's Angels'* self-consciousness about action movie conventions and, as I have argued, marks out precisely the identities associated with them as performances. As such, it also allows the film to comment on the construction of women as love interest and/or victims in the traditional action movie.

This is clearly indicated in a scene in which Jason sits at a café table with a woman who is seated with her back to the camera. From the woman's frame and long black hair we are clearly meant to deduce that this is Alex. Just as Jason proposes to her, however, she is shot in the back and, as he cradles the dead woman in his arms, he shakes his fist at the sky and damns her assailant in a histrionic gesture of revenge. Here, then, we are presented with a series of action movie stereotypes: woman as love interest and victim, man as avenger. But these fictions are revealed to be just that – stereotypes – as the camera pulls back to reveal that this is simply a movie set. The following scenes replace these with new fictions in which men are victims and women avengers. As Corwin (Tim Curry) is killed by the Thin Man (Crispin Glover) and Bosley (Bill Murray) is kidnapped by Vivian (Kelly Lynch), Alex survives a barrage of gunfire directed at the trailer and swears revenge, while Natalie delivers a knock-out kick to an assailant who calls her a bitch.

Elsewhere, male characters are made to look ridiculous in, for example, huge, padded sumo-wrestling suits, or are relegated to the role of dumb and/or dutiful love interest. It is perhaps for this reason that reviews of the film frequently likened the Angels to James Bond,[47] with Desson Howe and Melissa Wittstock both describing them as "James Bondettes." But the similarities here have less to do with the Angels' violence marking them out as figurative males and more to do with the way their relations with men reverses the Bond series' inherent sexism. Chad (Tom Green), for example, is frequently used, patronized, and dismissed by Dylan. As McRobbie has observed, this kind of reverse sexism, in which young women get pleasure from "subjecting men and boys to the kind of treatment they have come to expect, by virtue of being a girl," is a key aspect of girlie culture.[48] That said, shortly after Chad has taken the Angels to Carmel on his boat, the Angels are shown emerging "Bond-girl-like" from the sea. In this respect, the Angels perhaps owe something as well to the "'exotic' women gifted in equally 'exotic' forms of the martial arts . . . featured in such 1960s' and 1970s' products as the James Bond films."[49]

"I'm gonna moonwalk out of here": music, dance, and the aesthetics of violence in contemporary action/spectacle cinema

Despite the self-consciousness of the above reference, it could be argued that it merely sets us back onto the terrain mapped out by Inness, i.e., that the tough girl's eroticization functions as one of the ways in which her toughness is recuperated. Discussing the representation of violence in the original *Angels* television show, Cathy Schwichtenberg makes a similar point in relation to the connection between violence and dance:

> All the Angels' actions are choreographed and sanitized. The Angels dance their fights and in the process emerge as "tigresses" or "spunky little things." We see minimal struggle (fellow Angels always show up with guns) and the Angels never get dirty or dishevelled. Their confrontations with the villains usually appear short, neat, and clean. The "girls" remain statues – unruffled icons. Representative male shows of this genre – *Starsky and Hutch*, *Chips*, and *The Streets of San Francisco* – present more "realistic" violence with their action sequences. Men fight vigorously and often draw blood in the process, but this is not the case when women fight men, for the Angels are showcased as objects like aggressive Rockettes in their action sequences.[50]

Certainly, the film makes no secret of this connection between violence and dance. As noted above, it was made by a director of music videos, and its first set-piece fight sequence, in which the Angels take on the Thin Man, bears all the hallmarks of music video (though it is clearly inspired by traditional film musicals as well, specifically *West Side Story* [1961], in which violence is also represented through dance).[51] Set to the Prodigy's controversial number "Smack My Bitch Up" – although the Angels have evidently turned the tables in this respect – the sequence is clearly choreographed and edited to the rhythms of the music track and is punctuated by the Angels' iconic poses.[52] This match between image and music track is obviously not peculiar to *Charlie's Angels* but is a feature of New Hollywood's "High Concept" style of filmmaking and its reliance on synergy between different mediums.[53] Indeed, while the fight scenes were choreographed by Cheung-Yan Yuen, whose brother was responsible for *The Matrix* (1999), it is worth adding that these scenes perhaps owe something as well to the high-kicks and aggressive stances of post-feminist girlie icons like Spice Girls "Sporty" and "Scary." Consequently, the film's depiction of violence needs to be understood both in terms of the aesthetics of violence in contemporary action/spectacle cinema and in terms of the representation of women in contemporary popular music.

There are clearly some common influences at work here. For example, the choreography of action/spectacle films such as *The Matrix*,[54] and of girl bands such as the Spice Girls, both owe much to Hong Kong cinema, the former to the work of directors like John Woo and the latter to the success in the west of Hong Kong films starring female performers like Angela Mao Ying.[55] It may be that they both owe something to computer games as well. As Steven Poole observes: "In its exaggeratedly dynamic kung-fu scenes, in which actors float through the air and smash each other through walls, *The Matrix* contains the most successful translations to date of certain videogame paradigms to the celluloid medium."[56] Furthermore, the combination of excessive femininity and excessive violence found in computer games such as Tekken, where Japanese *kawaii* or "cutie" culture (most clearly visible in the west through the "Hello Kitty" merchandise mentioned earlier)[57] meets excessive violence, has also clearly influenced both the Spice Girls – Baby Spice (Emma Bunton), for example, combines childlike sweetness with a much-publicized blue belt at karate[58] – and, given the repeated references to Japan and Japanese culture, the contemporary Angels.

But unlike the individualized violence of most male- and female-centered action films and computer games, the Angels' violence is, at least in the first fight sequence, collective and co-operative. In this way, it is both informed by the choreographed dance routines of girl bands and reminiscent of the feminist-derived discourses of female solidarity and collective action such bands express. The continuing influence of second-wave feminism's critique of femininity has meant, however, that such discourses are commonly seen to be at odds with the sexualized and fetishized representation of women in such bands, particularly R&B bands like Destiny's Child, who provided the film's

23 No guns necessary. The woman warriors of *Charlie's Angels* (2000).

title track, "Independent Woman." As Jude Davies argues, though, representations of the Spice Girls – on which, as I have been suggesting, the Angels draw most clearly – "differ from the dominant ways in which women are represented as pop performers."[59] As Davies observes, for example, the video for the Spice Girls' first single "Wannabe" successfully "narrativized female collectiveness by dramatizing what looks like a gentlemen's club or an upmarket hotel being taken over by the Spice Girls *en masse*," while the group dynamic and the fact that they are often shown in active rather than static poses "disrupt[s] the singular focus of fetishism."[60] And in the film, the camp excess of Natalie's MGM-musical dream sequence and the self-conscious irony of her performance to Sir Mix-A-Lot's "Baby Got Back" clearly parody rather than replicate traditional depictions of the female body in musicals and music videos. It is worth noting, however, that such strategies for transgressing the traditional ways in which women are represented as pop performers are largely available only to white women. For the black female performers of Destiny's Child, for example, the images of sexual agency which performers such as Madonna mobilize with impunity are not available in the same way; this because, as bell hooks observes, such images have "been the stick this society has used to justify its continued beating and assault on the black female body."[61]

The connection between dance and violence is cemented later in the film when Dylan warns five male assailants that "by the time this is over, every one of you is going to be face down on the floor and I'm gonna moonwalk out of here." Furthermore, Dylan's detailed explanation of how she intends to achieve this aim serves to highlight the film's self-conscious foregrounding of the aesthetics of violence in contemporary action cinema, and indicates the way in which the gendered distinction Schwichtenberg makes between "choreographed" violence and "realistic" violence no longer holds in contemporary Hollywood action/spectacle films. As many scholars have recently observed, action sequences are now choreographed with the precision of song-and-dance routines in the old-fashioned musical. John Woo is perhaps the master of such hyper-aestheticized set-pieces of violence, as a review of his 1992 film *Hard Boiled* makes clear:

> The film's musical-like choreography and the overall rhythmic quality of the destruction suggest a directing style that has as much in common with Busby Berkeley as it does with Sam Peckinpah. It's an essentially decorative aesthetic of destruction in which pyrotechnics and firepower are celebrated for their own sake. In absurdly close proximity to each other, the leading characters shoot less to kill than to sustain their perverse dance-of-death courtship for as long as possible . . . As in a dance routine, it's the performance rather than it's goal that's important. The killing zone in front of the camera is like the endlessly extended stage in a vintage musical, its many disposable villains arrayed much as the scores of anonymous showgirls in a Busby Berkeley revue.[62]

As the term suggests, then, contemporary action/spectacle cinema problematizes the binary opposition between masculinity, activity, and narrative on the one hand, and femininity, passivity, and spectacle on the other as mapped out in Laura Mulvey's 1975 essay, "Visual Pleasure and Narrative Cinema," and which informs both Schwichtenberg's and Inness's critiques of the original *Charlie's Angels* TV show. As José Arroyo observes of the contemporary action set-piece, "their function as spectacle exceeds their function as narrative" such that "the viewer is too busy rushing through its aesthetics to think of anything but its erotics."[63] Like the visual presence of a woman in classical Hollywood cinema, the action set-piece in contemporary Hollywood's action/spectacle cinema, somewhat paradoxically, "tend[s] to work against the development of a story line, to freeze the flow of action in moments of erotic contemplation."[64] For example, Arroyo discusses the moment in *Mission: Impossible* (1996) where Tom Cruise's Ethan Hunt is suspended from the ceiling by wires just inches from an alarmed floor. At this moment, he argues, the film offers us both "the pleasure of Cruise's physique, his physical prowess" while simultaneously reducing his body to a two-dimensional "graphic element of the composition, albeit a gorgeous one."[65] In contemporary action/spectacle cinema, then, Schwichtenberg's distinction is no longer tenable. Instead, the spectacle of both male *and* female action bodies "gives flatness, the quality of a cut-out or icon rather than verisimilitude to the screen."[66]

If the aesthetics of violence in contemporary Hollywood cinema destabilizes the gendered distinction between narrative and spectacle, masculinity and femininity, activity and passivity, then the centrality of the gun and gunfire to those aesthetics might be seen as an attempt to restabilize this distinction.[67] As the phallic object *par excellence*, the gun helps to ensure that we read the action body, whether male or female, as masculinized. It also functions, much as the revelation of the "Full Monty" in the 1997 film of that name did, to allay any potential anxieties about the feminizing effects of spectacle on the male body. It is perhaps significant, then, that the contemporary Angels' violence is marked by an absence of the gun. Instead, and at a humorous level, the film's opening scenes recast the humble muffin as a lethal weapon when Natalie and Dylan start hurling Alex's rock solid and inedible creations at each other, thus giving a new meaning to "domestic violence." While this absence can be explained by producer Barrymore's well-documented dislike of guns, it is nevertheless significant for an understanding of the film's representation of violence and femininity.[68] For the elimination of such a privileged phallic signifier sets the contemporary Angels apart not only from the male action hero, but from their "figuratively male" action heroine counterparts as well as from the original Angels; the assumption that an active/violent female body is necessarily also a masculinized or a fetishized one is thereby problematized. Indeed, the film self-consciously foregrounds these assumptions when the Angels break into Redstar disguised variously as men (Natalie and Dylan) and as an eroticized dominatrix (Alex).

"Once upon a time there were three little girls . . . ": *Charlie's Angels* and the fairytale

If Charlie's Angels' refusal of the gun implies a refusal of the masculinization of earlier action heroines, do they simply represent the opposite extreme, a hyper-feminized and thus recuperated version of the action heroine? Kate Stab suggests that this is indeed the case:

Action heroines have traditionally been defined by their adoption or refusal of femininity, which surfaced as an issue for the make-a-man-of-yourself protagonists of the early and mid 90s. Thus Connor's attempts in *T2* to expunge female "weakness" with bodybuilding and macho posturing reached their logical conclusion in 1997 in *G.I. Jane*'s trial boot camp, where femininity was pared off in order that a hard-bodied male power could be assumed. This . . . pole of masculinized representation . . . has been countered in recent years by a girlier, post-feminist aesthetic most visible in the battling, lip-glossed Barbies of *Charlie's Angels* . . .[69]

For Stab, *Tomb Raider*'s (2001) Lara Croft (Angelina Jolie), with her combination of soft body – articulated through her "exaggerated curves" – and hard body – articulated through her "no-shit hard-ware" – represents a "third way."[70] What Stab's reference to the "girlier, post-feminist aesthetic" of *Charlie's Angels* points up but fails to investigate, however, is the argument explicated here. In short, the Angels are hyper-feminized only to the extent that their girlie identities simultaneously depend on and exceed traditional feminine identities; they are, to use Stab's term, "girl*ier*." Thus, for example, the Angels are no longer simply "three little girls" – they are "three *very different* little girls."

In this respect, the film also depends upon and exceeds the tradi-tionally feminine generic conventions of the fairytale which framed the original television series. Here Charlie's opening voiceover announces the show as a Cinderella narrative in which he is cast in the role of Prince Charming, rescuing the Angels from a life of drudgery: "Once upon a time there were three little girls who went to the police academy. Two in Los Angeles, the other in San Fran-cisco. And they were each assigned 'very hazardous duties.' But I took them away from all that and now they work for me. My name is Charlie." Schwichtenberg interprets this fairytale as an "all-too-real exploitation and recirculation of the female image for further ratings mileage."[71] Similarly, critics have read the references to fairy-tales (particularly *Cinderella*) in romantic comedies such as *Pretty Woman* as "a reversion to a pre-feminist narrative."[72] But I think one can argue – as Brunsdon does with respect to *Pretty Woman* – that in the film version of *Charlie's Angels* "the reference to *Cinderella* is contemporary and self-conscious."[73] So, for example, although the "once upon a time" remains intact, the reference to Charlie rescuing the Angels from a life of drudgery has been dropped. Indeed, just as in *Pretty Woman*, where Vivian (Julia Roberts) ends up rescuing Edward (Richard Gere), here it is the Angels who return the favor and rescue Charlie "right back" (although by the final scene Charlie is restored to the position of "guardian angel," as he tells the Angels he cannot join them because he has "some precious treasures to watch over").

Unlike *Pretty Woman*, though, *Charlie's Angels* does not offer the traditional fairytale ending of heterosexual union. The absence of the Angels' respective partners in this scene avoids the traditional recuperation of the violent woman through positioning her within a heterosexual romance, offering instead the perhaps more "feminist" pleasures of "sisterhood" – of female friendship and bonding (a preference also expressed in the defining anthem of "Girl Power," the Spice Girls' "Wannabe").[74] In so doing, however, it also fails to address the problem it repeatedly articulates and which is succinctly summarized in Alex's complaint in the opening scenes that men "come on all lovey-dovey until they find out I can shatter a cinder block with my forehead." The film continually dramatizes the problems of the post-feminist position – how to combine feminine desires for romance and domesticity with feminist desires for independence and a career – through the way in which the Angels' jobs, particularly their violent encounters, are constantly shown to interfere with their love lives.

A key moment in this respect occurs during the sequence at Carmel where Natalie attempts to conduct a conversation with paramour Pete (Luke Wilson) on her mobile phone while also fighting the villainess Vivian. The conversation comes to an abrupt end when Vivian grabs the phone and smashes it on the floor. Despite Natalie's complaint to Vivian – "Do you know how hard it is to find a quality man in Los Angeles?" – by the end of the film, the Angel's desire for heterosexual romance is replaced by desire for Charlie, figured here as a kind of father-figure. In this way, it could be argued that the film recuperates the threat posed by the violent woman by positioning her as a girl-child rather than as a woman. Stab makes a similar point about *Tomb Raider*, arguing that the film "neatly sidesteps the problems inherent in the screen representation of the action heroine – the terrifying issue of sexual difference in an empowered woman, the impossibility of portraying a sexual relationship, not to mention her fuck-you challenge to cinema's symbolic order – by positioning Lara firmly as a *girl*, not a woman."[75]

The film's penultimate sequence – in which the Angels, having been washed up on the beach, go in search of Charlie – would appear to reinforce this reading by situating its heroines, like the archetypal female protagonists of many fairytales, as little more than asexual "daddy's girls." However, like much else in the film, the explicitness of the reference to fairytale conventions here – the log cabin, the smoking chimney, the Angels' heads arranged vertically ("three little bears-like") as they peer around the door – is highly self-conscious and parodic. In this way, the film acknowledges the traditional fairytale's pleasures and the identities associated it while simultaneously exceeding them. Indeed, if the Angels are constructed as "daddy's girls," they are, by the same token, constructed as metaphorical "sisters" who, like their pop-music counterparts, the Spice Girls, privilege the feminist pleasures of female friendship and bonding over the imperative towards heterosexual romance inscribed in the traditional fairytale.

For this reason, however, the film only partially delivers on its promise to tell a tale of "three very different little girls who grew up to be very different women." As Davies points out in his discussion of the Spice Girls, "the central problematic here is maturation"[76] rather than recuperation. In other words, as "the pregnancies and marital arrangements of Mel B and Victoria signaled responsibilities which firmly distanced their 'real-life' selves from their performances as Spice girls . . . , the slippages between play and seriousness initially opened up by [their] multiple performances of identity" became more difficult.[77] Consequently, while the girlie identities of both the contemporary Angels and the Spice Girls exceed the identity "girl" in significant ways, they are also predicated precisely on *not* growing up and, in this respect, Charlie's Angels are destined to forever remain "three little girls."

On the one hand, this apparent retreat from the ostensible narrative of progress constructed in the film's opening voiceover need not be read as regressive since, in so doing, *Charlie's Angels* refuses to privilege the "new femininities" of the contemporary Angels over the "old femininities" of the original ones, instead pointing to the way in which (as I have been arguing) the girlie identity is simultaneously dependent on *and* disavowing of traditional femininity. The film can thus be seen as not only muddling the distinction between girls and power/violence, but between old and new femininities and between past and present. On the other hand, like the liminal space of the holiday in which the closing scene is played out, the girlie identity – dependent as it is on not growing up – can offer only a temporary reconciliation of femininity and violence. That is, if the film successfully reconciles girls with power/violence, it is only by retreating from the contradictory demands of adult femininity which might complicate such an equation. For this reason, while the Angels' girlie identities might resist the constraints of adult femininity, they also mask rather than confront the contradictions that growing up to be "three very different women" might involve.[78]

Notes

1 Charlotte Brunsdon, *Screen Tastes: Soap Opera to Satellite Dishes* (London: Routledge, 1997), 101.

2 Barbara Creed, *The Monstrous-Feminine: Film, Feminism, Psychoanalysis* (London: Routledge, 1993).

3 Carol J. Clover, *Men, Women and Chainsaws: Gender in the Modern Horror Film* (London: BFI, 1992).

4 Yvonne Tasker, *Spectacular Bodies: Gender, Genre and the Action Cinema* (London: Routledge, 1993); Tasker, *Working Girls: Gender and Sexuality in Popular Cinema* (London: Routledge, 1998).

5 Elizabeth Hills, "From 'Figurative Males' to Action Heroines: Further Thoughts on Active Women in the Cinema," *Screen* 40.1 (1999): 38.

6 Clover cited in Hills, "Figurative Males," 43.

7 Hills, "Figurative Males," 39.

8 Jacinda Read, *The New Avengers: Feminism, Femininity and the Rape-Revenge Cycle* (Manchester: Manchester University Press, 2000).

9 Hills, "Figurative Males," 42.

10 *Ibid.*, 38.

11 *Ibid.*, 42.

12 Read, *The New Avengers*.

13 Yvonne Tasker, "Approaches to the New Hollywood," in *Cultural Studies and Communcations*, ed. James Curran, David Morley and Valerie Walkerdine (London: Arnold, 1996), 226.

14 Joanne Hollows, *Feminism, Femininity and Popular Culture* (Manchester: Manchester University Press, 2000), 196.

15 Sherrie Inness, *Tough Girls: Women Warriors and Wonder Women in Popular Culture* (Philadelphia: University of Pennsylvania Press, 1999).

16 See, for example, *Action TV: Tough-Guys, Smooth Operators and Foxy Chicks*, ed. Bill Osgerby and Anna Gough-Yates (London: Routledge, 2001).

17 Susan J. Douglas, *Where the Girls Are: Growing Up Female with the Mass Media* (London: Penguin, 1995).

18 Peter Travers, "*Charlie's Angels* Review" (2000): www.rollingstone. com/mv_reviews/review.asp?mid=76365&afl=imdb (18 July, 2001).

19 Cathy Schwichtenberg, "A Patriarchal Voice in Heaven," *Jump Cut* 24/25 (1981): 13–16.

20 Inness, *Tough Girls*.

21 *Ibid.*, 31–49.

22 *Ibid.*, 33.

23 *Ibid.*, 36; 34.

24 *Ibid.*, 180.

25 Elyce Rae Helford, "Postfeminism and the Female Action Hero: Positioning *Tank Girl*," in *Future Females, The Next Generation: New Voices and Velocities in Feminist Science Fiction Criticism*, ed. Marleen Barr (Lanham, MD: Rowman & Littlefield, 2000), 296.

26 *Ibid.*, 304.

27 Inness, *Tough Girls*, 173.

28 Hollows, *Feminism*, 173.

29 John Storey, "The Sixties in the Nineties: Pastiche or Hyperconsciousness?", in Osgerby and Gough-ates, *Action TV*, 246. See Jim Collins, "Genericity in the Nineties: Eclectic Irony and the New Sincerity," *Film Theory Goes to the Movies*, ed. Jim Collins, *et al.* (New York: Routledge, 1993).

30 Jane Feuer, "Feminism on Lifetime: Yuppie TV for the Nineties," *Camera Obscura* 33–4 (1994–95): 133.

31 *Ibid.*

32 Anna Gough-Yates, "Angels in Chains? Feminism, Femininity and Consumer Culture in *Charlie's Angels*," Osgerby and Gough-Yates, *Action TV*, 93.

33 Tasker, "Approaches", 224.

34 See Rachel Moseley, "Glamorous Witchcraft: Gender and Magic in Teen Film and Television," *Screen* 43.4 (2003).

35 Cited in Moseley, "Glamorous Witchcraft."

36 Tamara Strauss, "Lipstick Feministas," *Metro Santa Cruz* (Nov. 29, 2000–Dec. 6, 2000): www.metroactive.com/papers/cruz/11.29.00 /feminism-0048.html (18 July, 2001): 2. See Jennifer Baumgardner and Amy Richards, *Manifesta: Young Women, Feminism, and the Future* (New York: St. Martin's, 2001); and Angela McRobbie, "Pecs and Penises: The Meaning of Girlie Culture," *Soundings* 5 (1997): 157–66.

37 McRobbie, "Pecs and Penises", 160.

38 *Ibid.*

39 *Ibid.*, 161.

40 Martina Ladendorf, "Pin-Ups and Grrls: The Pictures of Grrlzines," paper presented at the "Crossroads in Cultural Studies" Conference, Birmingham, UK (July 21–25, 2000): www.niwl.se/home/fornas /Research/digitalborderlands/inas/pinups_grrls.htm (18 July, 2001).

41 *Ibid.*
42 "Hello Kitty" is the star character and corporate symbol of the Tokyo-based Sanrio Company. Sanrio is a worldwide designer and distributor of character-branded stationery, school supplies, gifts, and accessories or "fancy goods" (*fanshi guzzu*). As Sharon Kinsella observes, "the crucial ingredients of a fancy good are that it is small, pastel, round, soft, loveable, *not* traditional Japanese style but a foreign – in particular European or American – style, dreamy, frilly and fluffy." Kinsella, "Cuties in Japan," *Women and Media Consumption in Japan*, ed. Lisa Skov and Brian Moeran (Richmond: Curzon Press, 1995), 226.
43 Brunsdon, *Screen Tastes*, 85–6.
44 Judith Butler, *Gender Trouble: Feminism and the Subversion of Identity* (London: Routledge, 1990).
45 Indeed, both in terms of the implication of "poshness" and in terms of costuming in which figure-hugging black leather clothing predominates, the figure of Alex clearly owes something to Posh Spice (Victoria Beckham), who was reportedly interested in the part (although she clearly also owes something to Ling Woo, the character Liu played in the TV show *Ally McBeal*).
46 Clover, *Men, Women and Chainsaws*, 40.
47 See Desson Howe, "*Charlie's Angels* Review" (2000): http://yp.washingtonpost.com/E/M/WASDC/0000/20/09cs1.html (July 10, 2001); Alexander Walker, "*Charlie's Angels* Review" (2000): www.thisislondon.co.uk/dynamic/film.html?in_review_id=336937&in_revie w_text_id (July 10, 2001); Christopher Goodwin, "Crouching Men, Flying Tigresses," *Sunday Times* (Feb. 11, 2001): 6; Melinda Wittstock, "Charlie's Angels Ride Again," *Observer* (Nov. 12, 2000): 22.
48 McRobbie, "Pecs and Penises", 160.
49 Tasker, *Spectacular Bodies*, 23.
50 Schwichtenberg, "A Patriarchal Voice", 13.
51 *West Side Story*'s logo, which features two dancing figures on a fire escape, is also reminiscent of the Angels as they exit Corwin's party via a fire escape in pursuit of the Thin Man.
52 In an article in *The Ottawa Citizen*, Janice Rocco, a spokesperson for the National Organization of Women, claimed that "Smack My Bitch Up" "teaches violence against women is a form of entertainment." "Music Group, Prodigy, Causing Controversy with its New Song and Video" (1997): www.media-awareness.ca/eng/news/news/two/music.htm (July 18, 2001). In addition, both Kmart and Wal-Mart removed the album featuring the single from their shelves "after determining that the collection's latest single 'Smack My Bitch Up' was inappropriate for its family-friendly policies." Marcus Errico, "Kmart, Wal-Mart Pull Prodigy Album" (1997):www.eonline.com/News/Items/0,1,2195,00.html (July 18, 2001).

53 Justin Wyatt, *High Concept: Movies and Marketing in Hollywood* (Austin: University of Texas Press, 1994).

54 It is worth noting that, just prior to *The Matrix*'s opening fight scene in which Carrie-Anne Moss's Trinity kicks, punches, leaps, and flies her way to freedom, she is referred to as a "little girl" by the police lieutenant whose men are pursuing her.

55 Tasker, *Spectacular Bodies*, 23.

56 Steven Poole, *Trigger Happy: The Inner Life of Videogames* (London: Fourth Estate, 2000), 87.

57 See n.42 above.

58 Jude Davies, "'It's Like Feminism, but You Don't Have to Burn Your Bra': Girl Power and the Spice Girls' Breakthrough 1996–7," *Living Through Pop*, ed. Andrew Blake (London: Routledge, 1999), 167.

59 *Ibid.*, 165.

60 *Ibid.*

61 bell hooks, *Black Looks: Race and Representation* (London: Turnaround, 1992), 160.

62 Tom Tunney, "*Lashou Shentan* (*Hard-Boiled*) Review," in *Action/Spectacle Cinema: A Sight and Sound Reader*, ed. José Arroyo (London: BFI, 2000), 73.

63 Jose Arroyo, "Mission: Sublime," in Arroyo, *Action/Spectacle Cinema*, 24; 25.

64 Laura Mulvey, "Visual Pleasure and Narrative Cinema" (1975), in *Feminism and Film Theory*, ed. Constance Penley (London: BFI, 1988), 62.

65 Arroyo, "Mission: Sublime," 24.

66 Mulvey, "Visual Pleasure," 63.

67 See Jason Jacobs, "Gunfire"; Arroyo, "Mission: Sublime"; and *Bang Bang, Shoot Shoot! Essays on Guns and Popular Culture*, ed. Murray Pomerance and John Sakeris (Needham Heights: Pearson Education, 2000).

68 Barrymore has stated, for example, that "I hate guns. There was no way we were running around with guns." Interview with Hilary Rose, "Heavenly Creature," *The Times* (4 Nov., 2000): 16. Barrymore's dislike of guns is also mentioned in several of the reviews I surveyed.

69 Kate Stab, "Run Lara Run," *Sight and Sound* 11.8 (2001): 20.

70 *Ibid.*

71 Schwichtenberg, "A Patriarchal Voice", 13.

72 Brunsdon, *Screen Tastes*, 94.

73 *Ibid.*

74 The song's lyrics privilege (female) friendship over heterosexual romance, as evidenced in the refrain: "If you wanna be my lover, you gotta get with my friends/Make it last forever, friendship never ends."

75 Stab, "Run Lara Run," 20.

76   Davies, "It's Like Feminism", 171.
77   *Ibid.*, 170–1.
78   I am extremely grateful to Rachel Moseley for her incisive and invaluable comments on drafts of this chapter.

11

Playing with fire: women, art, and danger in American movies of the 1980s

Susan Felleman

> Now at that time the men had no fire and did not know how to make it, but the women did. While the men were away hunting . . . the women cooked their food and ate it by themselves. Just as they were finishing their meal they saw the men returning, away in the distance. As they did not wish the men to know about the fire, they hastily gathered up the ashes, which were still alight, and thrust them up their vulvas, so that the men should not see them. When the men came close up, they said, "Where is the fire?" but the women replied, "There is no fire . . . " (Kakadu myth)

Martin Scorsese's contribution to the 1989 anthology film, *New York Stories*, cleverly acknowledged its director's digression from the kind of wiseguy theme for which he was, fairly or not, becoming known. The credit sequence of *Life Lessons*, his story of the relationship between two painters set in the somewhat rarefied New York City art world of the 1980s, runs over the image of "splattered" paint. This splatter simultaneously references the kind of visceral process-painting (à la Jackson Pollock) executed by the film's protagonist, painter Lionel Dobie (Nick Nolte), and the kind of viscera commonly associated with "execution" of a different sort, more commonly seen in other films, such as Scorsese's own *Goodfellas*, which would be released the following year. This pun suggests Scorsese's self-consciousness about both the violence with which his auteurism is marked and the mounting of a scenario (written by Richard Prince and based on Dostoevsky's *The Gambler*) that can so plainly be seen as autobiographical, focusing as it does on the outsized ego and desires of Dobie, a mature, celebrated, oft-married artist who is renowned for his big, colorful, violent, action-packed, gestural, almost baroque *tours de force*. And *Life Lessons* does feature its share of violence, though mainly of the sort expressed through artistic sublimation of powerful sexual impulses, and only occasionally of the more predictable sort associated with a virile temperament.

Life Lessons is but one of several American films released during the 1980s that mixes themes of art, sexual desire, and violence. But its picture of the New York art world is somewhat retrograde, focusing on an increasingly obsolescent – or at least atypical – master/muse theme, and featuring a kind of muscular, male, modernist painting practice that was experiencing a rather histrionic last gasp by the late 1980s with the overexposed careers of neo-expressionist artists like Julian Schnabel, Sandro Chia and Anselm Kiefer. The film does note, with some cynicism, the emergence of another art phenomenon: so-called "performance art," one of several relatively new and high-profile modes of artistic practice in that period which are by no means incidental to the disturbances that ripple through these films, as they did through the art world. As the film opens, Dobie's studio assistant-*cum*-mistress, Paulette (Rosanna Arquette), has been spurned by her choice of lovers, Gregory Stark (Steve Buscemi), a performance artist rather in the mold of Eric Bogosian. An unreconstructed, latter-day New York School type, Dobie is skeptical, to say the least, of this appellation. "Who is this guy?" he asks Paulette; "I know him, right?" "Gregory Stark," she replies. "That kid?" he responds incredulously; "the comedian?" "A performance artist," Paulette corrects. "*Performance artist*," sneers Dobie. "What the hell is a performance artist? The person's an actor, a singer, a dancer . . . I mean, do you call the guy who picks up your garbage a sanitary engineer? A *performance* artist!"

Dobie later accompanies Paulette to a Stark show, one really only distinguishable from stand-up comedy by its trappings. Set in an abandoned subway tunnel, Stark's performance ends with a monologue that voices stereotypical male preoccupation with issues of anger, conflict, and confrontation, and concludes with the sudden explosion of a bare, jury-rigged light fixture over his head. The film itself supports Dobie's suspicion of Stark and the very notion of a "performance" art by cutting away repeatedly during the scene in question to low-angle shots of Dobie's stony, imposing, judgmental visage. Later, in the film's most violent outburst beyond the action of the canvas, Dobie – in righteous, chivalrous indignation, supposedly in defense of Paulette (who is mortified) – assaults Stark in a coffee shop, giving large, histrionic form to the clichés disclosed in the stand-up performance. While

Stark plays with exposing, but does not deconstruct, the ways in which masculinity itself is a performance, Dobie performs the big burly myth itself, replete with all its concomitant imagery: beard, bourbon, cigarettes, penetrating insight, and sexuality.

The heroic, macho typology bodied forth by Lionel Dobie in *Life Lessons* may seem somewhat outmoded in terms of the art world of the 1980s. Indeed, when this narrative is seen in terms of the others I shall discuss, it seems positively quaint in its view of the gendered nature of art and inspiration.[1] This model, however, does not seem so obsolescent in terms of the sexual politics of New Hollywood feature filmmaking, a practice very much dominated in the 1980s, as before and after, in theory (auteurism) and in practice (the biz), by white men and their anxieties, which is very much to the point of this essay. Certainly, as a thinly-veiled autobiographical confession, Scorsese's film exposes some undeniable generalities regarding gender and power in the film industry, if not in the world of art.

The other films I'm concerned with here, including an earlier one by Scorsese, indeed reflect more centrally certain significant eco-nomic, demographic, and artistic changes in the 1980s art world, which included a boom, comparable to that on Wall Street, that was felt from the elite auction houses and blue-chip galleries uptown, down to the profusion of little upstart galleries and alternative venues in the East Village. Indeed, one key cinematic representation of both Wall Street and contemporary art is that offered by Oliver Stone's *Wall Street* (1987), to which half a dozen elite galleries – as well as a number of prominent artists and collectors (including Julian Schnabel) – lent artworks, used in the film mainly as décor for the home and office of millionaire corporate raider and junk-bond specialist Gordon Gekko (Michael Douglas).

I should like to pursue the broader issues relating to the represen-tation of art and commerce in movies of the 1980s. My interest here, however, is in three films – Scorsese's *After Hours* (1985), Ivan Reit-man's *Legal Eagles* (1986), and Dennis Hopper's *Backtrack* (a.k.a. *Catchfire*, 1989) – for the way that each of them conflates represen-tations of women and contemporary art, and of women artists par-ticularly, with danger: ranging from explosive passion, to kidnapping, fire, sadomasochistic acts of aggression, stalking, paralysis, murder, and annihilation. In all instances, the themes of art, femininity, and danger are imbricated and co-implicated. This essay seeks to identify why and how the women and the art, separately and together, seem to become sources of anxiety and loathing, and why, combined, they are wont to create an incendiary provocation. Problematic questions like "Is it art?" and "What does a woman want?" appear to entangle one another in the cinematic-cultural unconscious. I think the answers to these questions may be found in a peculiar nexus of psychological and socio-historical conditions.

Driving Mr Softie: *After Hours'* downtown odyssey

If Hopper's *Backtrack*, to which I shall return, is the most hallucinatory of these films, Scorsese's black comedy, *After Hours*, is the most fertile, especially in the psychoanalytic possibilities afforded by its many symptomatic moments. Written by Joseph Minion, *After Hours* actually plays like a combination of Homer's *Odyssey* and MGM's *The Wizard of Oz* (1939) adapted by Kafka and directed by Freud. Its protagonist, Paul Hackett (Griffin Dunne), a word processor for a generic, midtown-Manhattan corporation, is lured late one night downtown to SoHo by a chance encounter in a coffee shop and eventually finds himself trapped in a nightmarish half-world of unpredictable events and volatile characters, unable to get home. Arriving at a loft to which Marcy (Rosanna Arquette), object of his interest, has invited him, Paul finds her absent – gone on a mysterious errand to the "all-night drugstore" – according to her roommate Kiki Bridges (Linda Fiorentino), a "sculptress" whom Paul finds at work. The sultry Kiki persuades Paul to help dip papier mâché for her work in progress, a rather derivative, expressionist screaming figure which functions in the film as both an augury and index of Paul's dawning terror.[2] Kiki also induces Paul to offer her a massage, in the course of which the conversation turns ominously to the theme of burns, a major leitmotif of the narrative:

Paul: You have a great body.
Kiki: Yes, not a lot of scars . . .
Paul: It's true. It never occurred to me . . .
Kiki: I mean, some women I know are covered with them – head to toe – not me.
Paul: Scars?
Kiki: Uh-huh . . . horrible, ugly scars . . . I'm just telling you, now.
Paul: I don't know . . . I know when I was a kid I had to have my tonsils taken out. And after the operation, they didn't have enough room in pediatrics, so they had to put me in the burn ward. Well, before they

wheeled me in, the nurse gave me this blindfold to put on and she told
me never to take it off. If I did, they'd have to do the operation all over
again. I didn't understand what my tonsils had to with my eyes, either.
But, anyway, that night – at least I think it was night – I reached up to
untie the blindfold and I saw . . . [Kiki suddenly slumps back against
Paul; then snorts. She is asleep.]

Kiki's enigmatic intimations about scarred women and Marcy's
strange behavior upon her return compound Paul's discomfort. His
discovery in Marcy's bag of burn ointment and a medical text with
gruesome images of burn victims, along with her volatile personality, touch an obvious psychic nerve, inducing an increasingly anxious
Paul to conclude that Marcy has been disfigured by burns and (along
with us, the viewers) to actually perceive tell-tale scars with a quick
glimpse of her thigh. Only later, after Paul's erratic behavior and
sudden rejection have contributed to Marcy's unstable state of mind
and probably to her suicide, do we find that the film has imposed
Paul's delusion on us! When he examines her naked corpse, Paul
discovers with simultaneous relief and horror that Marcy is "disfigured" only by a tattoo (albeit one of a skull). That Paul and we are
led to conclude that a disfiguring wound is hidden from view, and,
more to the point, hidden in the vicinity of her genitals, points to the
underlying source of Paul's angst: a primary dread of the female genitalia. This is, of course, an essential aspect of the psychic content of
Paul's tonsillectomy memory, which is very like a screen memory,
the term Freud adopted to describe how the affect and power
attached to repressed ideas (in this case a thinly-veiled castration
scenario) are hidden behind suitable "screens" derived from actual
experience, enhancing them with their characteristic uncanny vivid-
ness. The death's-head iconography, another of the film's leitmotifs,
reinforces the ontological connection between the feminine and
death, which, according to Lacan, follows from the male subject's
recognition "that he is only a sexed living being, and that he is no
longer immortal."[3]

A psychoanalytic reading of this first episode of Paul's nightmare
is more than justified by the imagery connected with the subsequent
episodes, each one associated with a female figure of Medusal
horror.[4] Indeed, as Steve Reinke has pointed out, castration anxiety
is the explicit foundation of the film's scenario.[5] Scorsese foreshad-
ows Paul's subsequent after-hours odyssey with an image whose significance could not be *less* ambiguous. As Paul is resigning himself to

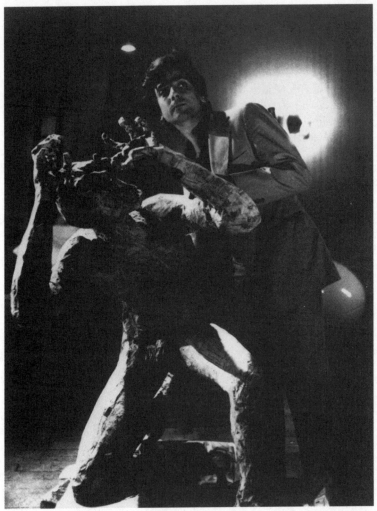

24 The papier mâché sculpture that serves as both "augury and index of Paul's [Griffin Dunne] dawning terror" in *After Hours* (1985)

charm Julie (Teri Garr), a cocktail waitress who has her eye on him, in hopes she might help him get home, he visits the men's room to pull himself together. There, next to the mirror, a graffito attracts his attention: a crude drawing of a man whose erect penis is in the jaws of a shark. And as it turns out, Julie – also a portrait artist and photocopy shop clerk, with a 1960s style and a circuit of mousetraps around her bed – does soon threaten to trap Paul with her guilt trips and her beehive hairdo and, of course, her mousetraps (real and figural). Shortly after Paul has extracted his finger from her hairdo, where it had become stuck, Paul observes a mouse, caught by the spring of a trap. There's no mistaking the expression of empathy on his face as he struggles to get away from Julie, who is loathe to release him.

Gail (Catherine O'Hara), the next potentially fatal female Paul encounters, in fact wounds him with a taxicab door. She drives a "Mr Softie" ice-cream truck – the phallic insult here has not been lost on all critics[6] – and represents a more menacing kind of castration threat. Not only is she shown as rather butch (she *drives* a Mr Softie truck and wears a studded belt) and therefore castrating, but also sadistic. She torments Paul by repeatedly making him forget a phone number he's obtained from directory assistance, demands to dress the wound she gave him, and then discovers, and reads from, a fragment of newsprint stuck as papier mâché to his arm: "a man was torn limb from limb by an irate mob last night in the fashionable Soho area of Manhattan. Police are having difficulty identifying the man because no form of ID was found on his shredded clothing and his entire face was pummeled completely beyond recognition . . . " "Wow!" she exclaims, "What does a guy have to do to get his face pummeled!?" Gail then tries to pull off the bit of papier mâché.

> Gail: Let me get it off for you.
> Paul: Ow! Just stop touching it.
> Gail: I want to get it off for you!
> Paul: Stop touching it!
> Gail: I know, I'll burn it off.
> Paul: No, you're not going to burn it off.
> Gail: Matches. I just need matches.
> Paul: No. No matches!
> Gail: I'm going to ask a neighbor.
> Paul: No, lady, no!
> Gail: My name is Gail.
> Paul: Lady, NO!

Just as Paul's "perception" of her wounds was later cast into doubt over Marcy's dead body, so are these scenes with Julie and Gail, although handled matter-of-factly, ambiguously open to being viewed as evidence of Paul's delusional dementia. Their incipient violence suggests that the repressed has returned, and is knocking at the door. The newspaper account of the man stalked by a vigilante mob presages plot turns yet to come in *After Hours*, when, through a series of mishaps, Paul comes to be suspected of a series of burglaries. This is not the first foretelling of events in this black, black comedy, in which such circularity can be seen alternately as magical or paranoid. In the aftermath of his narrow escape from Gail, Paul climbs, appropriately enough, a *fire escape*, from which he witnesses (or does he?) a horrifying act of domestic violence: a woman (blonde, like most of the film's "sirens") shooting a man at close range.

The last act of *After Hours* begins with the appearance of another female figure, utterly grotesque and yet totally realistic in terms of 1980s New York bohemia: a woman with orange dyed and sculpted hair, black lipstick, a black ring painted around her right eye, and punk regalia – stockings, garters, chains – who walks into a coffee shop and hands Paul an invitation to a "Club Berlin." She is a figure who reminds us that this nightmarish demimonde from which Paul cannot escape is (or at least overlaps with) the art world, a world Scorsese, manifesting some of his usual biases, draws as populated by gay men and Gorgons, although its borders and boundaries seem controlled by archetypically male authority figures: the cabby, token-booth clerk, cop, bouncer, bartenders, etc. But this is not quite the art world of *Life Lessons*: it produces baffling, nontraditional, often immaterial art; the announcement handed Paul is for a "conceptual art party."

Here the film's problematics of art, danger, and the feminine coalesce. Paul finds the Club Berlin empty save for a bartender and June (Verna Bloom), a quiet, self-effacing and seemingly benign older blonde, who, though bewildered by his interest in her, comforts him as they dance together to a song Paul selects from the juke box: Peggy Lee's "Is That All There Is?", an existential lament that begins with a spoken narration about a fire witnessed by a little girl. When the vigilante mob, led by Gail, closes in on him, June, who it turns out is an artist, steals away with the fugitive Paul to her underground atelier, attached to the club. Here in her cave – or womb-like lair – June, Calypso-like, "protects" Paul. Scorsese has said that a previous script ending had June "suddenly growing in size while people were banging on the door shouting, 'We'll kill him!' . . . , and then literally showed Paul climbing up into June's body to escape by 'returning to the womb'!"[7] But in the final version, the seemingly normative and maternal June turns into the most terrorizing gorgon of all, as Paul literally becomes the paralysed sculptural image of terror that had earlier augured his nightmare.

Paradoxically, it is as the subject-turned-object of art theft that Paul finally makes his escape, as Neil and Pepe (Cheech and Chong), the actual burglars, break into June's studio and remove him through the ceiling to their van above. Their discussion about the aesthetic merits of their loot reflects the film's consciousness of widespread public perplexity about postmodern art, as well as discourse about its value as a commodity in a changing marketplace:

> Pepe: Hey, man, is it worth taking this thing?
> Neil: What, are you crazy, man? This is art.
> Pepe: Art sure is ugly, man.
> Neil: That's how much you know, man, you know. The uglier the art, the more it's worth.
> Pepe: This must be worth a fortune, man.
> Neil: That's right. It's by that famous guy, Segal.
> Pepe: It is?
> Neil: Yeah, you seen him? He's on the Carson show, man, plays banjo all the time?
> Pepe: I never watch Carson.
> Neil: Yeah, well, that's how much you know about art.
> Pepe: I don't know, man, I'd take a stereo any day.
> Neil: What do you know, man? A stereo's a stereo. Art is forever.

These words – "art is forever" – are the film's last. *After Hours*' disturbing, mystifying mix of art, sexuality, and violence is resolved with a joke that puts art in its place, so to speak.

"I think I'm uncomfortable . . . ": performance art, radical narcissism, and *Legal Eagles*

The burgeoning market for art in the 1980s, and the high-profile attention to art as a commodity, is one of the central thematic concerns of another symptomatic film of the period, *Legal Eagles*, a convoluted thriller involving murder, arson, art theft, and fraud. Here, too, a sexy blonde artist is a potentially fatal femme. In the film's pre-credit sequence, back story is conveyed via dramatic images of an eight year-old Chelsea Deardon's (Daryl Hannah) birthday party and the fire afterwards that shattered her world, killing her father, a well-known painter. The grown Chelsea is a

25 The "savagely alluring and mystifying" Chelsea Deardon (Daryl Hannah) in *Legal Eagles* (1986)

performance artist who is arrested for theft in her attempt to reclaim a painting of her father's that was supposed to have been destroyed in the fire. But she is also rendered as a preternaturally, almost savagely alluring and mystifying woman. Robert Redford plays Tom Logan, an Assistant District Attorney who loses his job and becomes reluctantly involved in the case, thanks to Chelsea's spunky, resourceful lawyer, Laura Kelly (Debra Winger) and Chelsea's own dangerously seductive behavior. That the film, after unraveling a diabolical scheme on the part of the trustees of Deardon's estate to profit from arson, manslaughter and fraud, doesn't manage to convince of Chelsea's "innocence," only underscores the mythic anxiety with which this character is drawn (the broadcast TV version of the film, in fact, has a completely different ending in which she is *not* entirely innocent).[8]

Chelsea is presented as distraction personified. When she walks into the hall where Logan – introduced by the DA as his probable successor – is giving a speech, her appearance unnerves everyone in the room, as shown in a series of reaction shots strangely reminiscent of those attending the entrance of Marilyn Monroe and Jane Russell into the dining hall scene in *Gentlemen Prefer Blondes* (1953) some thirty years earlier. But Hannah's Chelsea Deardon lacks that parodic self-consciousness so abundantly manifest by those object lessons of the 1950s, as well as the "radical narcissism" characteristic of the feminist body artists of her own era, of whom she seems a faint echo.[9] The embodied distraction of this characterization is the narrative thread that ties together *Legal Eagles'* episodic moments of chaos, violence, and explosion. Chelsea's provocative, childlike presence is linked structurally, if not logically, to a series of disturbances, from the reluctant sexual entanglement of Logan, and ensuing implication of corruption, to murders, sabotage, and pyrotechnic destruction (the explosion of a warehouse and burning of an art gallery).

The mythic contours of this character are underscored through contrast. Debra Winger's role offers a constant, more earthly alternative and, inevitably, a less dangerous, more "appropriate love interest." Chelsea's narcissistic allure is countered by Laura's neurotic spunk; her arty obtuseness with the attorney's quick-witted intelligence. In her next film, Winger again played the down-to-earth, rather tomboyish alternative to a (blonde) woman of deadly allure, which she was pitted against Theresa Russell as the titular *Black Widow* (1987). Winger's function echoes that of similarly drawn characters in films that create an overwhelming and ominous sense of excessive, almost bestial feminine threat. *Cat People* (1942) and *Vertigo* (1958) are two that come immediately to mind. It should be noted that the characters played by Jane Randolph, Barbara Bel Geddes, and Winger in these films are not only spunky and down-to-earth: they are professionals (architect, designer, attorney, Justice Department investigator) – and therefore "masculinized" – while those played by Simone Simon, Kim Novak, Russell, and Hannah are described more by their aura, a large part of which is magical and cannot entail anything so mundane or practical as work, another significant part of which is feral, and therefore unemployable.

But, in fact, the mystification aroused by Chelsea Deardon flows as much from her chosen metier, performance art, as from the stunning, narcissistically seductive, statuesque yet childlike aura that Hannah lent to any number of roles in the 1980s (notably in *Blade Runner*, *Splash*, and *Clan of the Cave Bear*, in all of which she plays *femmes* rather *enfant* and *fatale*).[10] One of *Legal Eagles'* most memorable scenes is the supposedly spontaneous staging of a performance piece that could only happen in a movie. A multimedia extravaganza, it is all set up and ready to perform in Chelsea's loft when she is unexpectedly escorted home by Logan, this despite the fact that the piece involves carefully synchronized recorded and live sound, movement, projection, and the manipulation, ignition, and explosion of numerous props! "Hearts desire, hearts desire, never ever play with fire . . . ," echoes a childlike song. The performance proceeds, a kind of fugue on the theme of fire, one we know to have primary and traumatic meaning for Chelsea. A rather effective pastiche that borrows from a range of high-profile work of the period,[11] this performance makes evident how deeply imbricated is the film's understanding of art and femininity. It draws on manifold aspects of fire: its fascinating kinetic and formal properties, its erotic connotations, its consuming, destructive power – aspects contemplated by Gaston Bachelard in his *Psychoanalysis of Fire*[12] – and collapses all these properties of the performance into the performer, Chelsea herself drawn as a fascinating, erotic, dangerous flame.

At the end of the performance, Chelsea steps behind a large screen on which is projected an image of herself, just as a fuse she has lit burns down and the screen bursts open in flame. As the explosion subsides one sees a life-size figure engulfed in flames, and for a beat the audience – with Logan, who has grabbed a fire extinguisher (placed strategically near his seat) – must imagine that Chelsea has self-ignited. But the figure is revealed to be a mannequin, a prop, as Chelsea herself appears calmly next to Logan. "Well, what did you think?" she asks the stunned lawyer. He is speechless and then stutteringly replies, "I . . . think . . . umm . . . fine." "*What did you think?*" Chelsea repeats insistently. Logan's reaction is halting and baffled, "I think, uh . . . I think I'm uncomfortable," he finally admits. "Good," Chelsea remarks.

.*Legal Eagles* shares Logan's perplexity in the face of this spectacle. While it perfectly well understands, even if it does not sanction, the venal, material self-interest exhibited by the film's villains regarding traditional, material, saleable art objects,[13] it remains uncertain about a so-called art that can neither be sold nor exhibited in traditional ways, and one, moreover, that often derives its power from its very immediacy and immanence. As Carolee Schneemann, a pioneer of performance art, has stated, "there's something female about performance itself, I think, because of how it is ephemeral and close to the unconscious – involving display, use of the self."[14] These remarks underscore how close, too, performance is to cinema, also an ephemeral art of display that is "close to the unconscious," yet one that often claims not to be an art at all, or at least often seems unwilling to partake of that rubric, or to forego remuneration! Here we begin to see how the question, "But is it art?" as regards new and potentially subversive art forms is provocative and disruptive to cinema, another medium of which that question has historically been asked.

"Murder has its sexual side": *Backtrack's* hallucinatory postmodernism

That these new and potentially subversive forms are often associated with women and femininity is part and parcel of the disruption they constitute within a male-dominated industry. "Too close for comfort" expresses something of the crazy scenario at the center of Hopper's straight-to-video labor of love, *Backtrack*, a film which in fact takes me back to where I began, at least chronologically.

Released in 1989, the same year as *Life Lessons*, Hopper's scenario is like *Goodfellas* on acid.[15] Its protagonist is Anne Benton (Jodie Foster), a conceptual artist, whose work is not simply based on that of Jenny Holzer but was in fact made for the film by Holzer, one of the most prominent artists associated with postmodernist art practices in the 1980s. The resemblance between Holzer – who had already when *Backtrack* was produced been chosen to become the first woman to represent America at the 1990 Venice Biennale – and Foster's Anne, however, ends with their work. Holzer's "truisms" and other aphoristic texts, which add to seemingly authoritative, neutral, or received ideas a sharp, critical, often paradoxical twist, were originally conceived to be "exhibited" in the streets, subways, parks, and other public places of Manhattan, not in museums and galleries (though by 1989 they had certainly appeared in such); and they evolved in their presentation from simple Brechtian placards to billboards, urban furniture (for example, benches and bus shelters), and the LED signs employed in *Backtrack*.[16] The work doesn't seem quite as pertinent in the atomized, sprawling Los Angeles that is *Backtrack*'s background, though it does constitute a repeated and ironic disturbance to the scenario. In fact, twenty of Holzer's phrases appear in the film, mostly in LED form, shown in full or in part, including several that seem almost to comment on the clichés invoked by the action:

> SALVATION CAN'T BE BOUGHT AND SOLD
> MURDER HAS ITS SEXUAL SIDE
> I AM CRAZY BORED AND FAMILIAR WITH THE ENDING

LACK OF CHARISMA CAN BE FATAL
CLASS STRUCTURE IS AS ARTIFICIAL AS PLASTIC
GO ALL OUT IN ROMANCE AND LET [THE CHIPS FALL
WHERE THEY MAY]

But as a hybrid of a "real" conceptual artist and a fictional object of desire, Hopper's heroine is a paradoxical figure: tough, ambitious, skeptical but given (unlike Holzer) to wearing rather girlish, sexy short dresses and lingerie. Like *After Hours'* Kiki Bridges or *Legal Eagles'* Chelsea Deardon, Anne Benton suggests some popular fantasy of a woman artist: sexually provocative, mystifying, potentially dangerous; although as played by Foster, who is better suited to the sharp, spunky, tomboyish kind of alternative role, she lacks the preternatural narcissism of those others.

The film's plot is set in motion when Anne, victim of a blow out, stumbles upon a mob hit at a deserted petroleum plant near the freeway while looking for help. Having seen the face of the mobster who committed the crime and his henchmen, she is soon the object of an all-out mob search which claims the life of a boyfriend, and from which she cannot be protected by police or FBI. These organizations have been infiltrated by the mob and the faux-legitimate business which is their boss's cover. Through her wiles, Anne eludes her pursuers, collects some money, and skips town incognito. She adopts a new identity and gets a job at an ad agency in Seattle. Meanwhile, the mob has hired the best hit-man in the business, Milo (Hopper), to track her down.

Milo, a most improbable but inevitable movie figure, pursues his undertaking with the kind of passion, creativity, intelligence, and slightly lunatic insight that Hollywood generally ascribes to artists, very much in contrast to Anne, who is never shown working and whose actual practice is treated by the film with relative incomprehension and indifference. In order to hunt her down, Milo immerses himself in the study of Anne, much like a scholar, a lover, an artist, a connoisseur. He buys her work, surrounds himself with her aphorisms, contemplates her underwear and other effects, and locates her by recognizing an ad copy that, although uncredited, bears her "signature" (it reads, "PROTECT ME FROM WHAT I WANT," one of her "truisms"). That Milo might be taken as the "real" artist in this story is strongly suggested not only by Hopper's rather hackneyed manic intensity but by Milo's demonstrated affinity for the work of "real" artists: Charlie Parker and Hieronymous

Bosch. In fact, the film commits a profoundly counterintuitive role reversal: Anne, an artist and a woman, is the cool, composed, calculating character, while Milo, a hired gun and a man, is the intense, emotional, passionate virtuoso.

Anne just barely survives her first encounter with Milo but he eventually tracks her down in New Mexico after interviewing an artist friend whose work is plainly based on that of Frank Stella – with whom I doubt Jenny Holzer is close friends, but who is played by Bob Dylan (!) – and an encounter with an avatar of D. H. Lawrence (Alex Cox), seemingly conjured by Anne's imagination, at an annual pueblo Church festival (!!). When Milo finally catches up to his prey, this murder artist is loath to "finish" his work.[17] "I know everything there is to know about you," he tells her, revealing to a terrified Anne, whom he has surprised in bed, something of the fascination he feels with her. "You know nothing about me. All you need to know about me is that I'm giving you a choice: either I finish you now, or I let you live. And if I let you live, your life is mine and you belong to me."

From this point, the story becomes an embarrassingly unconvincing and perverse love story. Anne, who at first bristles at her captivity and virtual rape, soon chooses to stay with and love Milo, and with him plots to disable the Mafiosi who threaten their lives and happiness, clearly by the end taking pleasure in arming and defending herself with explosive fire power. Atmosphere associated with the visions of Georgia O'Keeffe and D. H. Lawrence (patron saints of the bohemian desert), her mystical discovery many miles apart of two shards of Indian pottery that fit together and the rescue of a trapped lamb from a rocky crevice, seem to signify Anne's deliverance from the cold, detached, cosmopolitan purgatory of life as a conceptual artist. The film ends with Anne and Milo blissfully sailing away from shore, presumably not long after having blown up a dozen armed Mafiosi and, it seems, an entire oil refinery in the climactic confrontation of this crazy, mixed-up story of art, sex, crime, and punishment. Where they're going is not at all clear.

What *is* clear is that the 1980s were years in which the worlds of art and business were in a volatile, even violent state of flux, as was public discourse about gender, sex, and sexuality. Films such as these captured some of the vicissitudes of the moment. Novel – often mystifying or perplexing – art forms and practices, like the performance art featured in *Legal Eagles* and the LED aphorisms in *Backtrack*, emerge as symptomatic of larger cultural and social problems, at the same time as they collapse into the insoluble riddle of femininity due to their otherness, immanence, irreverence, or mystery. An incipient flammability – an incendiary violence – rendered literal in the manifold explosions, flames and fires seen in these films, is associated with this riddle.

After all, one enduring collective identity crisis of the commercial narrative film is played out in the conflict between art and business, two poles of simultaneous identification and anxiety for popular film, especially in the 1980s, including the three on which I have focused here. Another source of enduring ambivalence and anxiety for Western (if not all) culture generally, as well as Hollywood cinema particularly, is, of course, Woman. Hollywood's most fervent devotion is to the depiction of feminine beauty as the cradle of heterosexual desire. But such devotion has always involved a suppression, a sublation of something horrifying in the ineffable sensuality of the feminine (*vagina dentata*, as illustrated in *After Hours*, or, as in the Kakadu myth related above, *vulva flammea*). These films, and others, suggest a slippage between two alluring, enigmatic, sometimes threatening terms – art and femininity – a slippage that is both a persistent structural attribute of the classical film ethos and a symptom of the sociopolitical cultural flux of the 1980s.[18]

Notes

1 For discussion of the artist couple in *Life Lessons* and two other contemporary films, see Susan Felleman, "Dirty Pictures, Mud Lust, and Abject Desire: Myths of Origin and the Cinematic Object," *Film Quarterly* 55.1 (2001): 27–40.

2 The sculpture is actually by Nora Chavooshian.

3 Jacques Lacan, *The Four Fundamental Concepts of Psycho-analysis*, trans. Alan Sheridan (New York: Norton, 1981), 205.

4 In his classic 1922 essay, "Medusa's Head," Freud analyses how that ancient apotropaic image "isolates" the "horrifying effects" of the female genital from the "pleasure-giving ones." *Collected Papers V*, ed. James Strachey (London: Hogarth Press, 1950), 106.

5 Steve Reinke, "Desire in Scorsese's *After Hours*," *CineAction!* (Summer/Fall 1986): 32–4.

6 See, for instance, Bryan Bruce, "Scorsese: *After Hours*," *CineAction!* (Summer/Fall 1986): 28.

7 *Scorsese on Scorsese*, ed. David Thompson and Ian Christie (London: Faber & Faber, 1989), 100.

8   In three of Hannah's roles of this era – this one, in *Splash* (1984), and in *Clan of the Cave Bear* (1986) – her character is introduced as a child, with primal-scene overtones. These prefaces underscore the narcissistic, childlike qualities of the grown character. The elements of *Legal Eagles'* plot relating to the fraudulent handling of the Deardon estate were inspired by and loosely based on aspects of the Rothko case. See Lee Seldes, *The Legacy of Mark Rothko* (New York: Da Capo Press, 1996).

9   See Amelia Jones, *Body Art/Performing the Subject* (Minneapolis: University of Minnesota Press, 1998), especially 151–95.

10 For a psychoanalytic reading of *Splash* and the mermaid myth, see Susan Felleman, "Fluid Fantasies: *Splash* and *Children of a Lesser God*," *Camera Obscura* 19 (1989): 108–33.

11 According to the film's credits, the performance was created by Arne Glimcher, Daryl Hannah, and Lin Hixson, a "legitimate" performance artist, and accompanied by "Put Out the Fire," written by Hannah and Michael Monteliere.

12 Gaston Bachelard, *The Psychoanalysis of Fire*, trans. Alan Ross (Boston: Beacon Press, 1964).

13 The film's associate producer, gallerist Arne Glimcher, ran Pace Gallery – the basis for the gallery in the film – one of the 1980s' bluest of blue-chip venues.

14 Quoted. in Jones, *Body Art*, 151.

15 The European release of *Backtrack* (titled *Catchfire*) was re-cut by the producers, disowned by Hopper, and is credited to Alan Smithee.

16 For a synoptic view of Holzer's career, see David Joselit, *et al.*, *Jenny Holzer* (London: Phaidon Press, 1998).

17 In *The Apostate* (1998) Hopper would play the role of a literal artist-murderer.

18 A version of this essay was first delivered at the University of Missouri-St. Louis "Violence, Cinema, and American Culture" conference (7 April, 2001). To the organizers, Frank Grady and Paul Roth, and to my fellow participants, I am most indebted. Thanks are also due to Jeffrey Hill, and to my husband, Peter Chametzky, who (as always) contributed much insight, support, and knowledge to this endeavor. For the grant that supported my participation in the conference and other aspects of this work, I thank Southern Illinois University-Carbondale's Women's Studies and University Women's Professional Advancement.

IV

Politics and ideology

12

From "blood auteurism" to the violence of pornography: Sam Peckinpah and Oliver Stone

Sylvia Chong

A tale of two censorships

A Hollywood conundrum: How can a film be branded with an NC-17 rating today when the movie was rated R in 1969? *— shows change*
Answer: When the film is Sam Peckinpah's *The Wild Bunch*. (Jane Galbraith)

In 1994, as Warner Bros. prepared to celebrate the twenty-fifth anniversary of Sam Peckinpah's *The Wild Bunch* (1969; hereafter *WB*), the Motion Picture Association of America (MPAA) derailed the re-release by giving the film an NC-17, a rating usually reserved for explicit sexual intercourse. Many were outraged by the absurdity of this rating, since the standards for screen violence had changed so drastically as to make *WB*'s stylized shoot-outs seem quaint and outdated, especially in contrast with the work of Oliver Stone's *Natural Born Killers* and Quentin Tarantino's *Pulp Fiction*, two other violent films released in 1994.

Ironically, when *WB* was first released in 1969, . . ., it also encountered controversy over its rating. During the period when it was under production, the American film industry was transitioning from the Production Code, a list of content restrictions that applied to all films, to the current MPAA ratings system, which restricts film viewing by age group.[1] Jack Valenti, who became MPAA President in 1968, helped introduce this new ratings system in order to rejuvenate a financially and artistically stagnant film industry, and to allow filmmakers more artistic license. Valenti saw the MPAA ratings system as a form of self-censorship which would allow the industry itself, rather than local and state governments, to draw the line between acceptable and unacceptable content. *WB* could never have been made under the Production Code, but even under the more permissive ratings system, Peckinpah still faced ratings trouble.

Threatened with an X rating, which would severely limit the film's release, Peckinpah deleted over six minutes of footage to reduce the graphic nature of the violence.[2] One of the more famous cuts involved the scene where General Mapache (Emilio Fernandez) slits the throat of Angel (Jaime Sanchez) to spark the Agua Verde shoot-out: the action is shown from a side angle rather than straight on, and a shot depicting blood spurting from the wound was removed.

Although these edits appeased the 1968 ratings board, they apparently did not pass muster in 1994. Judy Brennan remarked in the *Los Angeles Times* that "the MPAA's decision, Warner sources say, seems all the more intractable in light of the R rating given to *Natural Born Killers* – a film Warners considers much more violent than *The Wild Bunch*."[3] There was confusion as to whether the director's cut restored the censored edits. Finally, Peckinpah biographer David Weddle was able to help the studio prove that the director's cut was identical to the print reviewed in 1969 and rated R, and that the restored footage in question was taken out *after* its theatrical release, not before.[4] Finally, *WB* was screened on March 3, 1995 – twenty-six years after its original release.

The ratings game over *WB* highlights a change in the MPAA's stance towards film content between 1969 and 1994. When Valenti testified before Congress in 1968, he defended the then-new ratings system as a way of encouraging creativity of artistic expression in American film while still protecting its most sensitive audience – children – from the deleterious effects of "mature" content. Valenti spoke of a "new breed of filmmaker," one who is not bound "by the conventions of a conformist past" – particularly the conventions of the Production Code which presumably handicapped artistic creativity.[5] But despite Valenti's rhetoric of freedom, he turned away from this stance in the 1990s. What caused Valenti's reversal on this issue? In a word – violence. Commenting on *WB* in 1993, he stated: "In the last decade, there has been a public outrage about violence . . . and the judgment of the ratings board . . . is that the degree, the intensity and the persistence of violence is beyond the ken of young children."[6] Not only have representations of violence increased within films, but public opinion towards the film industry has also become more violent, more "outraged" by the industry's perceived irresponsibility towards the images it creates. Contrary to the conventional wisdom that society becomes more permissive over time, Valenti argues that we are actually less tolerant of violence in the media: "For twenty-five years, the rating system has tried to adjust to society's changing mores . . . Consider: Sam Peckinpah's *The Wild Bunch*, rated 'R' when it was released in 1969, was re-rated 'NC-17' . . . [T]he moral is clear: What was acceptable for children in one rating category more than twenty years ago may not be today."[7] Whereas in 1969 the greatest threat to these children was the loosening of sexual mores, in 1994 the threat comes from violence. Like a sexually-transmitted disease, film violence threatens to mimetically reproduce itself in the bodies of its young viewers and spill into social reality.

Perhaps two of those young people Valenti failed to protect were Mickey and Mallory Knox of *Natural Born Killers* (hereafter *NBK*), a movie often referred to during *WB*'s controversy.[8] Mickey (Woody Harrleson) and Mallory (Juliette Lewis) were Stone's allegorical figures for a society drenched in the discourse of violence, two children raised on the violent fare of post-1960s film and television. Against a backdrop of fake sitcoms, clips from the news, and images assembled from other Hollywood films, Mickey and Mallory go on a rampage and murder over fifty-two people – although during the course of the film, we see only a handful of these killings. Stone uses the media's various visual signatures to critique the glorification of violence which produced this murderous twosome – hence the irony of its title, since its killers are anything but "natural born."

Despite its graphic and controversial content, *NBK* received an R rating after excising only its most explicit scenes, such as a prison riot in which warden Dwight McClusky (Tommy Lee Jones) is decapitated, and a PoV shot through a wound in journalist Wayne Gale's (Robert Downey, Jr.) hand.[9] Overall, 150 cuts totalling just three minutes were cut from the film in order to obtain its R rating. While *NBK* generated a great deal of controversy, especially over a number of copycat murders reportedly influenced by the film, its rating received little public comment.

Why did *WB* re-release rate an NC-17 when *NBK* received an R? It is difficult to gauge which film actually contained more violent acts; both rack up the highest body counts in scenes of mass carnage – Agua Verde in *WB* and the prison riot in *NBK* – in which it is difficult to keep track of how many people actually die. From the reviews of Peckinpah's and Stone's works, one might believe that the two films represent violence in a similar fashion. However, the two director's styles are formally worlds apart, so much so that some scholars, such as Stephen Prince, classify Peckinpah as a modernist and Stone as a postmodernist.[10] A closer investigation of Peckinpah's and Stone's techniques highlights a paradox in the popular under-standing of obscenity as this term is applied to film violence. It is not simply that one film is more "obscene" than the other, but that the understanding of obscenity has changed between 1969 and 1994, reflecting a shift from pornography to violence as the "hard core" at the center of the obscene.

What follows is a Foucauldian analysis of the shifting discourses surrounding film violence, using *WB* and *NBK* as case studies. First, I look at the disjunctures between the discourses of film authorship and obscenity that produce the paradoxical term "blood auteur."[11] This necessitates expanding the definition of obscenity to include not only pornography but violence as well. Then, I return to the question of why *WB* rates an NC-17 by charting the transition from a "pornography of violence" to a "violence of pornography" – from a focus on the perverse pleasures of violent representation to an emphasis on pure aggression and violation. This transforms violence from a forbidden object of desire to the nature of desire itself, and helps to explain the increasing prominence of violence at the heart of current censorship debates.

Blood balletics: aestheticizing the obscene

> But this often-stated theme, that sex is outside of discourse and that only the removing of an obstacle, the breaking of a secret, can clear the way leading to it, is precisely what needs to be examined. Does it not partake of the injunction by which discourse is provoked? (Michel Foucault)
>
> The issue of violence is to this generation what the issue of sex was to the Victorian world. (Kenneth Keniston)

Obscenity has often been linked to pornography and other "low" forms of cultural production, and as such is viewed as incompatible with art. In fact, artistic value has often been used to defend texts from the charge of obscenity. As defined by the "Miller Test," texts with "serious literary, artistic, political, or scientific value" are pro-tected under the First Amendment, whereas obscenity, which lacks such value, is not.[12] A text's obscenity is linked to the obscenity of the sexual acts it represents, which collapses the difference between sign and referent and obscures the author's role in shaping the

Blood
Auteur

representation of the obscene. In cinema, the notion of an "auteur" implies that a director shapes his or her film through individual style. But the term "blood auteur" is problematic in part because here the notion of creator confronts the brute materiality of the obscenity of violence, which resists aestheticization by constantly gesturing outside the realm of discourse, into the "real." While few would suggest that there exists a pure, unmediated presentation of violence in film, the signifiers of film violence – forceful actions, blood, weaponry, wounds – are nonetheless overdetermined by a burden of meanings inherited not only from other films but from non-fictional film and television and from personal experience.

Link between violence + porn

Although violence has not traditionally been associated with obscenity, the two have become increasingly linked through the efforts of both anti-pornography feminists and anti-violence media activists. In an age of relative sexual permissiveness where the stigma of pornography has faded, feminists like Catharine MacKinnon have sought to regulate pornography by linking it with violence. In the anti-pornography ordinances MacKinnon helped to write, this link is doubled: the pornography industry is implicated in actual acts of violence against women, and the resulting pornography is presented as a "virtual" act of violence against all women.[13] Alternately, legal scholars such as Kevin Saunders have used existing obscenity laws to make a case for the censorship of violence. Responding to the popular perception that violent representations produce violent actions, anti-media violence laws in Missouri and Tennessee appeal to "community standards" and "prurient interest" in the language of the Miller Test.[14] Such links create the perception that violence is pornographic: that its audience derives a prurient pleasure from consuming its representations.

pain + pleasure

Although this connection may be purely coincidental or ideologically motivated, it indicates several formal similarities between film pornography and film violence. Both genres strive to make visible internalized affects – of pleasure and pain, respectively, although not exclusively. As the discourse of sexuality revolves around some hidden "truth" of pleasure which it seeks to expose, so does the discourse around violence resolve around a hidden "truth" of pain.[15] Because affects are situated inside the body, their translation requires a visible signifier to violate the boundary from within the body to without. In violence, that privileged signifier is blood, while in hard-core pornography it is semen.

Critical response to *WB* at the time of its initial release illustrates the primacy of blood in the film's perception: Judith Crist, for example, called it a "blood-lust slaughter-cult film"; Vincent Canby, a "blood ballet."[16] Even Charles Champlin's positive review of the film noted that it was "not so much a movie as a blood bath. We see the bodies flinch and the bullet holes appear and the blood explode from the exit wounds."[17] This last comment highlights the visceral link between blood, pain, and bodies. It is not simply that blood appears in copious amounts, but that the blood is *seen* to exit the body. And bodies literally dance in reaction to pain: they flinch and explode and gush. These ejaculations are analogous to the "money shot" in heterosexual hard-core pornography. Linda Williams notes that the money shot not only makes visible the "truth" of the man's pleasure, but also stands in for "the woman's invisible and unquantifiable pleasure."[18] Blood in screen violence enacts a similar transference of affect, with the blood spurting out of the victim standing in for the sadistic delight of the aggressor. However, blood also *transforms* affect, by changing the victim's pain into the aggressor's visual pleasure.

Mapache's death in *WB* illustrates the mechanics of blood and its ability to stand for both pain *and* pleasure. When Mapache slits Angel's throat, the first reaction shot from the Bunch is a close-up of Dutch's (Ernest Borgnine) face, his mouth wordlessly open in shock. But the silence does not last long, for Pike (William Holden) and Dutch respond by killing Mapache. Each shot is represented by an exploding squib followed by a spurt of blood, mimicking the mechanics of the "money shot." Peckinpah depicts each bullets' impact in slow motion, twirling Mapache's body around and visibly exiting his body. If the presence of blood symbolizes the affect of pain, then the amount of blood comes to stand in for the magnitude of that pain. But Mapache's pain does little to increase our sympathy for the character. If anything, his dying body is made to speak for the Bunch's anguish for their slain friend (juxtaposed against Dutch's silent cry), as well as for the mute pain of Angel's body, which only appears as a blur in the corner of our eye as it falls. (Remember that Angel's body is literally silenced by the ratings board, which demanded that the shot featuring blood gushing from his throat be cut.) Like the money shot, the bullet shot here signifies not the pain of the fallen body, but that of the Other whose affect is otherwise invisible to the camera. By being externalized in the form

26 Exploding squibs and spurts of blood: General Mapache's (Emilio Fernandez) "money shot" in *The Wild Bunch* (1969)

of blood, affect is freed from its originating subject and, like a dream-symbol, attaches to any number of the film's "subjects": Dutch, Angel, even the viewing audience.

An additional element of obscenity is excess – manifested in film as an excess of visibility defying the injunction to keep the obscene hidden. Whereas non-obscene sexual representations disguise the sexual object, obscene representations "let it all out": they glory in the "meat shots" (of genitalia) and "money shots" not allowed outside of pornography. This policy of full visual disclosure is at work in film violence as well. One early newspaper ad for *WB* dares the viewer: "If a look at the face of violence disturbs you, stay away from The Wild Bunch."[19] *NBK* adds an additional element of excess, not just in the *content* but in the *form* of the film. Although Stone employed Peckinpah's rapid-cutting montage style and use of exploding squibs, he also briskly juxtaposed the texture and appearance of his shots, mixing film speeds, animation and live-action, color and b&w, and other visual effects – resulting in what some reviewers called a "hyperkinetic" film with a "deranged energy."[20] *WB*'s visual excess lies within the spectacle of the physical body and its fluids, while the excess of *NBK* lies more within the spectacle of the spectacle itself.

Mickey's prison interview with Wayne Gale in *NBK* illustrates both the eruptive and excessive elements of Stone's style. As a prison riot interrupts the interview, Mickey entertains the remaining guards and television crew with a dirty joke: Little Bobby accompanies his older sister on a date to the drive-in, and reports on the date to his mother. Because Bobby can't talk, Mickey pantomimes the answers

– first the date drives, then kisses and fondles the sister, takes off her clothes, and has intercourse with her. At the joke's climax, the mother asks Bobby, "What the hell were you doing?", to which Bobby/Mickey replies by masturbating. Then Mickey segues from one phallic apparatus to another by grabbing a shotgun from one of the guards. In a departure from Peckinpah's style, Stone uses slow-motion, grainy, black and white film when Mickey shoots, and regular-speed, full-color, 35mm film when the guards are shot. The slow motion emphasizes the action of shooting the gun, while the full color calls attention to the red blood coming from those shot. However, Stone rarely employs squibs in *NBK*, and features fewer detailed shots than Peckinpah of exploding wounds. Although his technique may seem to link the viewer with Mickey's position, the narrative context places the viewer alongside the guards. The audience seems to be separated from *NBK*'s violent content until the film targets listening/viewing itself as a vulnerable position.

In much film violence, both the violation of the body's boundaries through blood and the excess of the visual spectacle contribute to what could be seen as a form of "de-humanization": the reduction of the human body to its material elements. Saunders, who champions the use of obscenity law against violent representations, argues that "what strikes us as obscene, in this non-legal sense, are actions or depictions in which people are afforded subhuman treatment or treated as nothing more than physical entities . . . [Violence] indicates the treatment of people as nothing more than meat."[21]

The metaphor of "meat" resonates with the "meat shot" of pornography, and applies as well to both Peckinpah's and Stone's aesthetics of violence. Prince notes that Peckinpah devotes "the bulk of the visual attention in the slow-motion inserts . . . to the body's loss of volitional control over its actions"[22] In violence, the body becomes incontinent; it is merely a body of physical laws rather than a body of agency and will. This reduction to materiality takes a different route in *NBK*, where multiple layers of images flatten subjectivity into a visual effect, a splatter of light from a projector. If Stone's film is postmodern, it is because it reduces the subject to a two-dimensional surface, denying both psychological depth and the substantive depth of the three-dimensional body. (As many reviewers have noted, *NBK*'s murders are relatively easy to accept because none of the victims have any real "subjectivity.") Differences aside, however, rather than reading "de-humanization" as a purely negative trait, I would argue that

27 In contrast with Peckinpah's style, Oliver Stone "uses slow-motion, grainy, black and white film when Mickey [Woody Harrelson] shoots" in *Natural Born Killers* (1994)

both Peckinpah's and Stone's attention to the material body confronts the mind/body duality which Saunders takes as given, attempting to reconnect the filmic body to the real body without resorting to a human "spirit" as an intermediary.

This connection between filmic bodies and real bodies threatens to bypass the workings of the rational mind, leading some critics to fear that audience members will directly imitate the violent acts viewed on screen. This "mimetic compulsion" is often used to indict both film violence and pornography: the obscene, visceral nature of the acts portrayed by these genres is seen as particularly amenable to imitation. This calls to mind both the Production Code's motivation for censoring detailed depictions of crime, as well as Robin Morgan's famous anti-pornography slogan: "Pornography is the theory, and rape the practice." According to this reasoning, film is little more than a "how-to" guide for rape, crime, and violation. Even Peckinpah acknowledged the seductiveness and excitement of watching violent acts: after *WB*'s opening robbery scene, he depicts a group of young boys who had witnessed the fighting now reenacting it in play, pointing their hands like guns at the camera. Stone parodies the mimetic impulse in *NBK* when he portrays a group of teenagers at Mickey's trial. "I'm not into killing," one of them claims, "but if I *were* a mass murderer, I'd want to be like Mickey and Mallory." Stone and *NBK* were actually accused of instigating a string of "copycat" murders, and in one case have been sued for damages with the claim that *NBK* was both obscene and inciteful of violence.[23]

Although none of the critics of obscenity propose a theory of how violence is mimetically transferred, it is likely that imitation (when it occurs) follows from identification with the characters in the text. It is instructive to compare the various arguments made against violence in films with Socrates' argument against poetry in *The Republic*. Socrates wants to exclude poetry from his ideal state because poetry imitates reality in such a way as to substitute itself for true understanding. Moreover, poetic mimesis – like cinema and unlike painting – is especially dangerous because of its *performed* nature, for it invites an active kind of participation from the listener. As Socrates describes this process,

> The best of us, I imagine, when we *hear* Homer or one of the tragic poets *imitating* some hero in a state of grief . . . well, you know how it is. We *enjoy* it, and *surrender* ourselves to it. We follow and *share the hero's sufferings, treat them as real,* and praise as an excellent poet the person who most affects us in this way.[24]

The familiarity with which Socrates refers to this experience points to just how persuasive mimesis is in this performed mode. As G. R. F. Ferrari notes, "'Imitation,' indeed, is too pale a word in English for what Socrates evidently speaks of here: 'identification' or 'emulation' would be closer to the mark."[25] Indeed, this type of mimesis is not merely an abstract process but involves the body – both that of the actor who imitates the character and that of the listener who identifies with that character. Our enjoyment of film narratives relies upon our identification with and vicarious enjoyment of the experiences of film characters.

But, as seen in the readings of *WB* and *NBK* above, is it ultimately possible to separate out identification with victims and identification with aggressors? Is it Mapache's pain or the Bunch's pleasure of revenge that we feel? Mickey's aggression or the guards' vulnerable shock of surprise? Although it is assumed that we always identify with the active role, we must remember that these positions are not stable, and that the agents of violence are often recipients as well: Mickey and Mallory are shot during the riot, and the Bunch is killed at the end of their shoot-out. Freud reminds us that sadism is contingent upon masochism, and that the enjoyment of inflicting pain requires a prior suffering of pain, so that even the sadist identifies with the suffering victim.[26] Therefore, the argument that one can lesson violence by showing "the face of human suffering" is disingenuous: it assumes that identification with *pain* leads to an ethical stance against *violence*. If anything, Mallory's abusive childhood in *NBK* encourages her later rampages.

This is not to say that violence necessarily begets violence, only that identification with the victim does not preclude identification with the aggressor. Likewise, the vicarious experience of pain can be transformed via masochism into a form of pleasure in and of itself. Describing his first viewing of *WB* as a teenager, screenwriter Charles Higson said, "Once the film was over, I was exhausted and in a state of high nervous excitement. I wanted to go out in a blaze of glory. I wanted a Gatling gun. I wanted to be pierced by a hundred bullets."[27] Higson's orgiastic pleasure – focused on pain and penetration – is masochistic, but it nonetheless valorizes the Gatling gun's phallic imagery. The controversy aroused by *WB* derives not only from its audacity in depicting graphic violence, but also from the visceral viewing pleasures produced by its aesthetic procedures.

In order to portray Peckinpah as an auteur rather than a pornographer, Stephen Prince goes to great lengths to distance him from this element of sadistic pleasure.[28] His book-length study, *Savage Cinema*, qualifies Peckinpah's "sensuous and kinetically appealing" screen violence by emphasizing the melancholy and suffering in his violence as a counterbalance.[29] The title of the concluding chapter, "A Disputed Legacy," reveals Prince's discomfort with Peckinpah's placement as the forefather of "ultraviolent movies." If we reject modern movie violence, Prince asks, "must we also, therefore, condemn and reject Peckinpah's work?"[30] But like the difficulty of separating sadism from masochism in the experience of film violence, is it possible to delineate between "good" and "bad" violence? Prince contrasts Peckinpah with such directors as Scorsese, De Palma, Tarantino, and Stone, concluding that Peckinpah's moral agenda and focus on suffering redeem his films against the dehumanized, superficial spectacles of these other directors. Stone's flaws, for Prince, are a lack of an "abiding moral perspective on its violence" and the "loss of control over the images he wishes to manipulate"[31] – both qualities that Peckinpah presumably portrays. These are also the qualities that separate the auteur, who retains mastery over the substance of his art, from the pornographer, whose representations are overwhelmed by their overdetermined significations.

For Prince, the difference between Peckinpah and his "legacy" lies not in the mere presence of violence, squibs, slow motion, montage editing, etc., but in the purpose for which they are used. But this begs the question of *how* any given viewer would ascertain this grand purpose, and whether this knowledge would change one's reception of the film. Thus, the defense of a "blood auteur" comes down to emphasizing the auteur over the blood. Echoing the legal language on obscenity, Prince invokes the power of authorial intent to defend Peckinpah: "[His] interest in violence was never *prurient*, and it was never conceived to stoke the extravagantly gory fantasies of its audience."[32] Yet this point is belied by Prince's own quote from Charles Higson, analyzed above. It is as if the powerful affects – both painful and pleasurable – generated by Peckinpah's work, and by *WB* in particular, overwhelm any moral intentions on the director's part. The sheer excess of bloody violence at *WB*'s end seems to obliterate any rational meditation on its cause or motivation.

Each of these techniques of the "blood auteur" seem to posit death as the "truth" of violence, the seeking of which ignites both fascination and revulsion. We might ask the same questions regarding violence that Foucault asks of sex. What is it about the truth of violence that both incites discourse around it and produces taboos and prohibitions against it? Violence, like sex, has been subject to the repressive hypothesis, in which we assume the existence of a repressive regime which censors and prohibits expression. Therefore, the very act of representing violence or sex seems transgressive. However, the act of transgression actually reinforces the repression or taboo which is purports to violate, thus instigating a vicious cycle in which even more discourse on sex and violence is produced. The hyper-visibility of violence reflects our anxiety to master it, to know it; the inaccessibility of death does not starve discourse, but in fact incites and produces it. Most modern censorship aimed at both sexuality and violence take for granted the power of their representations to reproduce themselves – that sex begets more sex, violence more violence. *NBK* and *WB* are not definitive statements of violence that silence their critics and competitors: they are incitements to more violence of a discursive nature, which proliferate out of their creators' control.

Thus, the power of the obscene implies both a material and stylistic excess that detracts from the mastery implicit in notions of authorship. This is not to say that either Stone or Peckinpah succeed in depicting an unmediated view of violence. Rather, the difficulty of the body in controlling its ejaculations and movements parallels the difficulty of the "blood auteur" in controlling the reception of his text. This applies even to the work of other directors who choose a less mediated, more "documentary" approach to representing violence, notably John McNaughton in *Henry: Portrait of a Serial Killer* (1986). Prince was correct in pointing out that Stone "could not divorce the style of [*NBK*] from the targets of his attack."[33] But this difficulty plagued Peckinpah as well, who reportedly vomited when he heard of Nigerian soldiers who fired their guns at the screen after watching *WB*.[34] The rhetorical force of Peckinpah's and Stone's obscene violence guaranteed a strong response from their audiences; however, the consequences of that response remain out of their control. The multiple levels of metaphor, mimesis, and identification between the film texts and the "real world" thus resemble the legal definition of obscenity, in that each seems to collapse the difference between sign and referent, fiction and fact, simulated and real violence. The failure of these artists to control violence and get at its "truth" derives from the very obscenity of their representations, blurring as it were the gap between materiality and textuality – transgressing the boundaries between inside and outside the body, victim and aggressor, and pain and pleasure.

The pornography of violence? Or the violence of pornography?

> In recent years the movies and television have developed a pornography of violence far more demoralizing than the pornography of sex which still seizes the primary attention of the guardians of civic virtue. (Arthur Schlesinger, Jr.)

> Under the influence of the ego's instincts of self-preservation, the pleasure principle is replaced by the *reality principle*. This latter principle does not abandon the intention of ultimately obtaining pleasure, but it nevertheless demands and carries into effect the postponement of satisfaction . . . (Sigmund Freud)

If analyzing *WB* and *NBK* under the rubric of obscenity brings them closer together, it may also obscure some crucial differences between them, particularly in their historical periodization. Because the styles of modern Hollywood film violence emerged at the same time the concepts of obscenity and pornography were being redefined by the courts and the film industry in the late 1960s, the discourse on violence was conveniently propped upon the rhetoric of the pornography debates. However, as the controversy over pornography has somewhat died down, the debate over violence took on some new rhetorical features in the 1990s, most notably an outcry against its "meaninglessness" and a focus on aggression rather than pleasure as the antithesis of societal order. I refer to the earlier attitude as the "pornography of violence" (POV), following historian Arthur Schlesinger,[35] and to the later attitude as the "violence of pornography" (VOP), thereby highlighting a reversal of affect around the two terms. Freud's schema of the reality principle versus the pleasure principle is helpful in delineating a crucial difference between these terms, for both POV and VOP revolve around different manifestations of the instincts of aggression and sexuality.

A crucial point in understanding *Beyond the Pleasure Principle* is that Freud's use of "pleasure" does not correspond to this word's everyday meaning. For Freud, pleasure is purely a discharge or "diminution" in "the quantity of excitation" in a psychic system, one which is often linked to the death drive – death being the cessation of all tension.[36] On the other hand, the reality principle refers to a deferment of pleasure for the purposes of sustaining life, conditioning the subject to postpone discharge of tension until the attainment of another goal. An increase in tension can be caused by something as simple as hunger; pleasure, in this case, is the cessation of hunger by consuming food. However, most circumstances in life require subjects to postpone immediate satisfaction for the sake of other activities or the needs of loved ones. Consequently, instincts such as aggression and sexuality can either be *bound* (harnessed under the reality principle) or *unbound* (left to discharge themselves freely under the pleasure principle).[37] Bound instincts might actually produce more pain than pleasure, as when tension is endured in order to reach a greater pleasure or goal, and therefore carry a sense of future temporality. However, unbound instincts seem to exist in a perpetual present; they demand immediate gratification. If we look at the types of media sex and violence that are most often censored, we will find that they are usually linked with the unbounded energy of the death drive: for example, non-reproductive sexual practices such as bondage, or anal and oral eroticism, and acts of violence that do not fall under either self-defense or sport.

The discourse around POV is linked to bound instincts, and the social violence referred to in Peckinpah's work was often of a political nature, harnessed towards the goals of social transformation, whether revolutionary (anti-war protests, violent overthrow of the government) or reactionary (the Vietnam War itself, police suppression of protests). Televised coverage of the assassinations of both John F. Kennedy and Martin Luther King, Jr., plus the on-air shooting of Lee Harvey Oswald, also provided an immediate cultural and visual context for Peckinpah's renditions of violence. Although he does not specifically cite any current events in *WB*, Peckinpah constantly refers to Vietnam, particularly the My Lai massacre, in his responses to critics. He also indirectly references these events in his film: *WB*'s opening bank robbery portrays the killing of innocent civilians by both sides of the shoot-out, and the final Agua Verde sequence depicts the mass destruction made possible by automatic weapons. In a 1972 *Playboy* interview, Peckinpah remarked,

> We watch our wars and see men die, really die, every day on television, but it doesn't seem real. We don't believe those are real people dying on that screen. We've been anesthetized by the media. What I do is show people what it's really like – not by showing it as it is so much as by heightening it, stylizing it.[38]

Peckinpah explicitly links the act of viewing with a moral imperative of seeking the truth, and he directs his "heightening" and "stylizing" towards making this truth more visible. The technical and economic (not to mention psychic) investments Peckinpah made towards showing this truth reveal his visual pleasures to be bound up with larger political agendas. Although critics may accuse him of making violence "pleasurable" to watch, he nonetheless succeeds in forcing those same critics *to watch* rather than to turn away – thus combating the greater "anesthetization" he locates in the media treatment of violence.

On the other hand, VOP is linked to unbound instincts; the violence Mickey and Mallory inflict is often not focused on any particular social structures, but simply on whomever happens to be in their way. They resemble the infants described by Freud throughout his work, who narcissistically view the world as an extension of themselves. The world exists only to satisfy their pleasures; when an obstacle appears, their first reaction is to obliterate it. The physical and visual exhilaration of violence thus becomes an end in itself.

"Killing you will send a message," Mickey tells Wayne Gale – "I just don't know what that message will be." Even sexuality and pleasure become subordinated as another means to violence: Mallory shoots a gas station attendant who didn't satisfy her sexually, and Detective Scagnetti (Tom Sizemore) murders a prostitute after having sex with her in order to better understand Mickey and Mallory. If we extrapolate from MacKinnon's concept of pornography as hate speech, the filmic representation of violence also becomes literally an act of violence on its viewers. Thus, *NBK* assaults its viewers both stylistically and narratively, by bombarding them with a profusion of colors, cuts, and textures.

Even when Stone employs Peckinpah's method of referencing current events, he further divorces the contents of his film from the outside world. At the end of *NBK*, Stone uses the evening news as a framing device to situate Mickey and Mallory among various non-fictional news figures: Tonya Harding, Rodney King, O. J. Simpson, the Menendez Brothers, Lorena Bobbitt, etc. In blurring the line between fiction and fact, Stone ends up making the real seem fake rather than making the fictional seem true; for example, he juxtaposes Bobbitt's retaliation against domestic violence and King's suffering of police brutality against Simpson's infliction of domestic violence and the FBI's use of unreasonable force at Waco, Texas, thereby flattening the context of each of these events under the signifier "violence." By erasing the differences between acts of violence, Stone promotes a sense that all violence is literally *meaningless* – that is, violence resides in a symbolic system where there no longer exist any distinctions between violent acts. This corresponds to the changing perceptions of violence from the 1960s, when the public feared an increase in politicized violence, to the 1990s, where the public reacts against random acts of violence.

The subtle reversal contained in this chiasmus – POV/VOP – suggests a societal context for the re-evaluation of the term "obscenity" in legal discourse. This is not to say that either *WB* and *NBK* belong solely to the categories POV or VOP; episodes in each film can be interpreted either way. But these categories locate a logical shift in the reception of violence, and help to explain why critics responded differently to each film at the time of their release. In fact, re-rating *WB* in 1994 forcibly severed its ties to any greater social context, promoting the belief that its displays of violence were meaningless and unbounded. The ratings board, being composed of parents rather than film historians, may not have supplied this missing context on their own, and thus viewed *WB* as another instance of unrestrained media violence. The pain experienced by the Bunch had no more meaning for the board than Mickey's murder of Wayne Gale – both were simply media events, purely spectacles. In fact, because *WB* relies more heavily on extended displays of ejaculating blood and spasming, incontinent bodies, it may have appeared *more* obscene than *NBK*, whose intentional irony and emphasis on active aggression focus more on mastery than masochism.

As the tide of public opinion leans towards approving the censorship of violence, we must ask ourselves whether the problem of violence lies in the films themselves or in their reception. In either condemning violence or celebrating it, we reify violence into a never-changing object, and risk collapsing the differences between types of violence and their deployment. Ratings boards or obscenity laws which seek to arrest the expression of violence in some forms always result in proliferating violence in other forms: bullet wounds censored because of their graphic nature morph into the pyrotechnics of exploding buildings where not a single person visibly dies. We will not stifle what seems to be the unceasing death drive of our popular culture by simply pretending that death does not exist; Freud's solution, rather, is to bind our instincts to the reality principle, to see what larger structures or purposes inform the manifestation of violence around us. The results of a strengthened censorship are not worth the foreclosure of these avenues of discourse, which can potentially restore context to seemingly meaningless representations of violence.

Perhaps our rallying cry could be a variation of Foucault's enigmatic conclusion to his *History of Sexuality*: rather than returning to "bodies and pleasure,"[39] we could return to *bodies and pain*, and examine the *affects* as well as the *effects* of violence. Whose bodies are produced, examined, incarcerated, or otherwise circumscribed by our deployment of violence in discourse? This would be one possibility for breaking out of the mimetic circle of violence surrounding our film texts – not by circumventing representation and discourse, but by forming links between different bodies and different texts. It is in our bodies, ultimately, and not simply our minds, that film reception takes place.

Notes

1 For more on the transition between the Production Code and the MPAA ratings system, see Jon Lewis, *Hollywood v. Hard Core: How the Struggle over Censorship Saved the Modern Film Industry* (New York: New York University Press, 2000), 135–91.

2 David Weddle, *"If They Move . . . Kill 'Em!": The Life and Times of Sam Peckinpah* (New York: Grove Press, 1994), 364; Stephen Prince, *Savage Cinema: Sam Peckinpah and the Rise of Ultraviolent Movies* (Austin: University of Texas Press, 1998), 22–4.

3 Judy Brennan, "*Wild Bunch*: In 25 More Years, It'll Be G-Rated," *Los Angeles Times* (Oct. 2, 1994): Calendar, 27.

4 See Weddle, "If They Move", 369–73; Judy Brennan, "R You Ready for the Reborn 'Wild Bunch'?", *Los Angeles Times* (Feb. 19, 1995): Calendar, 30.

5 "Statement before the National Commission on the Causes and Prevention of Violence" (Dec. 19, 1968). Reprinted in *Screening Violence*, ed. Stephen Prince (New Brunswick: Rutgers University Press, 2000), 65.

6 Qtd. in Jane Galbraith, "A Look at Hollywood and the Movies; Sam Peckinpah Meets the Mild Bunch," *Los Angeles Times* (March 14, 1993): Calendar, 21.

7 "Why Assault After Assault Can't Kill Rating System," *Los Angeles Times* (Nov. 20, 1994): Opinion, Part M, 2.

8 Both films were produced by the same studio, centered their narratives around similar themes of violence and social decay, were similarly innovative in its use of montage style, and came before the ratings board during the same year. In another strange coincidence, Stone boasted that *NBK* contained between 3,500 and 4,000 cuts, the most in any feature-length film to date. *WB* also boasted a similar number of cuts – around 3,642 – and made a similar claim to fame as being the most heavily-edited movie of its time. See Weddle, "If They Move", 362.

9 Donald Liebenson, "In all its gory glory; Director Stone says video release of 'Killers' lets him finish what he started," *Los Angeles Times* (July 30, 1996): Calendar, Part F, 1.

10 Prince, *Savage Cinema*, ch. 5.

11 Coined by Peter Keough in his "Introduction" to *Flesh and Blood: The National Society of Film Critics on Sex, Violence, and Censorship* (San Francisco: Mercury House, 1995), xi.

12 See Miller v. California, 413 US 15 (1973).

13 Catharine MacKinnon, *Only Words* (Cambridge: Harvard University Press, 1993). For an analysis of Mackinnon's construction of speech as conduct, see Judith Butler, *Excitable Speech: A Politics of the Performative* (New York: Routledge, 1997), 73–102.

14 Kevin Saunders, *Violence as Obscenity: Limiting the Media's First Amendment Protection* (Durham: Duke University Press, 1996), 21–2.

15 Michel Foucault, *The History of Sexuality, Vol. 1*, trans. Robert Hurley (New York: Vintage Books, 1978), 53–7.

16 Crist quoted in Marshall Fine, *Bloody Sam: The Life and Films of Sam Peckinpah* (New York: Donald I. Fine, Inc., 1991), 153; Canby, "Violence and Beauty Mesh in *Wild Bunch*," *New York Times* (June 25, 1969): Arts & Leisure, 45.

17 "Violence Runs Rampant in *The Wild Bunch*," *Los Angeles Times* (June 15, 1969): Calendar, 1.

18 Linda Williams, *Hard Core: Power, Pleasure, and the "Frenzy of the Visible"* (Berkeley: University of California Press, 1989), 113.

19 *Los Angeles Times* (June 18, 1969): Pt. IV, 10.

20 Janet Maslin, "*Natural Born Killers*; Young Lovers With a Flaw That Proves Fatal," *New York Times* (Aug. 26, 1994): Sec. C, 1; Craig Macinnis, "Cruising for a Killing; Stone's Otherwise Powerful Killers Declines into Farcical Rant," *Toronto Star* (Aug. 26, 1994): Entertainment, B1.

21 Saunders, *Violence as Obscenity*, 3.

22 Prince, *Savage Cinema*, 63.

23 See R. Robin McDonald, "Violent youths getting ideas from movie? In three murder cases, police cite Stone film," *Atlanta Journal and Constitution* (April 3, 1995): 4C; Curt Anderson, "Dole Cites Massachusetts Murder in Blasting Hollywood Mores Again," *Associated Press* (June 28, 1995); Joel Black, "Grisham's Demons," *College Literature* 25.1 (1998): 35–41.

24 Plato, *The Republic*, trans. Tom Griffith (Cambridge: Cambridge University Press, 2000), Book X, 605d; emphasis added.

25 G. R. F. Ferrari, "Plato and Poetry," *The Cambridge History of Literary Criticism, Vol. 1*, ed. George Kennedy (Cambridge: Cambridge University Press, 1989), 116.

26 Sigmund Freud, "Instincts and Their Vicissitudes," *General Psychological Theory* (New York: Simon & Schuster, 1963), 93.

27 Prince, *Savage Cinema*, 99.

28 Marsha Kinder also views Prince as struggling with this problem. See Kinder, "Violence American Style: The Narrative Orchestration of Violent Attractions," *Violence and American Cinema*, ed. J. David Slocum (New York: Routledge, 2001), 69–70.

29 Prince, *Savage Cinema*, 229.

30 *Ibid.*, 213.

31 *Ibid.*, 246–7.

32 *Ibid.*, 234; emphasis added.

33 *Ibid.*, 243.

34 *Ibid.*, 98.

35 Arthur Schlesinger, Jr., *Violence: America in the Sixties* (New York: Signet Books, 1968).
36 Sigmund Freud, *Beyond the Pleasure Principle,* trans. James Strachey (New York: W. W. Norton, 1961), 4.
37 *Ibid.,* 75–7.
38 Quoted in Prince, *Savage Cinema*, 49.
39 Foucault, *The History of Sexuality*, 157.

13

"Too much red meat!"

David Tetzlaff

Brothers and Sisters, students and teachers of the cinematic arts: do not view the popular culture as a force of good. Do not view the popular culture as a force of evil. In the culture, as in the human souls who made it, both good and evil are woven together.

When the righteous man looks at you, he does not ignore the evil within you, but neither does he dwell on it. Instead he seeks the seed of goodness in you, that he might help you feed, water, and care for that seed, for this is how we come to salvation. I tell you today that a movie, like a man, can be saved! I call on all of you, from this moment, to be missionaries of righteous interpretation. I call on you to go out into the marketplace where movies meet the masses and meaning gets manufactured, to seek out the evil moments of those meanings and smite them with the wit of your tongues and pens, yea, but I also call on you to seek out the moments of goodness in those meanings and nurture them with your words, that they may be fruitful and multiply.

Can I hear a little righteous revolution out there? Brothers and Sisters, each and every one of you you must decide whether you are going to be part of the problem or part of the solution. You must choose, yes, you must choose. Now, let's talk about violence . . .

In the 1985 action film *Commando*, the character played by Arnold Schwarzenegger sneaks up behind a man and slits his throat with a large knife, elbows the jaw of the man sitting next to him in an airplane hard enough to break the man's neck, delivers an uppercut that sends a large man flying backward through the air, landing so the leg of an overturned coffee table impales him through the stomach, smashes a man's forehead into an iron dumpster, stabs a man in the chest with a pitchfork, throws a tablesaw blade Frisbee-style, cutting off the top of a man's head, drives a hatchet into a man's groin, cuts off a man's arm with a machete, machine guns several men who die falling backward in slow motion with blood bursting from their bodies, fires a shot gun repeatedly into a man's chest, and drops another man off a cliff into a deep ravine.[1]

Following New Hollywood action film conventions, all of these acts of violence are shot with medium-close framing and edited in fast-paced sequences. The camera does not hide from the violence, but it does not linger on it. It has another moment of action to get on with. Even the slow-motion shots of the men being cut down by the machine gun last less than a second each. As such, I would characterize the violence as moderately graphic at most, and quite tame in comparison to *Bonnie and Clyde* (1967) or *The Wild Bunch* (1969). Although the descriptions indicate that some of these acts of violence tend toward the hyperbolic, the scenes are presented in a straightforward visual manner. I would not classify any of the images as "funny."

There are two basic paths of attack against cinematic violence in the scholarly literature. The first, based in media effects research, employs social learning theory to suggest that viewing violent images can lead individuals to be more likely to show aggression and commit violent acts. In his recent anthology *Screening Violence*, Stephen Prince draws on the social science literature to conclude that some forms of cinematic mayhem are far more unhealthy than others:

> Based on the empirical evidence, it is now possible to specify the program characteristics that are most implicated in the findings of aggression inducement. These involve violence that is relatively free of pain and suffering, victims who deserve what they get, stories that postulate righteous justifiable aggression, and a match between the cue properties of situations and characters on screen and the viewer's real world situation.[2]

A page later, he continues:

> The presence or absence of a victim's pain, and, when present, its degree of severity, tends to affect a viewer's disposition to aggress. One of the striking facts about much screen violence is its relatively pain-free quality. In the action epics of Arnold Schwarzenegger and Sylvester Stallone, the heroes massacre hordes of bad guys with little evident feeling and with no evident agonies on the part of those righteously dispatched.[3]

28 A typical scene of action-movie violence in the Arnold Schwarzenegger vehicle *Commando* (1985)

Of all of Schwarzenegger's films, the one that by far best matches this description is *Commando*. The plot concerns the efforts of retired US Army commando John Matrix (Schwarzenegger) to rescue his kidnapped young daughter from the clutches of a deposed Latin American dictator. All of the men the commando kills are henchmen of the dictator, and all the killing is contained within the context of the rescue mission. In terms of narrative convention, the melodramatically caricatured villains definitely deserve what they get. And get it they do. I covered only a fraction of the film's mayhem in the previous section. Matrix is shown killing something like eighty-eight people during the course of the narrative. This cavalcade of death is almost completely free of pain and suffering. The primary bad guys also have "cue properties" tying them to social groups that are likely targets of fear and/or hostility by mainstream audiences: two large African American men, an oily-looking Hispanic (also a drug dealer, of course), a kind of biker/punk, and a weaselly white guy who looks like a used-car salesman.

The second path of attack against screen violence is more interpretive, more concerned with ideological function. Devin McKinney draws a distinction between "strong" and "weak" forms of film violence, arguing that the former has the potential to disrupt the effects of an otherwise anaesthetizing popular culture that leaves us numbed of mind and spirit, while the latter only contributes to an apolitical passivity that, among other things, keeps us from facing up to the encroaching real violence around us. Strong violence "is piercing enough to shoot past the crap violence we all drink like beer."[4] It "acts on the mind by refusing it glib comfort and immediate resolutions."[5]

Weak violence, though, provides only superficial thrills. "Today's average violent movie doesn't ask suffering from those already aloof from it"[6] Weak violence allows an escape from emotional investment into mere entertainment, "trad[ing] flesh and blood for hamburgers and ketchup."[7] It wants "to look at horror," but not "to feel it, smell it, take the chance of getting sick from it."[8] This sounds like *Commando* again, and McKinney, too, makes specific reference to Schwarzenegger as an exemplar of "weak," and therefore bad, screen violence. Similar ideas are offered by Barry Grant, Annalee Newitz, and Philip Simpson in Christopher Sharrett's anthology, *Mythologies of Violence in Postmodern Media*.[9] For these authors, pleasurable film violence acts to mythify unjust uses of dominant social power, from Manifest Destiny to the Gulf War. In contrast, "progressive" violence breaks through comforting myths. Viewers are not just disgusted, but unsettled, opening a space for a critique of the dominant culture, in which representation may act to connect real-life violence to its social origins.

What interests me here is the contradictory trajectories these two lines of thought take to reach similar conclusions. Prince and the social scientists are concerned about film violence becoming a model for real violence. They believe watching violent entertainment may make viewers *do something* – something bad. In contrast, the progressive/ interpretive school is concerned about film violence promoting social passivity. They believe watching violent entertainments will make viewers *do nothing*, when something really ought to be done. Yet, for both camps, actions films like *Commando* are considered the greatest danger.

Perhaps the distinctions that ought to mark this contradiction have collapsed in some horrible postmodern implosion. Maybe the superficiality of violence in films like *Commando* has flattened the affect of an entire generation. So much so that a scene of gruesome violence wrapped in a transparently cheesy story caused the mythic bubble of resignation to burst for a couple of teenagers . . . who decided that something *did* need to be done to shake up the status quo . . . only their brains were too saturated with *Commando*-like images to conceive of their rebellion as anything but a full frontal assault against the bad guys with automatic weapons. And as their insurgency against a cartoon world came to be acted out in agitated imitation of those very cartoons inside a high-school cafeteria in Littleton, Colorado, the killers' schoolmates watched frozen in passive horror, having seen too many movies like *Commando* to believe that any of this could possibly be real.

Have I just shown an appalling insensitivity to real-life horror, or a laudable skepticism of media representation and ideological construction? Meaning is often hard to place when violence and humor come hand-in-hand.

What happens when violence and humor are laced together on the screen? What happens, furthermore when comedy pushes violence toward spectacle, and spectacle in turn pushes violence toward comedy? Both camps of violence critics could be expected to suggest that comedy will add to the negative effect – lightening the violence, making it too comfortable, desensitizing us – we'll either be more likely to emulate violence or less likely to be really moved by it if fun comes along with it. However, neither camp addresses the subject of humor explicitly, and perhaps for good reason. Most of us intuit that the violence in a Bugs Bunny cartoon, an Abbott and Costello film, or even in *Heathers* (1989) for that matter is of a different order than the violence in *Rambo: First Blood Part II* (1985) or *Dirty Harry* (1971). Equating these things would seem to miss some important point, even if we can't quite put our finger on it. Perhaps we feel we can't lump such different texts together without erasing important differences between the playful and the serious, between fantasy and reality. While social scientists studying the "effects" of media violence on children have often used animated cartoons in their research, it is no accident, I think, that studies of cinematic violence focused on adult fare almost always focus on more serious films. Humor muddies the waters.

While *Commando* presents a certain measure of its violence in a fairly straightforward manner, as described above, it also contains a great deal of humor. The film represents a key turning point towards the mixture of comedy and violence that has characterized the Hollywood action genre since the mid-1980s. This is the first movie where Schwarzenegger said "I'll be back" as a self-conscious joke, the movie where the silent Conan/Terminator killing machine first gave way to the pun-slinging persona that made Arnie a champion box office attraction. Highlights of the action genre before *Commando* include *The Dirty Dozen* (1967), *Dirty Harry*, *The French Connection* (1971), and *Rambo*. After *Commando* came *Die Hard* (1988), *Lethal Weapon 2* (1989), *Con Air* (1997), and Jackie Chan. Yet, while *Commando* served as a paradigm for action films to come in many ways, the humor in *Commando* goes in some directions that have largely been abandoned since. An exploration of these directions, though, suggests that humor and excess can be the building blocks of a more progressive action film – that these tools may serve a purpose beyond creating a merely spectacular "cinema of attractions."

In *Commando*, the male lead delivers groaner-quality puns:

• After Matrix dispatches his chaperone in the airplane – without anyone noticing – he pulls the man's hat down over his eyes, covers him with a blanket and tells the stewardess, "Don't disturb my friend. He's dead tired."
• Matrix kills the psychotic henchman Bennett (Vernon Wells) by ripping a piece of plumbing from the wall and throwing the pipe javelin-like all the way through Bennett's chest, penetrating the boiler behind him. The villain gasps, holding the pipe as fumes spill out the end, and Matrix says, "Let off some steam, Bennett!"

. . . witty repartee:

• Matrix jauntily inquires, "Como esta?" as he fires a powered knife into the chest of one of the dictator's guards.
• Cindy (Rae Dawn Chong), the flight attendant Matrix has shang-haied to help him escape the airport and follow the unsuspecting bad guys, asks him, "Are you going to kill me or something?" He answers, "No." She says "I suppose you wouldn't tell me if you were . . . " To which Matrix replies, "Sure I would!"
• As Matrix holds the weaselly henchman Sully (David Patrick Kelly) over the precipice, he smiles and asks, "Remember, Sully, when I promised to kill you last . . . ?" then adds, "I lied," before dropping him off the cliff.

. . . and more groaner-quality puns:

• After Matrix drops Sully to his death, Cindy – apparently having been out of sight of the just-concluded interrogation – asks him, "What happened to Sully?" Matrix replies, "I let him go."

Commando is not only spiced with verbal markers of burlesque, but also with slapstick action and comic excess in a variety of forms, including over-the-top levels of performance in the staging of scenes and in the portrayals created by the cast. Matrix is an impossibly strong and powerful hero, and the film revels in this exaggeration rather than trying to find ways to make it seem plausible. Schwarzenegger's strong-man star-persona is actually subverted by inflating it to the point where any reasonably intelligent viewer can see that much of the action is faked. Schwarzenegger's first appearance in the film comes in the form of a frame-filling close-up of a monstrous bicep. A cut back reveals Matrix walking down a mountainside carrying the entire trunk of a very large tree over his shoulder. He walks toward the camera, backlight flares into the lens, the frame tilts up and the horns swell on the soundtrack as Arnold momentarily blots out the sun.

In order to escape from an airplane, Matrix crawls onto the landing gear and jumps down after the wheels lift off. The cut back shows Arnold's stunt dummy falling a good ten stories or so, but Matrix lands in a clump of marsh and gets up running immediately. Commandeering Cindy and her little Sunbeam sportscar to follow Sully from the airport, Matrix effortlessly rips the passenger seat out of the car with one hand (and without establishing any leverage) to allow himself to fit into the car. Cornering Sully in a phone booth at the Galleria, Matrix rips it off the floor and hoists it over his head, with Sully still inside. Momentarily waylaid by eight keystone-cop security guards, Matrix stands up, throws his arms out, and sends all eight men flying backward in unison and in a perfectly symmetrical circle. In further defiance of the laws of physics, Matrix holds Sully over the cliff with one hand, standing straight up, feet together, his arm fully extended from his body. Breaking into a drug lab, he first opens a gate by ripping a stiff lock and chain apart with his bare hands, then simply tears off one of the building's corrugated metal walls panels to get inside.

Should the viewer wonder if such representations are meant to be taken seriously, *Commando* offers other cues. The before-credit sequence establishing the warm relationship between Matrix and his pre-teen daughter – the "softer side" inversion of Schwarzenegger's killing-machine persona – is overemphasized by showing him feeding a Bambi-like fawn by hand amidst verdant mountain greenery. Arnold not only gives the animal a series of cheesy lovey dovey faces, he actually kisses it at the end of the shot. Then we see the little family fishing. The daughter hooks one, but then the camera cuts to a tighter shot of Schwarzenegger giving a huge gentle laugh as the former Destroyer/Terminator *unhooks the fish and lets it slip back into the river!*

Then there are the bad guys: all broadly played, Snidely Whiplash melodrama villains, complete with comic opera foreign accents and dialogue like "Slitting a little girl's throat is like cutting warm butter!" Finally, there is the scene where Cindy rescues Matrix after he is captured by police while raiding an Army surplus store to gather weapons. As Matrix is being hauled away in the paddy wagon, Cindy drives up behind in and old Caddy convertible. She smiles at the donut-shop-comic-relief cops driving the van, then hoists a rocket launcher taken from the store to her shoulder. She fires, but she has pointed the weapon in the wrong direction, and the rocket blows up the storefront behind her. She turns the weapon forward, and (against all reason, given the size of the explosion she has just caused) fires again at the police van. This time the recoil from the launch knocks her comically into the back seat, and the rocket magically strikes just under the rear of the paddy wagon. This knocks the vehicle on its side and does no more damage than open a hole in the bottom just big enough for Matrix, completely unfazed, to crawl out and get into the Caddy, while the dazed but unhurt cop pulls himself up through the window and does a little take of comic surprise and confusion at the wreckage.

I suspect, in the absence of the actual clips, it may be difficult for readers of this essay to gauge the level of humor in these portions of the film. None of them quite approach the overtly comic nature of a *Monty Python* or *Saturday Night Live* sketch. I think it is best to say that if a viewer was resolutely determined to read *Commando* as a straight action film, the humor is not so outlandish as to prevent that. However, viewer responses gathered on The Internet Movie Database (IMDb.com) and Amazon.com indicate that while some fans evidently seeking straight action have been able to read *Commando* in that vein, and have thus enjoyed the film, others are just as likely (if not more so) to be put off by the excess and failed to enjoy the film as a result. On the other hand, while fans seeking entertainment and humor appear more likely to leave positive comments about *Commando*, viewers who believe the film is actively seeking this response seem to be in the minority, with the majority considering the humor to be at least in large part unintentional.

29 Hanging by a thread: Arnold shakes down one of the baddies in *Commando* (1985)

I would attempt to persuade you that *Commando*'s particular sense of let's-put-on-a-show fun cannot occur by accident, if I thought it really made any difference. But it doesn't. What matters is how the film *is*, and we can sum that up by saying that anyone open to having a few chuckles at comic images of hyper-masculinity can definitely find amusement in *Commando*.

Prince would have viewers (indirectly) experience the pain Arnold's victims suffer, to learn about the real human consequences of violence. Yet to show human pain and suffering for caricatures like the villains Matrix dispatches in *Commando* would be ludicrous. We might as well re-cut all the *Three Stooges* shorts to show Curly going to years of therapy to deal with the neuroses he developed as a result of Moe's abuse. It makes sense to argue that there is a problem when films portray violence without consequence done to *realistic* characters, as they certainly often do. However, if teenagers or adults fail to distinguish the characters and actions in films like *Commando* from real life . . . if they become agitated toward, or inured against, actual pain and suffering as a result . . . the problem is not these films. Rather, it is the fact that capitalism has spawned an empty and alienated real life that has in turn collapsed back into the ubiquitous media sphere of disconnected factoids and promotional discourse that drains sense equally out of melodramatic narratives, playful satire, going to your job in the morning and coming home at night.

The connection between empty, spectacular violence and consumerism is beautifully portrayed in a scene in *Repo Man* (1984). A convenience store hold-up goes awry and a group of characters with a variety of mutual hostilities gathered there by accident wind up with guns drawn on one another in a Mexican stand-off. As in *The Wild Bunch*, one shot breaks the pause, which leads, in chain reaction, to all the other weapons being fired, with most of the characters winding up dead or wounded. However, instead of portraying the damage of the violence with blood, the camera focuses on bottles of ketchup, liquor, and other consumer items (all with generic labels) being smashed in the process. As one of the robbers bleeds away in front of boxes of generic Instant Mashed Potatoes, his pain and suffering become represented in the form of an extended and definitely gross-sounding death gurgle. Otto (Emilio Estevez), the affectless teenaged protagonist, bends over him and says "You're gonna be alright, man." Then, after a few more seconds of gurgling, Otto adds "Maybe not . . . ," and turns to go.

I propose that we read *Commando* as closer to *Repo Man* than to *Rambo*. That is, I suggest that somewhere amidst those touches of burlesque are the seeds of a bit of cultural critique. In this, I suggest that the most significant aspect of *Commando*'s turn to humor – and what lifts it above the tide of the jokey action films that have followed it – is the presence of a central character whose gag lines articulate a critique of masculine aggression. Cindy, the flight attendant who becomes Matrix's helper, is given a privileged position by the narrative, acting as a kind of commentator and critic of the action.

After forcing his way into her car, Matrix explains his predicament as, "A guy I trusted for years wants me dead." Cindy replies, "That's understandable. I've only known you five minutes and I want you dead too." As Matrix faces off for his mano-a mano showdown with Cooke (Bill Duke), the guy who eventually gets impaled on the coffee-table leg, Cooke taunts him, "This Green Beret's gonna kick your big ass." Matrix replies, "I eat Green Berets for breakfast." Cooke tries to punch him but Matrix blocks the blow, delivers a hard jab into Cooke's nose, and quips, "and right now I'm very hungry!" This joke would be enough to complete the typical comedy/action beat, but *Commando* cuts to Cindy watching incredulously on the side as she replies, "I can't believe this macho bullshit." Cooke and Matrix continue fighting for a few minutes. Cooke says, "Fuck you, asshole!" Matrix replies "Fuck YOU, asshole!," flips Cooke by the arm, and then we cut back to Cindy who exclaims, "These guys eat too much red meat!" Later, after Matrix smashes the guard's skull against the dumpster a couple of times, Cindy inquires, "Did anybody ever tell you you have a lot of hostility?"

Now, I think what Cindy is commenting on in these scenes is not *real* masculine violence, but the *images* of manly aggression in movies. The unbelievable macho bullshit in question is the antics of male heroes in action films who take themselves seriously. By giving these critical jibes at its own genre such a prominent voice, *Commando* proclaims and revels in its own unbelievability. It becomes the bullshit of a shaggy dog story told with relish, as it condemns the bullshit of lies that masquerade as truth. *Commando* eats way, way, too much red meat, rejoicing in its theatrical excesses.

In the domestic sequence after the titles, Matrix sits down to lunch with his daughter, picks up her pop music magazine, and promptly makes a derogatory crack about Boy George. His daughter groans, "Dad, that is *so* old," and he pauses a moment with the magazine. Then he comments, "When I was a boy and rock and roll came to East Germany, the Communists said it was subversive . . . Maybe they were right."

The magazine is not *Tiger Beat* or even *Rolling Stone*. No, *Commando* actually presents us with a widescreen image of Arnold Schwarzenegger reading a copy of *Creem*. I believe this image is the key to interpreting the film, a sign of higher powers involved. The spirit of Lester Bangs is at work in this film. If *Commando* was a rock band, it would be The Dictators, or maybe The Ramones. Of course, The Ramones recorded a track called *Commando* on their second album back in 1977, and that song was loud, violent, funny, and self-aware too.

Okay, here's the editorial digression for readers who have never heard of The Dictators or The Ramones, never knew *Creem*, and (horrors!) have never read Lester Bangs.

- The Ramones: punk pioneers, frontman Joey Jewish kid from Long Island singing about Nazi Murders and Beat on the Brat with a Baseball Bat. Comic book shock theater peels away with a sense of humor and Herman's Hermits allusions, leaving just the energy of the chord, the beat, the feedback, the volume as a celebration of life wrested from the detritus of late twentiety-century culture:

First rule Is: The laws of Germany / Second rule Is: Be nice to Mommy / Third rule Is: Don't talk to Commies / Fourth rule Is: Eat Kosher salamis.[10]

- The Dictators: Bronx Jewish kids, mock-fascists working over the pompous macho of heavy metal rock pretending lead singer is a former pro wrestler. "Master Race Rock" almost sounds like legit metal-brag-bully-boy anthem but not quite:

  We are the members of the Master Race / We don't judge you by your face / First we check to see what you eat / Then we bend down to smell your feet / Hope that you don't pick your nose. / My favorite part of growin' up / Is when I'm sick and throwin' up / It's the dues you have to pay / For eating burgers every day . . . [11]

- Creem: "America's Only Rock and Roll Magazine," referring not to subject matter but to *being*. Enemy of aesthetic pretension Elephant Art rock looking for the true human spirit in the Termite Art trash of garage bands everywhere. Critical thinking about rock-'n'-roll culture but within its own terms, they might have called it stupidity as negation but if they'd actually read the Frankfurt school they weren't going to admit it.

- Lester Bangs: *Creem* editor, leading voice, tragic early death:

  > Number One. everybody should realize that all this "art" and "bop" and "rock-'n'-roll" and whatever is all just a joke and a mistake, just a hunka foolishness so stop treating it with any seriousness or respect at all and just recognize the fact that its nothing but a Wham-O toy to bash around as you please in the nursery, its nothing but a goddam Bonusburger so just gobble the stupid thing and go for the next one tomorrow; and don't worry about the fact that it's a joke and a mistake and a bunch of foolishness as if that's gonna cause people to disregard it and do it in or let it dry up and die, because its the strongest, most resilient, most *invincible* Superjoke in history, nothing could possible destroy it ever, and the reason for that is precisely that it *is* a joke, mistake, foolishness. The first mistake of Art is to assume that it's serious. I could even be an asshole here and say that "Nothing is true; everything is permitted," which *is* true as a matter of fact, but people might get the wrong idea. What's truest is that you cannot enslave a fool.[12]

When *Commando* was released, some commentators accused it of being a rip-off of *Rambo: First Blood Part II*, which had opened earlier the same year and made a ton of money. An angered

Schwarzenegger replied, "We probably kill more people in *Commando* than Stallone did in *Rambo*, but the difference is we don't pretend the violence is justified by patriotic pride. All that flag waving is a lot of bull . . . I've made a better film than Stallone's, and I'm happy to wait for time to prove me right."[13] Wait no more, Mr Schwarzenegger! Let us compare and contrast the two films.

On one hand, the similarities: both movies feature a lone warrior who must invade an enemy prison held by vastly superior forces in order to accomplish a rescue mission. Both protagonists are aided by non-white women who actively participate in the plot, free the hero from temporary capture and act as a combination sidekick/romantic interest. Both John Rambo (Sylvester Stallone) and John Matrix kill an awful lot of people, and both achieve vengeance.

On the other hand, the differences: Rambo attacks a socialist country, the recent real-life victim of American militarism, defined and demonized as "our enemies" in the dominant ideology of the time. Blatantly chauvinistic, *Rambo* portrays the Vietnam War as the betrayal of American masculinity by wimpy liberals. It marshals the inchoate paranoia produced by the inexplicable personal losses caused by the war into support for the feel-good saber-rattling of Reaganism. It rewrites the war with a fantasy ending where old-fashioned virility "gets to win this time," and ends with a call for increased militarism.

In *Commando*, the bad guy is a right-wing Latin American dictator, the sort of scum defined as "our friends" in the real political policies of the time. (One of the subtler jokes in the film is that the backstory posits a covert American force having supported a democratic revolutionary movement in its struggle against a brutal fascist strongman.) More to the point, Matrix's motives and actions in the course of the narrative exist completely outside any kind of geopolitical ideological framework. He just wants to keep his daughter from being killed, and to protect his own privacy. At the end he explicitly chooses domesticity over a return to militarist adventure.

In *Commando*, Cindy remains independent of spirit and mind. She responds to Matrix out of sympathy, poking fun at his masculine displays rather than swooning before them. Rambo's Vietnamese guide Co Bao (Julia Nickson) soon becomes besotted with her muscled hero, and after helping to free him from the prison camp falls into his arms in a submissive kiss. Narrative convention demands that anyone who gets too close to the lone hero must die, and die Co does. The woman in this tale exists only so that her death can provoke Rambo's anger. In perhaps the most mechanical and unintentionally hilarious execution of cliché ever put on celluloid, Co is cut down in a stream of machine gun fire exactly twenty-nine seconds from that first kiss.

Rambo actually asks us to take this seriously. It plays its melodrama deadly straight. As a result, serious issues are treated in an utterly simplistic manner. *Commando* refuses to take much of anything seriously, including itself, in a way that allows its lighthearted simplicities to become subject to further reflection.

But if *Commando* takes nothing seriously, doesn't that necessarily undermine any potentially progressive reading of the film that might focus on its narrative differences from *Rambo*? When the film presents the idea that the US should oppose right-wing dictators and support revolutionary freedom fighters, when Matrix rejects militarism for privacy and domesticity, when the story even turns a character type ("the stewardess") usually framed as a white bimbo into a witty, independent Afro-Asian woman, can't this all be read as part of the joke?

Sure.

Comedy is a destabilizing force on both sides of the discursive subjects its engages. Comedy needs some form of status quo (real or imagined) as a target, as it must invert the assumed or expected in order to create a laugh. From a well-dressed man taking a pratfall to cute cartoon children who curse like sailors, comedy's elements of inversion and surprise necessarily attack the ideological foundations of whatever the audience constitutes as normality. At the same time, the mercurial tone of these inversions, the tension-relief of laughter, prevent comedy from standing behind any alternative to the status quo.

While the joke would seem to prefer *some* kind of change from whatever is being made fun of, any possibilities in other directions are bracketed and undermined by the joking context. Humor undermines the seriousness of all perspectives, for and against. Still, many things may be broached in the context of humor that could never enter the conversation on a strictly serious note. Thus, as far as meaning is concerned, comedy is a double-edged sword. It subverts the dominant order but then subverts its own subversions. It softens and defangs disruptive ideas, but in doing so is often the only means by which these notions get out on the table.

In 1984, *Creem* writer Robert Duncan published a book called *The Noise*, which begins, "My father always blamed it on the rock-'n'-roll":

> The drugs, the sex, the faithless wild boys and girls obeying no authority and bearing no responsibility, playing havoc with America in a mindless quest for the good time they believed was owed them by the world. My father's not stupid.[14]

A year later, in *Commando*, Schwarzenegger utters a paraphrase of this passage while holding a copy of *Creem*. Bonusburgers, Kosher Salamis, Eating burgers every day . . . *Too much red meat!!!* Is this not revelation of a cosmic design? Is this not a Sign?

If anybody thinks I've been reading all sorts of things into *Commando* that may not really be there – well, damn right I have. Maybe *Commando* doesn't articulate a clear critique of other action films unless we make it do so. But the point is that we can, and we ought to.

The destabilizing effects of the humor and excess in *Commando* are readily evident in both the published reviews and in the user comments collected at Amazon.com and the IMDb. There are wide divergences of opinion not only about the quality of film, but as to whether or not it's funny, whether or not it's stupid, what the filmmakers intended, whether the tone is appropriate to the genre, and so on. This is one *very* open text. But then so are many other popular films. Which makes me wonder why so much academic film criticism today remains stuck in passive mode, trying to decipher *the* meaning of this or that text, not unlike the social scientists trying to locate *the* effects of cinematic violence, that they may be judged harmful on the one hand or harmless on the other.

There are lots of meanings hatching out there, struggling for light and life. The question is: what is at stake in arguments about meaning? Inside the academy, not much maybe . . . But if meaning matters, then activist critics ought to embrace any kind of small chaos that can provide opportunities to tip a few reified ideas on their side. If meaning matters, we ought to wade into the jokes and the excesses where sense is stumbling around and try to shove it in the right direction. If meaning matters, we ought to be doing this for as many people who go to the movies as possible.

Of course, that's not Cinema Studies, that's not "scholarship." That's being a preacher, a missionary.

I was in my early twenties when The Ramones released their first records. I loved the noise, and I could see the humor, but the references to violence scared me – high-speed pop songs about desires to emulate Manson and Nazis and Kill That Girl Tonight: *"You don't know what I can do with this axe / Chop off your head / So you better relax."*[15] The clue to interpretation is there, in the playful meter, rhyme, and irony of the last line. But pop culture, for all its alleged simple-mindedness, is often misinterpreted. Racist skinheads misread The Clash's "White Riot"; Bruce Springsteen's "Born in the USA" was appropriated for patriotic conservatism. It's a cultural studies cliché, but meaning *is* always up for grabs. It has to be fought for. The question is not so much which side are you on as whether you are on the front line or not.

What got me to understand The Ramones was interacting with the punk rock subculture. I found the one hip record store in town that had a lot of punk records, hung out, talked to the people working there who were all nerdy and cool and totally non-violent.[16] There was a context of interpretation available that framed the band's more outré references as Halloween-masquerade fun, and emphasized the egalitarian and ultimately humanist aspects of the punk stance. This context was in large part spread and nourished by a group of critics and publications, including but hardly limited to *Creem* and Bangs.

They were missionaries of righteous interpretation. That is what a critic should be. Pop music had them once, why can't pop film have them now? Where are the faithful who can fill the ranks of this crusade, bring a sharp intelligence to bear on the wobbly discourses of the culture, and build a revolutionary context of interpretation that can bump destabilized meanings over toward the side of the righteous? Brothers and Sisters, it only takes five seconds of decision, five seconds to realize your purpose here on the planet. It's time to move. It's time to get down with it! It's time to testify.[17]

Are you ready to testify?

Let me see a sea of hands . . .

Notes

1   All references to *Commando* are based on viewings of the DVD release, Twentieth-Century Fox catalogue number 4110424. The theatrical version of *Commando* was released by Fox in 1985.

2 Stephen Prince, "Graphic Violence in the Cinema: Origins, Aesthetic Design, and Social Effects," *Screening Violence*, ed. Stephen Prince (New Brunswick: Rutgers University Press, 2000), 21.

3 *Ibid.*, 22.

4 Devin McKinney, "Violence, the Strong and the Weak," *Screening Violence*, 100.

5 *Ibid.*

6 *Ibid.*, 109.

7 *Ibid.*, 108.

8 *Ibid.*

9 *Mythologies of Postmodern Violence*, ed. Christopher Sharrett (Detroit: Wayne State University Press, 1999).

10 "Commando" (The Ramones), originally issued on the Ramones LP *Leave Home* (Sire Records, catalogue # SA 7528), 1977.

11 "Master Race Rock" (Andy Shernoff), originally released on the Dictators LP *Go Girl Crazy* (Epic Records, catalogue # X598), 1975.

12 Lester Bangs, "James Taylor Marked for Death," in Bangs, *Psychotic Reactions and Carburetor Dung*, ed. Greil Marcus (New York: Alfred A. Knopf, 1987), originally published in *Who Put the Bomp* magazine (Winter-Spring 1971).

13 Quoted in John L. Flynn, *The Films of Arnold Schwarzenegger*, rev. edn (New York: Citadel, 1996), 96.

14 Robert Duncan, *The Noise* (New York: Ticknor and Fields, 1984), 1.

15 "You Should Never Have Opened That Door" (The Ramones), originally issued on the Ramones LP *Leave Home* (Sire Records, cataloge # SA 7528), 1977.

16 I refer here to Oarfolkjokeopus, at 26th and Hennepin in Minneapolis, MN, and especially to Ben, Pete, and Seth.

17 Parts of the introduction and conclusion of this essay quote or paraphrase the wording of Brother J. C. Crawford's introduction to the stage appearance of the MC5 at the Grande Ballroom, Detroit, October 1968, as heard on the Elektra record album *Kick Out the Jams* (cd re-issue Elektra 9 60894-2).

14

Tarantino's deadly homosocial

Todd Onderdonk

Rapper and accused homophobe Eminem's appearance with Elton John at the 2001 Grammies, a controversy perhaps already forgotten, highlighted the cultural prestige currently being enjoyed by the "gangster" ethos in American popular culture. Though depicting gang life is not really Eminem's lyrical province, his cultivated transgressions, violent postures, and famous association with Dr. Dre link him to the hypermasculine genre of "gangsta rap," for which Dre's best-selling 1992 album, *The Chronic*, might stand as a prototype. *The Chronic* was by no means the first gangsta rap album, but its wild success alerted the entertainment conglomerates (and upcoming rappers) to the marketing potential of the kind of black street "authenticity" that Dre performed with such menacing realism in his songs.

Quentin Tarantino's 1994 film, *Pulp Fiction*, also noted for its "authenticity" and (at the time at least) its shockingly realistic violence, mined the same vein of street credibility that gangster life has offered to consumers of pop culture since prohibition. Though the romanticization of male transgression is an old story in Western culture, from Zeus to Lord Byron to Billy the Kid, it should not be forgotten that the "bad-boy" brand of masculine authority is rarely accorded to real public malefactors. That is, it is fictive (or legendary) transgressions, rather than actual antisocial acts, that spark public fascination and garner cultural prestige. Thus a common confusion in the ongoing discourse concerning violence in the media, especially in the hubbub over Eminem (famous for his albums' over-the-top bluster and violence, including some horrific verbal depictions of murder), has been to confuse these *representations* of violence and transgression for the thing itself. In fact, Eminem and his producer, Dr. Dre, were no more gangsters coming up than was Quentin Tarantino: the real-life Marshall Mathers rapped in the Detroit music scene

30 *Pulp Fiction*'s (1994) infamous "war watch," symbolizing "the powerful solidarity between men." Notice how Captain Koons (Christopher Walken) looms close, while young Butch's mother hovers in the deep background out of focus, "a cipher, a negative value."

in his teens, while Dre was a DJ in high school and studied mechanical drawing; and everybody knows that Tarantino was a nerdy film fanatic working in a video store before he found Hollywood success. What these artists have in common – and with them the musical and filmic genres in which they made their reputations – is the exploiting of gangster life to create "realist" popular entertainments that use the "street" pose of intransigence and criminality to construct a kind of highly commercial, violent, masculine authority.

But beyond these shared rhetorical and commercial strategies, these genres also share a deep ideological commitment – to an ethos of violence and male social dominance energetically disavowed in the American mainstream, but resurgent in pop cultural representations. This essay looks at *Pulp Fiction* as a seminal example of that (disavowed) ideological project, questioning the film's depiction of male homosocial relations as a way of exploring the systematic gender bias and homophobia of American capitalism.

"Gangsta" performativity

The questions I raise here originated in juxtaposing *Pulp Fiction* and Dr. Dre's *The Chronic*. For the seeming paradox that struck me in the film, an ethos of intimate male bonds represented side by side with the most extreme male enmities and violence, was fascinatingly replicated on Dre's album, which I begin with as a point of entry. Like *Pulp Fiction*, *The Chronic* presents a world of a brutal and undiluted menace. So replete with armed threat and deadly swagger

– in short, with unmediated masculine aggression – is this aural mise-en-scene, that it obscures its own context, which is a commercial one. Competitors in the album's hellishly violent world are warned incessantly of the rapper's omnipotence, both by Dre himself and by a small coterie of associates such as Snoop Doggy Dogg (now Snoop Dogg), who take turns at the microphone in tight, textually interwoven support. Despite its manifest aggression, however, gangsta rap has always been a highly collaborative genre; that is, collaborative between men, who are joined in solidarity not only in the dangerous situations depicted in the songs themselves, but also in the musical and commercial solidarity necessary to face the hostile conditions of the marketplace. These bonds – and despite some famous feuds, many have been surprisingly stable over the years – are advertised on *The Chronic* by its intricate vocal interactions, and by the hyperbolic claims made by subordinate rappers about the unchallengeable power of Dr. Dre. This intensely homosocial hierarchy is set forward in opposition to the world of "bitches" and enemy "niggaz" against whom Dre contours his silhouette of phallic power, performing a kind of lyrical dominance in the songs. Importantly, this constructed dominance must always precede the "real," if transient, commercial dominance of making a hit record; indeed dramatizing some form of social or sexual mastery is increasingly prerequisite to scoring hit records in hip-hop today, both in the lyrics and the videos. But even for those artists with the best track records, the market, like the street, is precisely an *in*domitable thing: tastes are always shifting, hits come and go from week to week, and new faces and styles rise up to replace older ones. Just as Dre modeled a fictive street dominance as if he were a bona fide, Glock-toting gangbanger, he also modeled an equally fictive commercial dominance as the supreme rapper, though, when the album was produced, this was far from a sure thing.

What I am suggesting is that the performance of a "hard," or absolute masculinity – such as we see throughout both *Pulp Fiction* and *The Chronic* – paradoxically highlights its opposite, the sense of vulnerability and perceived social (or commercial) weakness that generates the need for the display. Such generative contradictions, I would argue, are fundamental to gender, which Judith Butler has theorized as an ephemeral and unstable cultural category, a "law" that must be continually "cited" in order to appear as a law at all.[1] For Butler, there is no ontological basis of gender, but only continually reiterated performances of it, producing not truth, but "truth effects" – constructed illusions of stable, gendered identity.[2] Where Dr. Dre helps us see the "performativity" of gender, then, is precisely in the way he constructs a particular or contingent version of masculinity in response to his particular cultural situation, for if masculinity were indeed the supreme mastery in which it so often garbs itself, there would be no need for performances of any kind.[3]

Of course this social constructivist viewpoint is nothing new, and is today even a feature of pop psychology. It now seems commonplace, for example, to recognize in overdetermined "macho" behavior a form of "protesting too much," revealing less the intended mastery or certitude than the deep insecurities that occasioned the display. But this pop version of performativity stops short of that insight's destabilizing and progressive potential, the leverage it gives us in considering how gender ideals *change*, how they shift locally and historically in response to different conditions and threats. For masculinity as an ever-changing cultural norm or ideology – norms here referring to the set of "ideal" identities we see privileged in our families, our schools, and (importantly for my argument) in the media – is a much more complex and deeply paradoxical concept than the term "ideals" might suggest. We can better understand the mutability of masculine norms as the result of a competition *between* ideals, a churning struggle for dominance between, as gender theorists suggest, "hegemonic and various subordinated masculinities."[4] One of the most truly subordinated of these is, of course, homosexuality, though theorists like Butler and Eve Kosofsky Sedgwick have argued that this subordination is central to the very structure of patriarchal society, and that homosexuality thus has a constitutive function that makes its repression a vital feature of patriarchy.[5]

Not surprisingly, then, such subordinations are visible wherever masculinity is powerfully asserted. Pop cultural representations have a crucial role in the cultural struggle over gender ideals, making intense arguments for certain modes of masculinity and femininity, and certain interrelations between the sexes. Due to their deep and generic investment in these issues, texts like *The Chronic* and *Pulp Fiction* can open up some of the deep structural contradictions of the gender system in a particularly revealing way. Turning to the film, we see a world similar to that of our rappers: extreme male intimacy and solidarity coupled with the same extreme enmities and violence that marked *The Chronic*. *Pulp Fiction*'s focus on the dynamics of male loyalty and betrayal is perfectly analogous to the rap world's bonds, breaks, and outwardly-focused hatreds. In my reading, Tarantino's film celebrates the hidden reality of, as singer James Brown has it, the "man's, man's, man's world" of American capitalism – a troublingly close-knit, misogynistic, often homoerotic homosociality that underlies the enabling façade of traditional heterosexuality. *Pulp Fiction* illustrates how women, and by extension, the institutions of marriage and the family, are granted no more than an instrumental function in the norms of a society that places most of its emphasis on male roles in the hierarchy.

But before examining these displacements in the film itself, let us briefly consider Sedgwick's theorization of male homosocial desire, which will be important to my discussion of its relationship to normative heterosexual desire and the proscription of homosexuality. In *Between Men*, Sedgwick uses René Girard's figure of the erotic triangle to suggest that desire for women is really a means of attaining and strengthening bonds between men. As the desired object, the woman allows the men to enter into the close relationship of rivalry, and she also helps them disavow the homoerotic aspects of that "love" relationship. As Sedgwick puts it, "the bonds of 'rivalry' and 'love,' differently as they are experienced, are equally powerful and in many senses equivalent."[6] I would suggest that in the competitive relationship (and in America, the competitive relationships that matter most are still between men), any desired object – whether it is a woman, or power, or a financial reward – can act as the third point of this triangle, which binds men together intimately and systematically while still preserving, through the surface emphasis on rivalry, a "deniability" for the intimacy of that bond. And that is the function of these objects in the systematic workings of American heterosexual culture, which sings of and cultivates the desire for women or power or riches – these terms and their connotations betraying a revealing slippage and exchangeability in diverse representations – while ideologically suppressing the knowledge that these desired objects are more important in how they bring men together than in themselves.[7]

But the argument seems counterintuitive, for what is the nature or attraction of this male bond that it takes structural precedence over such seemingly privileged objects as riches or romantic love? What does it promise? The answer, according to the most iterated

American social norms of masculinity, is that the male world is the only site for the realization of identity and self-actualization, and thus the only world, these representations tell us, that matters. If Butler is right, and gender (and especially masculinity) is at its heart a state of *disempowerment* – a lack that produces an incessant, almost squirming need for constant proofs of potency – then entering into what Sedgwick calls the male entitlement, or patriarchy, is represented and perceived as the only way for men to overcome that lack, that emptiness at the center of their beings. Of course this arrangement is a reductive fiction, a normative myth assembled of culturally cultivated anxieties and desires, but it has become one of the marketing obsessions of modern pop culture to offer consumers a way to fill that emptiness, that instability in the structure of gender, often through quite violent fantasies of masculine empowerment.

But these fantasies also serve another purpose, that of obscuring the real relationships of power – or powerlessness – in American society. Pop culture, and film especially, helps men (and possibly women) vicariously live out and satisfy desires for potency, for wild individualistic freedoms and for economic, romantic or sexual attainments. These fantasies, by fostering a false consciousness of freedom and self-realization just around the corner, serve actually to compromise and constrain all but a privileged few in a deeply hierarchical system that promises all to all, but delivers something quite different. The transformations offered in pop culture under the rubric of the American Dream are for most the false promises of an always-already foreclosed social mobility.

Homosocial *Pulp Fiction*

With Tarantino's devotion to genre and cinematic tradition, *Pulp Fiction* certainly fits in this category, offering up a number of appealing, if slightly ironized, fantasies of masculine potency and attainment. At another level, however, the film is instructive about the hidden dynamics of the gender system it wants to underwrite. I don't mean to suggest that *Pulp Fiction* is an analysis of this structure; but the suggestive ways that the movie mirrors gender relations in the US lets us explore the duplicity of the American Dream, complete with its exclusion of women, its systematic interworking of male bonds and betrayals, and the churning and destructive competitiveness the dream fosters in self-perpetuation.

I referred above to the deeply homosocial bias of traditional gender relations in American culture. *Pulp Fiction* treats heterosexuality precisely as an ideological façade, a veneer that the film's "realism" strips away, showing that the true basis for power lies in relations between men. This is most telling in "The Bonnie Situation," the episode where hit-men Jules Winnfield (Samuel L. Jackson) and Vincent Vega (John Travolta) arrive at an underworld colleague's suburban home with a blood-spattered car and the body of the accidentally-killed Marvin (Phil LaMarr) in the backseat. The comedic mock-drama of the episode results from the need to conceal this bloody evidence of the violent man's world from the absent Bonnie, the wife of Jimmy (played by Tarantino himself). Tarantino has discussed in interviews his satiric take on these "little boys with real guns," who in "The Bonnie Situation" are "afraid of their mom coming home," yet this is satire which has it both ways.[8] While the men bicker like little boys, exaggeratedly fearing the consequences of Bonnie's arrival on the scene, the lesser stakes here serve to heighten their "bad-ness" in later situations, and emphasize the marginal and hypocritical role of women in their lives.[9] Like his expensive coffee and respectable bourgeois surroundings, Jimmy's wife represents to him legitimacy and concealment, and is a necessary accessory for the middle-class lifestyle that veils his criminal activities.

More vitally communicated here than any particular foibles of masculinity is its utter separation from femininity, of course represented as a polar opposite. "The Bonnie Situation" illustrates an arrangement that scholars of nineteenth-century culture have dubbed the "separation of spheres." In this Victorian paradigm, male and female roles are held to be in complete opposition, with the "male sphere" being the world of business and the woman's sphere, the home, a supposed spiritual refuge from the brutalities of the world. The film rewrites this in 1990s terms, but doesn't change the essential arrangement. In *Pulp Fiction*, men participate in an exclusive and brutally real power game, in which the players move within a system of explicit and violent consequences. The code for men is one of dominance, subordination, betrayal, and retribution, and you play with your eyes open or you die. Women, on the other hand, either don't "get" this code or evade consciousness of it, and are more interested in consumerist nesting activities and pleasure, all of which can be threatened by the male "game" and the ethos of deadly competition driving it. Because they are aware of the feminine desire to repress knowledge of this ethos, the men openly conspire to keep it from women's view. Thus the emphasis is not on hiding the Marvin's body from the police, but on hiding it from Bonnie, who, Jimmy tells us, would divorce him immediately should she see it.

Yet Bonnie's position is more ambivalent, and even compromised, than it seems. With the image of Vincent absentmindedly bloodying that emblem of middle-class propriety, the guest hand-towels in Jimmy's bathroom, the film contrasts the grisly, blood-and-brain-splashed hit-men and Jimmy and Bonnie's immaculate and expensive suburban digs, generating mock urgency from the possibility of the male and female spheres ever touching. The men fear only disrupting the feminine-identified illusion of propriety – a propriety which is of course funded by whatever Jimmy does professionally that he would be referred to by Jules as his "partner." Yet as we see from Jimmy's eventual settlement with Mr. Wolf (Harvey Keitel), the bottom line of this clean domesticity is, just like the grittier male world, economic. When Jimmy complains that Bonnie would miss the sheets in which the men decide to dispose of the body, Mr. Wolf knows that there is no impropriety that cannot be finessed with that apparent guarantor of domestic security, plentiful cash. Bonnie may miss the sheets, but presumably, the film suggests, she'll be mollified by the money. Though Bonnie is one of only two working women in the film (the other is a sadistic cab driver, who pushes the boxer Butch [Bruce Willis] to describe what it felt like to kill a man), the implication is that women are just as venal and nihilistic as men, only more hypocritically invested in the concealment of the disgrace or criminality that makes their comfort possible. Amongst themselves, however, the men avow their criminal lifestyle honestly, and risk their lives to attain its rewards. Even if Jimmy is merely using Bonnie to work the situation, having donated sheets that wouldn't be missed, Bonnie benefits from the brutalities of the male world even in her ignorance, and is culpable in the world of the film to the degree she does not acknowledge this.

Three other wives fill similarly disingenuous positions in the film – benefiting economically from the brutalities of masculine aggression and competition while either cynically or childishly disavowing its reality. Rosanna Arquette's Jody, sensual and self-protective, and living off her drug-dealing husband, is the most vicious representation. One shot depicts her avid, sadistic anticipation of the large adrenaline needle about to be slammed into the heart of Mia Wallace

(Uma Thurman). Mia, pampered by her crime-boss husband, Marsellus Wallace (Ving Rhames), is discussed as a literal *femme fatale* by his subordinates; Fabienne (Maria de Medeiros), the childlike bride of Butch, lives in an insulated world provided by her husband's violent boxing career. These sheltered and expensive women endanger men by their sheer, childish irresponsibility. We first hear of Mia in the film's opening minutes, in a discussion of a rumored foot massage said to have resulted in the death of one of Marsellus's employees. As Jules and Vincent argue over the wisdom of performing such an act on the feet of one's boss's wife, it is clear that "woman" in their discussion represents one of the most ancient of Western stereotypes – danger or treachery. The latter is suggested explicitly by Jules when he characterizes Mia's role in the incident: "Bitch gonna kill more niggers than time."[10] Vincent, despite being anxious about his safety as a custodian of his boss's wife, and his best intentions to be loyal, is also exposed to danger by Mia's recklessness: she overdoses on heroin taken from his pocket as soon as he leaves the room.[11]

Like Marsellus, Butch also has custody of a helpless (if less avaricious) child bride, though Fabienne is just as self-absorbed, bent as she is on the nest and "oral pleasure." While Butch engineers and enacts a dangerous scheme to secure their future together, she moves about in a whimsical daze, dependent, undependable, and dreaming of blueberry pancakes. The script assigns her complete responsibility for the danger that Butch faces when he realizes she has left behind his most precious belonging (about which more presently) in her only assigned task in the film, that of fetching. Butch is enraged, yet manages paternally to contain his anger – child women are to be protected – until he can vent it in the car after he leaves her. *Pulp Fiction*'s nineteenth-century gender paradigm is differentiated from the Victorian model only in its hostility to euphemism. No mythos of angelic domesticity and feminine sexual purity here. The film's representation of heterosexual relations gleefully reveals these to be cosmetic adjuncts to the real "action" in this world, which is between men. Women are beside the point; they have their uses and willingly come along for the economic ride, but are excused in their obvious weakness and unworthiness from the consequences and dangers of the male world.

Having disqualified women, *Pulp Fiction*'s reactionary vision of gender equally exalts masculinity, if, in proper postmodern style, with some irony. The masculinity presented as "normal" in the film acknowledges few alternative modes. Its attributes are defined in relation to other men, and these relations exhibit two seemingly paradoxical tendencies: toward solidarity and competitiveness. These are each immersed in a medium of casual violence – casual precisely in how violence is taken for granted to be central to what masculinity produces and is produced by.

If male homosociality is our focus, then the movie's "heart" is the Gold Watch scene, in which Captain Koons (Christopher Walken) delivers to young Butch a "war" watch emblematic of these values of solidarity and competition. Koons' intense soliloquy, delivered in flashback, emphasizes both masculinity as a state of perpetual conflict – the watch being passed from generation to generation of soldiers who die in battle – and the tight bonds that such conflict engenders between men in response. The representation of this intimacy is pointedly homoerotic. The watch, symbolizing the continuity of male bonds, has been transferred from prisoner to prisoner in a North Vietnamese prison camp in the only "safe" place that men in such an environment can have – their anuses.[12] While this suggests some sublimation of proscribed desires, it also highlights the sexual and social exclusion of women, which is intensified with a low-angle shot which presents the speech from the boy's PoV: Koons looms close, while in the deep background over his shoulder, Butch's mother hovers uselessly and out of focus, a cipher, a negative value. The speech itself is a passing on of the values that we see are invested in the watch, of violence and love, of loyalty and cruelty, and of the powerful solidarity between men.

> CAPTAIN KOONS: The way your Dad looked at it, this watch was your birthright. He'd be damned if any slope's gonna put their greasy yella hands on his boy's birthright. So he hid it in the one place he knew he could hide somethin'. His ass. Five long years, he wore this watch up his ass. Then when he died of dysentery, he gave me the watch. I hid this uncomfortable hunk of metal up my ass two years. Then, after seven years, I was sent home to my family. And now, little man, I give the watch to you.[13]

Just as Butch receives the catechism and sacred relic of homosocial violence and solidarity, so do does the viewer, Koons delivering his speech directly to the camera in a long, static PoV shot. At the conclusion of the speech the boy's small hand enters the frame – as if it was our own – to grab his "birthright" with alarming alacrity.[14] Just as Koons' mission to the boy is one of transmission through representation, the exquisitely rendered capsule history of the watch, so does Tarantino transmit through representation in *Pulp Fiction* those identical and uncritiqued values. Though the scene is in one sense a moving and passionate portrayal of a proud and embattled masculine identity, its foreclosures and exclusions are indicative of a pathologically reductive single-mindedness about gender that pervades American culture at many levels. Of the many modes and variegations of masculinity we see in our daily lives, including broad ranges of traits displayed by effective and well-adjusted men somehow not obsessed with cultural definitions of maleness, pop culture reflects back to us precious few. Though Tarantino broadens this palette somewhat by giving his male characters engaging, self-conscious dialogue and musing pop culture sensibilities much like his own, their most basic motivations remain tied to the simpler and more restrictive hegemonic codes of masculinity which have always sold so well at the movies. For all its pleasures, *Pulp Fiction* offers these hegemonic fantasies in the exact same spirit, as empty consolations to a "castrated" American populace – and I use that term to suggest the psychic, economic, and social disempowerments that most moviegoers turn away from when they enter the theater.

Pleasures of sadomasochism

If Koons' speech celebrates a utopian solidarity between men, this must be reconciled with the film's representations of violent male competitiveness. Indeed, some form or threat of betrayal or violence marks every male–male relationship in *Pulp Fiction*. I would suggest that the seeming contradiction I have referred to between close male bonds and violent male betrayal and competitivity is only an apparent one. The masculine world depicted in the film is actually structured upon this dual dynamic, and depends on it for its continual reproduction. To explore this, I want to discuss the trope of sadomasochism that runs through the film, both implicitly and explicitly. The sadomasochistic relationship – where one person is the "dom," the other the "sub" – metaphorically suggests the hierarchical male relationship under capitalism. Yet sadomasochism as a sexual practice presumes that pleasure and pain exchanges are to be deeply enjoyed by each party. Does this mean that subordinated men in general revel

masochistically in their subordination? *Pulp Fiction* answers that economic rivalry and dreams of rising above one's class position give
meaning, and thus a sort of gnawing sustenance, to that pain. The
asymmetricality and competitivity of these hierarchical "bonds"
becomes a kind of "loving" intimacy between the male partners – a
tense, vying, often physical interaction that allows men to perpetu-
ally perform, if never permanently attain, that fugitive masculine
identity promised by cultural ideals. This is to say that the pleasure of
subordination is in the promise of future transcendence that structures the American Dream, however disingenuous that promise. Like
most films depicting male characters "going for it," *Pulp Fiction* suggests that the roles in these hierarchical relationships are fluid and
changeable, and that class position is no obstacle to the truly manly.

Here I am pointing to the role of competition in the film between
such "dom/sub" "partners" as Marsellus and Butch, Marsellus and
Vincent, Vincent and Butch, and the Americans and the Vietnamese
in Captain Koons' narrative. Thus, we see first Marsellus dominate
or, as it were, painfully "fuck" Butch in attempting to force him to
throw a fight. In the scene, Marsellus counsels the quietly bristling
fighter to swallow his pride and take the money (and the beating
from an inferior man), though such an act clearly would violate the
code of the film's ideologically preferred masculinity. Butch then
attempts to change his position by "dominating" or "fucking"
Marsellus, leaking the secret of the fixed fight in order to manipulate the odds, thus winning big by betting on himself as a long shot.
In the end, however, it is reaffirmed who is the real heavyweight.
Although Marsellus is swindled by Butch in the turnabout, their
bond as code-sharers impels Butch to return and rescue his "partner" from the obviously *non*-code-sharing Zed and Maynard (Peter
Greene and Duane Whitaker). This pair's difference from the film's
normative male relationship is marked by their "perversion" of the
code of masculinity, and not only in sexual (that is, homosexual)
terms. Instead of using leverage or strategy (the euphemized uses of
power employed by Marsellus and Butch in their rivalry), these players use naked force, raping the bound and ball-gagged crime boss
at gunpoint. And in overtly taking sexual pleasure in other male
bodies, with no excuse other than pleasure itself, they violate the
strict enjoinment to heterosexuality that makes "safe" the close male
bonds that structure the homosocial system. Thus their failure is in
not repressing the homoerotic nature of that system. They are

betrayers of a code that demands a euphemized version of both violence and sex in order to hide the real relations of power – those
brutal asymmetries that give the lie to *Pulp Fiction*'s assertions of
freedom, agency, and fair play among equals.

For in this game, power never *really* shifts, never is *really*
attained by subordinate males, though it is made to seem lavishly
available. When Butch drives off freely on Zed's phallic Harley, he
seems to have achieved the American Dream, taken on and dominated his nemesis to win complete freedom and masculine identity.
But in actuality nothing has changed – the utopian conceit that such
occasional and exceptional material rewards ever approach an
accession to or equalization of power in the overall hierarchy is a
lie. One image especially suggests that Tarantino was aware of the
erotics and fundamental unchangingness of the male power relationships depicted in the film. After Butch saves Marsellus from
Zed and Maynard in their basement, he stands before the crime
lord in an awkward and strikingly submissive pose, though Marsellus is unarmed and still bound, and Butch still bears the samurai
sword. Butch's devotion to the system is about to be rewarded.
Though he rides off into the sunset apparently having achieved
his dream by dint of masculine pluck, the real nature of this "transcendence" is that Butch has bowed to his superior and been
granted his life as payment not to reveal their common secret:
the false promises and repressed homoerotics of power and the
American Dream.

Justifying the code

But *Pulp Fiction*'s conservatism emerges most clearly in the way the
film's violence intersects with its representation of the idea of justice, a point of conjunction that emphasizes the silent class and
gender violence justified in the script. For it is important to note
that there are no victims in this hierarchical play; all accept the code
of violence and domination as a given in their circumstances, and
the uncritical viewer is persuaded to do so as well. Consequences
are in one's own control; one either (fearfully) plays it straight – as
Vincent tries to in the anxious date with Mia – or takes one's
chances, as we are led to believe the preppy white boys did in their
blundering transaction with Marsellus. In this spirit, the likeable
Vincent Vega's death at the hands of Butch (he has left his gun on a

counter while using the bathroom of the man whose apartment he is staking out) is to be accepted by the viewer as a blown assignment in an unforgiving game.[15]

Violent enforcements of this male code – presented as examples of living and dying by the sword – are elaborated with an almost erotic avidity in the film. The discomfiture of deserving "victims" is heightened and extended temporally, as when Jules delays Brett's (Frank Whaley) execution while he eats the doomed man's "Big Kahuna Burger," or when we are encouraged to savor the slow, "medieval" vengeance Marsellus plans to take on the avowedly homosexual and thus "perverted" male rapist, Zed. Since there is no question that Zed and Maynard's fates are condign, the vengeance can be relished. Tarantino's screenplay, a remarkably revealing document in its sheer excess and commentative brio, offers multiple fantasies of violent revenge to whet the erotic appetite for retribution against this pair of "pervs":

> On the counter is a big set of keys with a large Z connected to the ring. Grabbing them, he's about to go out when he stops and listens to the hillbilly psychopaths having their way with Marsellus.
>
> Butch decides for the life of him, he can't leave anybody in a situation like that. So he begins rooting around the pawnshop for a weapon to bash those hillbillies' heads in with.
>
> He picks up a big destructive-looking hammer, then discards it: not destructive enough. He picks up a chainsaw, thinks about it for a moment, then puts it back.
>
> Next, a large Louisville slugger he tries on for size. But then he spots what he's been looking for: A Samurai sword.[16]

Backed by the apparent justice of the masculine code he portrays, Tarantino is utterly sanguine about the violence that enforces it. My objection, however, is not to the violence so much as the ideological certitude it betrays with regard to "proper" masculinity. Those who fall short of the normative code espoused in the script are literally "written off." Indeed, the descriptions of such moments are almost pornographic in the way they clearly revel in the "just" death. Another example, with the typographic emphasis all Tarantino's:

FOURTH MAN

Die . . . die . . . die . . . die . . . die . . . die!

The Fourth Man FIRES SIX BOOMING SHOTS from his hand cannon in the direction of Vincent and Jules. He SCREAMS a maniacal cry of revenge until he's DRY FIRING.

31 For Tarantino, there can be no doubt: male pervs get all that they deserve,
here in the form of phallic (Sumarai) fury

> Then . . . his face does a complete change of expression. It goes from
> a "Vengeance is mine" expression, to a "What the fuck" blank look.
>
> FOURTH MAN
>
> I don't understand –
>
> The Fourth Man is BLOWN OFF HIS FEET and OUT OF FRAME by
> bullets that TEAR HIM TO SHREDS.[17]

The pleasure offered by this violence reminds us of the rightness of
the brutal code of intransigence and "personal responsibility" to
which the film is dedicated.

If *Pulp Fiction* truly advocates such gendered "justice" – and the
tenor of both the script and the film certainly suggests that it does –
how do we understand Jules' renunciation of violence and domination in the diner at film's end? Let us discount here the possibility that
the reversal was a lame gesture to propriety tacked onto the end of a
spectacularly violent film, with the sprung lateness of Jules' decision
allowing viewers to enjoy the full measure of transgressive thrills
before suddenly and vaguely reigning in the fun in time for the short
walk to the exits. Instead, I'd like to consider its implications seriously, for even in renunciation *Pulp Fiction* glories in the masculine
mystique of dominance and violence. Jules has been shaken by the
near-misses of the "Fourth Man's" bullets, and announces his intention to renounce "the life." Fearing that his professional use of power
has allied him with "the tyranny of evil men," Jules intends to "walk
the earth . . . You know, like Caine in *Kung Fu*," another pop cultural
figure engaged in redemptive violence excused by justice.[18] The
model of Caine suggests not that Jules will be a peaceable, wandering
Buddhist, but that he will redirect his violence to the ends of a new

code of justice, one more in accord with paternalistic social ideals. Indeed, social justice was always the necessary incentive to violence for the reluctant Caine (David Carradine) in the 1970s TV drama, which depicted a martial-arts-trained monk in the nineteenth-century American West.[19] The new way thus preserves much of the old: masculinity continues to claim violence, force, and domination as proprietary characteristics, and what pleasures it loses in outright transgression it gains in the legitimacy offered by paternalism, which allows the tradition of misogyny to remain intact. In this new chivalric model, women's weakness, not their avarice or moral corruption, justifies male excesses and the satisfactions of forceful justice.

We see this paternalism and its justification in action in the final diner scene, when Jules' objective is to manage the erratic, hysterical "Honey Bunny" (Amanda Plummer), who is trying gracelessly to do the "man's job" of robbery. Master of the situation, Jules benevolently saves the weak women and her ally, the weak man, from themselves – that is, from the violent consequences of their own weakness. Note that what saves the couple is their criminal (if inept) *aspiration*. They are "cute" armed robbers, pursuing, if incompetently, the nihilistic version of the American Dream privileged by the film.

In his discussion of the Western, Steve Neale could as well be describing *Pulp Fiction* when he says "these films are shot through with nostalgia, with an obsession with images and definitions of masculinity and masculine codes of behavior, and with images of male narcissism and the threats posed to it by women, society and the Law."[20] *Pulp Fiction* responds to these same threats in its devaluation of women and celebration of phallic individualism and casual criminality, though at the last second this is transformed into a newly legitimized, if still nihilistic, patriarchalism. *Pulp Fiction* employs its representations of violence to euphemize the male homosocial intimacies and desires that act as the engine of capitalism and masculine privilege. But violence also is used to legitimize the systematic inequities of these privileges, through the film's valorization of the masculine code advertised in every situation. The reactionary ideology depicted in *Pulp Fiction* as the pursuit of the "American Dream" is based upon an ethos of dominance as guilty as the male rape which Marsellus undergoes in the basement of the pawnshop, yet it sells at the multiplex as freedom for $10 a seat.

Notes

1 See Judith Butler, *Gender Trouble: Feminism and the Subversion of Identity* (New York: Routledge, 1990) and Butler, *Bodies That Matter: On the Discursive Limits of Sex* (New York: Routledge, 1993).

2 Butler, *Gender Trouble*, 136.

3 Though performativity does not exclude such conscious, strategic performances of gender – Butler's own parodic example of drag being just such an instance of the phenomenon – I am aware that the theory is more concerned with formative and normative effects at the unconscious and subconscious levels.

4 Tim Carrigan, *et al.*, "Hard and Heavy: Toward a New Sociology of Masculinity," *Beyond Patriarchy: Essays by Men on Pleasure, Power and Change*, ed. Michael Kaufman (Toronto: Oxford University Press, 1987), 178.

5 Eve Kosofsky Sedgwick, *Between Men: English Literature and Male Homosocial Desire* (New York: Columbia University Press, 1985), 3.

6 Sedgwick, *Between Men*, 21.

7 Consider how all three of these interchangeable objects are there to be "taken," the phallic connotations of that word implying conquest, penetration, and domination.

8 Gavin Smith, "'When You Know You're In Good Hands'; Quentin Tarantino," *Film Comment* 30.4 1994): 32–42.

9 Though Tarantino denies the connection with *film noir*, it is worth comparing his approach to masculinity with classic *noir* representations, from which *Pulp Fiction* draws both directly and indirectly. For Frank Krutnik, a defining characteristic of the "tough thriller" is the way these films undercut traditional masculine authority while constructing a new masculinity "turned narcissistically in upon itself" (*In A Lonely Street: Film Noir, Genre, Masculinity* [Routledge: London, 1991], 90). *Pulp Fiction* displays this same narcissism without any real undercutting. Despite getting some laughs at the expense of his male protagonists, their authority is never diminished by their slight embarrassments. For example, despite their ridiculous attire, Jules and Vincent still manage to off-handedly dominate the diner scene, and they emerge with professional reputations intact from the dangers of the "Bonnie Situation." Indeed, however they are dressed, they remain, as the screenplay tells us, "two bad-ass dudes."

10 Quentin Tarantino, *Pulp Fiction: A Quentin Tarantino Screenplay* (New York: Hyperion, 1994), 17.

11 Tarantino comments: "The guy takes out the mob guy's wife – 'but don't touch her.' And what happens if they touch? You've seen that triangle a zillion times" (*Pulp Fiction*, 68). The tension of this erotic triangle is greater between the two men than between either of them and

the woman. What is at stake between the men, and what fasinates Tarantino, are the defining characteristics of masculinity – loyalty, betrayal, and violence. The heterosexual tension between Mia and Vincent is not insignificant, yet the details of Mia's portrayal and the scripted events of the "date" itself emphasize less the erotic connection with the boss's wife than the peril she represents to Vincent.

12 A. Samuel Kimball notes the metaphorical equation of male anus and female vagina in his discussion of *Pulp Fiction*'s "abject . . . homophobic displacement on the one hand and . . . correspondingly abject counterphobic idealization of the heterosexual woman-as-wife on the other." Kimball links these displacements to the films psychosexual obsession with "regulatory heterosexuality," which defines homosocial masculinity as a commandment to every man "not only to 'cover his ass' but to cover the ass of his best friend and even his worst enemy, so long as he is heterosexual." Kimball, "'Bad-Ass Dudes' in *Pulp Fiction*: Homophobia and the Counterphobic Idealization of Women," *Quarterly Review of Film and Video* 16.2 (1997): 172.

13 Tarantino, *Pulp Fiction*, 68.

14 That Butch is dreaming of this intensely masculinity-invested object as he awaits the fight on which he is betting his life, shows the degree to which male identity, not life or death, is what is at stake in the film. The suggestively named "Butch," despite his "butchness," is worried more about his masculinity than his life, due to the pressure he feels to re-establish and perform it as if it was an ontological absolute.

15 And anyway, as hit-man-*cum*-working stiff, content with the small pleasures of his level in the hierarchy, Vincent lacks the aspiration we see in his nemesis, Butch, to sufficiently carry the burden of masculine ideality, and is expendable on that basis. In class terms, then, he is more likethe bulk of Tarantino's paying viewers, both male and female, who, inasmuch as they are unable to partake of the cultural imperative to "go for it," are normatively disdained.

16 Tarantino, *Pulp Fiction*, 105–6.

17 *Ibid.*, 126.

18 *Ibid.*, 146–7.

19 The figure of the reluctant hero, trying to evade his own violent tendencies but drawn back to the struggle by some exigent social injustice, is a favorite cliché used by New Hollywood filmmakers to justify their own violent representations. Recently both *Gladiator* and *The Patriot* (both 2000) have used this trope to ennoble their representational bloodsport.

20 Steve Neale, "Masculinity as Spectacle: Reflections on Men and Mainstream Cinema," *Screen* 24.6 (1983): 10.

15

Fight Club and the political (im)potence of consumer era revolt

Ken Windrum

> But if one fears or despises so much the philosophical foundations
> of a book, and if one demands so insistently the right to understand
> nothing about them, and to say nothing on the subject, why become a
> critic? To understand, to enlighten, that is your profession, isn't it?
> (Roland Barthes)

David Fincher's *Fight Club* (1999), adapted for the screen by Jim
Uhls from Chuck Palahniuk's novel, was a box-office disappointment considering the potential lucrativeness of re-teaming the director, whose last production *The Game* (1997) was financially
successful, with Brad Pitt, Fincher's star from *Se7en* (1995). The film
was a relative flop partially thanks to a critical-commercial backlash,
in the form of a well-publicized and hysterical discursive tantrum in
the press, against "dark," "violent," and "nihilistic" movies which
seemed unaware that scenes of men brutally pummeling each other
was hardly untrodden cinematic territory.[1] Since the corporate-
owned media is only willing to present aggression as autochthonous,
which ignores the socio-economic causes of violence, these attacks
(aided by the film's deceptive trailer) overwhelmed the political
valence of an unusually vivid attack, for a Hollywood production,
on the franchised, corporate culture of late consumer-era capitalism.
Demonstrations and rioting at the annual World Trade Organization
meeting in Seattle one month after the film's release, against the
World Bank's assembly in Washington, DC, at the 2000 Democratic
and Republic Conventions, and in Quebec City in 2001 certainly
were not directly influenced by *Fight Club*, but allow one to see the
ideological forest over some allegedly violent trees.

This defect on the part of "critics," therefore, highlights the need
for fresh and relevant inquiry concerning whether *Fight Club* actually posits a viable form of revolt through its "tough-guy" aesthetic

of bodily, phallic, masochistic, death-obsessed, atavistic group ritual. In other words, can the "tough guy" be politically potent? Or does this ethos, like Horkheimer and Adorno's conceptualization of the Enlightenment, dialectically include an auto-critique and contain its own antithesis either directly or as a structuring absence? Furthermore, can any American motion picture satisfactorily and practically posit a form of revolt which audiences can support, or are there severe limits to what Hollywood will bankroll, can imagine, and allow to be spoken? Finally, is *Fight Club* a failure or does its incoherence create a space for further discussion?

At first, *Fight Club* seems to imagine quite a bit and deliver a precisely articulated, vivid critique through the dialogue of both the unnamed Narrator[2] (Edward Norton) and his "friend" Tyler Durden (Brad Pitt). For instance, the former discusses his fetish for Ikea catalogue items and asks, "What kind of dining set defines me as a person? I had it all, even the glass dishes with the tiny bubbles and the imperfections, proof that they were crafted by the honest, simple, indigenous peoples of . . . wherever." With remarkable concision this statement includes many critical notions. At first it spoofs the sad juxtaposition of personal identity and consumer goods once reflected on by Guy DeBord when writing, "reified man proclaims his intimacy with the commodity. Following in the footsteps of the old religious fetishism . . . the fetishism of the commodity also achieves its moment of acute fervor. The only use still in evidence here, meanwhile, is the basic use of submission."[3] (This point about the inutilitarian nature of the commodity will be mentioned by Tyler later on when asking what, "in the hunter-gatherer sense," is the use of knowing what a duvet is?)

Next, this narration satirizes the kitschy, faux-rustic "authentic" products which exploit consumers' vague multi-culturalist liberalism and advertise the seller's enlightened, fair treatment of their indigenous suppliers. These far-off third-worlders are only an abstraction since, at the speech's end, the Narrator reveals his ignorance of their specific identity. An example of Tyler's critical discourse reveals a more pointed, obvious message, as when he intones "You're not your job, you're not how much money you have in the bank, you're not the car you drive, you're not the contents of your wallet, you're not your fucking khakis."

Furthermore, the film's narrative also includes a withering attack upon a society in which the Narrator labors for a major car company and decides whether to recall deadly defective models or, if financially expedient, simply pay off future victims' families. An insomniac who leafs through Ikea catalogues rather than porn, he finally achieves sleep through pretending to have serious illnesses and attending support groups to reach tearful catharsis. Ultimately, though, he "finds himself" through friendship with soap-maker and anti-consumerist provocateur Tyler. The two become roommates at the latter's dilapidated squat (a location which inherently evokes anarchist living practices) and form "Fight Club," in which young petit-bourgeoisie and service-working Caucasian men reach selfhood through bare-knuckle brawling. The group then begins perpetrating anti-consumerist pranks such as mass erasing the tapes at a Blockbuster video store, smashing the windows of luxury cars, and destroying corporate coffee franchises.[4] These guerrilla actions are the film's, and the Narrator's, joyous, libidinal, revolutionary peak.

At this point, further elucidation is necessary to precisely describe the aesthetic and nature of this putative radical movement. The film has provided pointed critique and shown defiant actions but can this nouveau-tough-guy cadre really prove successful or their activities and characteristics desirable?

The first problematic quality of Fight Club (which later morphs into "Project Mayhem") is its exclusively Caucasian and male membership; some characters, although not explicitly presented as such, could perhaps be read as Latino, but there are no African-American or Asian Fight Club members.[5] On the most obvious level, this ethnic and gendered "purity" denies the group's radicalism a significant degree of inclusion, thereby immediately eliminating the very potential of positive social change from the film. Furthermore, the organization is potentially placed on the political right by this racial homogeneity. Henry Giroux argues that the club's constituency also narrows the film's critique by ignoring "the broader material relations of power and strategies of domination and exploitation associated with neo-liberal capitalism," rebelling instead "against a consumerist culture that dissolves the bonds of male sociality and puts into place an enervating notion of male identity and agency":

> Fight Club has nothing to say about the structural violence of unemployment, job insecurity, cuts in public spending, and the destruction of institutions capable of defending social provisions and the public

good. On the contrary, *Fight Club* defines the violence of capitalism almost exclusively in terms of an attack on traditional (if not to say regressive) notions of masculinity.[6]

Perhaps expecting any Hollywood film to fulfill these daunting criteria is a bit naive, but Giroux' analysis still aptly describes the film's ideological defects.

Beyond their membership requirements, the Fight Club is also extremely macho. These men are muscular, violent, and highly body-oriented. After all, the whole project germinates with bare-knuckle, shirtless, sweat-drenched brawling. Tyler/Brad Pitt with his muscled physique, oiled, sweaty torso, and jeans hanging below the waist is the group's emblematic image. He also wears a *Hustler* tee-shirt which furthers a patriarchal machismo through valorizing a notoriously misogynist publication.[7] Giroux notes that such violence not only renders male-bonding a reductive act but ignores the fact that brutality is often suffered by "individuals, dissidents, and various marginalized groups" who hardly experience therapeutic release through physical punishment, instead being forced to endure "sheer acts of oppression deployed by the state, racist and homophobic individuals, and a multitude of other oppressive social forces."[8]

In fact, this form of male-bonding's inherent oppressiveness – beyond its homoerotic and misogynist exclusion of women – is reminiscent, in tandem with the group's ethnic composition, of a fascist aesthetic, one whose iconography is frequently reappropriated in gay-culture personae and pageantry via identities such as the "leather daddy" or by wearing police and military uniforms or other authoritarian costumes.[9] Similarly, as Hitler, Mussolini, and others found succor and lineage in ancient historical imagery, the activities of the Fight Club are quite resemblant of the male, aristocratic sporting practices of the first Olympic games and such repressive societies – often viewed now as hotbeds of homosexuality – as ancient Greece and Rome (hence the nomenclature "Greco-Roman wrestling").

Beyond these guys being buff, there is also an overhanging (pun intended) phallicism to *Fight Club*. For instance, the film contains loaded images such as the almost superfluous and plenitude-signifying lit cigarette Marla holds in front of Tyler's crotch while attempting to unzip his fly. Most noteworthy is the subliminal shot of a half-erect penis which Tyler, while working part-time as a projectionist, splices into a children's cartoon. This prank produces sobs from a little girl in

32 When is a gun not just a gun? And just whose gun is Ed Norton's narrator sucking?

the audience whose response may suggest female terror at being assaulted with such aggressive male imagery.[10]

Yet mere celebration of the penile would be dull if the inherent dialectic between macho steeliness and its opposite was not always present, as is revealed in the story of Bob (Meat Loaf) a former body-builder who suffers from testicular cancer, castration, and the presence of "bitch tits" (note the repulsed violence of this phrase), and who bemoans his fate while hugging fellow victims at support group meetings. This pitiable character hysterically wonders if "We're still men?" The Narrator responds by echoing "Yes, men is what we are" in a tone so blank and apathetic it foregrounds the impotence of a mere statement versus the punishing humiliations of biology gone awry.

More subversive to the phallic project, the threat of castration is ubiquitous here as the members of Project Mayhem put a rubber-band around the Police Commissioner's testicles and threaten their removal, only to repeat the action – like a hysterical leitmotif – against the Narrator himself, who manages to escape and spends the rest of the film in his underpants. Following this, Tyler stuffs a gun into the Narrator's mouth, which expands the punishment from cas-tration to having a phallus blow his head off. At this point, though, the film's key surprise – which is that Tyler is a figment of the Nar-rator's imagination – kicks in and our hero realizes he is basically sucking and holding his own cock! He accepts this and shoots or ejaculates into his mouth, thereby killing "Tyler" and liberating the Narrator from revolutionary machismo.

To continue down a path redolent of feminist theory, one can also note that if phallicism is textually desired at present, then the representation of woman – bearer of the lack and site of castration per Lacan, Laura Mulvey, *et al.* – should suggest threat and contamination. How else to account for Marla constantly being invoked by the Narrator as a destroyer, "a predator posing as a house pet," or at best a nuisance, "a scratch on the roof of my mouth that won't heal." She functions as his girlfriend when he is Tyler, and therefore confident enough to bear her onslaught, but as the Narrator he jealously rages at her invasion of both his home and the support groups which have given him rest.[11]

Furthermore, while considering feminist issues, we might ask "What is the film's gaze?" Does it suggest or invoke a lusting heterosexual female viewing oiled, lithe, sweating physiques, a gay male regard aimed at these pumped-up men, or perhaps both looks simultaneously? What about the narcissistic-masochistic pleasure involved in being a spectator at the film *Fight Club* or interdiegetically watching one of the brawls as a group member? Does the spectator narcissistically-masochistically identify with these guys as they are pummeled and – as when Tyler baits a mobster into giving him a beating – love the pain? Does the viewer look on helplessly while these events occur? Do progressive political notions get buried in the pre-Oedipal masochistic drive?[12]

While bandying about such terminology, though, one can certainly note another curious paradox. This seemingly macho film proposes a new, retooled tough-guy revolutionary aesthetic in line with the pumped-up musculature of Reagan-era action stars like Arnold Schwarzenegger and Sylvester Stallone[13] rather than the more traditional urban gangster/detective figure such as Humphrey Bogart, James Cagney, and Richard Widmark, or the large yet somnolent Robert Mitchum. Nevertheless, the production also helplessly or cunningly raises issues relating to feminist film theory or the ideas of post-feminist work concerning masculinity itself. Such a seeming contradiction, which may suggest an inherent dialectical antithesis for every concept or position espoused within this text, is significantly problematic, similar to the struggle to create oppositional or political cinema under capitalism.

Finally, characterizing the tough-guy aesthetic of *Fight Club* requires further noting its conversance with fantasies, whose political valence has previously been suggested, concerning the primitive and ritualistic. On the most obvious level is Tyler's Utopian vision, which intertextually invokes the character Pitt played in Terry Gilliam's *Twelve Monkeys* (1995), about ending civilization and creating a new Dark Ages in which the Sears Tower is covered in vines while gazelle, soon to be cooked and turned into life-long apparel (an obvious poke at the planned obsolescence of many current consumer goods), roam below the World Trade Center. Furthermore, the group forms a tribe with highly ritualized initiatory behavior. They chant tautological group slogans such as "The First Rule of Fight Club is you don't talk about Fight Club" or "His name is Robert Paulsen."[14] They also undergo a sort of manhood ritual of branding with lye since, according to Tyler, "without pain, without sacrifice, you have nothing." Finally, the Narrator survives a deliberate head-on car crash, courtesy of Tyler, which almost kills him but instead makes him stronger (and more aware), mirroring dialogue such as "Every evening I died and every evening I was born again, resurrected."[15] This crash leads to the film's longest fade-to-black, and when the Narrator awakens, he begins to discover that, technically speaking, his alter-ego does not exist. He eventually decides to regain his old identity, thereby defusing the group's radical agenda and returning us to the question of whether any true, potent revolt can be gleaned from *Fight Club*'s narrative and philosophy when the very aesthetic and group the movie celebrates is, as shown above, so ambiguously portrayed and fraught with problematic, contradictory tendencies.

Perhaps unsurprisingly, the answer to this question is basically "No," as the putative spectator (and I freely admit this is partially gleaned from my personal responses, ones observed at theatrical screenings and those of friends) becomes disenchanted with the group when Fight Club becomes Project Mayhem and begins resembling a Fascist organization even to the point of wearing black shirts. This shift had been symbolically anticipated already, as noted above, and since Tyler's livelihood involves rendering lipo-suctioned fat, stolen from hospital dumpsters, into expensive soap, the fate of Holocaust victims is immediately referenced.

The key turning point in terms of viewer sympathies occurs when Tyler drags a liquor-store clerk, who looks vaguely Asiatic but is ambiguously named Raymond K. Hessel (played by South Korean actor Joon B. Kim), into a parking lot at gunpoint and announces his imminent death, producing tearful sorrow. Terrifying a lowly pawn of the system differs from mass-erasing tapes or smashing cars. Spectatorial empathy is reinforced visually as many shots in this scene occur from a low angle, with both Raymond and the audience looking up at the gun and Tyler's menacing figure. Unlike the brawls under the Fight Club aegis, this is not an equal match. Furthermore, the group's putative ideology becomes concurrently incoherent since Tyler frees the clerk only on the condition that he return to college and work towards a professional career as a veterinarian. How does encouraging education and a productive, socially-acceptable vocation help to smash capital? Granted Tyler would claim that he is allowing Raymond to achieve his dream, but this action is still indefensible – a fact which, I suspect, is hardly accidental. Giroux, who views Hessel as "Indian," elides the spectatorial shift in sympathies and finds this scene problematic vis-à-vis espousing Tyler's apolitical notion that choice is "an exclusively individual act, a simple matter of personal will that functions outside of existing relations of power, resources, and social formations."[16] His neglect of formal analysis, which would reveal spectatorial suture with Raymond's viewpoint, and general dismissive disdain for the film, ignores the possibility that viewers cease sympathizing with Tyler at this point and that the narrative itself has shifted allegiances.[17]

After this episode, the group becomes known as Project Mayhem and would-be members begin appearing in droves to live military-style at Tyler's house; they wear black, carry out orders, and mindlessly repeat slogans such as "The first rule of Project Mayhem is you don't ask questions." At one point, the group had become almost leaderless and egalitarian with "Tyler" walking anonymously through Fight Club meetings. Now the recruits snap to attention whenever he or the Narrator passes by.

There are two possible explanations for this shift. I would argue that since the film is incapable of fulfilling its revolutionary potential, audience sympathy must eventually be turned away from the group. This could have been effected in a "liberal" manner, with the Narrator becoming morally indignant at Project Mayhem's destruction and either disbanding the organization or forcing Tyler to capitulate. Lip-service could thereby have been paid to the need for improvements in the consumerist system, yet the film would also have offered a cautionary tale about the need to respect others' lifestyles and points of views – an ideology suited to a society where multi-culturalism and anti-racism are gleefully used by multi-national corporations to effectively understand, coercively employ, and profit from the world's various ethnicities and cultures. Such a denouement would be a variation on Michael Douglas's increased disgust with Glenn Close – who at first provides him with therapeutic adultery – in Adrian Lyne's *Fatal Attraction* (1987); and it is a strategy that might well have been employed in Norman Jewison's *Fight Club*, or perhaps Sydney Pollack's *Fight Club*.

Fincher, though, is an unlikely director to resort to such sanctimony, especially after taking such obvious delight in Project Mayhem's pranks. Furthermore, this would seem a disingenuous tactic considering the director's oeuvre, one that consistently revels in sadistic, violent action such as Michael Douglas's subjection to a series of cruel ruses in *The Game* (which ends with him attempting suicide) or Brad Pitt's investigation of a serial killer in *Se7en* (culminating with the murderer presenting him with his wife's decapitated head). Granted, Fincher does usually extend the simulacra of an olive-branch and briefly strikes a moral tone at his films' – often abrupt – conclusions. For instance, Morgan Freeman quotes Hemingway at the end of *Se7en* about this being "a good world and worth fighting for," but qualifies the statement by only claiming agreement with its latter part. Similarly, Douglas's suicide was anticipated by those manipulating the eponymous "Game," allowing him catharsis and a seeming promise of future happiness. (Interestingly, the denouement of *Panic Room* [2002], Fincher's most recent production, eschews even this unconvincing solace. Whereas *Fight Club* provides at least some measure of [admittedly weak] reconciliation, *Panic Room* ends with Meg Altman [Jodie Foster] and her daughter, having survived a night of abject terror at the hands of burglars, simply looking nonchalantly through real-estate listings without any sense that the world has been righted or that their experiences have resulted in catharsis or instruction. A white screen, with blue stripes reading "generic and unsatisfying happy ending," could as easily have been projected at this moment.) Therefore, *Fight Club*'s audience must still turn against Project Mayhem, as will the hero, but without any speech-making or self-righteous disclaimers. Another explanation for this shift is that the group's nouveau-fascism could simply illustrate the point that extremism, either on the left or right, can bend back towards its alleged polar opposite.[18] Therefore, a leaderless and liberating group become indoctrinated jargon-spewers who, per the Narrator's words, state, "In Tyler we trust."

Giroux claims that the film continues to valorize the group and only poses a meager, ineffectual critique when, at the end, the narrator disavows his actions in "a meaningless gesture of resistance," since immediately following his disclaimer a massive explosion occurs in which a series of skyscrapers crumble as a result of Project Mayhem's terrorism.[19] A more nuanced reading, less indebted to old-school Marxist interpretation yet still ideologically aware, might suggest that the film posits a need for the group's activities but either simply "cops out" by vilifying their actions or shows that the cohorts' limitations are imposed by the narrowed options capitalism allows and hence function as critique through their obvious, glaring insufficiency for improving the socio-political system.

Ultimately, though, the biggest narrative twist is not the presence of incipient fascism but the non-existence of Tyler beyond his role as figment of the Narrator's imagination, a figure who appears Mr Hyde-like as an alter-id to his host's super-ego during periods (often lasting days) of unconsciousness. Therefore, every scene involving Tyler requires retrospective rewriting, with the Narrator either talking to himself or actually being responsible for his "friend's" actions.

Again, at least two feasible interpretations exist beyond simply discussing this development's gimmickiness or plausibility. I would argue that the resort to a mental crisis with a psychoanalytic explanation – the Narrator has two personalities – defuses and reduces the film's critique to the personal level, with the psychoanalytic approach and solution functioning as depoliticizing. This is in line with Gilles Deleuze and Felix Guattari's ideas, which criticize "concluding, for example, that fascists are mere paranoiacs":

> This would be an error precisely because . . . this would still amount to leading the historical and political content of the delirium back to an internal familial determination. And what is even more disturbing to us is the fact that the entirety of this enormous content disappears completely from Freud's analysis . . . everything is ground, squashed, triangulated into Oedipus; everything is reduced to the father, in such a way as to reveal in the crudest fashion the inadequacies of an Oedipal psychoanalysis.[20]

In contrast, and playing on the subtitle of Deleuze and Guattari's book *Anti-Oedipus* – "Capitalism and Schizophrenia" – the Narrator's split personality could also be attributed to the castrating, denaturing effects of consumerism, which has defensively created "Tyler"

33 An eerily prescient image of imploding skyscrapers at the conclusion of *Fight Club* (1999)

as a safety-valve for unacceptable feelings. (Similarly, if our society did not have real problems, he could hardly recruit followers.)

As this analysis, and the film's narrative, climaxes, we must consider the film's last scene in which the Narrator has killed off Tyler but "their" plan to destroy TRW and the major credit card companies is imminent. Suddenly Marla enters, like a *deus sex machina*, and, in stereotypical "female" fashion, sympathizes with the Narrator's head-wound and holds his hand. At this moment, the skyscrapers they are looking at implode and the not-so-subliminal image of the aforementioned half-erect penis Tyler had spliced into the cartoon is superimposed for three frames.[21]

This pornographic shot could be viewed as reinforcing the status quo, since the Narrator's return to heterosexual monogamy through reconciliation with his girlfriend – who has just behaved in a more normative manner than usual – may preclude further radicalism. This interpretation could satisfy a putative conservative spectator. In contrast, however, the Narrator has still managed to destroy world-wide credit without any likely punishment except for a nebulous, seemingly harmless head-wound. This double reading is furthered by the phallic subliminal image and the presence of the Pixies' song, "Where is My Mind?", on the soundtrack. The penile image is inter-pretable as the returning repressed/Tyler part of the Narrator sub-consciously (and subliminally) punching a hole in his defenses and reasserting the primacy of the macho Fight Club model. Whether or not the image simply represents his thoughts or is supernaturally spliced into the film, as Tyler did earlier with the cartoon, is another question.

Perhaps, though, Fincher is simply having fun, and this penis is simply a penis. As for the Pixies song, it literally asks a question – "Where is My Mind?" – which not only reprivileges the personalist discourse of psychoanalysis but raises questions concerning which side of the Narrator's consciousness – status-quo or revolutionary – has prevailed. Put crudely, the dialectic of Tyler/rebellion v. Narrator/ acquiescence is roughly synthesized at this point vis-à-vis how Fredric Jameson, by way of Claude Levi-Strauss, describes narrative performing an ideological service through "the imaginary resolution of" a "particular determinate real contradiction."[22] Therefore, warring impulses in society, the audience and the film's characters between the comfortable, plush life of consumerism (despite its castrating, dissatisfying nature) or the savage, masochistic, ascetic aesthetic of Project Mayhem are roughly synthesized into a potentially workable solution. Nevertheless, *Fight Club* as a film is either too incoherent or ambiguous, too multivalent and, to use Barthes' terminology, too "readerly" for such a pat solution.[23]

In fact, how tidily can a movie conclude which, in the manner of *The Wizard of Oz* (1939), suddenly reveals a key interpretive clue – that the Narrator has a split-personality – near the end? How can we truly reconcile smashing credit and tough-guy machismo with a renewed valorization of monogamy and heterosexual coupling? This neat synthesis is so transparently unsatisfactory that it foregrounds the rather cautious limits of the imaginable for any contemporary art text attempting to critique consumerism and capitalism.[24] Yet, unlike the naturalizing coherence of more ideologically certain narratives such as those found in *Forrest Gump* (1994), *Apollo 13* (1995), and *G.I. Jane* (1997), all of which close off discourse through their smoothed-out perfection, the "failure" of *Fight Club* allows for questions concerning both the validity of combining radical politics and the tough-guy ethos and whether any art in the "free world" – especially when produced under the corporate-industrial aegis of the American film industry – can ever satisfactorily, logically, consistently condemn capitalist consumerism and posit revolution.

Notes

1 Interestingly, only one person dies in *Fight Club*, yet unlike a James Bond or Schwarzenegger movie where mass slaughter is acceptable if bloodlessly rendered upon anonymous foes, Fincher's handling of violence requires one to observe the actual consequences of brawling and mayhem. Nevertheless, the film's release date was pushed back after the Columbine HS massacre even though teen angst and revenge killings scarcely figure into its revolutionary vision.

2 In a film about consumer-era depersonalization, onomastically reducing him to a function of discourse is a highly suggestive plot detail.

3 Guy DeBord, *The Society of the Spectacle* (New York: Zone Books, 1994), 44.

4 One may recall the mayhem visited upon Starbucks, Mc Donald's, and other corporate businesses in Seattle, London, and France in the last few years.

5 There are barely any other characters in the film except for a Police Commissioner they threaten, a terminally-ill female support-group member, rather cruelly mocked by the film's voice-over narration, and Marla (Helena Bonham-Carter), the only other notable female role and a potential threat to the group and Narrator's identity.

6 Henry Giroux, "Private Satisfactions and Public Disorders: *Fight Club*, Patriarchy, and the Politics of Masculine Violence," *JAC* 21.1 (2001): 1–31. Available online: www.gseis.ucla.edu/courses/ed253a/FightClub.

7 On the other hand, the shirt *could* be worn ironically, much as urban hipsters frequent kitsch-emporiums to purchase products associated with long-canceled 1960s television shows like *The Brady Bunch* and *Bewitched*.

8 Giroux, "Private Satisfactions."

9 Fascism, musculature, and homoeroticism are nicely compared in Leon Hunt, "Boiling oil and baby oil: Massimo Pupillo's *Il Boia Scarlatto* (*Bloody Pit of Horror*, 1965)." *Kinoeye: A Fortnightly Journal of Film in the New Europe* 2.2 (21 Jan., 2002): www.kinoeye.org/02/02 /hunt02.html.

10 What may be more unnerving is that each time I have seen *Fight Club* in a theater, this moment has produced gleeful, derisive spectatorial laughter.

11 There is much more to say about Marla, but it would blur this essay's major argument.

12 See Gilles Deleuze, "Coldness and Cruelty," in Gilles Deleuze and Leopold Von Sacher-Masoch, *Masochism: Coldness and Cruelty & Venus in Furs*, trans. Jean McNeil (New York: Zone Books, 1989), 55, 60–8. See also Gylyn Studlar, "Masochism and the Perverse Pleasures of the Cinema," in *Movies and Methods*, Volume II, ed. Bill Nichols

(Berkeley: University of California Press, 1985), 602–21 (esp. 603–7).

13 See Susan Jeffords, *Hard Bodies: Hollywood Masculinity in the Reagan Era* (Brunswick: Rutgers University Press, 1994).

14 In *Mythologies*, trans. Annette Lavers (New York: Noonday Press, 1972), Barthes notes the authoritarian nature of tautological speech (152–3).

15 For the sake of coherence, I will not discuss the film's religious symbolism or juvenile borrowings from Nietzsche.

16 Giroux, "Private Satisfactions."

17 In another fascinating expression of white male *ressentiment*, Joel Schumacher's *Falling Down* (1993), there is a similar point where the hero's anti-authoritarian, rebellious actions become unsympathetic.

18 Thanks to Beth C. Roberts for this point.

19 Giroux, "Private Satisfactions."

20 See Gilles Deleuze and Felix Guattari, *Anti-Oedipus: Capitalism and Schizophrenia*, trans. Robert Hurley, *et al.* (Minneapolis: University of Minnesota Press, 1983), 89.

21 Needless to say, this scene's resonance has dramatically changed since the September 11, 2001 bombings of the World Trade Center and Pentagon.

22 Fredric Jameson, *The Political Unconscious: Narrative as a Socially Symbolic Act* (Ithaca: Cornell University Press, 1981), 256.

23 See Roland Barthes, *S/Z: An Essay*, trans. Richard Miller (New York: Hill & Wang, 1974).

24 Giroux, in contrast, views this film as ideologically coherent. He grants that *Fight Club* could "be read differently by different audiences," but advocates analysis via "a pedagogy of disruption that would attempt to make students and others more attentive to visual and popular culture as an important site of political and pedagogical struggle."

Afterword

Stephen Prince

The essays in this anthology explore the topic of film violence in an impressive variety of contexts and according to numerous different issues. These include racial and gender politics, narrative structure, and the emotional and formal dynamics of mixing modalities, as when graphic violence is combined with comedy. David Tetzlaff, for example, offers a spirited defense of the comic value of graphic, cartoonish violence. Murray Pomerance develops a useful taxonomy of narrative structures that foreground violence. Paula J. Massood shows that the historical antecedents of John Singleton's work are much richer than the commonly proposed blaxploitation period of the 1970s. Sylvia Chong develops a provocative comparison of Peckinpah's squib effects and imagery from sexual pornography. Fred Pfeil shows us just why Terrence Malick's *The Thin Red Line* (1998) is a modern masterpiece whose stylistics and moral sensibility transcend the more conventional rendition of violence as found in *Saving Private Ryan* (1998) and *Full Metal Jacket* (1987).

These essays, and the others collected here, are symptomatic of a new interest among film scholars in the subject of movie violence. Indeed, the diverse nature of the essays in the present collection suggests just how widespread this interest now is. In this Afterword, I'd like to make a few comments about this development in the field and suggest some profitable directions in which inquiries might go.

Film studies has taken a very long time to reach its present level of interest in cinema violence. Scholars in other disciplines have been working on media violence for decades, whereas, until very recently, film studies has had little to say on the subject. The reasons for this seem fairly clear. Film studies evolved out of liberal-left currents in the humanities during the 1960s and 1970s, and the field has retained much of its originating political sensibilities, in particular, a

34 Terrence Malick's *Thin Red Line* (1998): an unconventional rendition of wartime violence on screen

commitment toward the progressive transformation of society. Much film interpretation, for example, is framed by this commitment and aims to show how movies are, or are not, complicit in the transactions of power ongoing in society.

Because of this orientation, and because the history of movie violence has been inseparable from struggles over censorship, film scholars have been slow to contribute to debates, especially heated since the emergence of graphic violence on screen, over the potential public consequences of a popular culture so geared toward imagery of death and destruction. Fearful of doing anything that might contribute, however inadvertently, to censorship, film scholars did not join in the debates. Paradoxically, the academic study of pornography has long claimed a place at the film studies table, but not blood and guts.

Anthologies like *New Hollywood Violence* point toward a change in the field, a willingness and interest among film scholars to take up the subject of movie violence. And yet, the movement in some ways is a halting one. A common theme in many of the essays collected here is a deep suspicion of the idea that the media might have social effects. Indeed, the word "effect" is often placed in quote marks by the authors, indicating that the reader should be properly suspicious of it. Controversies over the effects of movie violence are dismissed as "moralistic debates" (Geoff King), as squabbles pursued by those who mindlessly repeat that violence-is-bad in a "mantra-like" way (Martin Barker) and who believe "that every act of screen violence is indistinguishable from any other in perniciousness and corruptive effect" (Murray Pomerance). These allegations amount to a remarkable amount of distancing from media effects research and media effects controversies. It seems unlikely that film studies will assume its proper voice in these debates until it achieves a position of greater comfort with this research and these controversies. Standing off to one side can only help to reduce the ability of the field to participate in the ongoing controversies.

It also cuts us off from the ability to make ethical distinctions about the films that we examine, and discussion of movie violence gains much from such distinctions. By refusing these distinctions, we become cheerleaders for the film industry and its investment in bloody spectacle. My discussion of post-Peckinpah filmmakers in *Savage Cinema* has sometimes been criticized (Sylvia Chong's essay herein is one example) for being unduly harsh on directors such as Tarantino, Scorsese, and Stone, or for overlooking the merits of their handling of violence.[1] And yet Peckinpah's ability to be disturbed by the violence he depicted makes for a real difference with these other filmmakers, and it has ethical implications for the relationship between filmmaker and viewer surrounding graphic violence. It is unwise to turn away from such issues.

The tendency to simplify the questions involved in media effects and effects research is deeply rooted in film studies and is partially explainable in terms of the traditional rivalry between humanities and social sciences. Yet it has the consequence of cutting off film scholarship and film interpretation from the actual social context in which movies are produced and consumed. Do we really, as a field, wish to maintain as a kind of founding, first principle that the way in which films model the world exerts no influence over any viewers?

I doubt that few film scholars would actually affirm this idea, and, in any event, it is not the case that the field is antithetical to the prospect of media influence. Actually, the field's abiding suspicion is not that the media may have social effects but that these effects might go in certain directions, namely, ones that film studies scholars may find unpleasant. Effects of other kinds, provided they are not called "effects," are far from being problems. Indeed, uncovering and identifying them is the very object of interpretation and analysis. Writing about female action heroes in this volume, for example, Jacinda Read observes that "contemporary Hollywood cinema destabilizes the gendered distinction between narrative and spectacle, masculinity and femininity, activity and passivity" Does this idea not describe an effect of textual construction on viewer response? And Todd Onderdonk in this volume argues that *Pulp Fiction* (1994) promotes an ethos of violence and male social dominance that legitimizes the systematic inequities of capitalism. If this is not an effect – that is, if it doesn't influence, or have the potential to influence, a viewer's response or ways of thinking about the world – why should we care about it?

Thus, it is not that film studies finds no effects of the mass media. It is that the field seems to prefer that they remain in the realm of ideas rather than behavior, and that some other word besides "effects" be used to describe them. Future inquires, therefore, could be of great benefit if they would ease some of the repression in film studies surrounding the idea of media effects by creating a real dialogue over this issue, an informed discourse of pro and con, and situate the study of movie violence in relation to that idea and discourse instead of in flight from it.

I want to suggest a second profitable area of inquiry. Many of the essays in the volume examine violence in relation to macro-level social variables, like gender, sexuality, race, and so on. What does movie violence mean within these contexts? This is an important question, and these contexts are important, and the authors here do a very good job of explicating these dimensions of film violence. We also need, however, attention to the specifically cinematic components of movie violence. Violence, after all, appears in many of the arts, such as theater, painting, sculpture, and literature. Cinema arguably offers the most intense and dynamic depictions of violence, ones that carry a powerful emotional charge for viewers. Why?

To answer this question, we ought to look at the specifically cinematic elements of movie violence. In his essay in this volume, Geoff King writes, "Increased intensity is often as much a function of cinematic technique as it is of literal 'explicitness' in the depiction of violent acts." Indeed. This is a very important insight, and one that film scholars can profitably explore.

In *Classical Film Violence: Designing and Regulating Brutality in Hollywood Cinema, 1930–1968*,[2] I define film violence as "the stylistic encoding of a behavioral act." Movie violence has these two

components, the behavior that is depicted and its stylistic instantiation on screen. Much of the existing discussions of movie violence
focus, as did Hollywood's old Production Code, on behavior. They
examine who harms whom, in what ways, and within what socio-
cultural contexts or frameworks. But these are not the issues that
draw filmmakers to their work, not at the deepest level of the pleasure they derive from their craft. What draws and excites them
about doing movie violence is the pleasure they get from designing
new stylistic ways of doing death – rigging a set with squibs timed
to go off with a shower of glass and splintered wood; listening to a
magazine of film explode through a camera at high speed, capturing
bloody death in detail-laden slow motion; layering the audio over
images of gun battles and pumping it up with exaggerated intensity.
This level of pleasure is contagious. Viewers also feel it, and it
draws them to the designs that filmmakers have so lovingly crafted.

As a field, we need to come to terms with these pleasures, which
are lodged deep inside the formal structure of cinema and transcend
the socio-cultural categories on which much of the present scholarly
discussion of movie violence is focused. We need that discussion and
those categories, but without close attention to formal design – to
what filmmakers are actually doing with the audiovisual elements
of cinema – we will be unable to explain the elemental pull that
violence has within the history of cinema and for filmmakers and
audiences alike, or to explain how *movie* violence is different from
violent representations found in literature, painting, or theater.
Those are important questions and good places to begin looking.

Notes

1 *Savage Cinema: Sam Peckinpah and the Rise of Ultraviolent Movies*
   (Austin: University of Texas Press, 1998).
2 New Brunswick: Rutgers University Press, 2003.

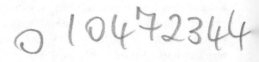

Index